Kumari Jayawardena received her secondary schooling in Sri Lanka before going on to the London School of Economics and the Institut de Science Politique in Paris. Until July 1985 she was Associate Professor of Political Science at Colombo University. She also taught on the Women's Studies Programme of the Institute of Social Studies in The Hague in 1981-82. The author of *The Rise of the Labour Movement in Ceylon* (Duke University Press) and *Ethnic and Class Struggles in Sri Lanka* (Colombo, 1985) and many publications in Sinhalese, she has been active in the women's movement and the civil rights movement in Sri Lanka.

"Seek out the book.... [Its] sheer scope ... not only allows for fascinating comparisons but also shows Third World women defining themselves and being influenced by other Third World women rather than in relation to the West.... The book proves that feminist ideas and movements are not an import from the West [and] shows clearly that the tradition of women's struggles is firmly embedded in these countries' histories."

Rahila Gupta, *Outwrite*

Feminism and Nationalism in the Third World

Kumari Jayawardena

Zed Books Ltd.
London and New Jersey

Feminism and Nationalism in the Third World was first published in India
by Kali for Women, N84 Panchshila Park, New Delhi 110 017, India,
and in the Rest of the World by Zed Books Ltd, 57 Caledonian Road,
London N1 9BU, UK and 165 First Avenue, Atlantic Highlands,
New Jersey 07716, USA, in 1986. All subsequent editions
by Zed Books Ltd.

Cover designed by Andrew Corbett.

Printed and bound in the United Kingdom
by Biddles Ltd, Guildford and King's Lynn.

Fourth impression, 1992.

British Library Cataloguing in Publication Data

Jayawardena, Kumari
  Feminism and Nationalism in the Third World.
  1. Nationalism—Asia—History—19th century
  2. Nationalism—Asia—History—20th century
  3. Women in politics—Asia—History
  I. Title
  322.4'2'095   DS33.3

  ISBN 0-86232-264-2
  ISBN 0-86232-265-0 Pbk

Contents

I am a new woman.
I seek, I strive each day to be that truly new woman I want to be.
In truth, that eternally new being is the sun.
I am the sun . . .
The new woman today seeks neither beauty nor virtue.
She is simply
crying out for strength,
the strength to create this still unknown kingdom . . .

Hiratsuka Raicho (1911) (Sievers 1983: 176)

To the memory of my mother, Eleanor (Hutton) de Zoysa,
and my aunt, Doris Hutton,
and for Doreen (Young) Wickremasinghe

Preface

This book is a revised and expanded version of *Feminism and Nationalism in the Third World in the 19th and early 20th Centuries*, published in 1982 by the Institute of Social Studies in the Netherlands, for its Women and Development Programme.

Here, I have dealt with the early years of feminism and the emergence of the 'new woman' in several countries of the East. Later periods are referred to, but the study is basically historical, set in the late 19th and early 20th centuries and is intended as an introduction to the subject of feminism in the Third World. Many people in the Third World are not aware that their countries have a history of active feminism, or of early movements for women's emancipation, that were supported both by women and men reformers. Moreover, as a result of a colonial-type education, many are not even familiar with the history of other Third World countries. I have, therefore, included some historical background in each of the country studies. Women's participation in revolutionary and democratic movements is also emphasized. Although many of these have been highlighted in history books, the role of women in such struggles has not been given adequate attention; one hears only of the 'heroes' and little of the numerous 'heroines' of Asia.

In analysing contemporary Asian women's movements, some understanding of the nature and content of feminist history in Asia is needed. This is important because those who want to continue to keep the women of our countries in a position of subordination find it convenient to dismiss feminism as a foreign ideology. It should, therefore, be stressed that feminism, like socialism, has no particular ethnic identity; further, any movement for liberation and social change in the Third World can be strengthened only by the participation of the women at all levels and, in so doing, they are able to free themselves from exploitation, oppression and patriarchal structures.

This book discusses the general issues of feminism, women's emancipation and women in political struggles, against a background of increasing activity by the Asian peoples against the domination of their countries by colonial rulers. The struggle for women's emancipation during this period was necessarily bound up with the fight for national liberation and formed an essential part of the democratic struggles of the period. It must also be emphasized that the book deals with a period when the bourgeoisies of some colonial or semi-colonial countries played a progressive role, and the women of this class, together with radical women of the petty-bourgeoisie and working class, came forward to fight in the various battles for democratic rights. Many of the 'new women' of the period, unfortunately, relapsed into their domestic roles or showed concern only with 'equal rights' struggles within the framework of capitalism and the post-colonial state in which the bourgeoisie retained power. Nevertheless, others continued the struggle, joined revolutionary movements for social and economic change, and brought a revolutionary feminist perspective into political movements. Their struggle still continues in many countries, where women militants participate in movements for national liberation, women's liberation and socialism.

The material for this study has been gathered from a wide range of sources that are indicated in the bibliography. In compiling that material I had the invaluable assistance of Alem Desta (of Ethiopia) who unearthed several rare books from the Women's Archives in Amsterdam and other libraries in the Netherlands. I am also grateful to those who commented on sections of the study, made valuable suggestions, and helped in finding material. I am particularly indebted to Maria Mies, who pioneered the women's studies programme in the ISS and inspired many Third World feminists. I must thank Kamla Bhasin, Susan Ekstein, Swarna Jayaweera, Donovan Moldrich, Cecilia Ng, Chitra Maunaguru, Howard Nicholas, Rhoda Reddock, Rosalynd Tibalgo, N. Sanmugaratnam, and several other friends, as well as the students of the Women and Development Programme of the Institute of Social Science, and women in Sri Lanka with whom I had many discussions on issues concerning feminism and Third World women. They are, of course, not responsible for my errors. I would also like to thank Robert Molteno of Zed Books for his encouragement, and all those who, in many ways, have helped in the editing and publication of the book, especially Jean Sanders, Rosalynd Paine, M. Jacob, and other staff members of Zed Books.

Kumari Jayawardena
University of Colombo
Sri Lanka

1. Introduction

> I see here the representatives of only half the population of
> Egypt. May I ask where is the other half? Sons of Egypt, where
> are the daughters of Egypt? Where are your mothers and
> sisters, your wives and daughters?
> *Bhikaiji Cama of India*, at a meeting of the Egyptian National
> Congress at Brussels in 1910. (Kaur 1985: 102)

This study deals with the rise of early feminism and movements for
women's participation in political struggles in selected countries of the
'East' in the late 19th and early 20th centuries. The developments in the
countries chosen — Egypt, Iran, Turkey, India, Sri Lanka, China, Japan,
Korea, the Philippines, Vietnam and Indonesia — show certain parallels
and similarities of experience as well as some clear differences of strategy
based on their specific historical backgrounds, and provide interesting
material for comparative study.

The countries dealt with have one factor in common: they have
either been directly subjected to aggression and domination by imperialist
powers interested in establishing themselves in the region, or indirectly
manipulated into serving the interests of imperialism. While India, Sri
Lanka, Indonesia, Vietnam and the Philippines became part of colonial
empires, Egypt and Iran were reduced to semi-colonial status, the Turkish
Empire was progressively dismembered, Japan was put under pressure
from Western countries to open up the country to trade, and China
became prey to the encroachments of foreign trading powers who wanted
to exploit Chinese resources. Although all these countries fall into what,
for the sake of convenience, has been termed 'the East', they also present
certain specificities linked to their cultural and ideological backgrounds.
Egypt, Turkey and Iran have an Islamic history that has shaped their
attitudes and responses. India and Sri Lanka inherited civilizations based
on Hindu and Buddhist doctrines and show similarities with, and differences from, one another. Further East, China, Japan and Korea have
certain common characteristics that are partly due to their Confucian
ideology. In between, such countries as Vietnam, the Philippines and

1

Indonesia have felt at various times the pressures of the two dominant ancient civilizations of Asia: the Indian and the Chinese. In responding to the pervasive presence of imperialism, their attitudes showed the different influences of their ideological heritages — ideologies which had an impact on the position and role of women as well as on the modes and characteristics of women's movements, as the detailed country studies in this book reveal.

The words 'feminism' and 'feminist' have become emotive words that often evoke hostile reactions. Feminism is generally thought of as a recent phenomenon, rooted in Western society, and people tend to overlook the fact that the word was in common usage in Europe and elsewhere in the 19th and early 20th centuries, to signify agitation on issues concerning women. The meaning of the word has now been expanded to mean an awareness of women's oppression and exploitation within the family, at work and in society, and conscious action by women (and men) to change this situation. Feminism, in this definition, goes beyond movements for equality and emancipation which agitate for equal rights and legal reforms to redress the prevailing discrimination against women. While such movements often advance the struggle for equality, they do not tackle such basic issues as women's subordination within the family or challenge the existing framework of men-women relations in which the subordination of women is located. In this study the word 'feminism' is used in its larger sense, embracing movements for equality within the current system and significant struggles that have attempted to change the system.

The concept of feminism has also been the cause of much confusion in Third World countries. It has variously been alleged by traditionalists, political conservatives and even certain leftists, that feminism is a product of 'decadent' Western capitalism; that it is based on a foreign culture of no relevance to women in the Third World; that it is the ideology of women of the local bourgeoisie; and that it alienates or diverts women, from their culture, religion and family responsibilities on the one hand, and from the revolutionary struggles for national liberation and socialism on the other. In the West, too, there is a Eurocentric view that the movement for women's liberation is not indigenous to Asia or Africa, but has been a purely West European and North American phenomenon, and that where movements for women's emancipation or feminist struggles have arisen in the Third World, they have been merely imitative of Western models.

As a result of this, I have thought it necessary to take up some of these issues and to show that feminism was *not* imposed on the Third World by the West, but rather that historical circumstances produced important material and ideological changes that affected women, even though the impact of imperialism and Western thought was admittedly among the significant elements in these historical circumstances. Debates on women's rights and education were held in 18th-century China and there were movements for women's social emancipation in early 19th-century India; the other country studies show that feminist struggles originated between 60 and 80 years ago in many countries of Asia. In a way, the fact that such movements for emancipation and feminism flourished in several non-European countries during this period has been 'hidden from history'. Only recently, with the rise of feminist movements all over the world, has attention been directed to early feminists and feminism in the Third World.

The movement towards women's emancipation described and analysed in this book was acted out against a background of nationalist struggles aimed at achieving political independence, asserting a national identity, and modernizing society. During the period dealt with in this study, the countries under consideration were trying to shake off imperialist domination. All had faced the reality of foreign conquest, occupation or aggression. They had resisted in diverse ways, but their resistance had three common facets: first, the desire to carry out internal reforms in order to modernize their societies, it being felt that this was necessary if they were successfully to combat imperialism; second, the dismantling of those pre-capitalist structures, especially ruling dynasties and religious orthodoxies, that stood in the way of needed internal reforms; and third, the assertion of a national identity on the basis of which people could be mobilized against imperialism. These forces can be seen to be at work in all the countries studied.

The external and internal forces were thus closely interlinked. The forcible domination or opening-up of the countries to capitalist penetration had created unequal trading relations and promoted the expansion of a local class of merchants, commission agents and collaborators of foreign capitalists. In all the countries under consideration, some sections of the capitalists, primarily those who went into industry and whose products had to face foreign competition, conflicted with imperialism; their dissatisfactions were shared by intellectuals and professionals who had studied abroad or were products of the modern schools and colleges that had been started in the 19th century. This local bourgeoisie and petty bourgeoisie faced the continuing fact of foreign occupation and economic domination. In some countries, they attempted to throw out the occupiers and to develop on a basis of autonomy; in others, they tried to negotiate more advantageous positions for themselves. In all cases, however, they felt the need to sweep away crumbling ruling groups and monarchies which tended to submit to imperialism (the Qajars in Iran, Manchus in China, the sultanate in Turkey and the Shogun in Japan); this was considered a necessary step towards the modernizing, reforming and strengthening of internal structures which were essential if an effective opposition to imperialism were to be mounted.

This resistance, which used the paradoxical strategy of adopting

Western models in order to combat Western aggression, reinforce cultural identity and strengthen the nation, took various forms. Japan, for example, industrialized rapidly, becoming a powerful country within the framework of a highly authoritarian imperial system and a traditional hierarchy. China, in contrast, swept away the feudal monarchy and challenged Confucian attempts in order to modernize the country, resist imperialism, and build up democratic forces. India, while purifying internal structures of the worst excesses, concentrated on the political struggle and achieved a political, but not a social revolution, and in Sri Lanka the emerging bourgeoisie successfully negotiated a transfer of political power which left the existing social structure unchanged. Turkey and Iran associated 'civilization' with capitalist development and Europeanization, programmes that were carried out by dictatorial regimes which imposed the necessary reforms on the people. Egyptian reformism and nationalism developed within the framework of the prevailing class structures and the monarchical system.

As nationalism grew, the struggle of the local bourgeoisie in most of these countries developed on two fronts simultaneously: internally against the pre-capitalist structures, and externally against imperialism. In this agitation, which took on a bourgeois democratic form, the bourgeoisie had to assert the national cultural identity in the form of patriotic appeals intended to unite and arouse the consciousness of the people, while also promoting reforms aimed at educational, scientific, technological and industrial advancement. The liberal slogans of democratic rights, including representative government, universal suffrage, the rights of man and the rights of nations, which were used in the struggle, thus had a material base in the striving of the local bourgeoisie to gain political and economic power.

The creation and assertion of a cultural identity was itself dialectically related to the growth of imperialism. One of the by-products of imperial aggression was a mutual interaction between the cultures of Europe and of the non-European world. Eighteenth-century Europe experienced a new wave of interest in the 'Orient', which led to voyages of further discovery and colonial conquest, and to an interest in Eastern cultures and social structures. The Orientalists, as the new scholars became known, were particularly active in India after Britain gained its initial foothold in the 1750s and the colonial scholar-officials began to 'discover the East', as well as in France, where Napoleon's 1798 expedition to Egypt was accompanied by a shipload of French scholars who set about studying all aspects of Egyptian society. Similar studies undertaken in other Asian countries helped to uncover much of their history through archaeological and historical research; in the course of time they also led to the creation of a concept that became an instrument of cultural domination — a concept of non-European cultures seen through the prism of European cultural and intellectual development. This is the construct that Edward Said has called 'Orientalism':

4

The Orient is an integral part of European *material* civilisation and culture. Orientalism expresses and represents that part culturally and even ideologically as a mode of discourse with supporting institutions, vocabulary, scholarship, imagery, doctrines, even colonial bureaucracies and colonial styles . . . a Western style for dominating, restructuring and having authority over the Orient. (Said 1979: 2–3)

The interaction between cultures proved to be a two-way process, however. The beliefs that the older cultures of the East were the 'source of civilization', that the quest for origins lay in the East and that European languages were linked to Sanskrit, were to have a profound influence on Western political thinking in the 19th century. Similarly, in those countries of Asia and Africa which had been exposed to 'Occidentalism', the attempts to emulate Western economic development were associated with an appreciation of Western cultural values and specially of such concepts as natural rights, liberalism and parliamentary democracy, which were perceived as the foundations for such growth.

Within this framework, those nationalists who challenged foreign aggression had to tackle the problem of asserting a national identity by combating obscurantism, and by reforming and rationalizing existing structures and religious and cultural traditions. In short, they had to challenge and change the old order, sometimes radically, while reviving what were defined as the true and pristine traditions of a distant and independent past. In doing so, they were influenced by European Orientalists who had glorified Asian civilizations and cultural traditions, as well as by Western political thought. In particular, they were inspired by the slogans of liberty, equality and fraternity and the anti-religious views of French revolutionary thinkers of the 18th century.

In addition, the 19th-century flowering of liberalism, especially associated with the ideas of Jeremy Bentham and John Stuart Mill in Britain, and the socialist challenge of the French Utopians and later of the Marxists, were to strongly influence sections of Asian intellectuals. One must also stress the influence in Asia of Darwinism, the freethinkers, theosophy, and all the anti-Christian, anti-clerical movements of the 19th century, including the bitter political struggles between state and church, the separation of religion and politics, and the secularization of society which occurred in many European countries. In a colonial or semi-colonial context, resistance to Christianity and to missionary activities had anti-imperialist implications, and the challenge to Christianity in Europe gave an impetus to national movements of cultural revival that already existed (as in India and Sri Lanka). Similarly, European rationalism, Freemasonry, secularism and positivism were also to influence those liberal and socialist groups in Asia and Africa who were less concerned with religious revival than with social change.

Religious revival and opposition to tradition generally took the same form in most Asian countries, linking together the reinterpretation of sacred texts and the reform of clerical structures; this led, in some cases, to the reduction of clerical influence. In the Middle East, Islam as it existed was seen as an obstacle to nationalist political and economic development; much was written not only about the need to return to the 'pure' Islam of an earlier period, but also about the idea that Islam, if reinterpreted correctly, was a rational religion compatible with social advance. Similar movements were at work with regard to other religions in Asia. In India, there was an attempt to reinterpret Hinduism on the basis of the concept of one God and the unity of all humans; repugnant social practices such as caste and *sati* were seen as the result of accretions or misinterpretations. In Sri Lanka, reformers went back to the texts of Buddhism and reinterpreted them as being indicative of a rational system of ethics, totally compatible with modern scientific knowledge.

In many Asian countries, clerical authority was seen as retrograde and supportive of corrupt feudal regimes and, therefore, as conducive neither to the growth of nationalism nor to necessary superstructural reforms of the social system, such as measures to emancipate women. Efforts to reduce the power of clerical authorities were perhaps most marked in those countries with well-established hierarchies as in Islam. The drive towards a secular state was seen particularly in the 'Young Turks' movement of the early 20th century, which in turn influenced policies in the neighbouring Muslim countries. The anti-Brahmin content of religious and political reformism in India shows another facet of this same tendency.

We thus have a situation where Western secular thought is a crucial factor in fashioning a consciousness and in devising structures that would make possible an escape from the domination of Western political power. The traditional political and religious élites were well aware of the dangers of this emerging consciousness and tried to meet the challenge in various ways: total isolationism in some countries, a return to fundamentalism in others. But in almost all the countries under study, the new body of ideas was seized on by the bourgeoisie and used as an instrument in their attempt to forge a new national consciousness and modern secular political structures. It must be noted, however, that the early fervour with which such ideals were pursued has now somewhat diminished; the old pre-capitalist dogmas and religions have proved to be surprisingly enduring.

Another important factor in the formation of this consciousness was education. In almost all the countries under consideration, education had been closely linked with religion and generally confined to the religious and upper strata of society. Mass education was a concept of the bourgeois world, brought into these countries by the colonizing powers. Even though in most cases education began as a process of proselytization, and for the training of local administrative cadres, it paved the way for the spread of literacy among the masses. Ultimately this education also became the means of imparting a knowledge of modern science. The spread of literacy in turn formed the foundation on which newspapers and

6

journals could be established. The specific ways in which women's consciousness was fashioned by education will be made clear in the following case studies.

The spread of literacy and of newspapers had another far-reaching effect. Political events in one country can have a rapid effect on nationalists and revolutionaries in another. An important turning-point in Asian nationalism, for example, was Japan's victory in 1905 over Tsarist Russia in the Manchurian war. Asians had admired Japan for the success of her rapid modernization and industrialization policies, and many students and political exiles had been attracted from neighbouring countries (especially China, Korea and Vietnam). Japan's military victory showed that Asians were able decisively to challenge and defeat Europeans in armed warfare. Sun Yat-Sen claimed that the Japanese victory gave 'unlimited hope' and 'raised the standing of all Asians' (Spector 1962: 30), and Nehru declared that Japan was 'the representative of Asia battling Western aggression. If Japan could make good against one of the powerful European countries, why not India?' (Nehru 1949: 440–4). The Russian revolution of 1905 also gave Asian democrats and revolutionaries the conviction that absolute governments, however firmly entrenched, could be toppled:

> The Russo-Japanese war underlined the possibility of the overthrow of Western imperialism. The Russian Revolution of 1905 indicated the feasibility of the overthrow of autocracy, native or foreign. In most Asian countries, where the two objectives were fused, Russia's defeat and Russia's revolution together produced a resounding and durable impact. (Spector 1962: 30)

Other striking events which evoked a strong response among Third World nationalists included the struggles of the Irish against British domination, especially the martyrdom of the freedom fighters and hunger strikers. Many Asians and Africans who were in Europe in the early 20th century made a point of visiting Ireland; Nehru did so in 1907, and the visit strengthened his 'extremist sympathies' (Gopal 1975: 22). Moreover, the political changes that occurred in some countries of Asia and Africa caused hope to grow in other areas where the struggles continued. The deposition of the Manchu dynasty and the proclamation of the Chinese Republic by Sun Yat-Sen in 1912 had a tremendous impact on nationalists in other countries. Similarly, the Young Turks' revolution of 1908 and Mustapha Kemal's declaration of the republic in 1922 were dramatic events which influenced other struggles, while news of nationalist upsurges in India, Egypt, Iran, Vietnam and many other countries, which were constantly highlighted in the newspapers, served to provide mutual encouragement. Perhaps the most influential event was the Russian Revolution of 1917 which caused reverberations throughout the non-European world, and in the colonized countries aroused hopes of major change. At the time, a Sri Lankan radical journal expressed the enthusiasm of young Asian nationalists and revolutionaries: 'Czardom that for ages manacled human liberty has vanished from unhappy Russia with the heralding of the dawn of a better day' (Jayawardena 1972: 227). Influenced by the events in Russia, Communist parties which had arisen in Asia by the early 1920s — in China, India, Japan, Iran, Egypt and Turkey among others — launched revolutionary movements for social and political change.

It is in the context of the resistance to imperialism and various forms of foreign domination on the one hand, and to feudal monarchies, exploitative local rulers and traditional patriarchal and religious structures on the other, that we should consider the democratic movement for women's rights and the feminist struggles that emerged in Asia. The country studies, in which we examine the situation of each country in detail, will show that struggles for women's emancipation were an essential and integral part of national resistance movements. In all these countries, the 'woman question' forcefully made its appearance during the early 20th century. The debate on the role and status of women had of course started earlier, but in the era of imperialist and capitalist expansion the question assumed new dimensions; the growth of capitalism changed the old social order and gave birth to new classes and new strata whose women had to pose the old question in a new dynamic. In short the issue was one of democratic rights.

To foreign and local capitalists and landowners, women were the cheapest source of labour for plantations, agriculture and industry. To the colonial authorities and missionaries, local women had to be educated to be good (preferably Christian) wives and mothers to the professional and white-collar personnel who were being trained to man the colonial economy. To the male reformers of the local bourgeoisie, women needed to be adequately Westernized and educated in order to enhance the modern and 'civilized' image of their country and of themselves, and to be a good influence on the next generation; the demand grew for 'civilized housewives'.

The importance of female labour under conditions of capitalist development in Asia has to be stressed. While it is true that women had toiled in the fields and plantations and domestic industries in the pre-capitalist phase, it was with the development of capitalism in a colonial or semi-colonial context, that they were to become available as potentially the largest and cheapest reserve army of labour. Women's labour was therefore very important to local and foreign capitalists; traditions and practices which restricted women's mobility or enforced their seclusion were thus detrimental to capitalism in its search for cheap 'free' labour. With the growth of industries — especially those associated with the textile trade — the demand for women's labour grew in all the countries under consideration: China (silk and allied manufactures), Japan (textiles and consumer goods), Iran (carpets), Egypt (cotton), India (textiles) and

Turkey (rugs and textiles). Women's labour was also crucial in the plantation sector (tea, rubber, coconut, sugar, etc.) and in farm and domestic agriculture in these countries. Moves towards the further 'emancipation' of women to enable them to work and to better serve the needs of industrialists, planters and farmers were therefore to be expected.

The process of capitalist expansion also created an emerging bourgeoisie which arose partly from the needs of the imperial administration, i.e. local administrators and professionals, and partly from the needs of the new forms of economic organization that served foreign capital. The men of these emerging groups, however, saw the 'woman question' in a very different light. While the women of the peasantry and working class were being proletarianized, those of the bourgeoisie were trained to accept new social roles in conformity with the emerging bourgeois ideology of the period. For example, the bureaucrats, missionaries and male reformers of the local bourgeoisie were convinced that women had to be emancipated from the social abuses of a 'savage' past, from practices that were defined as repugnant by the prevailing norms of European society. Obvious areas of violence and oppression were highlighted, such as widow burning in India, veiling, polygamy, concubinage and seclusion in Egypt, Turkey, Korea, Vietnam, Iran and Indonesia, and foot-binding in China. But to these were added other so-called 'barbaric practices' that went against the Christian ideas of monogamy and sexual control that Europeans enforced upon their own women. For example, vestiges of matriarchy, tolerant sexual mores, polyandry and divorce by mutual consent, all of which existed in the Kandyan regions of Sri Lanka, were criticized not only by the foreign rulers and missionaries but also by men of the local bourgeoisie. Many of the reformers among the indigenous bourgeoisie were men who saw the social evils of their societies as threats to the stability of bourgeois family life, and who therefore campaigned for reform in order to *strengthen* the basic structures of society rather than to change them. There was thus an in-built conservative bias in many of the reform movements.

The nature of the resistance movements in these countries and of the feminist struggles within those movements varied with the balance of forces that resulted from capitalist expansion. In most countries, they were dominated by the local bourgeoisie. Again, there were two types: those in which the bourgeoisie found it necessary to mobilize the masses in the struggle, as in India and Indonesia, and others, in which the local bourgeoisie replaced the imperialist rulers through a process of negotiation and gradual reforms as in Sri Lanka or the Philippines. The women's struggles associated with both types of resistance movements did not move beyond the sphere of limited and selected reforms: equality for women within the legal process, the removal of obviously discriminatory practices, the right to the vote, education and property, and the right of women to enter the professions and politics, etc. These were reforms which had little effect on the daily lives of the masses of women; neither

9

did they address the basic question of women's subordination within the family and in society. Even where women of the working classes were involved, the specific character of the struggles was determined by that of the larger struggle; equal pay and similar demands were usually their main objective.

In a few countries, however, the involvement of peasants and workers in the resistance movements pushed the struggle on to a broader front. Not content with replacing the pre-capitalist or imperialist regimes with a local bourgeoisie, they aimed at a more radical transformation of society, at the establishment of a socialist society, a trend that is illustrated by the country studies of China and Vietnam. The feminist element in these movements was able to become a revolutionary force that simultaneously helped to transform society and to improve the position of women. In this context, examples of revolutionary feminism during the early 20th century provide valuable evidence that feminism was not a diversion, a bourgeois aberration, nor a matter to be considered only after a social revolution; on the contrary, it was a process which had to be continuous and permanent during all stages of the struggle.

Women's movements do not occur in a vacuum but correspond to, and to some extent are determined by, the wider social movements of which they form part. The general consciousness of society about itself, its future, its structure and the role of men and women, entails limitations for the women's movement; its goals and its methods of struggle are generally determined by those limits. Mention will be made in the country studies of courageous women who consciously strove to move beyond those limits in the pursuit of goals that today would be defined as feminist, but who failed because of the lower levels of general awareness.

It is appropriate at this stage to discuss women's consciousness as it emerged in the countries under study after the impact of colonialism and the experience of Western society and thought. Of all the religious ideologies discussed, Islam has the longest contact with Europe. From its very beginnings it has fought continuously with Christianity. What challenged Islam in the 19th century, however, was not Christianity but European secularism. As Bernard Lewis says:

> A philosophy free from visible Christian connotations and expressed in a society that was rich, strong and rapidly expanding, it seemed to some Muslims to embody the secret of European success and to offer a remedy for the weakness, poverty and retreat of which they were becoming increasingly aware. In the course of the 19th and 20th centuries, European secularism and a series of political, social and economic doctrines inspired by it, exercised a continuing fascination on successive generations of Muslims. (Lewis 1982: 184)

Muslim travellers to Europe who tried to understand this secular society were particularly interested in the position of European women. The fact that women seemed relatively free of the social restrictions of Islamic society, that they were allowed to move about, that they were respected in society and deferred to by men, struck them forcibly. The institution of monogamous marriage and the fact that the family was the basic unit of society were also alien concepts that provoked discussion. Evliya Celebi, an 18th-century Turkish traveller and observer of European society, wrote:

> If the emperor encounters a woman in the street . . . he halts his horse and lets the woman pass. If the emperor is on foot . . . then he remains standing in a polite posture . . . takes his hat off . . . and shows deference to the woman, and only when she has passed does he continue on his way. This is a most extraordinary spectacle. In this country, and elsewhere in the lands of the infidels, women have the chief say and they are honoured and respected for the sake of Mother Mary. (Lewis 1982: 287)

The freedom displayed by women in their social intercourse with men was commented on by many; witnesses to grand balls were compelled to think that such intimacy also meant sexual liberty. The 18th-century travellers were sometimes so struck by the ostensible freedom of women that they tended to exaggerate:

> In France, women are of higher station than men, so that they do what they wish and go where they please; and the greatest lord shows respect and courtesy beyond all limits to the humblest of women. In that country their commands prevail. (Mehmed Said Effendi in Lewis 1982: 289)

These travellers were struck by the openness of a society that permitted some men and women to take part in easy social intercourse; it might be said that they found this so surprising because the Islamic élite at that time was accustomed to seclude its women in the *zenana*. However, non-Muslims were equally impressed. Yu Kil-Chun of Korea went to the USA at the end of the 19th century as his country's ambassador and published an account of his travels in 1892. One of the things that struck him most was the position and status of women in American society and their employment in various activities and professions outside the home. Moreover, he was singularly intrigued by the marriage pattern which ideally permitted women to choose their husbands on the basis of love. Yu finished his account by advocating the equality of men and women. Even though he made it obvious that this was not due to any concern for the human rights of women, but rather because equality would promote the welfare of children, homes and country, it is still remarkable that he should single this factor out for particular attention. Asian women too were influenced by the myth that all Western women were 'free'. To give one example, around 1900, Kartini, the pioneer of female education in Indonesia, was to envy the 'free, independent European woman' (Geertz 1964: 137).

Faced with societies that were sufficiently developed and powerful to subjugate them, and with the need to modernize their own societies, many reformers of Asia seized on the apparent freedom of women in

Western societies as the key to the advancement of the West, and argued that 'Oriental backwardness' was partly due to women's low status. For example, Fukuzawa Yukichi, an interpreter with the first official Japanese mission to Europe in 1862, advocated equality between the sexes. In *The Encouragement of Learning*, he criticized the traditional relationships between men and women, advocating monogamy and freedom of choice in marriage in order to make Japanese society more 'presentable' and 'civilized'. Fukuzawa said frankly: 'I shall attempt to make our society more presentable if only on the surface . . . I should like to put my future efforts towards elevating the moral standards of the men and women of my land to make them truly worthy of a civilized nation' (Fukuzawa 1968: 306, 336).

Since the status of women in society was the popular barometer of 'civilization', many reformers agitated for social legislation that would improve their situation. In India, in 1818, Raja Rammohan Roy led a campaign against what the missionaries called 'certain Dreadful Practices'. This was followed by actions led by many other social reformers, including Vidyasagar, K.C. Sen, Ranade and Phule. Similarly in the Meiji era, Japanese intellectuals such as Fukuzawa and Soho condemned Confucian traditions of family life and advocated rights for women. The Young Turks of the early 20th century, Ziya Gokalp and Ahmet Agaoglu, pleaded for women's emancipation: Gokalp expressed the general current of opinion among male reformers when he wrote: 'In the future, Turkish ethics must be founded upon democracy and feminism, as well as nationalism, patriotism, work and the strength of the family' (Ahmed 1982: 155). Another Turkish writer, Tevfik Fikret, expressed the sentiment prevalent among Asian reformers of the time that 'when women are debased, humanity is degraded' (Ahmed 1982: 155). In China, reformers of the later 19th century such as Kang Yuwei and those of the early 20th century grouped around Sun Yat-Sen opposed the constraints on women that traditionally existed in Chinese society, as did nationalists Dr So Chae-p'il in Korea, and José Rizal in the Philippines who strongly advocated a secular education for women. Education and freedom of movement for women, and monogamy, were thus seen as marks of modernity, development and civilization. Reformers tried to embody these factors in their political platforms and activities, striving to make their own wives and daughters embodiments of the new ideal.

This new consciousness demanded an 'enlightened' woman. The new bourgeois man, himself a product of Western education or missionary influence, needed as his partner a 'new woman', educated in the relevant foreign language, dressed in the new styles and attuned to Western ways — a woman who was 'presentable' in colonial society yet whose role was primarily in the home. These women had to show that they were the negation of everything that was considered 'backward' in the old society: that they were no longer secluded, veiled and illiterate, with bound feet and minds, threatened with death on their husband's funeral pyre. The concept and terminology of the 'new woman', so fashionable in Europe in the 19th century, was eagerly adopted by both men and women of the educated class. For example, Kassim Amin's book on women's emancipation published in 1901 was called *The New Woman*; in 1919 Egyptian women formed the 'Société de la Femme Nouvelle'. In the same year an 'Association of New Women' was established in Japan, while in China and Korea, in 1919 and 1920 respectively, feminist magazines called *The New Woman* were published.

Though the terminology was similar, the various regions showed differences in this concept of the 'new woman'. In certain Islamic countries the emphasis was on copying European styles of dress for women including the latest fashions, and discarding the traditional dress. The modernists saw the veil as a mark of women's seclusion and backwardness; Jamal Sudki Azza Khawy who, in Iraq in 1911, advocated doing away with the veil, was imprisoned for sedition (Woodsmall 1936: 69). The act of throwing off the veil, regarded as a symbol of feudalism, was given great significance, and occasions when prominent women appeared unveiled became dramatic moments of defiance of the old order. Some examples include the fearless behaviour of the Babi woman leader of Iran, Qurrat ul Ayn, who fought in battles and caused a scandal in the 1840s by going unveiled; the first unveiled public appearances of Queen Surayya of Afghanistan in the 1920s and the Queen of Iran in 1936; the marriage ceremony of Mustapha Kemal at which his bride, Latife Hanem, was not veiled (1922); and Huda Sharawi's boldness in publicly flinging her veil into the sea (1923).

In other Asian cultures defiant women sometimes wore masculine attire — a challenge to all traditional views of feminine conduct and deportment but not unknown in literature in which heroines lead men into war wearing male battledress (e.g. Mulan in the Chinese story of the 6th century). In real life, too, inspiring women warriors had fought on the battlefield wearing male clothing. One of the best known of these was the Rani of Jhansi who, in the war of independence against the British in India in 1857, led her troops into battle on horseback, Lord Canning remarking that 'she used to dress like a man (with a turban) and rode like one too' (Hibbert 1980: 385). Kalpana Dutt, the Bengali revolutionary, took part in the Chittagong Armoury raid of 1930 disguised as a man. In China, too, the tradition persisted: the Chinese revolutionary Jiu Jin (inspired by the Mulan story) often dressed in male attire during her stay in Japan (around 1905), and Chinese women fighting in the revolutionary liberation armies of the 1920s wore male army dress. The tradition of seeing women's hair as a symbol of beauty also became an issue, and many feminists and 'emancipated' women in the Muslim world, Japan, China and Korea defied tradition and cut their hair short in keeping with modern fashion. During periods of counter-revolution, however, as in China and Iran in recent years, a backlash occurred and women who had discarded the old customs became targets for physical violence.

13

A striking example of the impact of Western ideas on the new consciousness concerning women's emancipation is provided by Ibsen's play *The Doll's House,* written in 1879. The theme caused a scandal in both Europe and Asia for it challenged all accepted social norms concerning the role of women, In the play, Nora slams the door shut and walks away from her husband and children on the grounds that over and above her 'moral' duty as wife and mother she had a 'sacred' duty to herself. In the context of the times, Nora symbolized the struggle to break out of traditional constraints and orthodox morality and achieve a conscious identity of self. In China, Japan, Korea, India and many other Asian countries, Nora became a topic of discussion and a symbol not only for women, but for intellectuals struggling for emancipation from the 'old order'. The play was translated into Chinese and in 1918, a special issue of *New Youth* was devoted to Ibsen; moreover, the word 'Ibsenism' was frequently used by Chinese intellectuals to express their ideological revolt, and Nehru, in 1928, mentioned *The Doll's House* in a speech to women students. In China and in other countries where the debate went beyond bourgeois democracy, Nora's defiance stimulated controversy among the revolutionaries. It was argued that her gesture was purely individualistic, meaningless unless social changes were introduced which would make real emancipation possible. For example, Lu Xun, in his 1923 article 'What Happens after Nora Leaves?', predicted that she would be compelled either to return home or to become a prostitute, since capitalist society would allow her no other alternative (Schwarcz 1975: 3).

But this was not the total picture. In their search for a national identity, the emergent bourgeoisies also harked back to a national culture: the new woman could not be a total negation of traditional culture. Although certain obviously unjust practices should be abolished, and women involved in activities outside the home, they still had to act as the guardians of national culture, indigenous religion and family traditions — in other words, to be both 'modern' and 'traditional'.

To seek legitimacy for this position, many reformers idealized the civilization of a distant past, speaking of the need to regain the lost freedom that women were said once to have possessed in their societies. In Turkey, Gokalp, Ataturk and the intellectuals asserted a specific Turkish identity and ethnicity, and referred to pre-Islamic Turkey, where freedom for women was said to have existed among the nomads of Central Asia. Similarly, Iranian reformers spoke of the early history of the country and of its Zoroastrian traditions which accorded a high status to women; the Japanese referred to their sun goddess and empresses; Egyptians were proud of ancient Egyptian history when women had held high positions and the country was ruled by famous queens such as Nefertiti and Hatshepsut. In India, social reformers and politicians not only constantly harked back to the golden age of Vedic culture when women were said to have been free, but also frequently referred to the goddesses of mythology, warrior queens and famous women of history to show that India had a tradition of according women a high status in society. In Sri Lanka, the Sinhalese evoked a mythical Aryan past in which women had been held in high esteem and claimed that Buddhism had accorded women equal rights. In Indonesia and the Philippines, the reference back was to a tribal past in which some women were said to have held power.

The objectives of the reformers were thus twofold: to establish in their countries a system of stable, monogamous nuclear families with educated and employable women such as was associated with capitalist development and bourgeois ideology; and yet to ensure that women would retain a position of traditional subordination within the family. This was an echo of earlier events in Europe where the development of the factory system during the Industrial Revolution had changed the nature of the home and the family which, in pre-capitalist times, had been a centre of production. Capitalism had drawn women of the poor from the home into the factory as wage labour, while the women of the bourgeoisie were confined to the home as housewives and the family was idealized in all the propaganda of the bourgeois media. The bourgeoisies of the Third World, as part of their strategy for achieving economic growth, 'civilization' and reform, also began to propagate the concept of a family system based on strict monogamy for women, monogamy in theory (if not in practice) for men, and the abolition of 'feudal' extended-family relationships. In India, reformers campaigned against the tortures and restraints imposed on widows and against polygamy and child marriage. In Sri Lanka, they called for an end to the 'brutal' practice of polyandry. In all Islamic countries, from Turkey to Indonesia, polygamy was denounced and laborious attempts were made to prove that the Islamic tenet that a man might have four wives was so hedged by conditions that fulfilment was impossible in a modern society. In China, Korea and Vietnam, concubinage was attacked as well as the tyranny of the Confucian family. In Japan, too, the reformers denounced Confucian family oppression and called for a nuclear, modern system of family life. Thus, the ideal of monogamy, with bourgeois women confined to a housewife's role, became almost universal in reformist circles in the countries under study.

Education then became a crucial problem. Many women of royal families, the aristocracy and the merchant class had earlier asserted themselves in the intellectual sphere, proving by their exceptional nature the rule that women in general were deprived of access to formal education. As the rise of the bourgeoisie in Europe brought demands for democratic rights, the issue of equal educational opportunities became a major demand of European bourgeois women. Similarly, with the growth of local bourgeoisies and the rise of nationalism in non-European countries, women's emancipation and education became primary issues, both for the women of the bourgeoisie and for male reformers, including

15

intellectuals and national leaders. The motives of the male reformers were varied but education was a crucial issue for the women; lack of it had denied them employment, income and social recognition, and had kept them intellectually subordinate to men.

The first modern girls' schools were established in India in 1820, in Sri Lanka in 1824, in China in 1844, in Egypt in 1846, in Turkey in 1863, in Japan in 1870, in Iran in 1874, in Korea in 1886 and in Indonesia in 1904. Girls began to move on to higher education: the first Sri Lankan girl sat for the Senior Cambridge Examination in 1881. Women graduates appeared in India from the 1880s onwards, and women in all these countries started to enter the professions as teachers, nurses, midwives, lawyers and doctors. Medicine was the first prestigious profession in which women made a breakthrough. The first Indian woman doctor qualified in 1886; the first woman student from Sri Lanka entered the Medical College in 1893, and from both these countries women went to Britain and the USA to qualify as doctors in the last decades of the 19th century. Similarly, the first Korean woman qualified abroad in medicine in 1896, and in 1900, the first women's medical college was established in Japan. In later years the ultimate in female achievement and a symbol of courage and emancipation was to become a pilot and to fly single-handed. Those who did so became national heroines, e.g. Wang Guifen (daughter of the revolutionary Jiu Jin) who became China's first woman pilot (Gipoulon 1976: 158); Mustapha Kemal's adopted daughter was Turkey's first woman pilot; and Lutfiya El Nadi became the first Egyptian woman to fly solo in 1934. The education of girls placed new emphasis on gymnastics, sports and other outdoor activities: in several Muslim countries such as Turkey, Iran and Egypt, where such activities had earlier been disapproved of, displays of gymnastics by girls' schools were held in public, the first in Cairo in 1929.

The content and nature of women's education reflected the ambiguities inherent in the new concept of 'woman'. The missionaries had been primarily concerned with producing Christian wives and mothers for the new male converts in order to prevent the latter from lapsing into their former beliefs, which was thought to be more likely if the women remained 'heathen'. This kind of education was unable to satisfy the nationalists for long. Reformists stressed the democratic right to education for all, irrespective of sex, so as to achieve a strong, monogamous (and preferably nuclear) family system which would be the foundation of a stable society.

But what type of education was advocated? To start with, it was class biased, since it was geared to providing good wives and mothers for those men who had risen on the economic and social ladder of colonial society. As in early 19th-century Europe, the education given to girls consisted of basic subjects and 'accomplishments' considered necessary for a girl to make a good marriage, as demonstrated in several countries. 'Modernity' meant educated women, but educated to uphold the system

16

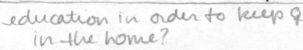

of the nuclear patriarchal family. The missionary schools not only trained girls to be good wives, but also introduced them to the 19th-century European code of female virtue and correct behaviour, a limited view that was contested by many women who were themselves products of the new education. Similar to European women who demanded equal access to higher education, bourgeois women in Asia began to agitate for further educational opportunities that would give them access to new avenues of income-earning opportunities and, hopefully, greater freedom. The bourgeois males of these countries were faced with the usual liberal dilemma: the democratic rights championed by followers of the Enlightenment in Europe, though ostensibly 'universal', were intended for bourgeois males to the exclusion of the workers, colonial peoples and women (Mies and Jayawardena 1981: 5). Similarly, the indigenous bourgeoisies, while willing to grant some concessions to women of their own class, had no intention of applying the concepts of natural rights, liberty, equality and self-determination to the masses of women or to the workers of their own countries.

It is impracticable, however, to expect to launch slogans that are claimed to be universal and to mobilize people around these banners for political causes without the oppressed groups taking up the issues on their own behalf. In spite of efforts to 'Westernize' and educate women within the confines of a traditional patriarchal framework, further demands were made by those women who had already benefited from educational opportunities. Women reformers, for instance, were interested in emancipating women from certain social customs that were detrimental to them, and from legal, economic and political constraints which, in spite of their education, kept them in a subordinate position. But the more radical women were to take the struggle further, basically challenging the oppressive patriarchal structures of their societies and advocating revolutionary political and social alternatives.

With the spread of education and literacy, feminist literature in the form of books, journals and magazines became an important aspect of the women's movement. In several Asian countries, there was a flowering of books, novels, journals and articles in the late 19th and early 20th centuries, written both by women and men and dealing with issues concerning women's role in society. While many of these publications discussed traditional 'women's' topics, they could not avoid getting involved in the ongoing debate on women's subordination. In many cases they reported developments in the sphere of women's emancipation in other countries. Egyptian women, for example, were told of innovations and legislative reforms in Turkey; such journals also informed their readers about the suffragist and feminist struggles in Europe. They included *Al Fatah* in Egypt (1892), the Turkish weekly *Newspaper for Ladies* (1895), the *Chinese Women's Journal* (1907), *Knowledge*, an Iranian women's journal (around 1906), *Yoja Chinam* ('Women's Guide') in Korea in 1909, *Seito* ('Bluestocking') in Japan (1911), and *Nu Gioi*

Chung ('Women's Bell') in Vietnam in 1918. These journals covered a wide range of views: the Turkish journal stressed women's education and the need for women to be good mothers, good wives and good Muslims (Ahmed 1982: 155), while the *Chinese Women's Journal* was both revolutionary and feminist in content. There were 15 Arabic journals for women in Egypt around 1914.

While women's magazines and writings helped to arouse women's consciousness, male novelists, poets and journalists also wrote on issues concerning women. In several countries, concern about women's role in traditional society was first expressed by male writers whose books on this theme achieved popularity and sometimes notoriety. In China in the 18th century Ch'en Hung-mou wrote a book on the need to educate women, and in 1825, Li Ruzhen wrote the first Chinese feminist novel (*Flowers in the Mirror*) in which sex roles were reversed in a society where women ruled and men had bound feet. In Egypt, too, the earliest book in support of women, *One Leg Crossed over the Other*, was by a male author El Shidyak (1855), while Kassim Amin's books on women's emancipation and the new woman, written in the 1890s, also created a stir. Amin's books, with their liberal views, are looked upon in the Arab world as the seminal works on feminism, and can still rouse considerable hostility among conservative and religious elements (Ahmed 1982: 159). In India, the issue of the status of women occurs in Rabindranath Tagore's novels as well as in other literature of the period dealing with social questions; Sarachchandra's *Biraj Bahu* dramatized the plight of child widows, and Chandu Menon's *Indulekha* the need for female education, preferably in English. In Turkey, many male writers, including Halil Hamit, Celal Nuri and Ahmet Agaoglu, wrote books in the early 20th century on women's rights. Even more remarkable was the emergence of the new generation of Third World women writers and poets, the products of 19th-century educational reforms, whose writings reflect the feminism of the period. These included Malak Hifni Nassif and May Ziada in early 20th-century Egypt; Jiu Jin in China, author of a feminist book *Stones of the Jingwei Bird* written around 1904; the Filipino women writers of the 19th century such as Leona Florentina; Swarnakumari Devi's novel *An Unfinished Song* of the late 19th century; the Turkish writer Fatima Aliye, whose novel *Womanhood* appeared in 1892; Halide Edip, author of several successful novels on women's issues; the 'new wave' feminist writings of Yosano Akiko in early 20th-century Japan; the Korean women writers of the 1920s, Kim Won-ju, whose novels were on women's liberation from male domination, and Na Hye-Sok, who wrote a poem on Ibsen's Nora.

The education of women also gave an impetus to the struggle for suffrage, which became an important issue in the campaign for democratic rights. The issue of voting rights had been one of the great battles fought by the European bourgeoisie against aristocratic privilege, and the question of suffrage rights for other groups, especially the working class, formed the next stage of the struggle. By the late 19th century, women's suffrage had become a major issue, and prior to the outbreak of World War I the militancy and violent tactics used against the state apparatus by British women suffragists became world news. In several countries of the Third World the question of voting rights for women was posed, especially during heightened phases of the nationalist struggle, when the issues debated included the right to self-government and equality. Some of the early and unsuccessful attempts to obtain female suffrage were made by male reformers, for example in Iran (1911 and 1920) and the Philippines (1907), but the women themselves were also to lead the agitation as in China (1911), India (1917), Japan (1924) and Sri Lanka (1927). In some cases the agitation was peaceful, but in others it was less so. Women organized demonstrations and stormed the legislatures when these bodies failed to grant female suffrage; such militant agitation occurred in China in 1911 and 1924, and in Japan and Egypt in 1924.

Education for women in Asiatic countries thus had a dual function. It brought bourgeois women out of their homes and into various professions, into social work, and into the political sphere claiming the right of suffrage. It transformed them in the image of the 'emancipated' women of Western society. On the other hand, as nationalist reformers took over, education also became a conservative influence; it began to hark back to traditional ideals, to emphasize the role of women as wives and mothers. It is hardly surprising, therefore, that this sort of education was by and large incapable of pushing the consciousness of women beyond the appearance of legal equality.

In the country studies that follow, the specific situations under which mass education for women became a significant factor will be discussed. It needs to be said, however, that during the period under discussion, education remained largely the privilege of the bourgeoisie and the petty bourgeoisie. The role played by such women in contributing to the nationalist movements as well as to the social advancement of women, is discussed. But another class of woman was drawn into the movement, not by reason of education but by the very nature of their class position. These were the working-class women who, becoming aware of their exploitation within the colonial system, began to struggle for their economic rights, as well as against imperialism and the prevailing capitalist system. The achievements of women in working-class and revolutionary struggles have been recorded in some of the studies in this book. The apparent gap in other country studies is not due to the fact that there were no such women in those countries, but to the paucity of material. One has to remember that such women often belonged to left-wing movements which, in many of these countries, were crushed by repressive governments. The history of such movements has often been suppressed, and thus the history dealing with women in such movements also disappeared.

19

While emphasizing the internal factors that led to the rise of the feminist movement in Asia, recognition has to be made of the role of Western women, who introduced various ideological strands of opinion which influenced Asian feminist consciousness. For example, women missionaries played a significant part in the process of education, in mitigating discriminatory practices and in putting forward alternative religious ideologies and social practices. From the early 19th century, women missionaries had been active in condemning social evils, in exposing 'barbaric' customs, and in setting an example (especially among Christian converts) of a lifestyle in which women were not secluded. Their behaviour and moral standards served as a model for respectable bourgeois housewives. Other European women who lived in Asia as the wives of colonial officials and professionals (doctors, nurses, teachers), as supporters of local religions or esoteric movements, or as feminists, suffragists, pioneers of birth control and activists in nationalist and revolutionary struggles, also played an important part. Many of these European women were dissidents in their own societies, such as socialists, theosophists and freethinkers who preferred to live in and participate in anti-imperialist movements in the colonies. These included Annie Besant, Margaret Cousins, Sister Nivedita (Margaret Noble) and many others. Moreover, the frequent visits to Asia by foreign women who belonged to feminist and suffragist movements) Mary Carpenter (Britain), Margaret Sanger (USA), Ellen Key (Sweden), Dr Aletta Jacobs (Holland) and Carrie Chapman Catt (USA) — provided Asian women with direct knowledge of the struggles experienced by women in other parts of the world.

The contribution made by foreign women in leftist circles to revolutionary struggles and to the women's struggle in Asia and Africa should also be mentioned. Dutch feminists in the socialist movement helped to arouse early feminism in Indonesia, the best-known being Ms Ovink-Soer, wife of a colonial official, who influenced Kartini, Indonesia's pioneer feminist. Another outstanding woman was an American, Agnes Smedley (1892–1950), who worked with Vir Chattopadhyaya's group of Indian revolutionaries abroad, spent many years in China with the revolutionary army, and was better known in China, Japan and India than in the United States.

Among Japanese women participating in progressive political causes, Agnes Smedley was admired as a Socialist from humble origins who had grown up in a capitalist society, as a person who had spent her lifetime fighting oppression, as an adventurous woman, as a feminist, and as a foreigner who sympathised with the struggles of oppressed peoples in Asia. (Pharr 1981: 120–1)

Foreign wives of several left-wing leaders also made remarkable political contributions. Evelyn Roy was an American radical who helped her husband M.N. Roy (India's best-known Communist of the early years) to organize Indian revolutionaries in New York and later was active in Mexico; in 1920, she and Roy were members of the Indian delegation to the Second Congress of the Communist International in Moscow where, according to all accounts, she played an active part (Overstreet and Windmillar 1959: 27). An English woman, Doreen Wickremasinghe, née Young (wife of the Sri Lankan Communist leader, Dr S.A. Wickremasinghe), was active in the India League in London in the late 1920s and was a pioneer of the socialist and anti-imperialist movement of the thirties and of the first socialist feminist association in Sri Lanka, the Eksath Kantha Peramuna (United Women's Front), formed in 1946.

Mention should also be made of the influence that certain outstanding women in other countries had on Asian women. Popular examples were women of the French Revolution, such as Madame (Marie Jeanne) Roland (1754–93) who was active in politics and died on the guillotine, and Madame (Germaine) de Staël (1766–1817), a novelist and literary critic who was renowned internationally for her books and her love affairs with famous men of the time; both these women were frequently quoted by feminists in Japan, Vietnam and China. Similarly, heroines of the Russian revolutionary movement such as Sofia Perovskaya and Vera Figner were often cited in these countries; and the writings of other Western women, Harriet Beecher Stowe, Emma Goldman, Olive Schreiner and British and American suffragists, were known in Asian feminist circles. Among Asians themselves, Pandita Ramabai of India was to influence Kartini in Indonesia; articles by Jiu Jin of China were translated into Tamil; the Japanese women's university made an impact in India; the Turkish experience influenced women all over the Muslim world; and in Vietnam, inspiration was drawn from feminists in Japan and China.

From the time of Mary Wollstonecraft and Flora Tristan, European feminists were great travellers within their countries and abroad (Mies and Jayawardena 1981: 17 and 61). Likewise the pioneer feminists of the Third World, despite all constraints placed on their physical mobility, were able to find the resources and opportunities to travel widely at home and abroad, and contact women's associations and political groups. To give a few examples: Pandita Ramabai travelled widely in India and went to Europe and North America, returning in the 1880s via Japan, after having met many foreign feminists during her travels. In the early 20th century, Bhikaiji Cama travelled in Europe and the USA, and lived in Paris where she became a focal point for organizing revolutionary Indian groups in Europe, and in the same period, Jiu Jin was one of several Chinese feminists who studied in Japan, as did many Korean women writers. Around 1920 Mao Zedong was active in organizing groups of Chinese radical women to study in France, while many Egyptian, Turkish, Iranian, Japanese and Filipino feminists of the time also travelled to other countries.

During the Second Congress of the Communist International (Comintern) in Moscow in July 1920, a Communist Women's International was formed on the initiative of Clara Zetkin. Its secretariat included the leading women Communists of the period such as Krupskaya (Lenin's wife) and Alexandra Kollontai. The conference adopted resolutions on future work that was to be done among women; these were presented by Zetkin to the full session of the Comintern and approved. Clara Zetkin's dynamism kept the movement alive in the 1920s and it is interesting that several Asian women participated in its activities. The subject has yet to be researched, but their journals of the years 1921–25 include material on China and on women in Muslim countries. Varsenika Kasparova, a Bolshevik militant from Armenia, headed the Eastern section of the Women's Secretariat, and Lu Tain (China), G. Nasarbekowa (Armenia), S. Zalukidse (Georgia), Mussabekowa (Azerbaijan), Nam-Mantschun (Korea) and Dcevad-Sade (Persia) were all members of this Communist Women's International (Kommunistische Fraueninternationale 1921–25).

The most important development in Asian feminism during that period, however, was the emergence of autonomous women's organizations and associations of women linked to political groups which played an important part in nationalist struggles. In some cases, the women were merely involved in promoting handicrafts made by women (e.g. Sakhi Samiti in Bengal in 1886); in the colonial period, however, even such simple activities had political overtones since local products were encouraged in order to counteract the import of goods from Europe. In Korea in 1898, a women's organization that was linked to the liberal political movement agitated for women's rights, especially for education. In 1905, an organization for women's education and suffrage was formed in the Philippines, significantly called Asociacion Feminista Filipino. The first Turkish women's club, named Red and White (1908), was associated with the politics of the Young Turks movement; the Persian Women's Society (1911), which came into being during a period of heightened political agitation and was linked with those struggles, was in contact with British suffragists; the Japanese women's association, Seito (Blue Stocking, 1911), had a strong feminist bias, while the earliest Egyptian women's group, Mabarat Mohamed Ali (1909), was concerned solely with establishing health clinics for women. In contrast, the first Chinese women's association formed by Jiu Jin and other Chinese women revolutionaries studying in Japan in 1904, was consistently feminist and simultaneously agitated for the overthrow of the Manchu dynasty.

The most striking factor about early nationalist and revolutionary agitation in all these countries is that women of all classes went out into the streets to demonstrate on issues of national concern; for example, in India in the nationalist struggles of 1905, 1909 and 1930; in Iran, in 1906 and 1911, during constitutionalist agitation; in China, from 1907 to 1911, during the democratic revolution; in Egypt, China, Turkey, Iran and

Korea, in the 1919 nationalist upsurges after their betrayal by Western powers in the post-World War I treaties; and in Japan, when socialists and anarchists demonstrated in the streets. The Third World in that period produced many pioneering women — including Huda Sharawi (Egypt), Halide Edip (Turkey), Sadiqa Daulatabadi and Khanum Azamodeh (Iran), Kanno Suga and Hiratsuka Raicho (Japan), Pandita Ramabai and Bhikaiji Cama (India), Kartini (Indonesia), Jiu Jin and Xiang Jingyu (China), Minh Khai and Nguyen Thi Nghia (Vietnam), Agnes de Silva (Sri Lanka), and Trinidad Tecson and Conceptión Felix (Philippines) — whose courageous activities have not been adequately recognized but unfortunately remain confined to the footnotes of history. In many cases, their achievements are barely known even in their own countries and their names are seldom commemorated alongside male national heroes.

The development of capitalism in Asia brought the participation of women in the labour force, and women's emancipation struggles were geared towards further acceptance of such participation in all major sectors of the economy. As Shah Reza Khan stated, when promoting measures to bring women out of seclusion, 'one half of the population has not been taken into account . . . *one half of the country's working force has been idle*' (Elwell-Sutton 1955: 34; emphasis added). The presence of women wage-workers in the labour forces of the countries under consideration led to their incorporation into trade unions and other associations of workers, and to their participation in strikes and industrial disputes.

The 1918 Rice Riots in Japan were triggered off when women port workers refused to load rice and were joined by other workers; this led to a long struggle and a political crisis. In China in 1922, many thousands of workers in 70 Shanghai silk factories went on strike, calling for increased wages and a ten-hour working day; this was the first important strike by Chinese women workers. In India and Sri Lanka, in the years after World War I women workers were active participants in militant industrial agitation and strikes. To give only one example from the region, the most militant activists of the Ceylon Labour Union which led the strikes in Sri Lanka in the 1920s were women factory workers in Colombo; they used to dress in red, were the most vociferous of the strikers and picketers, and formed a bodyguard for male trade union leaders during demonstrations. In Iran, Egypt and Turkey, women were to join with men in the formation of left-wing political groups and trade unions, in spite of repression and adverse conditions for mobilizing the people.

Finally, this study attempts to examine a period of Asian history from the perspective of women's participation in feminist movements for emancipation and their simultaneous involvement in struggles for national liberation and social change. This has included an evaluation of the contribution and motives of male reformers and political leaders who championed 'women's rights'. The study is limited in scope, being necessarily confined to countries for which material is available. I must also emphasize that a comprehensive history of the participation of the poverty-stricken masses of women in various forms of agitation in Asia has yet to be attempted. While material is available on movements that involved women of the bourgeoisie and petty bourgeoisie of Asia, an intensive search would be necessary to unearth detailed information on the participation of women of the working class and peasantry in class struggles and anti-imperialist agitation. (This is a task which perhaps can be done only by motivated researchers in their own countries.) It will be evident that in each of the country studies, certain specific aspects have been highlighted and discussed at some length in this book, for example, education in Sri Lanka, social reform movements in India, revolutionary struggles in China, and the struggle against religious constraints in Turkey. This has enabled particular aspects to be discussed in greater depth, according to material available.

Another area on which there is insufficient research is the role of women in the pre-capitalist societies of Asia before the impact of colonialism. There are some studies that deal with the impact of ideology on women, but such conclusions as can be drawn from these studies remain rather abstract. The level at which ideology affected women in real life and was really operative are matters on which our knowledge is insufficient.

The women's movements in many countries of Asia achieved political and legal equality with men at the juridical level, but failed to make any impression on women's subordination within the patriarchal structures of family and society. Feminist consciousness did not develop, except in rare exceptions, to the point of questioning traditional patriarchal structures. The conclusion to the book is an attempt to assess the basis of these successes and failures.

2. 'Civilization' Through Women's Emancipation in Turkey

> I see women covering their faces with their head scarves or turning their backs when a man approaches. Do you really think that the mothers and daughters of a civilised nation would behave so oddly or be so backward?
> *Mustapha Kemal* (Minai 1981: 64–5)

The movement towards women's emancipation in Turkey was closely integrated with successive waves of modernization and secularization and with the ideology of Westernization and social reform. The political ideology of the country had passed through several phases. The intellectuals and reformists of the 19th-century Ottoman Empire were inspired by liberal, Masonic and internationalist ideas, derived from their links with France. The Young Turks, the reformers of the early 20th century, were also strongly influence by currents of opinion in France, especially of the positivist school, and also by Islamic and Turkish nationalism. When Mustapha Kemal took power in the 1920s, the dominant ideology became one of secular modernization. The ways in which women's rights were closely linked with these changes will be considered in the following pages.

At the end of the 19th century, the Ottoman Empire, which had at one time threatened Central Europe, was in the process of disintegration. Externally, it faced pressure from the European powers who wished to expand their influence into the Middle East; internally, the pressure came from two sources: growing feelings of nationalism among the non-Turkish population of the Empire (Greeks, Armenians and people of the Balkans), and a desire for modernization and democratic institutions among the Turks themselves.

Its proximity to, and domination over, parts of Europe had brought Turkey under the influence of European thought from an early period. The strongest influence in the 18th and 19th centuries was that of France, the impact of the French Revolution being felt in the post-1789 period: 'while the Revolution itself was still in progress, the first vital penetration of ideas took place, opening the way to the great flood, which . . . transformed the outlook, thought and self-awareness not only of Turkey but of all Islam' (Lewis 1965: 55). The dangers of such heresies from France were clearly recognized by the *ancien régime* in Turkey. A memorandum drafted in 1798 by the Ottoman Chief Secretary for the High Council of State said:

> The known and famous atheists, Voltaire and Rousseau and other materialists like them, had printed and published various works consisting, God preserve us, of insults and vilification against the pure prophets and the great kings, of the removal and abolition of all religion, and allusions to the sweetness of equality and republicanism, all expressed in easily intelligible words and phrases, in the form of mockery, in the language of the common people. (Lewis 1982: 182–3)

These ideas were further pursued in a warning proclamation to the Sultan's subjects: 'They assert . . . that all men are equal in humanity and alike in being men, none has any superiority of merit over any other and everyone himself disposes of his soul and arranges his own livelihood in this life . . . (Lewis 1982: 183).

Nevertheless, a conscious effort was made to modernize along European lines. In 1792, Sultan Selim III established a 'New Order' (*Nizam-i Cedid*) in administration and in the armed forces, the latter being reorganized on the European model with military and naval schools where instruction was given in French by French officers.

> The result . . . was to create a new social element — a class of young army and naval officers, familiar with some aspects of Western civilisation through study, reading and personal contact, acquainted with at least one Western language — usually French — and accustomed to look up to Western experts as their mentors and guides to new and better ways. (Lewis 1965: 59)

The reforms also included the appointment of ambassadors to the major capitals of Europe; they were instructed to acquire foreign languages and knowledge that would be useful to the empire. Gradually, however, propaganda from orthodox and conservative sources against French influence and against the reforms increased, until, in 1807, a backlash occurred when a section of the Turkish army revolted, deposed the Sultan, and massacred many of the people who had foreign inclinations.

The second wave of reform, which began during the rule of Mahmud II (1808–39), was intended to strengthen the state apparatus against foreign invasion. Naval and military students were sent to France and other European countries for training: 'the first outriders of a great procession of Turkish students to Europe, who on their return played a role of immense importance to the transformation of their country' (Lewis 1982: 82). In 1827, an army medical school was established, followed by a music school, and in 1834 a school of military sciences, modelled on the lines of St Cyr in France. In 1839, preparations were made for civilian education and two grammar schools were established to produce civil servants. In 1838, in his speech at the opening of a new medical college, the Sultan stated: 'You will study . . . in French . . . my purpose . . . is not to educate you in the French language; it is to teach you scientific medicine and little by little to take it into our language (Lewis 1965: 83–4).

The reform of feudal and religious privileges and reform in dress were also attempted in the early 19th century. In 1828, the fez was introduced from North Africa into the Turkish army together with European-style tunics and trousers; in 1829, officials had to wear the fez with trousers, frock coats and boots. The Sultan set an example and even adopted European protocol when receiving foreign diplomats; he 'gave receptions and chatted with his guests, and even went so far as to show deference to ladies' (Lewis 1965: 98–101).

The Tanzimat (Reorganization)

When Mahmud II died in 1839, he was succeeded by his son, Abdul Majid, who, under the influence of Mustafa Rashid Pasha, former ambassador to France and Minister of Foreign Affairs, inaugurated a further set of reforms. These reforms, promulgated in 1839 and known as the Tanzimat, marked a fundamental change in Turkey from a theocratic Sultanate to the beginnings of a modern state. The security of the subject's life, honour and property, and fair and public trials were guaranteed, and a new penal code was formulated. The principle of equality of all persons of all religions before the law was considered a very bold move for the times (Lewis 1965: 105). The tax structure was reformed, tax farms were abolished, and a new provincial administration based on the centralized French system was set up, replacing the earlier semi-feudal system.

Controversy arose, however, over a new commercial code derived from French law on grounds that it did not conform to holy law. 'The Holy Law has nothing to do with the matter', was Rashid Pasha's reply to the *ulemas* (religious leaders). In this instance, however, the *ulemas* proved more powerful; Rashid Pasha was dismissed and the reforms appeared to suffer a setback. But ultimately the processes of modernization were to prove stronger. Rashid Pasha returned as Grand Vizier in 1845. With the help of some convinced and Westernized supporters, he made a great effort to enforce the new principles in every sphere of government. The reforms were extended into the educational structure. A Council of Education established primary and secondary state schools alongside the religious schools, and tried to unify the system. Progress was slow, however, and by 1850 there were only six secondary schools with 870 pupils. In 1847, the creation of a Ministry of Education effectively took away the *ulemas'* power of sole jurisdiction in this field (Lewis 1982: 111–12).

In the years following Rashid Pasha's death in 1858, two younger reformers, Ali Pasha and Fuad Pasha, continued the policies of the Tanzimat; both had acquired some knowledge of French and had been diplomats before holding high office in government. As Lewis has shown, in Turkey at that period 'the new elite of power came not from the army, not from the Ulema, but from the Translation Office and the Embassy secretaries' (Lewis 1965: 116).

Abdul Aziz became Sultan in 1861 and in 1867 visited London, Paris and Vienna. In 1868 a French *lycée* was opened, giving Western secondary education in French. The most important reform of the period, however, was the new civil code completed in 1876 and drafted by Ahmed Cevdet, who 'preferred to remain within the Islamic tradition, and to prepare a code, which while modern in form and presentation would be firmly based on the Seriat . . . It remained in force in Turkey until . . . 1926' (Lewis 1965: 121).

The Young Ottoman Movement

At the time that European ideas were spreading in Turkey, a new literary movement arose which broke from the classical Turkish style and was inspired to some extent by French writing. The pioneers were Ibrahim Sinasi (1826–71), Ziya Pasha (1825–80) and Namik Kemal (1840–88), all writers who tried to reconcile the Turkish Muslim identity with the pressure for modernization. Sinasi had studied in Paris, and is said to have taken part in the 1848 revolution there; in 1862, after returning to Turkey, he began a journal which influenced Turkish intellectuals. Ziya Pasha, also a student of French, was exiled in Europe because of his criticisms of the regime. He constantly wrote about the need to learn from the West while not imitating Western models and was a fierce critic of his own society. In 1870 in Geneva, he wrote: 'I passed through the lands of the infidels, I saw cities and mansions; I wandered in the realm of Islam, I saw nothing but ruins' (Lewis 1965: 22). Namik Kemal also studied French; he went into the Translation Office and also worked for Sinasi's journal. In exile in Europe, he published journals that opposed the regime. His principal ideas, expressed in poems, plays and novels, were of freedom and the fatherland 'in a form adapted to Muslim traditions and attitudes' (Lewis 1965: 138). These liberal reformers, known as the 'Young Ottomans', had to live in exile while opposition against them increased in Turkey, but their influence was felt and they paved the way for the more radical reformers of later years.

Women and Education

The issue of women's education was the subject of much debate in the Ottoman Empire in the 19th century, and the decision was taken that education should be extended to women. Sultan Abdul Aziz opened middle-level schools and a teachers' training college for girls in 1863, but the education provided was a very basic one, mainly religious in orientation, with the aim of creating good Muslim wives and mothers. Some upper-class girls, however, were given a cosmopolitan education at home by foreign governesses, or attended foreign schools in Turkey. In 1871, for example, the American College for Girls was started; for two decades attendance was restricted to Christians, the first Muslim girl to complete her studies there being Halide Edip, a future women's leader. Thus with the emergence of a Western-educated Turkish aristocracy and bourgeoisie in the 19th century, the issue of educated wives had already arisen:

> Though Turkish fathers . . . had their women wear the best Paris fashions . . . and took them to the most elegant capitals of Europe, they expected the governesses to give their daughters much more than charm-school training. They wanted their daughters to have serious Occidental and Oriental education, *as befitted the future spouses of important men*. (Minai 1981: 49; emphasis added)

Many women educated in this manner were to make their mark as novelists and writers on women's emancipation.

> Unlike their mothers, who expressed themselves through the nightingales and roses of formal Turkish poetry, the daughters wrote letters, memoirs, newspaper articles and novels . . . prose freed women's thoughts . . . it created a psychological climate for social change, all the more powerfully because their writings could be printed and circulated to help unite harem-bound women. (Minai 1981: 50)

The first woman novelist of this epoch was Fatima Aliyé (born in 1862), daughter of Ahmet Cevdet, a historian who was also active in politics; she was educated at home in French and first achieved success as the translator of a French novel in 1890. In 1892, she wrote a novel *Muhadarat* ('Womanhood'), a story of a gifted woman whose development was stunted by traditional society. This was followed by another publication, *Nisvani Islam* ('Islamic Women'), which denounced the misinterpretation of Islam and urged women to become educated and to participate in society. In 1895, Aliyé published and wrote extensively in *A Newspaper for Ladies*, 'one of Turkey's first and longest-lived newspapers for women by women', which was an outlet for a spate of women writers and journalists. Another woman writer, Zeyneb Hanoum, who had travelled in France and Britain, wrote of the contradictions faced by those Turkish women who had received a European-style education but yet remained confined by tradition. The details of harem life that she gave to Pierre Loti, the French writer, led to his novel *Les Désenchantées* (published in 1906) which 'describes the malaise of a Turkish woman whose brain had leaped to the twentieth century while her body remained imprisoned by medieval customs' (Minai 1981: 52–4).

The Young Turks Movement

Opposition to the Sultan's despotism manifested itself in 1889, when the 'Young Turks' group was formed by four medical students; this group, officially called the Committee of Union and Progress (CUP), soon had within its ranks many minor officials, small traders and Istanbul students. Groups of exiled Turks were also organized in Europe and Egypt. Young Turks were active among the army officers; one group, set up in Damascus in 1906, had Mustapha Kemal, the future Turkish president, among its members. In France, the Young Turks were led by Ahmed Riza (1859–1930), who had come under the influence of the positivist French philosophy of Auguste Comte (1798–1857). Writing in a period of rapid industrial transformation of society, Comte rejected supernaturalism and the orthodoxy of the church and advocated the adoption of the positive or scientific method, emphasizing the need for a basic social science which would study society and explain social organization (which he called 'sociology'). He rejected the Christian god in favour of a new, secular religion of humanity and a new social system based on political, social and economic justice. The emphasis was on universal education, the monogamous family and the use of empirical data rather than metaphysical speculation. Moreover, positivism with its scientific perspective, replacing religion with notions of social progress, influenced many social reform and secular movements in Europe, and had an impact on students from Asia who were challenging their own religious and feudal hierarchies.

One of the principal tenets of the Young Turks was the need for modernization and Westernization, and they expressed themselves forcibly against the orthodox elements. To some, it was a matter of survival and not choice: 'Either we westernize, or we are destroyed' was the view of Ahmed Muhtar the scholar and soldier, who formed the government in 1912. Similarly, Abdullah Cevdet, one of the founders of the movement, wrote: 'There is no second civilization; civilization means European civilization and it must be imported with both its roses and thorns'. This civilization meant a new status for women; a journal edited by Cevdet published an interesting article in 1912, describing a vision of the future Westernized Turkey, where, among other things, the Sultan would have one wife and no harem, the fez would be abolished, women could wear what they wanted and could choose their spouses, and matchmaking would be prohibited (Lewis 1965: 231–2).

It must be remembered that the process of Europeanization was not only ideological; it also meant the forging of economic links with the capitalist countries of Europe. In the 50 years between the Tanzimat reforms and the Young Turks revolution of 1908, according to Keyder: 'central authority was strengthened while the country fell gradually under the political control of the imperialist powers' but 'the successive waves of modernization could not achieve a permanent balance in favour of a modern state mechanism conducive for the sustained development of capitalism' (Keyder 1979: 4–5).

The Young Turks' actual take-over of power began with a mutiny in the Turkish army in Macedonia in July 1908; this was led by Major Niazi and Mustapha Kemal was one of its participants. The revolt spread through all major cities, and Sultan Abdul Hamid was compelled to restore the Constitution and grant certain democratic rights. He attempted a counter-coup in 1909; but this failed and resulted in his deposition and succession by Mohamed V. This was the last attempt to restore absolutism in Turkey.

The Young Turks initiated many political and administrative reforms with the intention of modernizing the empire. The financial administration was reorganized and measures were taken to extend the education of women. However, their reforming zeal was contained by the Balkan wars and by the World War of 1914–18. The great powers of Europe, which had contemptuously referred to Turkey as 'the sick man of Europe', took this opportunity to dismember the Ottoman Empire. They not only attacked Turkey but also fomented revolts among its non-Turkish elements. Under the Treaty of Sèvres (1920), Turkey lost all its European and Arab possessions, while the Dardanelles and the Bosphorus were internationalized.

Although they visualized a modernized empire within which its many peoples could live, the Young Turks were essentially Islamic and supportive of the sultanate. The growth of nationalism among the non-Turkish peoples, however, and the nation's defeat in war, caused a new group to emerge among the Young Turks, a group which advocated the building of a modern Turkish national state that was 'republican, secular and non-imperialist' (Keyder 1979: 9). Following the Sultan's capitulation to the Western powers, this new group led various protests and uprisings.

The Young Turks and Women's Emancipation

During the period of Young Turk dominance, more high schools and teachers' colleges for women were established, and the first university for women was set up in 1915. With the spread of education for women and with greater concern for a democratic reorganization of the state, the issue of women's emancipation was extended beyond the question of education. Their status in both the domestic and political spheres was widely discussed in journals, literature and drama. Many leading intellectuals became involved in these discussions. In 1910 Halil Hamit published *Feminism in Islam* which supported women's suffrage; in 1915, Celal Nuri wrote *Our Women*, in which he urged that polygamy be banned. Another leading politician and intellectual of the period, Ahmet Agaoglu, who had studied in Paris, argued in favour of women's rights and encouraged his daughter, Sureyya, to become Turkey's first woman lawyer. Like many other intellectuals in Muslim countries, Agaoglu associated the denial of rights for women with backwardness, and claimed that women's rights were 'in accordance with the tenets of pure Islam cleansed of misinterpretations' (Minai 1981: 48).

The country's best-known writer and sociologist, Ziya Gokalp (1876–1924), often referred to as the theoretician of Turkish nationalism, writing around 1915, also advocated equality in marriage, divorce and succession rights for women (Abadan-Unat 1981: 9). He further argued that women's emancipation was part of an early Turkish tradition of the free nomads of Central Asia (Minai 1981: 48). Expressing himself in poetry, Gokalp wrote:

All must be equal, marriage, divorce, wealth
No nation can ever bloom if its daughters
Are not given the weight they deserve.
We have fought for and won all our other rights.
Only the family is still in its dark age.
Why do we still turn our backs on women?
Tell me, have they not a part in our struggles?

In this period, when the role of women was eagerly debated in intellectual and reformist circles, there was also a flourishing feminist press. Between 1908 and 1919, nine women's papers were published, some in both French and Turkish. They catered to educated women and highlighted the freedom that women were said to have had in the days of the Prophet. In their advocacy of women's emancipation in Turkey, these papers were motivated by their Western bias and knowledge of European feminist movements. They

interpreted Western ideas for Turkish women's consumption, [and] they also became a forum to unite the readers, each of whom had thought that she was alone in her frustration and confusion. The women enthusiastically took up the chance to communicate with one another. 'For the first time I feel proud to be a woman' wrote one of them. (Minai 1981: 61)

From the early years of the century Turkish women began to be active in the social, political and economic life of the country, as well as in education and journalism. The deposition of the Sultan in 1908 gave an impetus to their activities. In that year, the first women's club was formed in Salonika, with the name Red and White (the colour of the Young Turks); other women's organizations of the period included The Association for the Betterment of Women, led by Kadriye Ihsan, and the more radical Ottoman Association for the Defence of Women's Rights led by Nuriye Ulviye Mevlan, who in 1913 began a journal *Women's World* (Abadan-Unat 1981: 7–8).

This period also witnesses renewed intellectual and cultural activity among the Turkish intelligentsia. The journal *Türk Yurdu* ('Turkish Homeland'), edited in 1912 by Ziya Gokalp, became the rallying point for Turkish nationalists. Associated with this, the *Türk Ocaği* ('Turkish

Hearth') movement was formed in 1912 to 'advance national education and raise the scientific, social and economic level of the Turks, who are the foremost of the peoples of Islam, and to strive for the betterment of the Turkish race and language'. Many such clubs were formed throughout the country and became centres of debate and educational and literary activity. Women participated in the gatherings on terms of equality with men, and for the first time were able to speak on a public platform as well as to perform in amateur dramatics (Lewis 1965: 344).

In general conformity with the ideology of the Young Turk movement, however, the question of women's emancipation was debated within the limits laid down by Islam and by Turkish nationalism. Some proponents of women's rights based their case on a rereading of Islamic texts: it was argued that the severe limitations on women in the Ottoman Empire resulted largely from various misinterpretations of Islam. Even Ziya Gokalp found it necessary to locate his arguments for women's emancipation in the context of the nomadic ancestors of the Turkish nation. Thus, the basic thrust for women's rights based on the needs of a modernizing society and its demands for women's participation, was given legitimacy by reference to religious and nationalist traditions.

The Kemalist Revolution

The leader of the Turkish nationalists was Mustapha Kemal (1881–1938), an army captain who had fought in the Turkish army during World War I but had opposed the Sultan's defeatist policies and set up a revolutionary government in Ankara in 1920. Kemal's men forced the French, Italians, Greeks and British to terminate their occupation of parts of Turkey, and a peace treaty was signed with the British in 1922. Soon afterwards, the Sultanate was abolished and the Turkish Republic was established in 1923 with Kemal, the leader of the Republican People's Party, as President. He remained in this office until his death in 1938.

Mustapha Kemal (referred to subsequently as Atatürk, 'the father of the Turks') began a more deliberate process of Europeanization which meant not only economic development along capitalist lines, but also an effort to secularize and modernize the state by separating politics from religion, attacking tradition, Latinizing the alphabet, promoting European dress, adopting the Western calendar, introducing civil marriage and divorce, and banning polygamy.

The fetish of Europeanization, which had existed in Turkey in earlier periods, was to become part of the new ideology. To be European was equated with being 'civilized', and Turkish 'backwardness' was contrasted with Western 'progress'. The country's leading nationalist intellectual, Ziya Gokalp, urged the Turks to 'Belong to the Turkish nation, the Muslim religion and European civilization'; in similar vein, another Turkish writer, Sadri Etem, asserted: 'We are Europeans, to be

European is our ideal' (Rodinson 1974: 127). To be European also meant taking the capitalist road of development. In the absence of entrepreneurs, the state had to assume the task of developing industry in order to pave the way for capitalist growth. As Gokalp wrote in 1923:

> If the new Turkey is to be a modern state it must above all develop a national industry. Just as we have done in the field of military technique, so in industry we must reach European levels by an effort undertaken on a national scale. (Rodinson 1974: 126)

The promotion of a national economy built on capitalist lines was advocated, the principal beneficiaries of this effort being naturally the commercial bourgeoisie. In spite of a burst of rapid accumulation during the war, however, this class was not well developed in Turkish society, and when the 'difficulties characteristic of a trade-oriented peripheral capitalism, hit the economy', the state stepped in 'to act once again as the redistributing centre which collected and disposed of the surplus according to its own conceptions of the national economy' (Keyder 1979: 11).

The Turkish state became totally secularized with the abolition in 1926 of the *sharia* (Islamic holy law), which freed the civil and penal codes of their last vestiges of religious influence. In Turkey, as in many Asian countries, clerical authority was seen as retrograde and supportive of corrupt, feudal regimes, and therefore as not conducive either to the growth of nationalism and capitalist development or to (what were considered) necessary superstructural reforms of the social system, such as measures to emancipate women. The tendency towards secularism and rationalism was seen not only in the Young Turks movement of the early 20th century but also in many of Mustapha Kemal's reforms in the 1920s which, in turn, influenced policies in Iran, Afghanistan and other Muslim countries. In 1930, Mustapha Kemal made it clear that he associated secularism with progress:

> The Turkish Republic has no official religion. In state affairs, all legislation is drafted and applied according to the spirit, form and universal necessity as seen by science and contemporary civilization. Since religion is merely a matter of personal conviction, the Republic sees in the separation of religious ideas and affairs of State a principal factor in the progress of our nation. (Aksan 1981: 49)

Dissident views of minorities and leftists, however, were vigorously suppressed by Kemal. When the Kurds revolted in 1925, he took the opportunity to crush not only this minority uprising but all opposition to his regime. This included the left, which Kemal had tried to eliminate from the early years of his regime, while maintaining a policy of friendship with the Soviet Union. The Turkish Communist Party had been formed in 1920 in the Soviet Union and was led by Mustapha Suphi; before it could develop, however, 'Turkish communism was stifled at birth by the prior success of Kemal Ataturk's independence movement' (Samin 1981: 64–5). Kemal did not hesitate to liquidate such opposition.

The 'Green Army', a guerrilla peasant force whose objective was to expropriate the village rulers, had at first allied with Kemal, but was later crushed by his troops in January 1921. In the same month Suphi and other Turkish Communists were trapped into visiting Turkey, only to be killed by drowning. As Samin writes: 'Thus both the founding Turkish communists as well as the most militant class force were cut down within weeks.' He adds that the Turkish Communists 'instead of recognizing the "Bonapartist" character of the Ataturk regime, with its state-organized primitive accumulation . . . insisted on seeing the Kemalist movement as a petty-bourgeois force which could be influenced in radical directions. In fact, it was Ataturkism which made use of them, not the other way round.' It must be noted, however, that men and women of the left did play a political role in subsequent years. Nazim Hikmet, 'Turkey's supreme poet', was a Communist Party member from the 1930s, and much of the creative input into modern Turkish culture has been 'socialist or Left-populist in character' (Samin 1981: 64–5). Hikmet, who was tried and imprisoned in 1938 for his political views, expressed sentiments in favour of women's equality and 'was the first Turkish poet to attribute to woman such qualities as friendship and solidarity' (Altiok 1981: 224).

Kemal and the Emancipation of Women

An important element of Mustapha Kemal's vision of the modernization of Turkey was the emancipation of women from the rigid shackles of orthodoxy. He had been particularly impressed by the courage and militancy of Turkish women during the Balkan wars and World War I. Turkish women had then taken up new avenues of public employment as nurses on the war fronts, and had worked in ammunition, food and textile factories, as well as in banks, hospitals and the administrative services. Political events caused their involvement in militant activities. For instance, the occupation of various parts of Turkey by European troops in 1919 aroused protests in which women joined, and women in Anatolia were part of Mustapha Kemal's army which had launched a war against the invaders. In 1919, the 'Anatolian Women's Association for Patriotic Defence' was formed with many branches: 'They became the female counterpart of the core group of Mustapha Kemal's bureaucrats, soldiers and merchants' (Abadan-Unat 1981: 10).

In his speeches in later years Kemal constantly referred to the role played by Anatolian women in the nationalist struggle. In his speech, 'The Turkish Woman', made at Konya in 1923, he said:

> The Anatolian woman has her part in these sublime acts of self-sacrifice and must be remembered with gratitude, by each one of us. Nowhere in the world has there been a more intensive effort than the one made by the Anatolian peasant women.
> Woman was the source of a vital dynamism: who ploughed the fields? She did. Who sowed the grain? She. Who turned into a woodcutter and wielded the

35

axe? She. Who kept the fires of home burning? She. Who, notwithstanding rain or wind, heat or cold, carried the ammunition to the front? She did, again and again. The Anatolian woman is divine in her devotion.

Let us therefore honour this courageous and self-sacrificing woman. It is for us to pledge ourselves to accept women as our partners in all our social work, to live with her, to make her our companion in the scientific, moral, social and economic realm. I believe that this is the road to follow. (Atatürk)

Kemal's ideas about the position of women in society were quite advanced. In a speech at Izmir in 1923 he said, 'A civilisation where one sex is supreme can be condemned, there and then, as crippled. A people which has decided to go forward and progress must realise this as quickly as possible. The failures in our past are due to the fact that we remained passive to the fate of women.' (Atatürk)

He kept reverting to this subject in his speeches and was tireless in spreading his views on the equality of women. Speaking to the people at Kastamonu, he said:

Let us be frank: society is made of women as well as men. If one grants all the rights to progress to the one and no rights at all to the other, what happens? Is it possible that one half of the population is in chains for the other half to reach the skies? Progress is possible only through a common effort, only thus can the various stages be by-passed. (Atatürk)

While having advanced views on the one hand, Kemal also continued to stress the importance of motherhood. In 1923 he said:

History shows the great virtues shown by our mothers and grandmothers. One of these has been to raise sons of whom the race can be proud. Those whose glory spread across Asia and as far as the limits of the world had been trained by highly virtuous mothers who taught them courage and truthfulness. I will not cease to repeat it, woman's most important duty, apart from her social responsibilities, is to be a good mother. As one progresses in time, as civilisation advances with giant steps, it is imperative that mothers be enabled to raise their children according to the needs of the century. (Atatürk)

But Kemal was also adamant that Westernized Turks should have wives who were equally 'civilized' and modern in outlook and appearance. He followed this precept in his own personal life. His wife Latife Hanem (whom he married and divorced in the early 1920s) was educated in Britain and France, and appeared with him, unveiled, on public occasions.

In keeping with these views, Kemal was a great supporter of the movement for a modern secularized education for women. He argued that society could not function efficiently if women remained uneducated: 'if only some of the members of a social body are active while others remain inert, the social body is thereby paralysed'. He claimed that if Turkey was to become a strong modern nation, the education of women was necessary since children receive their first lessons from their mothers: 'hence, our women have the obligation to be more enlightened, more civilized and wiser even than the men' (UNESCO 1963: 45–50). His campaign resulted in the expansion of educational opportunities for women, with coeducational university education being allowed in 1921. In 1924, an Education Bill brought religious schools under government control, secularized education, and made provision for equal educational opportunities for both sexes. These measures were not enacted without opposition. In 1921, the Minister of Education was forced to resign after being criticized in the National Assembly for holding a Teachers' Congress, attended by male and female teachers (Toprek 1981: 286–7). Some women, however, benefited from these measures: the first woman doctor in Turkey, Safiye Ali, opened a clinic in Istanbul in 1922, and by the 1930s many others had entered the well-paid professions; but women's education in Turkey has remained class-bound and very uneven. In the 1970s women formed 20% of the legal profession and 17% of the medical profession; these figures are higher than those in the USA, France and many other European countries, yet the general illiteracy rate for Turkish women was as high as 52% (Öncü 1981: 181).

Another reform of the Kemalist period which had great significance for women was the introduction of a new civil code in 1926, based on the Swiss model. Under the new law, polygamy and marriage by proxy were declared illegal, women were given equal rights regarding divorce, custody of children, and inheritance, while minimum ages for marriage were raised to 18 for men and 17 for women. More daringly, a Muslim woman could legally marry a non-Muslim, and adults were legally allowed to change their religion. The courts also accorded equality to women in respect of testimony, instead of the earlier practice whereby the testimonies of two women equalled that of one man. The separation of property and goods, and the right of the woman to freely dispose of her property, were also introduced (Abadan-Unat 1981: 13–14).

The reforms caused a sensation at the time, and Turkey became the first Muslim country to adopt a civil code in place of the *sharia*, or Muslim legal code. In his speeches, Kemal had referred to the need to 'reach a level of contemporary civilization', and this was to be the keynote of the discussion justifying the changes. In introducing the code, Mahmud Esad, the Minister of Justice, stated that 'the Turkish nation has decided to accept modern civilization and its living principles without any condition or reservation' (Rodinson 1974: 127). Another speaker stated: 'The new law incorporates such principles as monogamy and the right to divorce — principles, which are required for a civilized world' (Öncü 1981: 181).

Kemal had indicated that it was not the reform of the God-given religious law, but its replacement by a new family law that the country needed. In 1924 he declared, 'The basis of civilization, the foundation of progress and power, are in family life. A bad family life leads inevitably to social, economic and political enfeeblement' (Lewis 1965: 266–7). It was on the legal front that the religious authorities suffered their most serious defeat, the whole sphere of family law being taken away from them. In 1925, in an attack on these conservative forces, Kemal said:

> The efforts made by the Turkish nation for at least three centuries to profit from the means and benefits of modern civilisation have been frustrated by painful and grievous obstacles . . . the greater and . . . most insidious enemies of the revolution are rotten laws and their decrepit upholders. It is our purpose to create completely new laws, and thus to tear up the foundation of the old legal system. (Lewis 1965: 268–9)

Thus, the whole system of law was changed in Turkey and in addition to the new commercial, maritime and criminal laws, a new system of civil law was introduced. However, those reforms involving personal law did not question the continuation of patriarchy. For example, the husband remained the head of the family, alone entitled to choose domicile; the wife had to obey him and needed his consent to work outside the home. The new laws proved insufficient to change the force of tradition which ruled in the countryside. Even with such limitations, Turkish women intellectuals claim that the reform 'was a great step forward as far as women's status was concerned' (Tekeli 1981: 297). The code was certainly a step forward, as was the subsequent enfranchisement of women in local elections in 1930 and in the national elections in 1935. In the 1935 elections, 18 women (4.5% of the Assembly) were elected, the highest number of women deputies in Europe at that time, when many European countries, including France and Italy, did not even have female franchise (Tekeli 1981: 299).

Dress Reform

The imposition of dress reform was an integral part of Mustapha Kemal's policy of 'Westernizing' and thereby 'civilizing' the country and abolishing some of the superstructural symbols of the caliphate; for example the fez, which was introduced in Turkey only in 1828, had become a symbol of the Ottoman Empire and of its Islamic heritage. In the 19th and early 20th centuries, many Turks had adopted European clothes but 'even among the immaculately trousered and jacketed dandies of the capital, one badge of distinctness had remained — the fez' (Lewis 1965: 262).

Kemal consistently emphasized the issue of dress in his tours around Turkey. In Kastamonu he exclaimed:

> I see a man in the crowd in front of me; he has a fez on his head, a green turban on the fez, a smock on his back, and on top of that a jacket like the one I am wearing. I can't see the lower half. Now what kind of outfit is that? Would a civilised man put on this preposterous garb and go out to hold himself up to universal ridicule? (Lewis 1965: 264)

The issue of the fez and Turkish dress became a political one and Kemal used the prevailing emergency laws to pass decrees on dress reform. 'We did it while the law for the Maintenance of Order was still in force . . . the existence of the law made it much easier for us and . . . prevented the large-scale poisoning of the nation by certain reactionaries' (Lewis 1965: 265). Kemal not only hit at symbols of the old Ottoman society, but also enforced a 'secular' dress which did not proclaim religion or ethnicity. He led the way, wearing a European hat and clothes and giving orders that the Turks, including religious leaders and government servants, should discard the fez and wear European-style hats, on the grounds that 'we have to resemble the civilized world in our costume' (Bisbee 1951: 23). In a defiant mood, Kemal stated that the dress of the 'civilized' world was suitable for Turkey and declared:

> We will wear boots and shoes, trousers, shirts, waistcoats, collars, ties . . . we will dress in morning coats and lounge suits, in smoking jackets and tail coats. And if there are persons who hesitate and draw back, I will tell them that they are fools. (Wortham 1931: 193)

Women's dress also became a controversial issue. Turkish women were requested, but not compelled, by the government to abandon the veil and to wear Western clothes. Even Kemal hesitated to flout traditional opinion by using emergency laws to abolish the veil, but he campaigned vigorously on the issue. The women of the bourgeoisie did not hesitate to adopt the latest European fashions, but the dress reform hardly affected the rural women.

Kemal's view of 'civilized' behaviour also included discarding old forms of salutation (the salaam), encouraging Muslim women of good families to become actresses, discouraging Turkish music and propagating Western music, and popularizing European social etiquette, including ballroom dancing. Kemal himself gave regular dances and ordered his officers and their wives to dance; this resulted in a craze for ballroom dancing in the major cities, which outraged the traditionalists. In his personal life, too, Kemal challenged Muslim orthodoxy by marrying in a ceremony where no religious *imam* was present and the bride was unveiled, and encouraging his adopted daughter to become a pilot. It is interesting to note that Kemal is supposed to have considered his wife to have had ideal feminine virtues such as the ability 'to talk, dance, and drink cocktails' (Wortham 1931: 167).

This forcible imposition from above of Western dress and social graces on a population with its own distinct culture caused only a superficial change, however. It was not easy to revolutionize social customs by decree, especially customs that involved religious orthodoxy, although a powerful cultural organization was used to make propaganda in favour of the new changes through schools, books, dramas and films. In addition, an inquisitional committee was formed, called the Tribunal of Independence, which went from village to village punishing those who did not conform to the new dress regulations: 'the rumour of its approach might cause the veils to disappear and the baggy Turkish trousers . . . to vanish until these dreaded gentry left the neighbourhood. Things could then return to their comfortable ways' (Wortham 1931: 203).

Several other reforms represented major attacks on tradition and orthodoxy. In 1928, the clause in the Constitution of 1924 that 'The religion of the Turkish State is Islam' was deleted by a vote in the Assembly, thereby finally disestablishing Islam and making Turkey a secular state. The other assault was on a remaining symbol of Islamic identity, namely the Arabic script. In 1928, the Latin script was introduced and the Minister of Education stated: 'The adoption of Latin letters is for us a necessity. The old literature is doomed to moulder away.' Again, Kemal made the point that the changes were part of the 'civilizing' process; announcing the new script he said:

> Our rich and harmonious language will now be able to display itself with new Turkish letters. We must free ourselves from these incomprehensible signs that for centuries have held our minds in an iron vice. You must learn the new Turkish letters quickly. Teach them to your compatriots, to women and to men, to porters and to boatmen . . . for a nation to consist of 80 per cent of illiterates is shameful. Now is the time to eradicate the errors of the past . . . *Our nation will show, with its script and with its mind that its place is with the civilised world.* (Lewis 1965: 272; emphasis added)

Halide Edip

The effects of the Kemalist reforms on women in Turkey can be illustrated by the life of Halide Edip (1883–1964), the woman nationalist who had served in Kemal's forces. Edip came from a traditionally influential family, her father being at one time the Sultan's secretary. She had received a European education, both at school and at home, and was a frequent contributor to liberal journals on literary subjects and on women's issues. Her greatest successes were as a novelist and political agitator. In her novels, which are mainly concerned with women's rights (the best-known being *Sinekli Bakkal*), she tries to synthesize the two prevailing ideologies of the time, Turkish nationalism and the Westernization ideal:

> As she began writing in the pre-republican period and continued to do so during the period of Ataturk's reforms, the problems she approached and the images of women she created show great variety . . . images of nationalistic women, modernised women, women with a strong personality, women rising up against oppression and idealistic women striving to educate the masses. (Altiok 1981: 226)

Halide Edip was active in the nationalist movement in the years 1910–12 and was the only woman member of the council of Ojak, the nationalist organization which had branches all over Turkey. During

World War I, she organized schools and orphanages in Syria and Lebanon. She joined the army, becoming one of the leading writers and public speakers in Mustapha Kemal's forces, and was one of several nationalists to be sentenced to death by the Sultan's government. That the daughter of a former palace official should challenge the system made her a target for attack and praise. 'As an eloquent public speaker and an adviser to Kemal, she was the most visible woman of the revolution' (Minai 1981: 62). Her writing and activism had an important impact at the time and also in later years:

> During Halide Edip's lifetime her influence was great; it continues to be today. Her novels are still read in Turkey. Her life spanned one of the most dramatic periods in Turkish history, from the crumbling of the old Ottoman Empire to the emergence of an independent nation. Her example helped prepare the way for the appearance of a new kind of Turkish woman. (Fernea and Bezirgan 1977: 167–8)

Conclusion

The Kemalist reforms in Turkey were cited all over the world as successful attempts at achieving women's emancipation by decree from above. As we have seen, the reforms were an integral part of an attempt to force Turkey into the 20th century through the modernization of all its institutions. The reforms covered not only economic activities and the legal structures, but were extended into areas of ideology and even dress and social behaviour.

These changes have been analyzed by many women political scientists of Turkey, who were themselves the products of these reforms. Dr Nermin Abadan-Unat, a professor of political science, claims that though Kemal 'focused his attention mainly on the elimination of polygamy, sex-differentiated legislation and traditional ethical norms', an assessment of these changes 'indicates that revolutionary efforts through law have only resulted in partial changes both in the status and role of women in Turkish society'. She adds that the principal progressive changes were not fought for but were given by the government in order to prove that, in granting equal rights to women, the new Turkey was 'reaching a level of contemporary civilization', and was 'a symbol to the world'. Abadan-Unat concludes that 'the major rights conferred on Turkish women were much more the result of unrelenting efforts of a small revolutionary elite, rather than the product of large-scale demands by Turkey's female population' (Abadan-Unat 1981: 12–13).

Another woman academic, Dr Sirin Tekeli, a political scientist who analysed Kemal's reforms, has shown that the model followed was one based on capitalist ideology. She writes:

The objective of the revolutionaries was to create a modern Turkey and 'modernity' was defined as the social organisation prevalent in the West, i.e. capitalist social formation. The forces of production that the new state inherited from the Ottoman Empire were not developed enough to be historically determining: therefore one had to start with modernising the superstructures. The new 'civil code' adopted in 1926 reorganised civil and property relations on the basis of the model relationships dominant in capitalist states. (Tekeli 1981: 294)

Despite the undoubted breakthrough in Turkey, the reforms remained class-bound, barely affecting the masses of Turkish women. As Dr Fatma Mansur Cosar has written:

The sudden changes . . . thrust upon Turkish society in the early 1920s were made bearable and did not dislocate the social structure because, in the final analysis, only a very small number of women were able to use the rights granted to them by Ataturk. The vast majority of women are still tied to the land and under the social control of men. (Cosar 1980: 138)

Nevertheless, however class-determined in the final analysis and limited in their scope, the Turkish reforms created an international sensation. Just as Japan had inspired wonder at the rapidity of its transformation from feudal society to industrial capitalism, Turkey's political transformation from the sultanate to the republic and its attempts at drastic social reform caught the imagination of the 'modernizers' and nationalists of other Middle Eastern and Asian countries. The example of Turkey, especially in respect of women's rights, became one of the most discussed issues in the Muslim world, and efforts were made to emulate it in Iran and Afghanistan.

3. Reformism and Women's Rights in Egypt

> To leave our girls a prey to ignorance, and taken up with stupid pursuits, is indeed a great crime.
> *Mohamed Abduh* (1849–1905) quoted in El-Saadawi 1980: 171

Egypt was, in many respects, the forerunner of 'Eastern' countries in the spheres of modernization, reform and education, as well as in developing movements of nationalism, of resistance to imperialism and of feminism. It also took the lead in the reform of Islam. Situated strategically between Europe and Asia, and exposed to radical movements of change including the French Revolution, Cairo had become a cosmopolitan centre of new ideas and movements. The stirrings of reformism and feminism in Egypt were linked to attempts by successive rulers to modernize the country's educational, cultural and administrative structures, and also to the growth of nationalism and anti-imperialism under British occupation in the post-1882 period. The early debates on women's rights in Egypt, the emergence of male reformers championing women's rights and the role of 'the new women' who pioneered ideas of female equality must be assessed in the background of these historical events.

Egypt can lay claim to one of the oldest civilizations, as attested to by the remains of numerous temples, cities and burial sites as well as by sculptures, paintings and writings. The people of Egypt had a developed religion, in which female gods played a role almost equal to that of male gods. Goddesses like Mut (the goddess of Truth), Isis and Hathor ruled over and controlled many areas of human activity. The existence of such goddesses has been seen by some scholars as a reflection of the high status of women in Pharaonic society. Records generally depict women as highly cultured, practising such sports as swimming and acrobatics in the same way as men. Paintings of the earlier eras show men and women as being of equal size; it is after about 2000 BC that women are often depicted somewhat smaller than males, probably indicating a diminution of their status. Socially and politically, women appear to have enjoyed a relatively equal status. Egypt has been ruled by many queens, such as Nefertiti and Hatshepsut, as well as Cleopatra in later times (1st century

43

BC); women are also recorded as having occupied positions as ministers and rulers of provinces.

From the time of Cleopatra's death (in 30 BC) up to AD 642, Egypt was under Roman domination except for brief periods, as in AD 270, when it was annexed by Zenobia, Queen of Palmyra. In the 7th century, the Arab conquest and the consequent Islamization of Egypt took place and in 1517 the country became part of the Turkish Ottoman Empire. From being an independent sultanate, it became a province of the Ottoman Empire, but this caused little change to its traditional administrative or power structures. Moreover, the change to Ottoman suzerainty had very little influence on Egyptian society and culture, and commercial and trading links with European countries were continued more or less on an autonomous basis.

It was with the intention of consolidating these links that Napoleon Bonaparte and the French army invaded Egypt in 1798. Their occupation lasted three years, opened up a two-way interaction between the countries, and marked the beginnings of the modernization of Egypt. Napoleon had brought with him 120 scholars and scientists who embarked on a comprehensive study of Egyptian society and culture. To this end, the French established the Institut d'Égypte in Cairo in order to study the country's antiquities, languages, agriculture and medical knowledge; the institute's library was open to Egyptians and printing presses turned out publications in both Arabic and French. As the Egyptian historian al Jabarti (1745–1825) wrote:

> The French were particularly happy if a Muslim visitor showed interest in the sciences. They immediately began to talk to him and showed him all kinds of printed books with pictures of parts of the terrestrial globe and of animals and plants. They also had books on ancient history . . . (Lewis 1982: 295)

The first French-language journal in Egypt, *Courrier de l'Égypte*, was also started during this period. French intellectual activities also brought the publication in Paris, between 1809 and 1828, of an encyclopaedia *Description de l'Égypte* which was responsible for arousing interest in Europe in Egyptian civilization and Islamic studies, and also the first Arabic-French dictionary written by an Egyptian Copt in 1828.

The influence of France caused a rapid flow of European ideas into Egypt, including the ideology of the French Revolution. The position of women was affected in this way and some intermarriages even occurred. General Menou married an Egyptian woman and is said to have treated her with the French 'chivalry' of the period; he 'led her by the hand into the dining room, offered her the best seat at the table . . . if her handkerchief fell to the ground he would hurriedly pick it up'. This caused other women to petition Bonaparte 'to have their husbands treat them in the same manner'. When the French left Egypt, however, repercussions occurred and a French observer of the time reported that 'women were massacred, poisoned, or drowned in the Nile'. The historian al Jabarti wrote of the 'pernicious innovations' and 'corruption of women' caused by the French occupation, and related how the daughter of a leading religious figure, Shaykh al-Bakri, was killed because she had dressed in the French style and mixed with the French (Ahmed 1982: 154). It is significant that one does not hear of such violence being used against Egyptian men who had adopted European ways.

Reformism in Egypt

The French were compelled to evacuate Egypt after their defeat by the British navy at Abukir, their departure being followed by a period of instability during which the British, the sultans of Egypt, and representatives of the Ottoman Empire vied with each other for control of the country. The British were in turn compelled to leave Egypt in 1805, and authority was finally established by the Albanian General Mohamed Ali, under the suzerainty of the Ottomans. Mohamed Ali ruled Egypt from 1805 to 1848, introducing a series of reforms which gave the various departments of state a recognizably modern form. The country was given a Constitution and a consultative council was established, action being taken simultaneously to reduce the powers of provincial lords. In the economic sphere, tax-farming was abolished and a system of fixed taxes introduced; foreign trade was taken over by the state, which resulted in increased agricultural and commercial revenues, and agricultural wages were increased. The cultivation of export crops such as cotton was encouraged and many industries started up, including armaments, textiles, machine tools and glass.

Mohamed Ali's reforms also extended to education. A Ministry of Education was established and the first schools of engineering and medicine were set up. Those who needed skills that could not be acquired in Egypt were sent abroad. In the years between 1813 and 1849, 311 Egyptian students were sent on state scholarships to France, England, Italy and Austria (Hitti 1961: 433). However, Mohamed Ali generally conceived of education as a means of fitting young men for the public service and his reforms have to be seen in this context. Another of his innovations was the establishment of a government printing press whose output was not confined merely to government gazettes and returns, but included works of learning in Arabic, Turkish and Persian. He also started publication of the first Middle Eastern newspaper and established a translation bureau which, between 1822 and 1842, published 243 books, mostly translations. This programme was mainly responsible for the spread of European thought in Egypt during this period. It was reinforced by the experience of students and diplomats who went to Europe and became influenced by France and French culture. By the end of Mohamed Ali's reign, 'Egypt consisted of a rich, alien ruling class and a bureaucracy which was also largely alien, a substantial . . . population of foreign traders and technicians, and a subservient population of Egyptian farmers and peasants, labourers, craftsmen and petty traders' (Little 1967: 36).

Female education also became a significant issue during this period and many advances were made. The daughters of rich families had been educated at home; girls from poor families could attend the *kuttabs* where the Koran was taught by rote together with some reading and writing. In 1832, Mohamed Ali built a school at which girls (mainly slaves and orphans) were taught to be midwives. The missionaries were also active, opening schools such as the 'Dame du Bon Pasteur' in 1846, followed by an American Mission School for girls in 1859.

Another area of reform was among the armed forces. By 1826, Mohamed Ali had created a powerful army, French-trained and well-equipped, as well as a small naval force. The armed forces successfully extended the national territory and restricted Turkish inroads into Egypt's relative autonomy. Eventually, however, they became a drain on the country's revenues and exposed Mohamed Ali to renewed intervention by the British, who had begun to be apprehensive of his power, particularly because he demanded commercial independence from the Ottoman Empire with which Britain had beneficial trading concessions. The Treaty of London of 1841 reduced Egypt's army to a force of 18,000 and restricted his independence within the Ottoman Empire. Egypt, though nominally a province of the Empire, anticipated many of its Tanzimat reforms of 1839 to which we referred when discussing Turkey.

The process of modernization continued and economic development accelerated during the rule of the Khedive Ismail (1863–82) who introduced strategies of modernization, the diffusion of technology and scientific knowledge, and made changes in education, administration, irrigation and public works. Modernization was considered to be the panacea for Egypt's 'backwardness' and necessary for the country's greater prosperity and power (Vatikiotis 1980: 117–18). But the Egyptians who had studied abroad, especially in France, were from the higher echelons of society, and on their return they continued to work within the framework of an authoritarian state structure and monarchical system, which they did not challenge.

The Khedive Ismail continued the educational policies of his predecessor with some beneficial results for women. In 1873, his third wife, Jashem Afet Hanum, started the Suyfiyya Girls School which soon had 400 pupils, and provided instruction in arithmetic, geography, history and religion as well as needlework and domestic skills; in 1875, the government opened another such school, giving girls a Western-style primary education. The purpose of female education was restricted to preparing girls to be efficient mothers and good wives, however, and it was mainly the girls of urban bourgeois families who benefited (Abdel Kader 1973: 118–19).

The last decades of the 19th century, a period of aggressive imperialism and competition among European powers, saw the re-establishment of British control over Egypt. In the 1870s, the financial problems of Khedive Ismail's government led to several political changes. To avoid bankruptcy, new and unpopular taxes were devised which mainly burdened the peasantry; the Khedive's shares in the Suez Canal were sold to Britain, and British and French officials were allowed to oversee the economy.

Economic developments during this period brought into existence an Egyptian urban middle class, influenced by European political thought. This class became the basis of a popular nationalist movement: dissatisfaction with the rule of the Khedive and resentment of foreign control brought matters to a head, resulting in the revolt led by Arabi Pasha in 1882. This was crushed by an Anglo-French force, after which Egypt was occupied by the British forces. This was to last until 1922, when after a series of protracted struggles, a nominal independence was granted; Egyptians were allowed administrative power but effective military and political control remained in the hands of the British.

The Influence of Al-Afghani - reformation of Islam

The transformation of the country into a semi-colony of the British, together with the influence of liberal thought, the movement for reform and the growth of nationalist consciousness, formed the background to the intellectual debates that took place in Egypt in the late 19th century. Great influence was exercised over the intellectuals of the period by Sayyed Jamal al-din al-Afghani (1839–97), who was born in Iran, educated in the rationalist tradition of Avicenna, and became the best-known radical agitator, social reformer and pan-Islamist of the Muslim world. Afghani lived in turn in India, Afghanistan, Turkey, Egypt, Russia and Europe, and was expelled from many of these countries because of his agitational activities against their regimes. In Paris, in 1884, he edited an anti-British, pan-Islamic journal which was influential among the Arab intelligentsia; he also distinguished himself by indulging in polemical discussions on Islam with French academics. Returning to Iran, he became involved in bringing together Iranian reformists and in conspiracies to overthrow the Shah. He was also a stern critic of the absolutist monarchy in Turkey. Afghani advocated the reform of traditional beliefs and structures; he argued for a return to the 'pure' Islam of an earlier period, explaining that Islam, if interpreted correctly, was a rational religion capable of providing an ideological basis for social advance and for the unity of all Muslims. He promoted alliances of religious and radical forces in society, and opposed feudal oppression and corrupt governments. His role in the reformation of Islam cannot be overemphasised:

> As in all the countries attacked by Europe, people were looking for the secret of European success. Jamal al-din [al-Afghani] believed that the key to this secret was modern science and technology. He argued that a return to primitive Islam, the rational and reasonable religion which had subsequently been so

47

grossly distorted and rigidified, would enable the Muslim world to adapt to the new conditions. *But the old structures were upheld by the European powers who benefited from their sclerosis. The independence of the Muslim world and a struggle against the European imperialists were therefore necessary if Islam was to be purified.* (Rodinson 1979: 79; emphasis added)

Afghani's consistent anti-imperialist and nationalist stand, as well as his inclination towards socialism, made him the most inspiring of the Muslim reformers of the 19th century and his 'appeals to unity around Islam to fend off the West had a multi-class appeal' in the Muslim world (Keddie 1981: 189, 65).

Afghani's ideas gained him followers in all Muslim countries. His views on the modernization and liberalization of Muslim societies, on the promotion of Western science and technology, and on the establishment of Islamic unity under one empire with the strength to resist European imperialist domination and exploitation, were of great appeal to young reformers. In Egypt, Turkey and Iran, many leading intellectuals became his collaborators and disciples. Afghani's influence in Egypt was particularly crucial. He had lived in Cairo and taught at Al-Azhar University in 1871. His nationalism and ideas of resisting European domination through the adoption of Western methods gained popularity and even inspired Arabi Pasha's 1882 revolt against the British.

Male Reformers and Women's Rights

Although nationalism grew in Egypt during the late 19th century, it did not take on any radical form, but operated within the framework of the existing structures. Several moderate reformers and nationalists appeared on the scene, one of the best-known being Mustapha Kamal (1874–1908), who had been educated in France and was a Francophile; he was a talented writer and speaker, and formed the National Party which demanded constitutional government and independence for Egypt. However, the movement co-operated with the conservative religious leaders and with the ruling Khedive, while supporting French interests against the British. Kamal published a newspaper (*Al-Lewa*) in English and French: 'he became the most powerful influence among the literate Egyptians and through *Al-Lewa* he raised enough money to start a number of independent national schools which became hotbeds of schoolboy extremism' (Little 1967: 62). Kamal was against any idea of women's emancipation but his contemporaries were to take up the issue.

It is not surprising that during the second half of the 19th century, a period of intellectual discussion and reformist activity, the debate on women's rights was also heard in Egypt, its first advocates being male reformers. These included Ahmed Fares El Shidyak who, in 1855, had published *One Leg Crossed Over the Other*, one of the first books to support women's emancipation. Others, like Rifaa Rafii El-Tahtawi (1801–71), wrote on the need for women's education and for the redress of injustices to which women were subjected. Tahtawi, a high-ranking government official, had studied in Paris from 1826 to 1831 and was a leading Egyptian intellectual and reformer. In France he had been influenced by the writings of Voltaire, Rousseau and Montesquieu. On his return to Egypt he became part of the campaign to modernize education, helping in 1835 to establish the School of Languages which trained translators, jurists and administrators. In his own writings, Tahtawi popularized concepts of secularism in politics and in law, and also ideas of liberty and political rights.

> He was the first Egyptian to report fairly systematically and intelligently to his compatriots on the general outlines of European political institutions, the ideas of the enlightenment and the French Revolution . . . Above all he advanced the idea of the rule of law and a stable order as the most important manifestations of a civilised society. (Vatikiotis 1980: 115)

Tahtawi was also a pioneer of women's education in Egypt, putting forward his views on the need for female education in *A Guide to the Education of Girls and Boys* which he published in 1872. This was a period when the debate on women was in full swing: 'Every shade of opinion regarding the emancipation of women was represented and nationalists were far from agreeing on the matter. The issue was an essential one, directly touching the life of everyone. An increasing flow of books and articles about the topic gives evidence of its importance' (Philipp 1978: 278).

As in many Asian countries, the Egyptian reformers tried to show that it was not the tenets of religion that subordinated women, but rather an incorrect interpretation of that religion, and corrupt practices and additions which later contravened the purity of the original faith. Muslim reformists started a debate on religion and on the rights of women in Islam, one of the pioneers being Sheik Mohamed Abduh (1849–1905), who had studied in Paris and had come under the influence of Afghani. Abduh and Afghani together formed the Free National Party in Egypt which attracted many prominent soldiers, officials and teachers. However, its views on pan-Islamism did not find favour with the authorities who suppressed the party, expelling Afghani in 1879 and Abduh in 1882. The two joined forces again in Paris where they published a journal, *al-Urwat al-Wuthqua* ('The Indissoluble Bond'), which attacked British imperialist intervention in Islamic countries and called for an Islamic revival. Though banned in Egypt, the journal achieved a wide circulation and influence. After returning to Egypt, Abduh became a leading reformer, influencing a generation of intellectual nationalists. Like many others of this period, however, he was essentially a moderate rather than a revolutionary reformer. 'His ideology aimed at a gradual transformation of Egyptian society by means of an education programme geared to slowly changing the people it reached, through free universities, benevolent societies and organs of the Egyptian state, still controlled by the British' (Rodinson 1979: 24).

Abduh was outspoken on women's status, denouncing polygamy as against Islam and condemning the prevalent practices of concubinage and women's slavery. Citing the Koran as in favour of women's education, he claimed that the backwardness of Arab women was detrimental to the future of the Arab peoples (Philipp 1978: 278). He stated:

> We wish that our daughters should be educated. For Allah the Almighty has explained, "To them are due the same goods that we expect from them". There are many sacred verses that . . . clarify that both man and woman share in fulfilling the same duties towards life and towards religion. (El-Saadawi 1980: 171)

Abduh pioneered a flexible interpretation of the Koran in the light of modern thought, and his work became known in other Muslim countries, including Indonesia. Rather than denouncing religion, reformers like Abduh tried to separate religious and political questions, and attempted to find new explanations of traditional texts which were in keeping with the times. Abduh founded the Salafiyah movement which called for a return to the purity of primitive Islam and for a restatement of its teaching in terms of modern science. In Egypt he was bitterly attacked by religious leaders and conservatives who opposed not only the foreign occupation in their country but also the encroachment of Western civilization: 'But he did not retreat or hesitate to continue propagating his ideas. He maintained that one of the most important sources of the weakness and passivity which had assailed the Arab peoples was the backwardness of women' (El-Saadawi 1980: 171).

It was Abduh's disciple, Kassim Amin (1865–1908), educated in France and a judge by profession, who created a furore in 1899, with his book *Tahrir al Mara* ('Women's Emancipation'). On the basis of religious texts, Amin argued that female seclusion, the veil, arranged marriages and the prevalent divorce practices were un-Islamic. He advocated women's right to work as well as legal reforms to improve their status, claiming that there could be 'no improvement of the state of the nation without improving the position of women' (Philipp 1980: 279). Amin stressed the importance of women's education not only for bringing up children but also for creating a better relationship between husband and wife on the basis of mutual respect (Abdel Kader 1973: 11). Not unexpectedly, his book was denounced in orthodox Muslim circles and his views were refuted. Opposition was also voiced by those nationalists who held that issues of women's emancipation weakened and diverted the campaign against foreign domination. Kassim Amin answered his critics in a second book, *Al-Mara Al Jadida* ('The New Woman'), basing his arguments less on religion than on the doctrine of natural rights and the concept of progress (Philipp 1978: 279).

50

The debate was carried further by such male reformers as Lutfi Ahmed El-Sayed (born in 1872), and a group of intellectuals who expressed their liberal views on women's rights in *Al Gareeda*, a paper which was edited by Lutfi (El-Saadawi 1980: 172). This discussion of the position of women took place within the context of a debate on secular reform and religious orthodoxy. Lutfi El-Sayed, who had known al-Afghani, was a liberal writer and teacher who advocated not only British withdrawal from Egypt but also a limitation of the Khedive's powers. He favoured a secular state, and did not link progress to a reform of Islam. Like Taha Husein, another intellectual of the period, he sought to reform and modernize the Muslim University of Al-Azhar, and expressed these views in the journal *Weekly Politics*, which not only criticized Al-Azhar but advocated a separation between religion and politics (Little 1967: 129).

Nationalism and Protests by Women

The turn of the century saw a growing national consciousness and the emergence of a group of politicians, led by Saad Zaghlul, who demanded self-determination for Egypt. These demands intensified after World War I when the victory of the allies raised the issue of Egypt's political future. Zaghlul and his group of Egyptian lawyers, officials and land-owners, and those with interests in commerce and the cotton industry, formed a delegation to present Egypt's case to the British. This group, which emerged as the Wafd Party, had the support of intellectuals, teachers, students, peasants and women. The British refusal to negotiate and their exile of the Wafd leaders led to demonstrations, strikes and assassinations. In 1922, the British eventually recognized Egypt as an independent state but they retained absolute control of the Sudan and of Egyptian defence, imperial communications and foreign interests. After a period of difficulties and a new Constitution, the 1924 elections gave the Wafd 90% of the seats in the Egyptian parliament, with Zaghlul forming the government and Fuad I as king.

This was the political background to the rise of women's activity in Egypt before and after World War I. Saad Zaghlul and his group, who were secularists, had earlier been identified with the promotion of women's education, and many influential women writers used their talents to write extensively on feminist issues in the first decades of the 20th century. They included Malak Hifni Nassif (1886–1918), the most force-ful woman writer of her time, who, under the pen-name of Bahissat El Badia (Searcher in the Desert), wrote in the contemporary press on marriage, divorce, veiled seclusion and women's education. Her father, a university lecturer in Arab studies, had been a disciple of Mohamed Abduh, and she was one of the first women in Egypt to qualify as a teacher in 1900. After her marriage, she moved away from Cairo and lived near the desert where she began to criticize the seclusion and patriarchal subjection under which women lived. A victim of her husband's polygamy, she was particularly articulate on the evils of the system. Her fame was such that in 1911 she spoke in the Egyptian Legislative Assembly, putting forward a programme for the improvement of the situation of women. This included demands for universal elementary education for girls, with emphasis on religious education, hygiene, first aid and child rearing, and the training of women as doctors and teachers to fulfil their medical and educational needs. El Badia's work was praised by contemporary male reformers. Kassim Amin supported her ideas on women's liberation, and Lutfi El-Sayed described her as 'a true example of those women authors who have surpassed many of the men writers living during the same period' (El-Saadawi 1980: 172).

Another woman writer of the period was May Ziada, who held a literary salon in Cairo in 1915–16 and led a life of independence. 'She was able to impose her personality on literary circles in Egypt, to mix and talk freely with men, and to correspond regularly with them at a time when the veil still hung heavily over the faces of many Egyptian women in the same sector of society' (El-Saadawi 1980: 122). The proliferation of women's journals and of women who wrote on various issues was striking: prior to 1914 there were 15 Arabic women's magazines, many of which were edited by Syrian Christian women (Philipp 1978: 280).

Another area of activity for middle-class women was philanthropy. For example, Hidiya Afifi (1898–1969), the daughter of a high-ranking official, educated at a French convent and related by marriage to the nationalist leader, Saad Zaghlul, is best known for her work in health-related charities. In 1909, together with other wealthy women, she formed the Mabarat Mohamed Ali which ran a network of women's clinics. In 1919, the same group formed the Société de la Femme Nouvelle, concerned with girls' schools, orphanages and child-care centres (Marsot 1978: 272).

Open political agitation and action on the part of women began with their participation in the nationalist movement against the British after World War I. British repression and the exile of Zaghlul and other Wafd leaders in 1919 led to violent demonstrations which marked the beginning of militant nationalist agitation. The dissatisfaction was not only political but also economic:

> Discontent had accumulated during the war. In the cities inflation had hit the lower classes, and in the villages the peasants had suffered from such measures as mobilization of draft animals, forced labour, and confiscation of products. The tax burden had increased. The frustration and disaffection of the various classes found an outlet in the general demonstrations of 1919. (Philipp 1978: 288)

It was during this nationalist upsurge, in which all classes participated, that political demonstrations by women occurred on four occasions in 1919. The women were organized by many of the wives of the Wafd founders, and middle-class women were seen protesting for the first time in public. Particularly active was Huda Sharawi (1882–1947), who came from a wealthy family, had been educated at home in French, Turkish and Arabic, and was widely read. In 1910 she had opened a school which provided a general education for girls. Sharawi's husband was a founder member of the Wafd and she moved in nationalist circles; she organized women to demonstrate during the agitation of 1919, and collected women's signatures to a petition to the British High Commissioner in which they condemned the shooting of demonstrators and the exiling of Egyptian leaders: 'We the women of Egypt, mothers, sisters and wives of those who have been the victims of British greed and exploitation . . . deplore the brutal, barbarous actions that have fallen upon . . . the Egyptian nation. Egypt has committed no crime except to express her desire for freedom and independence' (Fernea and Bezirgan 1977: 193–6).

There are many contemporary accounts of women's participation in the 1919 demonstrations. Sir Valentine Chirol (to whom there were only two categories of women: 'good' and 'bad'), wrote in the London *Times*:

> In the stormy days of 1919 [the women] descended in large bodies into the streets, those of the more respectable classes still veiled and shrouded in their loose black coats, whilst the courtesans from the lowest quarters of the city, who had also caught the contagion (of political unrest) disported themselves unveiled and arrayed in less discreet garments. In every turbulent demonstration women were well to the front. They marched in procession — some on foot, some in carriages shouting 'independence' and 'down with the English' and waving national banners. (Philipp 1978: 288–9)

The presence of both bourgeois and poor women has been noted by many writers: 'The veiled gentlewomen of Cairo paraded in the streets shouting slogans for independence and freedom from foreign occupation. They organized strikes and demonstrations . . . boycotts of British goods and wrote petitions . . . protesting British actions in Egypt' (Marsot 1978: 269).

It was not only the 'veiled gentlewomen' who participated in the upsurge but also working women in both industrial and agricultural occupations who were active in the 1919 struggles:

> They went on to the rural roads, side by side with the men, cut the telephone wires and disrupted the railway lines in order to paralyse the movement of British troops. Some of them participated in storming the improvised camps and jails in which many of those who had led the uprisings or participated in them had been imprisoned. Women were killed or injured when British troops fired on them. Some of them are known such as Shafika Mohamed, Hamida Khalil, Sayeda Hassan, Fahima Riad and Aisha Omar. But hundreds of poor women lost their lives without anybody being able to trace their names. (El-Saadawi 1980: 176)

In Egypt in the 1920s there were also small groups of socialists and Communists who were active in the period of post-World War I political and industrial unrest. During these years, there were strikes over wages and hours of work among factory workers as well as among other groups such as tram drivers, waiters and lamplighters, culminating in demonstrations in Cairo and Alexandria and a general strike in 1924. The Socialist Party founded in 1920 by Joseph Rosenthal (an Alexandrian jeweller of Jewish origin), which became the Communist Party in 1922, came under suspicion and its leaders were frequently arrested. While the Communist Party remained an urban-based movement of intellectuals, professionals and trade union leaders, its leadership was mainly based on minority support. There is also evidence of participation of at least one woman in the leadership of the movement, for in 1925, when the party leaders were arrested, they included Charlotte Rosenthal (Laqueur 1956: 36), wife of Joseph Rosenthal.

Huda Sharawi

In 1923, when the female militancy of the earlier phase had died out, Huda Sharawi and other middle-class women formed the Egyptian Feminist Union, which became the main women's association concerned with education, social welfare and changes in private law, to provide for equality between the sexes. Sharawi is best remembered for the gesture she made against tradition by throwing her veil into the sea on her return from Rome, where she had attended the International Conference of Women in 1924. 'This naturally caused a scandal, particularly as Huda was an eminent pasha's wife. Undaunted, other prominent women cast off their veils, one after another' (Minai 1981: 69).

In drafting the new Constitution of 1924, Egyptian politicians chose to ignore the question of women's political rights, making only changes such as raising the age of marriage for girls to 16, but not giving women the right to vote or to divorce. A protest demonstration was held in March 1924 at the opening of Parliament, when some feminists demanded the right to vote, but this seems to have been the last spark of revolt on the issue (Philipp 1978: 289).

In 1925, Huda Sharawi started a journal in French, *L'Égyptienne*, edited by Ceza Nabarawi, who had also been at the women's conference in Rome. The élitist nature of the venture is clear in that it catered only to the French-speaking women of the Egyptian bourgeoisie. Nevertheless, the issues discussed included Turkish reforms regarding women, which had also influenced Egyptian women, and the question of Islam. The journal's editor stated in 1927 that 'We, the Egyptian feminists, have a great respect for our religion . . . In wanting to see it practised in its true spirit . . . we are doing more for it than those who submit themselves blindly to the customs that have deformed [Islam]' (Minai 1981: 72). The issue of polygamy also evoked little response from the legislators. In 1928, a new law limited it to those who could look after 'the family they already have charge of' — a measure which could hardly be seen as a restriction.

Egypt, although the intellectual leader of the Muslim world, remained very conservative with regard to the reform of personal law, and on the question of polygamy did not reach the level of progress achieved in Turkey. In 1935 when Huda Sharawi lectured at the American University of Cairo on the status of women and called for the abolition of polygamy, two sheiks from Al-Azhar University protested; but it was perhaps a sign of changing educated opinion that the audience sided with Sharawi. Her speech on this occasion was 'received with enthusiasm in the university gathering . . . was printed in full in a leading newspaper and thus widely circulated through the Arabic-speaking world' (Woodsmall 1936: 121–2).

But the rise of feminism was stunted by the climate of political opinion and the class bias of the women's movement. As Nawal El-Saadawi has written of the reformist women's activities:

> The movement was not representative of the overwhelming majority of toiling women, and its leadership ended, just as the political leadership did, by seeking accommodations with the British, the Palace and the reactionary forces in the country. The women's movement . . . kept away from an active involvement in the national and political life of the country and limited its activities to charitable and social welfare work. (El-Saadawi 1980: 176)

The activism of the earlier phase thus petered out. The admission of a few women to the University of Cairo in 1928 caused an outcry in orthodox circles and a crisis within the government. It was only in 1962 that Al-Azhar University admitted women students. Nevertheless, new generations of educated Egyptian women arose, making inroads into some of the professions. In 1934, Lutfiya El Nadi, a graduate of the American Girls' College of Cairo, was the first woman pilot to make a solo flight (Woodsmall 1936: 81). But the majority remained unschooled; in 1975, 25% of the girls attended school as opposed to 49% of boys. Religious interests and masculine opposition remained strong and it was not until 1956 that women obtained the right to vote; in 1979, Parliament reserved 30 of the 392 seats for women, and in the same year marriage and divorce laws were liberalized to benefit them (Minai 1981: 74, 78).

In conclusion, the earlier democratic and nationalist struggles in Egypt gave rise to an intellectual debate on the status of women, to moves to give women access to education, and to the rise of a feminist consciousness which expressed itself in a feminist press, in women's organizations, in demands for suffrage and other rights, and in the appearance of women of all classes in agitations and street demonstrations against the British. However, expectations of the early years were not fulfilled and feminism did not survive into the 1930s. Although Egypt had been among the first countries of Africa and Asia to be exposed to European currents of thought, the internal structures of traditional society — including the monarchy and religious orthodoxy

— continued to dominate during the period under consideration and attempts to achieve radical changes for women were therefore unsuccessful.

4. Women's Struggles and 'Emancipation from Above' in Iran

> Because women in these states are not being fitted for any of the human virtues it often happens that they resemble plants.
> *Ibn Rushd (Averroes)*, 12th century Persian scholar
> (Fischer 1978: 190)

Women's participation in political struggles and the question of their emancipation first arose in Iran in response to foreign domination and as part of the nationalist reaction both to the foreign powers and to the ruling dynasty. Although Iran was not colonized during the imperialists' expansion in the 19th century, it nevertheless came under their 'sphere of influence', the two notable foreign powers exercising such control being Britain and Tsarist Russia. Russia was continuously involved in aggression against Iran, including the annexation of territory and the extraction of concessions, while British policies were based on the belief that imperial supremacy in India required control of Iran and of the Gulf.

Due to its geographical location Iran had always been exposed to invasions and cross-currents of influence from Europe and Asia. During the phase of European colonial expansion, the Portuguese were the first to make their appearance in the Gulf, capturing the island of Hormus and part of the mainland in the early 16th century. The British were also active in the area trying to promote trade, and in 1599 Shah Abbas I was able to enlist the help of British adventurers in reforming his army. Abbas also gave trading rights to the Dutch and British East India Companies and later, with British help, expelled the Portuguese from his domains. The Russians made their presence felt in the early 18th century: their invasion of northern Iran in 1721 under Peter the Great gave rise to an agreement between the Ottoman Empire and Russia by which the latter was allowed to occupy parts of Iran.

Monarchs of the Qajar dynasty who ruled the country from 1794 until 1925 were constantly involved in intrigues and manoeuvres with foreign powers. This was a period of expansion for imperialism, and Iran, being on the overland route to India, became an important area of conflict among rival European powers, especially Russia and Britain.

The winds of modernization which swept the Islamic world in the 19th century and led to some internal reforms were also felt in Iran. Attempts towards some kind of liberal reform were made during the rule of Shah Nasir ud-Din (1848–96) who had absorbed liberal ideas from his vizier Mirza Taqi Khan, who in turn had been influenced by liberal movements in Turkey. Under this regime, some progress was made towards modernization: the army was reformed and the sale of offices and titles was stopped; the first Farsi newspaper was established, and an *école polytechnique* at which science and other subjects were taught along modern lines was opened in Tehran; communications were also improved through roads, a postal system and the telegraph. These reforms proved unpopular in certain quarters, however, and Taqi Khan was executed on the grounds that he was becoming too powerful. By this time the reform movement in Turkey had also failed; Sultan Hamid had reverted to absolutist rule and the Shah Nasir ud-Din followed his example.

In the 1870s and 1880s, the Shah made three visits to Europe. He made no attempt, however, to implement the reforms demanded by liberals who had begun to agitate from abroad and who were influenced by Afghani's reform movement. Under his successor, Shah Muzzaffar ud-Din (1896–1907) agitation for reform spread rapidly and by the early 20th century had become a serious challenge to the regime. The Qajar rulers maintained feudal structures and despotic rule and had bartered the country away to foreign interests. The resistance movement and agitation that began in the 19th century was aimed both at opposing the monarchs' habit of acting alternately as agents of Tsarist Russia and of imperialist Britain, and at opposing their autocratic powers.

In economic terms Iran was reduced to semi-colonial status, forced to give concessions to foreign entrepreneurs and unable to protect its own markets from foreign competition. Between 1885 and 1900, 15 countries extracted concessions from Iran: 'The effect of foreign competition was greatly increased by the concessions that were granted to foreigners by virtue of their political predominance, while in turn, the country's state of economic underdevelopment caused it to be politically helpless in relation to the West' (Rodinson 1974: 125).

As in other Asian countries, contact with Europe led to the growth of technical education. The polytechnic, which opened in 1851 and whose students came mainly from aristrocratic families, gave courses in military science, engineering, medicine and pharmacy. The director was Reza Quli Jhan, an Iranian scholar, and the teachers were Austrians, assisted by Iranian translators. For about 50 years, Western ideas were transmitted mainly through this institution (Hitti 1961: 410). In the latter half of the 19th century, many translations, including the works of Molière, Alexandre Dumas and Jules Verne, were published, and writing of a high standard also began to appear among exiled Iranians abroad.

Around the turn of the century, an Iranian bourgeoisie emerged, as a result of activities such as importing foreign goods, exporting domestic produce, investments in mining, and a few industrial activities. Sections of this bourgeoisie thus developed contradictions not only with foreign capital over the home markets, but also with the feudal interests that ruled the country. The agitation that took place between 1906 and 1909 is seen by some as 'bourgeois democratic' in character while others disagree.

> The weakness of the bourgeoisie in tackling the bases of feudalism and its lack of decisiveness in facing colonialism, the absence of a properly formed working-class movement as well as the absence of peasants in the Revolution, do not exclude it from being regarded as a bourgeois democratic revolution, albeit in its elementary form as was the case with the Turkish revolution of 1908 and the Chinese Revolution of 1911. (Jazani 1980: 6)

The agitation for democratic rights was led by the Constitutionalists who included sections of the bourgeoisie, the clergy and urban intellectuals; the movement drew inspiration from the Russian revolution of 1905 against the Tsar.

In 1906, popular demonstrations were organized by the Constitutionalists throughout the country: merchants, bankers, *ulemas* and others took part. The Shah arrested many of the leaders but was unable to quell the protests. Eventually, he was compelled to accede to some of their demands, including the establishment of a national assembly (Majlis). The first Majlis was convened in October 1906 and drew up a Constitution which was enacted as a fundamental law. Five days after signing the law the Shah died, to be succeeded by his son Mohamed Ali who was bitterly opposed to the reform movement and attempted to subvert the Constitution. This led to conflict with the nationalists who retaliated. It was at this point that Britain and Russia, faced with the growth of the new nationalist forces in Iran, got together in a bit of horse-dealing which resulted in the Anglo-Russian Convention of 1907. This pact ostensibly recognized and guaranteed the independence and integrity of Iran, but in reality was an excuse to keep the unpopular monarch on the throne and to divide the country into two spheres of influence: Russian in the north and British in the south-west.

Using this opportunity, the Shah renewed his efforts to turn back the tide of reform, and attacked Parliament. This led to an armed struggle with the nationalists in which the Shah was supported by Russian forces. Almost the entire country rose in protest, however, and Tehran was recaptured and the Shah replaced by his son. But the Russians again invaded the country in 1911 and served a further ultimatum on the Constitutionalists who were forced to acquiesce in Russian domination of the north. In the south, the British position was strengthened by the discovery of oil.

During the 1914–18 War, Iran became a battleground for Turkish, British and Russian forces, and after the 1917 Russian revolution, White Russian and Bolshevik forces also fought each other on Iranian soil. Iran sent a delegation to the 1919 peace conference to demand political and economic independence for the country and the abrogation of the 1907 convention, but it was not even given a hearing. In 1919, the British imposed the Anglo-Persian Treaty on the country, which was in a state of economic collapse, thus turning it into a British protectorate. The Soviet government renounced all Tsarist claims on Iran, and Iranian rebels, led by Kuchik Khan, formed the Soviet Republic of Gilan in the north. It was at this point that an army officer, Reza Khan of the Iranian Cossack Brigade, deposed the brigade's Russian commander and led the successful march on Tehran in 1921. Reza Khan reorganized the armed forces, crushed the Soviet in Gilan, suppressed tribal revolts and, making himself Prime Minister, established his rule over the country. In 1925, rule by the Qajar dynasty was brought to an end by parliamentary decision. After some hesitation as to whether the country should be declared a republic following the example of Turkey, it was decided to preserve the monarchy; the religious leaders, noting the action of the Turks in divesting Islam of some of its traditional characteristics, strongly opposed the idea of a republic. Reza Khan was therefore crowned Shah of Iran, founding the Pahlavi dynasty which was overthrown in 1979.

Women Leaders

As in many parts of Asia and the Arab world, the 19th century and early decades of the 20th century saw the emergence of women activists in Iran during a period of increased national awareness which culminated in the constitutional agitation of 1905–11. Even in earlier periods, however, there had been queens, women religious leaders (both saints and heretics), women warriors and militants who had challenged the existing norms of society. In fact, the early religion of Iran, Zoroastrianism, gave certain rights to women over property and in the performance of religious ceremonies, and equal status in law. In the Sassanian period of Iranian history (AD 224–651) there had been two famous queens, while the country's national epic deals with the bravery of Gordafarid, a woman warrior who led the Iranians against a Turkish invasion (Sanghvi *et al.* 1967: 10). In the 12th century, there seems to have been a discussion on the status of women during which the Iranian scholar, Ibn Rushd, criticized their restriction to child-bearing on the grounds that this denied the country half its labour power and the potential for a better standard of life (Fischer 1978: 190).

Ancient Persia was a country of many beliefs and heresies which gave rise to women saints and legendary women who inspired religious fervour amongst the masses. The Zoroastrians had many shrines for female saints and many holy women were worshipped by the Shiite Muslim believers. For example, Fatimeh (daughter of the Prophet and wife of Ali) is 'constantly invoked in prayer and parable'; Bibi Shahrbanu (wife of the Iman Hosein) has a shrine at Rey that is open only to women;

Fatimeh Hazrat-e Masumeh (sister of the Imam Reza) has a shrine in Qum and there is another shrine for the Forty Virgins (Chehel Dokhtaran) who had been 'miraculously taken into the earth to escape Zoroastrian armies' (Fischer 1978: 213).

Women's participation in religious heresies has been observed in many countries. In Iran, too, in the 1840s, a heretical movement, Babism (later known as Baha'ism) advocated reforms including greater social justice, freedom of trade and rights of personal property, the reduction of unjust taxes, a higher status for women, limits on polygamy, a prohibition on violence against women and measures for their education (Keddie 1981: 50). The Babi movement was founded in Iran by Muza Ali Mohammed of Shiraz (1820–50) who proclaimed himself the 'Bab' (gate) to the truth; since Shiite Islam believed in the coming of great religious leaders or imams, the Bab was able to gather a following among the people. This reformist movement was seen as a threat by orthodox Muslims and by the government, and the Bab was arrested. A wave of violent uprisings followed, and the Bab and about 28 of his followers were executed in the early 1850s. His authority passed to another disciple and Babism, though subject to persecution, continued to attract support among dissident Iranian minorities, intellectuals and women.

The best-known woman of the movement was Qurrat ul Ayn (1815–51); she came from a family of mullahs, was a poet, well-versed in religious questions, who took part in intellectual debates with religious leaders. She joined the Babi movement, leaving her husband and relatives, and became active in the cause, preaching in public, fighting on the battlefield, and ultimately dying a martyr.

> She was apparently quite a remarkable, intelligent woman . . . she devoted her life to missionary activism, not only converting but also assuming leading roles on the battlefield when the Babis revolted . . . her memory and especially the poems she wrote kept alive the Babi spirit of revolt. (Bayat-Philipp 1978: 296)

Qurrat ul Ayn evidently attracted much attention at the time; the French diplomat Comte de Gobineau, writing in 1866 on religions and philosophies of Central Asia, mentioned the Babist crusade of Qurrat ul Ayn:

> Not content with a mere passive sympathy, she publicly professed her master's faith. She turned not only against polygamy but also the veil, and she appeared with face unveiled in public places, causing much fright and scandal amongst her kin and amongst pious Muslims. Her public preaching, however, was applauded by an already great number of persons who shared her enthusiasm and [helped] widen the circle [of followers]. (Bayat-Philipp 1978: 296)

Male Reformers and Women's Rights

Babism, along with Freemasonry, also attracted several male intellectuals and radical reformers of the 1880s and 1890s, who took up the cause of women's rights. Many of them were associates of the famous scholar al-Afghani, and included Mirza Malkom Khan (1833–1908), an anti-clerical Armenian Iranian who had been educated in Paris and had been exiled from Iran for forming a society based on Freemasonry. While in London in 1890, he edited *Qanun* ('Law'), a journal to which al-Afghani contributed. In an issue of *Qanun* in 1890, Malkom Khan contributed an article advocating women's education (Bayat-Philipp 1980: 306). The journal called for democratic rights: 'It stressed the people's grievances and in unmistakable terms spelled out their demands: a fixed code of laws and a parliament wherein people's representatives would be free to discuss all matters related to the welfare of the state'. Another important writer of the period was Mirza Aqua Khan Kermani, a Babi who had become a radical freethinker. As editor of the newspaper *Akhtar* and collaborator of al-Afghani, he was forceful in his criticisms of conditions in Iran: he glorified the pre-Islamic past, criticized orthodox Islam and represented the current of anti-religious nationalism which existed at that time. Linked with similar activities was Shaikh Ahmad Ruhi, also a Babi and a writer, teacher and freethinker who, in 1891, together with Kermani, grouped together the Iranian reformist supporters of al-Afghani, who was then in Istanbul. Another influential writer was Fathali Akhundzadeh, an Iranian of Azerbaijan origin who lived in Russian Transcaucasia. In the late 19th century, Akhundzadeh wrote a series of letters in which he denounced conditions in Iran: these formed part of the considerable output of critical writings by Iranian radicals in exile (Keddie 1981: 68, 71, 191).

These four writers favoured women's emancipation, supported their right to education, and were opposed to polygamy. 'Their primary concern seems to have been the necessity to breed a new generation of Iranian patriots, and they felt that only with a proper "healthy" family environment where the mother is educated and given a prominent role as the first educator of the child, could this be achieved' (Bayat-Philipp 1978: 296–7).

Iranian writers and poets of the early 20th century rejected the tradition of Persian poetry in which women were portrayed as beautiful playthings and also as devils, snakes and dragons; they took up the theme of women's equality and emancipation, challenging the prevailing view that woman was inferior to man, and especially criticized polygamy and the veiling of women. Muhammed Hashim Mirza Afsar (born 1880) made the point:

> Thy left hand is not inferior to the right;
> had it worked it would have been as strong as the right;
> if woman is not like man, the fault is yours;
> we should demand education and art for women.

(Bayat-Philipp 1978: 304)

Iraq Mirza, a Qajar prince, wrote on similar themes: 'Are women not human amongst us, or is there in women no power of distinction between good and evil?' 'You and I are both human after all, equal in creation' (Bayat-Philipp 1978: 304).

The poet Lahuti rejected the classical view of female beauty and projected a new image for women: 'I don't appreciate the beauty of one who is ignorant; fascinate me no more by beauty, rather show thy worth.' Together with many other poets of the period, Lahuti campaigned for the removal of the veil. 'O Lift thy veil . . . I long to see thee free in the community' (Bayat-Philipp 1978: 304). Similarly, the poet Ishqi wrote of the need for action:

> If two or three speakers join their voice with me,
> an agitation will gradually start in the country,
> and by this agitation the faces of the women will be unveiled.
> Pleasure will be derived from social life.
> Else, so long as the women hide their heads in this shroud,
> half of the Persian nation remains dead.
>
> (Bayat-Philipp 1978: 305)

The intellectuals of the early 20th century, many of whom had studied in Europe, were at the forefront of the nationalist and democratic agitation and established secret societies to debate political issues. As Bayat-Philipp has written:

> They were used as platforms to sound the alarm and to call for revolt against the corrupt Qajar government, as well as for the dissemination of new concepts and ideas . . . The new mood of rebellion caught and met a corresponding and equally legitimate desire for change among a small but then growing number of Iranian women. (Bayat-Philipp 1978: 296)

Education and Agitation

It was in such a climate of opinion that education for women was expanded. In 1874, an American Presbyterian Missionary School had been started in Tehran and was attended at first by non-Muslims; two Muslim girls entered the school in 1891, however, and their numbers rose to 120 in 1909. In 1907, the first Iranian girls' school, and in 1908 a French girls' school were founded in Tehran. By 1910, there were 50 girls' schools in Tehran and increasing numbers of women teachers, journalists and activists in women's organizations (Bayat-Philipp 1978: 300). One of these was Khanum Azamodeh whose husband held liberal views and believed in education for women. In the early 20th century, Asamodeh started a school in her home for 20 girls; this grew into a large middle school for girls with 400 pupils (Namus School), a venture which inspired the creation of many more girls' private schools in Iran (Woodsmall 1936: 145–6).

As in other countries, women in palace circles and in the royal harem were involved in political intrigue and protest, harems being 'rarely the dens of idleness and iniquity imagined by Westerners' (Keddie 1981: 34). It is claimed that Anis Ud Daula, Shah Nasir ud-Din's third wife, conspired to secure the downfall of the Prime Minister whom she held responsible for her recall from Europe in 1872, where she had been on a visit with the Shah. Since the Prime Minister was also under attack for selling the country to British interests, the incident was politically important. 'Thus . . . a member of the Qajar harem became involved in one of the first important nationalist political movements' (Bayat-Philipp 1978: 297). The harem was also active in the first expression of Iranian opposition to foreign economic domination in 1890 when the entire tobacco monopoly, including the production, sale and export of the country's tobacco crop, was given to G.F. Talbot, a British capitalist (Rodinson 1974: 126). The protests included a boycott of tobacco launched by the women of the royal harem: 'The successful boycott was to be a prelude to the constitutional revolution in 1905' (Bayat-Philipp 1978: 298).

During the constitutional agitation that erupted in 1905, women joined the protests on the streets and were very effective in this form of demonstration. They also took part in the agitation against the Shah in 1906, when they demonstrated in the streets, surrounded the Shah's carriage and handed him a petition with their demands. One woman gave him a letter saying 'Fear the time when we shall finally take away the crown off your head and the royal cane off your hand'. It is hardly surprising that such activities brought hostile reactions and that when Iranian women marched unveiled in Tehran shouting, 'Long live the Constitution, long live freedom . . . We must free ourselves from religious obligations to live the way we want!', they were denounced as prostitutes hired by reactionaries to discredit the 1906 revolution (Bayat-Philipp 1978: 298, 302).

The new Constitution of 1906 did not grant suffrage to the women. Article 10 stated that 'Those deprived of the right to vote shall consist of all females, minors . . . fraudulent bankrupts, beggars, murderers, thieves and other criminals punishable under Islamic law' (Sanghvi 1968: 300). During this period a number of women's secret societies came into being, whose prominent members included Malikiya-yi Iran, Safia Yazdi, Sadiqa Daulatabadi and Badri Tundari, wives or relatives of constitutionalist leaders. One of these societies published a weekly paper, *Danish* ('Knowledge'), which was edited by the wife of a doctor and was said to be 'the only newspaper written exclusively for women, and discussing topics of special interest to women'. One of the principal activities of the women's groups was propaganda regarding the need for education for girls and the opening of girls' schools. The nationalist and feminist nature of their agitation can be seen in the appeal against Russian threats to Iranian independence made by the Persian Women's Society in 1911 to British suffragettes: 'The ears of the men of Europe are deaf to our cries; could you women not come to our help?' — to which the

British women replied: 'Unhappily, we cannot make the British government give political freedom even to us, their country women. We are equally powerless to influence their action towards Persia' (Bayat-Philipp 1978: 298, 307).

When conservative forces attempted to destroy the constitutional government, however, women joined the resistance, demonstrated on the streets and fought in battle. In the second attempt against the Majlis in 1911, the women's participation in mass protests was noted by the London *Times*:

> The patriotic demonstrations continue. A curious feature is the prominent part taken in them by women. At a large meeting of women held in the great mosque . . . addresses were delivered by female orators; it is said that they were very eloquent. One lady announced that, although the law of Islam forbade it, the women would . . . take part in a holy war. (Bayat-Philipp 1978: 303)

The participation of women in the 1911 demonstrations after the Russian invasion of North Iran is of particular interest because they staged separate demonstrations of their own. Their revolutionary zeal during this period of crisis, though hidden in official history, has been documented by eyewitnesses. For example, Morgan Shuster, the American financier whose employment by the Constitutionalists had caused a Russian ultimatum for his removal and thus provided a pretext for the Russian invasion, witnessed the women's action. In his book *The Strangling of Persia*, he recounts that when rumours spread that the deputies of the National Assembly had capitulated to Russian demands, the question arose of what could be done to prevent this humiliation.

> The Persian women supplied the answer. Out from their walled courtyards and harems marched three hundred women . . . many held pistols under their skirts or in the folds of their sleeves. Straight to the majlis they went and gathered there, demanding of the President that he admit them all . . . they confronted him . . . exposed threateningly their revolvers, tore aside their veils and confessed their decision to kill their own husbands and sons and leave behind their own dead bodies, if the deputies wavered in their duty to uphold the liberty of the Persian people and nation. (Sanghvi *et al.* 1967: 15–16)

Among the women activists of the period, Sadiqa Daulatabadi, an early pioneer of women's education, was particularly important. Her father, a leading *mujahid* of Isfahan, was said to have 'advanced' ideas and she attended her brother's school dressed as a boy. In the early 20th century, she opened the first girls' school in Isfahan and later became a government inspector of girls' schools. Sadiqa Daulatabadi was also active in women's journalism; she published a bi-monthly 'The Tongue of Women' (*Zabaun-i-Zanan*) in Isfahan, which took a strong nationalist stance on political issues and protested very strongly against the treaty with Britain in 1919; this 'stirred up such strong opposition that the magazine was finally closed' (Woodsmall 1936: 145, 365).

An interesting factor is that as early as 1911, when the Constitution was being discussed, Hadji Vakil el Roaya proposed in Parliament that women should be allowed to vote. According to a report in the London *Times*, he asked why women were deprived of the vote: 'are they not human beings, and are they not entitled to have the same rights as we have? I beg the ulema for a reply'. The religious leader Sheikh Assadollah replied, 'we must not discuss this question, for it is contrary to the etiquette of Islamic Parliament. But the reason for excluding women is that God has not given them the capacity needed for taking part in politics' (Bayat-Philipp 1978: 301).

The activities of Iranian women during this period were noted by foreign correspondents. 'The movement is in its infancy, but the fact that last April for the first time Persian women held a large meeting in Tehran to discuss problems of education seems to suggest that the education of women will play an important part in the future evolution of Persia' (London *Times*, quoted in Bayat-Philipp 1978: 300); an American writer commented on the role of the 'veiled women who overnight became teachers, newspaper writers, founders of women's clubs', rapidly absorbing 'absolutely new ideas . . . with the elan of the crusader who has a vision' (Shuster, quoted in Bayat-Philipp 1978: 300).

The defeat of the Majlis in 1912 led to a period of reaction, but the lessons of women's participation in the agitation of the period, though ignored by historians, were not forgotten. An Iranian woman scholar, Dr Mangol Bayat-Philipp, has commented:

> In most of the historical accounts of revolution subsequently published, the women's role is either severely underestimated or overlooked altogether. Their participation in the 1905–1911 political events seems to have been a spontaneous, free move on their part . . . the role of women clearly reveals not only a new nationalist feeling that suddenly overwhelmed them and spurred them to action, but also a nascent though strong desire for official recognition . . . The revolution therefore turned out to be a fertile ground for their experimental struggle for emancipation. It did not bear immediate fruit, but the seeds were planted. (Bayat-Philipp 1978: 305–6)

In the years after World War I there was an upsurge of reformist and revolutionary feeling in many countries of Asia and it seems that certain Iranian women had also hoped for radical changes:

> The fact that great post-war changes abroad were making no difference to women's status in Iran disappointed Mohtaram Khanum (a woman pioneer) even more and convinced her that it was her duty to intervene directly in the struggle. She contacted a small number of other freedom-seeking women, and in 1922 they formed a society which they named the Patriotic Women's League. (Yeganeh 1982: 30)

The Policies of Reza Khan

In the next historical phase, Reza Khan, the soldier who became Shah in 1924, ruled despotically, crushing dissent, preserving the internal class structures in the 1930s taking the country towards Fascist Germany in his effort to steer clear of the traditional enemies, Britain and Russia. In his career, Reza Khan had been influenced by the Turkish experiment in secularization and modernization. In 16 years of autocratic rule, his policies were to strengthen his hold on the country by modernizing the state apparatus, especially through army reforms — introducing conscription and establishing military academies, medical corps, military police and other ancillary services. With the aid of the army and police, rebellions were crushed and nomadic tribes were disarmed and forcibly settled. The Shah's dictatorial policies included repression of his political opponents, especially the Communists.

The proximity of Iran to the USSR and the presence there of migrant Iranian workers in the early 1920s meant that events in the USSR influenced Iran. The Iranian Communist Party, formed in 1920, was mainly active in Gilan province where a Soviet republic under Kuchik Khan had been proclaimed. But the crushing of the Gilan republic weakened the Communist movement and many activists died in the struggle. A renewed attempt to develop the party occurred after 1922 when a legal party paper *Haqiquat* ('Truth') was started and achieved considerable success. The Communists also set up women's and youth societies as well as trade unions and cultural groups and tried to co-operate with nationalist forces. The women's section had contact with Clara Zetkin's Communist Women's International (formed in 1920) and an Iranian woman, Ms Dcevad-Sade was on its committee (*Die Kommunistische Fraueninternationale*, 1921–25).

But Reza Khan's repressive policies after 1925 weakened the party. In 1931, the Communist Party was banned and a period of severe repression followed. Many women were among the militants thrown into jail during this period, among whom were Jamileh Sadiqui and Shokat Rousta who earlier had established an organization in Rasht (the capital of Gilan province) advocating the abolition of the veil for women (Roshanak and Faramarz 1982: 159). In 1932, Taqi Arani and other students who had been influenced by Marxism while abroad formed a study group of 53 intellectuals and writers; they were arrested and imprisoned, but some later joined with Communist activists to form the Tudeh Party.

During Reza Khan's regime, a rigid bureaucracy was enforced to keep the people under control; financial and tax reforms as well as judicial reforms were introduced and a network of major roads and the Trans-Iranian railway were built. Policies for industrializing and modernizing the country were implemented through the imposition of new structures on the traditional economy and society. Consumer industries (textiles, soap, glassware and matches) were begun and by 1939 there was an industrial workforce of

650,000 (Roshanak and Faramarz 1982: 158). Interaction with the West influenced the direction of change. In addition to pressures from the small middle class, 'modernisation from above was seen by Reza Shah and those around him as the only way to make Iran a strong, self-respecting nation that could hold its own in the modern world' (Keddie 1981: 93).

Paradoxically, the Shah's policy of crushing all opposition was executed simultaneously with his efforts to 'free' women and to bring them out of seclusion and into society and the workforce. Inspired by Mustapha Kemal, Reza Khan, who had visited Turkey in 1934, made efforts towards modernization which included the separation of religion from politics, law and education, and the emancipation of the women of Iran through a few reforms from above, which included the encouragement of women's education and measures of dress reform such as a ban on the veil. Twelve women were permitted to enter the university for the first time in 1935. Delivering an address to the students of the first women's college, the Shah said, 'The women of this country, because of their being aloof from society, could not show their abilities and personal qualities. They could not play their role in the building of their beloved country and as a result they could not perform their duties towards their country' (Sanghvi *et al.* 1967: 25).

Not surprisingly, the issue that aroused hostility among religious interests was the Shah's efforts to compel women to give up wearing the *chador* (veil). An apocryphal story runs that the Queen Mother appeared at a shrine in Qom in 1928, wearing a light veil in place of the orthodox black *chador*. The religious *ulema* reprimanded her, and so Reza Shah beat the *ulema* after striding into the mosque with his boots on. In 1934, women teachers and students were ordered to appear unveiled, and in February 1936 the wearing of the *chador* was prohibited. This made Iran the first Muslim country to outlaw the veiling of women officially. Government officials were not allowed into cinemas and public places if their wives wore the *chador*, and 'taxi and bus drivers were liable to fines if they accepted veiled women as passengers' (Savory 1978: 98).

It was in 1936 that a concerted effort was made to highlight the issue, the intiative being taken by the palace. In January that year when the Shah attended the presentation of awards at the Normal School in Tehran, the Queen and princesses appeared in public unveiled and in European dress — a fact that was publicized as an important milestone in women's emancipation. The Shah spoke to an audience of 500 women and declared: 'we must never forget that one-half of the population of our country has not been taken into account, that is to say, one half of the country's working force has been idle.' However, he stressed the familiar theme of the need for women's education in order to benefit the next generation: 'The happiness of the future is in your hands. You are the educators of the coming generation, you have the possibility to become good teachers and to bring up good citizens' (Elwell-Sutton 1978: 34).

A contemporary account of the event states that all the women present on this occasion were unveiled, and that the streets were lined with crowds of unveiled women who had come to see the royal procession:

> The repercussion of this event was felt all over Iran. Emulating the Shah's example, in many places the Governor with the Chief of Police and School Superintendent held meetings in girls' schools to promote the progress of women . . . and pupils threw off their veils. The Iran Press after the eventual day of emancipation (8 January 1936), was filled for days with news articles and pictures on women's advance. Photographs of schoolgirls' athletics, Girl Scouts, Women's Club activities, held the front page. The forward movement was also promoted through the theatre by a special play depicting social advance with two Iranian girls in the contrasting roles of the old and new women of Iran. (Woodsmall 1936: 44)

In 1935, at the Shah's insistence, a 'Ladies Centre' was formed to organize 'lectures, adult classes, exhibitions and sports clubs for women, and . . . to promote the abandonment of the veil' (Yeganeh 1982: 32). The following years saw an active campaign to encourage women to discard their traditional clothes in favour of European styles. There was such a demand for women's coats, dresses and hats that rules against profiteering by Tehran tailorshops had to be introduced. Newspapers kept women informed of 'correct' social etiquette linked to the new fashions.

> Ladies in public meetings should not remove their hats; they may or may not take off their coats and gloves . . . Those who have always put their hand-kerchiefs, cigarette cases and other articles up their sleeves must now use their hand-bags for such things . . . To take fruit or sweets with gloves on is forbidden. (Woodsmall 1936: 45)

Although the legal abolition of the veil was a superstructural change which did not reflect any basic change in society, for most women it represented a welcome reform. The country's leading woman poet, Parvin-i I'tisami (1907–41), wrote a poem on this occasion called 'Woman in Iran' (*Zan dar Iran*):

> It is as if the woman in Iran was not an Iranian before.
> She had no pursuit other than misfortune and distraction.
> She lived and died in a solitary corner.
> What else was a woman in those days if not a prisoner?
> No one like a woman dwelt in darkness for centuries.
> No one like a woman was sacrificed in the temple of hypocrisy.
>
> (Bayat-Philipp 1978: 306)

However, measures from above that affect social customs can also have negative long-term results. Writing of the outlawing of the veil, an Iranian woman scholar commented: 'The brutal enforcement of this law until 1941 was one reason for a later pro-veil backlash, and many now doubt that legislation is a useful approach to veiling.' She added that the measures taken during Reza Shah's regime nevertheless introduced some changes:

> There was a *de facto* decline in upper-class polygamy and in inequality in marriage and divorce in the modernised classes, and a rise in paid work for women. These trends affected primarily middle and upper-class women, who nevertheless did not obtain political rights or complete economic and social equality, though their advanced in a decade was considerable. (Keddie 1981: 108–9)

Under the Pahlavi dynasty, women's emancipation remained a purely bourgeois urban phenomenon. Unfortunately, the militancy of the early 20th century, when the question of women's rights was keenly debated and women formed organizations, started newspapers and came out in public demonstrations, gave way to a period of reaction under Shah Reza Khan and his son, Shah Mohamed Reza Pahlavi. Nevertheless, some gestures were made: in 1963, the Shah gave franchise rights to Iranian women, and the Family Protection Law of 1967 made polygamy a possible reason for divorce and gave women more opportunities to initiate divorce. But even the right to vote in a situation where women had few other rights meant little to the majority of Iranian women. Their first experience with feminist activity in the years before 1920 were short-lived; the reforms of the following period were class-biased, and the association of 'women's emancipation' measures with the Shah's unpopular and repressive regime led to further deterioration in the position of women under the new rulers, after the Shah was deposed in 1979.

5. Attempts at Women's Emancipation in Afghanistan: A Note

Turkey's and Egypt's attempts at modernizing their economies and social structures, and consequently the movement towards women's emancipation, had an influence on other countries in the region, including Afghanistan. Lying geographically at the crossroads between Central Asia, the Middle East and India, Afghanistan has been a battleground for centuries. Islam became the predominant religion in the 10th century AD, but it was not until the 18th century that Afghan tribes tried to assert their own identity and establish their national independence. This process was hampered by the interests of various outsiders, the Turks and the Persians at one level and the British and Russians at another. These powers encouraged and sponsored various tribal groups, and continuous warfare among them was the result, with various expeditions being sent out, particularly by the British from India, in support of their nominees.

This state of affairs was brought to an end by Amanullah Khan who succeeded in uniting many of the tribes and seized the throne in February 1919. One of his first acts was to declare the complete independence of Afghanistan in its internal and external affairs. The British were not happy with this declaration of independence and tried to negate it by force. However, the British could not defeat the Afghan armies and were forced by the peace accords signed at Rawalpindi to accept Afghanistan's independence.

As in Turkey and Egypt, Amanullah Khan then set out to modernize the country. He developed close ties with Turkey, Iran and the Soviet Union, visited these and other countries, and referred to himself as a 'revolutionary'; in 1921 he signed a treaty with the Soviet Union calling for 'the liberation of the peoples of the East', and attempted several internal reforms. These included general conscription (to replace tribal levies), legal reform and in 1923 a proposed new Constitution with a national assembly and voting rights for women (in this respect he was ahead of Mustapha Kemal and Reza Khan). Claiming that 'the keystone of the future structure of the new Afghanistan will be the emancipation of women', he introduced a Family Code in 1921 forbidding child marriage; he also encouraged girls' schools, sent some Afghan girls to Turkey for education, banned polygamy for government employees, and ordered them to wear Western dress; in 1928, his wife Queen Surayya appeared unveiled in public and it was decreed that women should in future discard the veil (Halliday 1978).

Afghan society was, however, still organized on tribal lines and conservative in its attitudes. Tribal leaders were rigidly opposed to the process of modernization and reform because it affected their powers. Civil war resulted and Amanullah was dethroned and forced into exile. The swift pace at which he tried to introduce reforms was, in a sense, counterproductive. Some aspects of the reform, such as those regarding dress, were seized upon by the reactionaries as weapons: Amanullah himself offended the traditionalists by wearing European dress; he is reported to have attended the Azhar mosque 'in a grey top hat of fashionable shape in which to the scandal of the *ulema* he performed the ritual genuflections of Muslim prayers'. It was also said that in religious centres like Kandahar, 'the news that the Queen was appearing unveiled and in European evening dress caused much resentment' (Fraser-Tytler 1953: 208, 210). When tribal conflicts broke out, Amanullah, who had not built up a strong army, was easily ousted and exiled in 1929. Reaction set in and the succeeding kings, Nader Shah (1929–33) and Zaher Shah (1933–73), annulled the measures beneficial to women in order to please orthodox religious opinion; schools for girls were closed, women were refused the vote, wearing the veil was made compulsory, Islamic law was stressed and the power of the mullahs over the legal system was re-established (Halliday 1978: 10–14). The failure of the Afghan experiment resulted in some Islamic countries exercising caution on reforms affecting the status of women.

6. Women, Social Reform and Nationalism in India

> I should like to remind the women present here that no group, no community, no country, has ever got rid of its disabilities by the generosity of the oppressor. India will not be free until we are strong enough to force our will on England and the women of India will not attain their full rights by the mere generosity of the men of India. They will have to fight for them and force their will on the menfolk before they can succeed.
> *Jawaharlal Nehru*, speech at Allahabad, 31 March 1928

The issue of women's emancipation in India under British colonial rule, which also included today's Pakistan and Bangladesh, was closely linked with two important movements: one, a political movement of challenge and resistance to imperialism, and the other, a social movement to reform traditional structures. Both these movements were, however, integrally connected with the concept of a free and modern India.

The religious base on which these traditional structures rested was Hinduism, which had more or less acquired its present form in the 5th and 4th centuries BC. Hinduism has some characteristics that set it apart from other religions: it is not derived from a historical person, nor does it spring from any divine revelation. Instead it 'grew and evolved from a variety of cults and beliefs' (Thapar 1966: 132). Some of these cults had their origins in the Vedic religion practised by the first immigrants into India from the north-west. Others had flourished among the people and were gradually absorbed into organized religion.

Hinduism was basically monotheistic, but this was expressed in a *tri-murti* or trinity of gods: Brahma who creates the universe, Vishnu who preserves it, and Shiva who destroys it when it becomes degenerate and has run its course. This concept was a reflection of the natural order with its cycle of birth, life and decay. However, at a later period, Brahma lost his prominence and Hindu devotees were followers of either Vishnu or Shiva, both seen as manifestations of the Absolute. Together with this trend, there also evolved the cult of *bhakti* or personal devotion to the God.

The doctrine of karma is of central importance in Hinduism, a person's actions conditioning his status in succeeding lives. Whether an action is morally correct and results in good is dependent on its conformity with *dharma*, the sacred law. If one does one's duty as prescribed by the *dharma*, then the result is good. The social organization of Hinduism was based on the four caste structure: *Kshatriyas* (warriors and aristocrats), *Brahmins* (priests), *Vaisyas* (commoners — in the agrarian economy, cultivators) and the *Shudras*. A late hymn from the Rg-veda legitimizes, in a myth, the origins of the hierarchic caste system:

When they divided the man, into how many parts did they divide him?
What was his mouth, what were his arms, what were his thighs and his feet called?
The brahmin was his mouth, of his arms were made the warrior
His thighs became the vaisya, of his feet the shudra was born.

(Basham 1954: 240–1)

As society developed, various sub-castes grew up in association with different types of work; the continuance of the system was ensured by caste being made hereditary, and the performance of one's caste duty being synonymous with righteous action. Inter-caste commensality and marriage were forbidden. With occupation and caste being linked, social mobility within the hierarchic structure became severely restricted. The accent on heredity made the family the unit of society. Since the family was patriarchal, women were generally subordinate to men. Male children were greatly prized, for important religious rituals could be carried out only by a son. The practice of self-immolation by a woman on the death of her husband seems to have been merely symbolic at the early stages, for there are references to widow remarriage, but later, the practice of a widow burning herself on the husband's funeral pyre became real and widow remarriage was forbidden; women appear to have had some degree of choice in marriage in the early periods, as the story of Sita choosing Rama at a *svayamvara* (self-choice ceremony) would appear to indicate. Later developments, however, restricted this practice and made the choice of husband subject to caste and parental control. It was against most of these highly ossified caste and ritual practices that the Hindu social reformers were to struggle in diverse ways, which are considered later in this chapter. However, it cannot be forgotten that a sizeable section of the population of India was not Hindu, having converted to Islam.

Muslim dynasties from Afghanistan and Turkistan had occupied the Punjab in the 10th century and had extended their control to Delhi by 1192. Most of the rulers of this period in North India were zealous Muslims, ardent warriors against the Hindus, whom they regarded as idolatrous heretics. However, the real foundations of Muslim rule were laid in the middle of the 16th century, when Babur occupied Delhi and created the basis for the Mogul Empire that was to cover a large part of the Indian sub-continent. Religious policy under the Moguls assumed a different aspect. Akbar realized that it was impossible to rule over India

74

as an orthodox Muslim potentate whose basic role was to spread the Islamic faith; instead he adopted a policy of reconciliation and even toyed with the idea of creating a new syncretic amalgam of the two religions. Various sections of Hindus converted to the new faith, some under force, but many voluntarily; the latter included those who converted because of the privileges and positions to which Muslims had access, those who wished to avoid the poll tax on non-Muslims, and some members of the lower castes who wished to escape from their disadvantaged position in society. Despite some clashes, coexistence in the same society forced Islam to adopt some of the features of Hinduism and Hindu society, including caste and some forms of ritual worship. This cultural cross-fertilization also made some difference to the status of Islamic women. Practices such as the wearing of the veil were not very widespread among Indian Muslims although the institution of purdah or seclusion did apply, at least at the level of the higher groups; yet Muslim women became subject, just as much as Hindu women, to all the oppressions of a patriarchal, caste-bound society, and 19th-century Islamic reformers fought against many of these practices side by side with Hindu reformers.

The other movement which influenced the growth of feminism in India was the struggle to assert and obtain national independence from Western imperialism. European aggression in India dates back to the 16th and 17th centuries when Portuguese, Dutch, French and British trading posts were established in the coastal regions. British involvement in India was through the East India Company, founded by royal charter in 1603. At first the East India Company was primarily a trading concern; it had no territorial interests beyond its trading posts, although it made use of military power to keep the trade routes open. The victories at Plassey over the Nawab of Bengal in 1757 and at Buxar over the Mogul emperor brought enormous territory into the hands of the company, some of which it held independently and some under the nominal sovereignty of the Moguls. Pitt's India Bill, introduced in 1784, separated the trading activities of the East India Company from the political administration of the country, and policies of expansionary conquest and control were followed.

By 1823, almost all of India had either been directly annexed by the British or was under their indirect control through their alliances with princely states. The last aggressions were the conquest of Sind in 1843 and of the Punjab in 1849. In order that the sub-continent might be more easily exploited and controlled, the British army was strengthened, roads and railways were built, a civil service was formed to administer the country, and the infrastructure of a colonial economy was established. The administration of these vast territories required local officials, and an English educational system was introduced to create this class. The first province to be subjected to these policies was Bengal, where the Hindu (later Presidency) College was established in Calcutta in 1817.

That English education and involvement in government would favour the creation of a Westernized élite was to be expected. To quote Macaulay in 1835: "We must do our best to form a class who may be interpreters between us and the millions we govern; a class of persons Indian in blood but English in taste and opinion.' Two factors worked against the whole-hearted adoption of this policy: first, job opportunities for the British had to be kept open, and second, the British feared that education of Indians would in the long term be detrimental to the continuation of their own control.

However, it was necessary to recruit Indians at least for the lower rungs of the administration. By the early 19th century, an English-speaking Bengali petty bourgeoisie and bourgeoisie had arisen, sections of whom sponsored movements of reform, cultural revival and nationalist agitation, in which both liberal and orthodox Bengalis played an important part. Education had exposed Bengalis to the late 18th-century European ideas of the Enlightenment which emphasized the inalienable rights of man, and opposition to tyranny; they were also influenced by the views of political thinkers on government by consent, representative parliamentary government, and the right to opposition and rebellion. These ideas gained popularity in Bengal, first through the impact of Rammohan Roy (1772–1833) who had been influenced by the thinking of James Mill, and Jeremy Bentham whom he met in London in 1831. Bengalis were also introduced to radical thought by Henry Vivian Derozio (1809–31), a Eurasian teacher at Calcutta's Hindu College who had an 'academic association' (on the line of Plato's Academy) where continuous discussion among Bengali students took place. Derozio popularized the work of Bacon, Locke, Hume, Paine and the French 18th-century thinkers, and encouraged his students to doubt and question everything and accept no authority but reason. He became the 'youthful prophet of the new youth', the founder of the iconoclastic movement known as Young Bengal which attacked religious orthodoxy. Throughout the 'stormy decade' of the 1830s after Derozio's death, his disciples continued the movement, promoting rationalism, individualism and nationalism, even going to the extent of welcoming the July Revolution in France in 1830 by planting the French tricolour on a building in Calcutta (Haldar 1972: 21).

Forms of Resistance

Resistance to British imperialism was long and continuous, lasting almost 200 years. In 1757, the ruler of Bengal attacked the foreign aggressors, and the British under Robert Clive won their first major victory at the famous Battle of Plassey. In 1764 the princes of Bengal and Oudh joined in, unsuccessfully challenging the British, and in 1780 the King of Mysore (Hyder Ali) also tried to oust them. In the late 18th and 19th centuries, there were frequent skirmishes under the leadership of the Mahrattas who opposed foreign rule, and bitter warfare between 1846 and 1848 in the Punjab which ended in its annexation. But resistance against the imperialists climaxed in the 1857 Indian 'Mutiny' — the first war of independence — which started when Indian soldiers in the British army mutinied and then spread to a large area of North India covering Meerut, Delhi, Cawnpore, Lucknow and Allahabad. Peasants joined in the struggle and managed to evict the British from many of their strongholds. The struggle failed to spread to other parts of India, however; also, it was opposed by many of the landholders and tax-gatherers who had been appointed by the British. The struggle was crushed by the British, who retaliated severely and brutally against combatants and civilians alike; there was general and indiscriminate burning and pillaging of villages and numerous executions. One result of this struggle was the end of the East India Company; the Indian Act of 1858 abolished the company and established the direct rule of the British government.

The challenge of imperialist domination and the attempted imposition of an alien culture, ideology and religion on India produced, in its turn, several movements of religious and social reform among Hindus and Muslims. These reformist movements — such as the Brahmo Samaj which started in Bengal in 1828 — were intended to cleanse Hinduism of certain corrupt and decadent practices and to counteract missionary propaganda by presenting the Hindu religion as one that was compatible with progress and change. Social reform also became a popular issue among Indian intellectuals, who, inspired either by liberal views of social change or in the hope of preventing drastic social change, were to launch movements to abolish or correct some of the worst abuses that prevailed in the society of the period.

The political response to imperialism was initiated late in the 19th century with the growth of Indian nationalism, centred on the Indian National Congress (formed in 1885). In the early years, the Congress was led by moderates, but by 1900 more militant elements, inspired by B.G. Tilak in Maharashtra and Aurobindo Ghosh in Bengal, had become influential. Mass-based nationalist agitation spread throughout Bengal after its partition in 1905, including a campaign for *swaraj* (home rule) and *swadeshi* (promotion of local products), and a boycott of British-run institutions and British goods (the boycott of British imports having a special appeal to the Indian bourgeoisie). The militants in Bengal also had recourse to violent actions, labelled 'terrorist'. In the following years there were several waves of agitation, notably after Gandhi's return to India in 1915 and his assumption of the leadership of the Congress. Another period of political upheaval occurred in 1919 after the Congress rejected reforms proposed by the British. Gandhi launched a campaign of non-cooperation which included *hartals* (mass work stoppages), the boycott of all legislatures, foreign goods and official functions, and the refusal to pay taxes. The subsequent repression, including the massacre of an unarmed crowd at Amritsar in 1919, and the imprisonment of

77

Gandhi, Nehru and other leaders in 1921–22, served only to strengthen the movement in the 1920s. By the beginning of the next decade, the agitation climaxed again over the issue of *swaraj*; Gandhi led the famous Salt March in 1931, thereby launching a movement of civil disobedience, non-cooperation and non-violent resistance. From then until independence was achieved in 1947, the nationalist struggles were continuous and involved large masses of men and women.

Agitation Against 'Certain Dreadful Practices'

The status of women in India has varied in different historical periods and in the different regions of the country, and has also been subject to differentiation according to class, religion and ethnicity. The general situation, however, was one of suppression and domination within the bounds of a patriarchal system. Whether the woman in question belonged to a peasant family and was compelled to drudgery in the field and home or to a high-caste family and living a life of leisure, she was the victim of a set of values that demanded implicit obedience to male domination, and of many other social practices that circumscribed her life.

In the early 19th century, the glaring social evils that affected women were subjects of discussion among administrators, missionaries and concerned members of the local bourgeoisie. The Europeans emphasized the low status of Indian women as a reflection of the general backwardness of the country, but the Indian reformers were keen to show that, whatever the current position, women's status had been high in ancient India and many outstanding women had made their mark on Indian history. These included the warrior-queens: Sultana Razia, who succeeded to the throne of her father, the King of Delhi, in the 13th century and led her troops into battle, and Nur Jehan who exercised real power and led the army to war in the early 17th century during the reign of her husband, the Emperor Jehangir. The best-known, however, was the legendary Lakshmi Bai, the Rani of Jhansi who, during the war against the British in 1857, rode on horseback in fierce battles against the foreigners and died in combat. 'It was the Rani of Jhansi's custom to lead her troops dressed in military uniform . . . a crimson jacket, crimson trousers and a white turban, which made it impossible to tell her sex' (Madhavananda and Majumdar 1953: 397).

Movements of reform against the social evils that affected women began in India in the early 19th century. They have usually been attributed to external factors such as the impact of English education, missionary activities, the promotion of the nuclear, monogamous family, and liberal ideas from the West, and to internal movements such as the nationalist agitation against imperialism and a religious-cultural resistance to the challenge of Christianity and Western culture.

From early on, the missionaries were active in drawing attention to

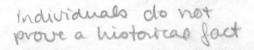
Individuals do not prove a historical fact

what a Baptist had, in 1796, termed 'certain Dreadful Practices' (Potts 1967: 140). These included infanticide, self-torture, exposure of the sick and dying on the banks of the holy rivers (Ghat murders) and *sati*, the practice of burning Hindu widows on the funeral pyres of their husbands. The latter practice, in particular, provoked continual protest from the missionaries; William Carey of the Baptist mission in Serempore studied the prevalence of *sati* around Calcutta in 1803 and recorded 430 cases that year (Potts 1967: 146). In Britain, the support of William Wilberforce, the slave abolitionist, and of other social reformers of the period was enlisted and missionary agitation also evoked, in turn, a response from Indian social reformers who were anxious to redeem the reputation of their society.

The issues tackled by the reform movement — including *sati*, widow remarriage, polygamy and women's property rights — were problems of a certain stratum of society, being mainly confined to Hindus of the higher castes and classes. They were raised by bourgeois, male social reformers from urban areas who tended to idealize women's role as wife and mother in the context of patriarchy. Whether, like the orthodox reformers, they looked back to a Vedic golden age, when women were supposed to have had high status, or whether they looked forward to a new society based on liberal principles which negated the 'barbaric' heritage of the past, their basic assumptions were that social reform and female education would revitalize and preserve the patriarchal family system, produce more companionable wives and better mothers, and therefore have a stabilizing effect on society.

Some reformists also felt that middle-class family structures were endangered by the prevailing social evils. The fact that some high-caste widows who had been ill-treated and prevented from remarriage had turned to prostitution was an example of such a threat. One reformer commented that, 'Social rigidity, child marriage with its necessary consequences, child-widows, the social taint involved in widow re-marriage, all combine to create in society a new class of women whom we are prone to call fallen' (Asthana 1978: 8). This concern to prevent the disintegration of family life, which existed among the English-educated and also among the non-Westernized intelligentsia, was a theme in the literature of North and South India. As Vina Mazumdar writes:

> With increasing urbanisation, prostitution became more commercialised . . . the large number of young high-caste widows, helpless victims of family neglect and even torture, was an obvious recruiting ground. This was a threat that could not be ignored by those who wanted to preserve the family and its economy from destruction. The debate on ill-treatment of widows, the denial of re-marriage, child marriage and polygamy . . . which raged in the newspapers and journals of the 19th century bear ample testimony to this fear among reformers (Mazumdar 1976: 49).

Under the influence of liberalism or using slogans of cultural revival, the bourgeoisie in India were thus enabled, through the reform movement, to prohibit the more extreme abuses affecting women. But the questions were taken up individually and fought as single issues, with success measured by each legislative act that was passed. Since all areas of social reform concerned the family, the effect of the reforms may have been to increase conservatism and, far from liberating women, merely to make conditions within the family structure less deplorable, especially for women of the bourgeoisie. It is clear that, while some Indians fought for social reform on the principle of liberal values, many conservatives felt otherwise; for example, the famous reformer, M.G. Ranade (1841–1901) who was a lawyer, judge and legislative councillor in Bombay, expressed the view that social reform was in the 'great Hindu tradition' of 'seeking out ancient principles in order to restate them'. Instead of destroying the structure, the reformer should 'lop off the diseased overgrowth and excrescences and . . . restore vitality and energy to the social organism' (Mazumdar 1976: 43). Moreover, many social reformers themselves condoned child marriage and opposed widow remarriage in their own families. Even before the nationalist movement had become politically active in India, the social reformers had started to agitate on two of these issues — the practice of *sati* and the ban on widow remarriage. These could safely be tackled because they had not existed in very early times, were confined to the upper castes and classes and, if remedied, would given India the appearance of being 'civilized' without endangering the traditional family structures.

Apart from attempting to persuade people to give up such practices, the reform movement also sought the help of the British administration in India, hoping to prohibit them by law. Initially the British administration followed a policy of non-interference, but its attitude changed in 1817, when Mrikyunjaya Vidyalankar (the Chief Pandit of the Supreme Court) announced that *sati* had no religious *shastric* authority, and other Bengali intellectuals joined in the clamour for legislation against *sati* (Potts 1967: 142–8).

Raja Rammohan Roy

The poineer in the agitation for women's rights in India was Raja Rammohan Roy (1772–1833), a Bengali who had been influenced by Western liberal thought and had attempted to reform and revitalize Hinduism. His family were Radi Brahmins, a group which had for several generations been involved in administration and higher learning and were to figure prominently in the 19th-century social reform movements. Roy's early classical education had included Sanskrit, Arabic and Persian, and by 1800, he was fluent and well-read in English. He was exposed not only to the dissident Calcutta British radicals, Unitarians and advocates of free-trade, but also to liberal political thinkers of Europe — Locke, Bentham, Montesquieu and Adam Smith among others. This was a period when the question of women's emancipation was eagerly discussed in Europe, especially by the radicals and Unitarians in Britain; while the

British radicals were directly influenced by the philosophers of the Enlightenment in France (Voltaire, Montesquieu and Rousseau) and by the events of the French Revolution, the Unitarians (liberal Christians who believed in the single personality of God the Father as opposed to the Trinity) advocated reason and tolerance in the religious sphere and civil liberty in politics, and were at the forefront of reformist and democratic movements. Associated with radicals and Unitarians was Mary Wollstonecraft (1759–97), the best-known feminist of the time who had made an impact with her famous book *Vindication of the Rights of Women* (1791) (Mies and Jayawardena 1983: 13). It is interesting that Mukherjee who describes Roy as 'one of the male feminist thinkers of the 19th century' remarks that Roy's arguments on women's status 'were like those of Mary Wollstonecraft', and one can only speculate that, living at that period, he had been exposed to her writings. It is known, however, that on his visit to London, Roy met the radical Unitarian, Harriet Martineau (Mukherjee 1982: 161–5).

Roy championed women's rights on four issues: *sati*, polygamy, women's education and women's property rights. In 1818 and 1820, he published pamphlets against *sati* (which were translated into English). Criticizing the oppression of women, he wrote:

> At marriage the wife is recognised as half of her husband, but in after-conduct they are treated worse than inferior animals. For the woman is employed to do the work of a slave in the house . . . to clean the place . . . to scour the dishes, wash the floor, to cook night and day, to prepare and serve food for her husband, father, mother-in-law, brothers-in-law and friends and connections. (Nag and Burman 1977: 156)

Roy's mobilization of Hindu thought against the system of *sati* created the necessary public opinion to enable the government, which was also under pressure from missionaries on this issue, to make the practice a criminal offence in 1829. Although ancient Hindu law had made provision for widows to remarry in certain circumstances, by the medieval period of Indian history the higher castes had prohibited remarriage. The issue came up between the 1830s and 1850s, and agitation for a reform of the law was taken up in many parts of India. The Young Bengal Movement, founded in the 1830s, for example, was a proponent of social reform and women's emancipation; its journal, *The Bengal Spectator*, came out in 1842 in strong support of widow remarriage (Haldar 1972: 45). Rammohan Roy was particularly horrified by the various types of violence used against women, which he vividly described in 1820:

> Amongst the lower classes, and those even of the better class . . . the wife, on the slightest fault, or even on bare suspicion of her misconduct, is chastised as a thief. Respect to virtue and their reputation generally makes them forgive even this treatment. If unable to bear such cruel usage, a wife leaves her husband's house to live separately from him, then the influence of the husband with the

purify Hinduism →
resist Brit. domination

magisterial authority is generally sufficient to place her again in his hands; when, in revenge for her quitting him, he seizes every pretext to torment her in various ways, and sometimes even puts her privately to death. These are facts occurring every day, and not to be denied. What I lament is, that, seeing the women thus dependent and exposed to every misery, you feel for them no compassion, that might exempt them from being tied down and burnt to death. (Nag and Burman 1977: 157)

There was a lively debate on the religious texts. Rammohan Roy and the liberals challenged the interpretation of Vedic texts on the question of *sati*: they were also eager to counteract the missionary view that Indians were barbarous and uncivilized, and referred to 'cruel murder, under the cloak of religion' which had led to Indians being regarded with 'contempt and pity . . . by all civilised nations on the surface of the globe' (Nag and Burman 1977: 163).

The reform of Hinduism became a vital issue if the Indians were to counter the attacks and criticisms of the British, and ultimately if they were to resist British domination. In 1828, Roy and other enlightened Bengalis formed the Brahma Samaj, which drew inspiration from many religions and aimed at changing the debased form of Hinduism that prevailed. The 'Brahmos', as they were called, challenged all forms of obscurantism and ritual, as well as female oppression associated with orthodox beliefs, and many of the later activists who took up issues of women's emancipation were from this group of Brahmo Samaj reformers.

Roy and the Brahmo Samaj had been given valuable financial support by Dwarkanath Tagore, a rich landowner of Bengal. His son Debendranath Tagore (1817–1905) succeeded Roy as head of the movement and carried on Roy's campaigns to purify Hinduism. He founded Shantiniketan as a religious retreat in 1886; it was his son Rabindranath Tagore who transformed it into a university in 1901.

Growth of the Reform Movement

The reformist campaign increased in fervour during the 1850s. The most active campaigners on widow remarriage during this period were Iswar Chandra Vidyasagar (1820–91), a Bengali who, in 1856, published a pamphlet 'Marriage of Hindu Widows' and presented a petition to the government on the issue; Debendranath Tagore, an activist of the Brahmo Samaj, who formed an organization to campaign for widow remarriage and against other evils affecting women, and Dayananda Saraswati (1824–83), a North Indian social reformer who founded the Arya Samaj, another movement for the purification and revival of Hinduism. With support from the press and British officials, the agitation led to the Act of 1856 which legally permitted the remarriage of widows. Social custom was difficult to change by legislation, however, and it was only the very daring who defied tradition.

As in many Asian countries at this time, the reformers' ideal was the monogamous, nuclear family. Polygamy in India was practised by both Muslims and Hindus of 'high' caste and class, the Muslims being allowed four wives; the Kulin Brahmins, for example, were permitted an indefinite number of wives. The issue of polygamy was first raised by Hindu reformers who campaigned for its abolition and by Bengali playwrights and writers who satirized the practice; in the 1850s, many petitions against polygamy were presented to the government, one being from the Maharaja of Burdwan in 1855. The campaign was continued, especially by Vidyasagar who, in the 1870s, wrote tracts exposing the evils of polygamy. Government policy at that time, however, was against too much interference in traditional practices affecting family life.

The issue of child marriage was also taken up by social reformers of the 19th century. Unlike *sati*, polygamy and the ban on widow remarriage, which affected the upper segments of society, child marriage was widespread among Hindus (but not practised by tribal groups). The practice was considered a religious and social obligation by 'higher' castes, and a means by which to protect their daughters from men with economic power by the 'lower' castes. It was also an economic saving, since male children commanded lower dowries (Mazumdar 1976: 52). The reformers best known for their agitation on this issue were Keshab Chandra Sen (1838–84), Vidyasagar and Gopal Hari Deshmukh. As a religious reformer and leader of the Brahmo Samaj, K.C. Sen argued that the practice of child marriage was a corruption of the scriptures and wrote, 'the custom of premature marriage, as it prevails in this country, is injurious to the moral, social and physical interests of the people and is one of the main obstacles in the way of their advancement' (Basu 1978: 46–7). Vidyasagar pointed out in 1850 that child marriage was linked to the problem of Indian widows because many of the child brides were widowed at an early age. Dayananda Saraswati urged that girls should be educated and only allowed to marry at 16 or 18, arguing that because of child marriage, the Hindus were the 'children of children' (Heimsath 1964: 120).

In 1872, some success was achieved with the Marriage Act which set higher age limits for marriage, 14 for girls and 18 for men. Further agitation and publications by reformers like Behramji Malbari, who had used the press (including his own *Indian Spectator*) for the campaign against child marriage, led to the Age of Consent Bill of 1891, which raised the legal age of consent for sexual intercourse from 10 to 12 for girls. Even this was achieved only after bitter controversy since it was opposed by political radicals like B.G. Tilak as being an unwarranted interference by the British in local customs.

Another area of agitation for the social reformers was that of property rights for Hindu women. Existing unwritten practice was particularly harsh on the Hindu widow who had no claim on her husband's property except the right of maintenance, as a result of which she was at the mercy of her husband's relatives. In 1874, the Right to Property Act gave a widow a life interest in her husband's share of the property and a share equal to that of a son; however, the Act did not give a widow the right to own or dispose of this property, and daughters continued to be excluded from rights of inheritance.

Omvedt has pointed out that the subordination of women is 'crucial to the general hierarchical organisation of caste society' and the anti-Brahmin movement in India was consequently also linked to the women's struggle. One of the first to make the connection between caste oppression and women's oppression was the most radical social reformer of the 19th century, Jotirao Phule (1827–90), a Maharashtrian of 'low' caste who led the anti-Brahmin struggle, also opposing polygamy and child marriage and advocating women's education and widow remarriage. In the 1850s, Phule had set up a school for girls in Pune and two schools for 'untouchables', and in 1863 he started a Home for the Prevention of Infanticide, to care for the unwanted children of widows. He founded the Satyashodhak (Search for Truth) Samaj in 1873, an anti-Brahmin movement aimed at saving the 'lower castes from the hypocritical Brahmins and their opportunistic scriptures'; this movement heralded the struggles of non-Brahmins of later years. Phule's forceful writings in Marati had an impact, especially works like *Gulamgiri* ('Slavery'), published in 1872. In opposing *sati*, Phule speculated about whether any husband would become a *sata* by being immolated on the funeral pyre of his wife (Heimsath 1964: 102, 248). Omvedt has written on Phule's concern for women's rights:

> Phule was capable of becoming emotionally involved over the issue — one of his polemical articles involved a scathing attack on one of his own colleagues for sexist behaviour and showed an awareness of the issue of language-embedded sexism that has only become more general today. In his final book, *Sarvajanik Satyadharma*, an effort to create a secular ethics, he strives throughout to use non-sexist phraseology; instead of the Marathi equivalent of a phrase such as 'all men are equal' he used instead and very consistently, the term *sarve ekander stri-purush*, 'each and every woman and man'. (Omvedt 1975: 46)

The Marati and Gujarati reformers of the 19th century were in the forefront of several controversies over women's rights, and important public debates on caste and women's oppression raged in western India. An influential Gujarati reformer was Darsondas Mulji (1832–71), who had a newspaper, *Satya Prakash*, which led an attack on the immorality of maharajas and Hindu priests and supported widow remarriage, women's education and foreign travel. His denunciation of the maharajas led to a libel case against him in 1861 which he won. Another of the early Maharashtrian reformers was Gopal Hari Deshmukh (1823–92), known as 'Lokahitwadi', who in the 1840s had begun to attack Brahmin traditional practices, including the caste system, child marriage and the treatment of widows. Deshmukh urged the use of English texts or translations to foster scientific thought and advocated the rejection of Brahmin learning. Writing in Marati he said: 'I think that the misery of women is so great that when I remember it my hair stands on end. These Brahmins instead of killing their daughters, put them into greater misery . . .' (Heimsath 1964: 102). The woman question remained an important issue in the non-Brahmin movement of later years. In 1920, for instance, the non-Brahmins of Pune, together with Brahmin liberals, held a meeting at which free compulsory female education was demanded. The nationalist leader Tilak was violently opposed and driven away from the meeting when he argued that there were funds only for male education (Omvedt 1975: 46).

Another element in the continuing expansion of education for women was in the creative fields. Rabindranath Tagore (1861–1941) had transformed Shantiniketan (founded by his father) into an institute for the regeneration and revival of Indian culture and art, while being open to influences from all other cultures. Shantiniketan was open to women and Rabindranath placed great emphasis on the conditions necessary for the release of creative potential in women. This was evident, not only in his educational work, but also in his well-known poems and short stories. He came out strongly against traditional customs and practices, while adopting a modern attitude to the role and status of women in society; the women in his creative writings are 'drawn more vividly and with a firmer hand than the male characters' (Naravane 1980: 94). An example is his story 'Devi', later made into a film by Satyajit Ray, where a woman is driven to insanity by a tradition-ridden father-in-law who believes, on the basis of a dream, that she is the reincarnation of a goddess. However, while attacking such practices, Tagore was, at the same time, a believer in the unique contribution of woman, through her special qualities, to the harmonious continuance of human society. His vision in this respect was essentially traditional and sentimental:

> If the human world becomes excessively male in its mentality, then before long it will be reduced to utter inanity. For life finds its truth and beauty, not in any exaggeration of sameness, but in harmony . . . It is their instinct to perform their services in such a manner that these, through beauty, might be raised from the domain of bondage to the realm of grace. (Naravane 1980: 94)

In these attitudes, Tagore was at one with most male reformers of the time.

In South India too the non-Brahmin movement had originated against Brahmin hegemony 'questioning the right of the Brahmins to dominate top-class jobs and to perpetuate the myth of a superior culture' (Lakshmi 1984: 9). The 'self-respect movement' in the 1920s against the Brahmins, led by E. V. Ramaswami Naicker, known popularly as *Periyar* (the Great), attacked the caste system and all forms of religious ritual and idol worship. Equal rights for women were advocated and marriages based on 'self-respect' were popularized: this meant that there should be equal consent between the man and the woman, and that there should be no priests present to officiate at a marriage (Ram 1979).

There were several male writers and poets in South India who were forceful proponents of women's emancipation. One was the leading Tamil poet Subramaniya Bharathi (1882–1921), who belonged to that stream of radical thought in Asia and the Middle East which advocated modernity and reform, while asserting a cultural identity against imperialism. He was active in many areas of political and social reform, and was influenced by foreign radical and revolutionary movements, welcoming the Russian Revolution in 1917. He championed Indian independence while denouncing caste oppression, the ill-treatment of immigrant Tamil workers in Fiji, the inequitable distribution of wealth in India and the subordination of women.

Bharathi was especially insistent on female education and the rights of women, and criticized Tamil conservative society for keeping women in subjection. He often used the image of 'Mother India', and linked the subjection of India with the subjection of women, describing the awakening of all oppressed groups that was taking place. He was impressed by the agitation for women's voting rights in Europe and in a journal he edited called *India*, he wrote a note in 1906 on the struggle for women's suffrage in Britain. He also edited a monthly journal for women, *Chakravarthini* ('Empress'). It is also interesting to note the influence of early Chinese feminism on Bharathi, who translated two articles on the famous woman martyr entitled 'The Story of a Chinese Woman called Jiu Jin' and 'A Speech by Jiu Jin'. Bharathi's poems in Tamil also frequently dealt with issues facing women, one being significantly entitled 'Pudumai Pen' ('New Woman'), the popular slogan of the period. Themes of marriage, free love and chastity also occur in his poems.

While many Indian nationalists like Gandhi chose to idealize Sita, 'the monogamous, chaste, self-sacrificing spouse of Rama', as the model for Indian womanhood, Bharathi in contrast wrote poems on Draupadi, 'the strong-willed, passionate, revengeful, polyandrous wife of the five Pandavas of the Mahabharata' (Mies 1975: 57). He translated his own poem 'Kummi of Women's Freedom' based on the 'kummi', a woman's dance in South India, from which a few verses are given below:

Dance the Kummi, beat the measure;
Let this land of the Tamils ring with our dance.
For now we are rid of all evil shades;
We've seen the Good.

Gone are they who said to woman: 'Thou shalt not open the Book of
    Knowledge'.
And the strange ones who boasted, saying:
'We will immure these women in our homes' —
Today they hang down their heads.

And they talk of wedded faith;
Good; let it be binding on both.
But the custom that forced us to wed, we've cast it down and trampled it under
  foot;
Dance the Kummi, beat the measure;

To rule the realms and make the laws
We have arisen;
Nor shall it be said that woman lags behind man in the knowledge that he
  attaineth.
Dance the Kummi, beat the measure;

Another South Indian who similarly wrote on women's oppression was the well-known poet Kumaran Asan (1873–1924). His controversial poem *Chintavishtayya Sita* ('The Brooding Sita'), written in 1919, is an interpretation of the legend of Rama and Sita, where Sita instead of submitting obediently to tests of fire to prove her chastity, strongly protests 'Does the King think that I should once more go into his presence and prove myself a devi? Do you think I am a mere doll . . . my mind and soul revolt at the thought'.

There were other novelists of Kerala who in the 19th century spoke out on women's issues, including Chandu Menon (1847–99), who advocated women's education, stressing the importance of English education. His famous Malayalam novel *Indulekha* (1889) concerns, in the author's words, a story of a woman who although left 'helpless by the untimely death, first of her father and then of her uncle' was able to marry a man of her choice because of 'the firmness and strength of mind she had acquired through education'. Menon also adds, addressing Indian women:

If you wish to really enlighten your minds, you must learn English, whereby alone you can learn many things which you ought to know in these days and by such knowledge alone can you grasp the truth that you are of the same creation as man, that you are as free agents as men, that women are not the slaves of men. (Menon 1965: 369)

Female Education

Since the reform of 'social evils' was linked to the issue of preserving and strengthening basic family structures and creating good wives and mothers, the question that frequently arose was that of female education, a policy supported by both progressive and orthodox reformers. There had been many educated women in the upper classes, including famous women writers and poets, but no general education was available to women. This became an issue on which there was broader agreement than on such issues as widow remarriage, which had touched religious sensibilities. Many liberal reformers campaigned in favour of female education. Vidyasagar was at the forefront of the movement and established 40 girls' schools in Bengal between 1855 and 1858 (Asthana

1974: 27). Conservatives also joined the campaign for female education. Ramakrishna Paramhamsa, the Hindu philosopher who popularized the concept of a 'Supreme Mother' and her worship in the form of the goddess Kali, said: 'I worshipped all women as representatives of the divine mother. I realised the Mother of the Universe in every woman's form' (Everett 1979: 55). Ramakrishna's renowned disciple Vivekananda, however, a radical on many issues, believed that a woman should not be educated in the modern sciences but should be trained to achieve fulfilment within the family.

In the 19th century, as in other countries, Indian reformers thought that social evils could best be eliminated through education; however, the concept of education was limited to producing good home-makers and perpetuating orthodox ideology. 'Education would not turn the women away from their familial roles, but improve their efficiency as wives and mothers and *strengthen the hold of traditional values on society, since women are better carriers of these values*' (Mazumdar 1976: 49–50; emphasis added). In addition, Christian missionaries were keen to use education for proselytizing and for ensuring that, if the women became Christians, there would be no lapses back to the old beliefs by male converts. Girls' schools were started by missionaries and British residents in the leading cities, especially in Bengal where the British had made their first inroads in the mid-19th century. In 1820, the first girls' school was founded by David Hare in Calcutta; Professor Patterson founded a girls' school in Bombay in 1848, and in 1851 J.E.D. Bethune started the Bethune Girls' School in Calcutta, which later became the first women's college. Many Indian reform groups like the Arya Samaj and Brahmo Samaj ran educational institutions for women, and Indian women such as Pandita Ramabai and Ramabai Ranade were involved in projects for female education. The visit to India of Mary Carpenter, a well-known British social reformer, who made a report on women's education in India, resulted in the establishment of a teachers' training college in 1870 (Asthana 1974: 135). By 1882, there were 2,700 educational institutions for girls with 127,000 pupils; the majority were primary schools, but there were also 82 secondary schools, 15 teachers' training institutes and one college.

By the 1870s, women had begun not only to write literary works in English, but also to translate works from other European languages, a notable example being Toru Dutt (1856–77), born to a wealthy, literary family of Bengali Christians. She travelled with her parents to Europe in 1869, attending school in France where she not only learnt French but also developed an abiding interest in French culture. In 1870, they went to England, where the poems of the family were published that year by Longmans, Green & Co., under the title *The Dutt Family Album*. In 1871, the Dutts went to Cambridge where Toru and her sister 'sedulously attended the Higher Lectures for Women, with great zeal and application' and also took French lessons (Das 1921: 39). Returning to Bengal in 1873, she continued to write and translate. She published her first book of verse translations from French poetry at the age of 20 (the year before her death in 1876) under the title *A Sheaf Gleaned in French Fields*; this has been described as 'an amazing feat of precocious literary craftsmanship' (Das 1921: vii).

In the 1880s, Indian women also started to graduate from universities, the first being two students of the Bethune school, who completed their studies at Calcutta University in 1883. By 1901, there were 256 women in colleges, the figure rising to 905 in 1921. In 1916, the Indian Women's University was started in Bombay by D.K. Karve, who had read about the Japanese Women's University (Heimsath 1964: 241). In the same year the Benares Hindu University was founded with an affiliated women's college.

Although some women thus benefited from access to schools and universities, even in the most educationally advanced states of India the vast majority of girls did not attend school (Asthana 1974: 135–7). Moreover, education for women was mainly confined to the larger cities and towns and served the needs of the bourgeoisie and petty bourgeoisie. The policies of promoting women's education and the type of education provided were not intended to promote women's emancipation or independence, but to reinforce patriarchy and the class system. 'The class bias of the reform movement was most pronounced in the field of education. The plea that education would only improve women's efficiency as wives and mothers left its indelible mark on the educational policy' (Mazumdar 1976: 53).

However, education enabled some women to break into avenues of employment that had previously been denied to them. In 1902, 242 women were attending medical schools and many had been trained as teachers, nurses and midwives. Cornelia Sorabjee, a Parsee, was the first Indian woman to graduate in law at Oxford in 1882, although it was not until 1923 that women were allowed to practise law. Another category of pioneers were the Indian women who challenged convention by studying medicine, either in India (where Madras and Bombay Medical Colleges had admitted women in 1875 and 1883 respectively) or by going abroad to medical colleges in the West, where women were accepted. Among the early women doctors were Anandibai Joshi who graduated in 1886 from the Women's Medical College in Philadelphia and worked as a physician in the women's ward of the Kohlapur hospital; Kadambini Ganguli (b. 1862) who had been educated in Britain and was the first woman graduate of Calcutta University and Bengal's first woman doctor; Annie Jagannadhan who studied in the newly founded Edinburgh School of Medicine for Women in 1888 and in 1892 became a house surgeon in a Bombay hospital; and Rukmabai who obtained a medical degree from London University in 1895 and later worked in the Women's Hospital in Rajkot. These women had to battle against the full weight of conservatism. To give one example:

Rukmabai rebelled against Indian traditionalism, in order to study medicine. She left her husband who filed a suit against her. She was bitterly criticised and even sentenced to six months imprisonment if she did not agree to live with him. A compromise was finally reached whereby she had to pay a large sum of money to her husband. It was, however, decreed in accordance with Hindu Law, that Rukmabai could never marry again. (Asthana 1975: 54–5)

Agitation by Women

Pandita Ramabai

Although the leading social reformers in the 19th century were males whose objectives were to cleanse and reinforce family life, the women themselves started to overstep the home and family limits envisaged for them by the reformers:

> For the early pioneers of social and religious reform, women were at first objects of their emancipatory efforts, but in the course of the 19th and 20th centuries they became more and more subjects in the political and social sphere. (Mies 1980: 117)

There were several women activists and pioneers in the 19th and early 20th centuries, the majority of them linked by birth or marriage to families in which the men had participated in religious or political reform movements. Many examples of protest by women have been lost to history, however. Omvedt has written: 'Phule had referred to a Marathi book written by a non-Brahmin woman, Tarabai Shinde, "The Comparisons of Men and Women" but both this 19th century woman and her writings have disappeared from available records' (Omvedt 1975: 46).

One of the most notable pioneers among the women we do know of was Pandita Ramabai (1858–1922), a reputable Sanskrit scholar, whose courageous and independent activities on behalf of women's causes made her the foremost female agitator of her time. Her life was unusual for a woman of that period. Her father, a Sanskrit scholar of Maharashtrian origin, believed that women had as much right to knowledge as men. He is said to have been 'cast out by society for teaching Sanskrit to his wife Lakshmibai against the established social convention'. Although orthodox on other issues, he took an 'uncompromising attitude towards the education and the marriageable age of girls (Madhavananda and Majumdar 1953: 403). Because of such views, the family was hounded from place to place and lived the life of nomadic scholars, wandering all over India. As a child, Ramabai not only acquired mobility and experience, but learnt Sanskrit and theology from her parents. The family went through many misfortunes and it was said of Ramabai that 'the persistent social persecution that ultimately led to the death of her parents and sister . . . reinforced by the famine of 1874, steeled her heart against the Hindu religion and society, neither of which she could ever forgive' (Madhavananda and Majumdar 1953: 404).

In 1878, Ramabai went to Calcutta together with her surviving brother. Her critique of Hinduism made her known in Bengali reformist circles and, because of her knowledge of Sanskrit, she was given the title of 'Pandita'; she also went on a tour of Bengal and Assam, lecturing on social injustice. For a woman to be well-versed in theology, in a society where religion is all-pervasive, has always been an advantage when challenging social evils that are disguised as religious orthodoxy; and Ramabai used her knowledge in the cause of women. She had two unique advantages that are usually denied to women who are physically and intellectually confined, namely an understanding of social reality gained through her nomadic travels and a command of Hindu ideology gained through her knowledge of the scriptures.

Using the argument that women had held high positions in ancient India, Ramabai made an all-out attack against the orthodox priests. Having been widowed (in 1882) with a new-born daughter, she had to fend for herself and to face criticism for not conforming to the traditional deportment of a widow. She began a life of travel and agitation, starting a series of Mahila Samaj (women's organizations) in Bombay state, and campaigning for women's education and medical training. She wrote a book, *Sthri Dharma Neeti* ('Women's Religious Law'), which advocated women's emancipation and attacked traditional practices harmful to women. By this time she had also learnt English, having come into contact with Christian missionaries in Pune. In 1883, she travelled to Britain, where she met Dorothea Beale, a pioneer woman educationalist and principal of Cheltenham Ladies College, where Ramabai spent some time studying and teaching. She went on the USA and Canada in 1886, where she studied and lectured, returning to India in 1889 via Japan. Her book on the status of women, *The High Caste Hindu Woman*, was well received in America and led to the formation of the Ramabai Association, one of whose objectives was to collect funds for women's activities in India. She later converted to Christianity and began a series of projects involving girls' schools, orphanages and widows' homes. Pandita Ramabai was also politically active, being one of the few delegates to the Indian National Congress sessions in 1889. Her life and work not only inspired many other women, but also influenced many male reformers such as M.G. Ranade and D.K. Karve (Asthana 1974: 41–8).

The other area of activity that permitted women to leave the confines of the home was social work. As in Victorian Britain, some women of the bourgeoisie and wives of male social reformers were active in social work among the poor and destitute. To give one example among many, Ramabai Ranade (wife of M.G. Ranade) held free classes for women in sewing and first-aid, visited hospitals and prisons and distributed food during crises such as the 1913 famine (Asthana 1974: 50–1). The proliferation in the 19th century of social reform activities among various groups resulted in the formation, under M.G. Ranade's guidance, of the Indian National Social Conference in 1887. The aims of this organization were to 'strengthen the hands of the local associations and to furnish information to each association . . . as to what is being done by others . . . and to stimulate active interest by mutual sympathy and co-operation'. Up to 1917 the Conference met separately but concurrently with the political organization, the Indian National Congress, but after that date, its activities were merged into the general political agitation of the Congress (Desai 1957: 123–34).

Muslim Women and Social Reform

While the early agitation for social reform came from Hindu males and was concerned with the status and role of Hindu women, the Muslims also began action on social reform in the late 19th century. Many of the issues that agitated the Hindus did not apply to Muslim women since Muslim law allowed for widow remarriage, divorce and a share of parental property. However, concern was expressed by Muslim male social reformers on issues such as polygamy, purdah and female education.

The most prominent Muslim reformer was Syed Ahmad Khan (d. 1898), who pioneered Muslim higher education and, in 1875, founded a Muslim university college at Aligarh. Khan wrote in his journal *Tahzib-ul-Akhlaq* on all aspects of social reform. Believing that the decline of the Muslims was due to their reluctance to adopt Western-style education, Khan advocated modern education for both men and women. He also opposed polygamy, taking the view that since a man could not treat all his wives equally (as enjoined in the Koran), polygamy was not permissible under Islam. On this question Syed Ahmad Khan went against the strong current of orthodox opinion, declaring that, 'Polygamy must be absolutely and definitely restricted . . . monogamy should be the rule.' He also challenged the orthodox views that Islam advocated purdah (seclusion) for women or that it discouraged women's education (Bhatty 1976: 101, 107). Other Muslim male reformers included Badruddin Tyabji (1844–1909), a Bombay businessman who campaigned against the purdah system; Syed Imam who financed a Muslim girls' school in Patna, believing that the country's progress was linked to women's education; and Hydari, a well-known writer, who expressed the prevailing views on the need for educating girls: 'while the education of a boy helps him only, the education of a girl lifts the whole family to a higher state of mental and moral life' (Desai 1957: 112).

Some attempts to promote education were made by Muslim women: Amina Tyabji, wife of Badruddin Tyabji, started a Muslim girls' school in 1895 and Begum Abdullah managed a similar school in Aligarh that was founded by her husband, Sheik Abdullah in 1906; this school later became a woman's college affiliated to the Aligarh Muslim University. Other

Muslim women pioneers included members of the Tyabji family: Begum Nawab Misra, who founded an orphanage, and Shareefa Hamid Ali, who began a nursing centre. In several urban centres, Muslim women of well-known families began local women's associations, and in 1916, the Begum of Bhopal formed the All-India Muslim Women's Conference. Such activities were not wholly approved by the traditionalists, however, who showed their opposition to Muslim girls' schools and were angered by the resolution passed by the Muslim Women's Conference in 1917 that polygamy be abolished (Everett 1979: 63).

As the political struggle began, however, Muslim women began to take part in the agitation. The Khilafat movement among Muslims in India (protesting against the dismemberment of the Turkish Empire) brought the female relatives of the leaders of the movement on to the public platform. Mohamed Ali's mother, Bi Amman, as well as his wife and Hasrat Mohani's wife, for example, addressed women's meetings during this campaign; when the brothers Mohamed and Shaykat Ali were imprisoned, Bi Amman appeared in public at the joint Muslim League and Congress Sessions of 1917. In later years, many Muslim women joined the *satyagraha* and non-cooperation movements. Thus while participation in political activities was more easily tolerated, Muslim opinion was not prepared for changes in laws regulating women's social position.

Women and Nationalist Agitation
It was in the political struggles against imperialism that Indian women (both Hindu and Muslim) began actively to participate in life outside the home; and in doing so, they had the support of many nationalist political leaders. The expansion of women's education and their admission to universities had produced a number of English-educated, middle-class women by the late 19th century, and they made their presence felt in political activities. The Indian National Congress, founded in 1885, allowed women to become members and ten women participants from Bombay and Bengal attended the sessions in Bombay in 1889.

Bengal had been exposed to British influence from the 18th century and was in the vanguard of both Westernization and political and reform movements linked to national revival and nationalism. The women of the Bengali bourgeoisie were also among the earliest pioneers of reform and political agitation, one of the best known being the writer Swarnakumari Devi (1885–1932), Rabindranath Tagore's sister, who together with her husband edited *Bharati*, a Bengali journal. In 1882, she started the Ladies Theosophical Society for women of all religions, during a period when Indian intellectuals had shown some interest in the theosophical movement founded by Colonel Olcott and Helena Blavatsky. In 1886, Swarnakumari also began a women's association (Sakhi Samiti) which was concerned with promoting local handicrafts made by women, and in 1889 she was one of the first women to attend the sessions of the Indian

National Congress. She was also a well-known novelist; her novels reflected the thinking of Bengali reformers, both men and women, who had been educated in English but had retained traditional values. In *An Unfinished Song*, the heroine is Westernized and marries a doctor who has studied in England and is supportive of women's rights, but she adheres to certain orthodox values and to 'the traditional ideal of female religious devotion' (Everett 1979: 54).

Women continued to participate in Congress politics in the 1890s, including activists like Pandita Ramabai and women professionals such as Dr Kadambini Ganguli. In the early 20th century, women became more involved in politics with the increase in nationalist activities. Mass struggles for self-rule, including the boycott of British goods, took place during this period. There was also increased militancy, bomb throwing and assassinations, especially in Punjab and Bengal; violence occurred after the partition of Bengal in 1905, and events such as the deportation of the 'extremist' leader B.G. Tilak in 1908 led to strikes by Bombay workers. Women joined the agitation, organized *swadeshi* meetings, boycotted foreign goods, and donated money and jewellery to the nationalist movement. As part of the campaign, a pamphlet *A Vow for Bengali Women* was circulated, explaining the *swadeshi* movement to village women, calling upon them to participate in certain rituals which had political significance and to boycott foreign goods. Protest meetings were held throughout Bengal, some of them exclusively for women. The most active women's leader of this period was Swarnakumari's daughter, Sarala Devi, who started physical exercise clubs and a *swadeshi* store for products made by women.

Many foreign theosophists also participated in the nationalist and women's movements, the foremost being Annie Besant (1847–1933), feminist and former Fabian socialist who, in the 1880s, had created a stir in Britain with her campaign for birth control and her leadership of the match girls' strike. Besant came to India in 1893 and was active in the theosophical movement and in education and not only formed the Home Rule League in India but also became the first woman president of the Indian National Congress in 1917. Other theosophists who were concerned about Indian women's status included Margaret Cousins, an Irish feminist, who arrived in India in 1915 and participated in many of the social and political reform movements of the time, being one of the founders of the All-India Women's Conference in 1927, and Dorothy Jinarajadasa (the wife of a Sri Lankan theosophist) who, together with Besant and Cousins, formed the Women's Indian Association in 1917. Also active in the early 20th century nationalist upsurge was a militant Irish woman, Margaret Noble (1867–1911), who arrived in India in 1895, and under the influence of Swami Vivekananda, took on the name of Sister Nivedita and worked in Bengal. She is said to have had links with Irish revolutionaries, and her work in education, cultural activities and agitation for *swaraj* was characterized by revolutionary zeal.

Gandhi and Women's Rights*

The Congress leaders saw the advantages of mobilizing women and always exhorted them to join the nationalist struggle as equals. We shall examine in some detail the ideas of Mahatma Gandhi and Jawaharlal Nehru as they pertain to the role and status of women; the similarities and differences of their ideas reflect the many currents of thought that were then prevalent on the issue of women's emancipation.

Gandhi's basic ideas on women's rights were equality in some spheres and opportunities for self-development and self-realization. He believed that 'woman is the companion of man, gifted with equal mental capacities', and realized that her contemporary subordinate position was the result of domination by man. He said 'woman has been suppressed under custom and law for which man was responsible and in the shaping of which she had no hand.' He argued that the rules of social conduct must be developed only on the basis of co-operation and consultation, and should not be imposed by one sex on the other. In this connection, Gandhi said, 'men have not realised this truth in its fullness in their behaviour towards women. They have considered themselves to be lords and masters of women instead of considering them as their friends and co-workers.' Gandhi was equally aware that the position and role of women differed from class to class and that, for example, 'in the villages generally they hold their own with their men folk and in some respects even rule them.' But he was convinced that 'the legal and customary status of women is bad enough throughout and demands radical alteration.'

However, Gandhi's view of women's equality was located within a religious sense of the word and within the patriarchal system, projecting a concept of women's role as being complementary to that of men and embodying virtues of sacrifice and suffering. In 1921 he stated: 'To me the female sex is not the weaker sex; it is the nobler of the two: for it is even today the embodiment of sacrifice, silent suffering, humility, faith and knowledge' (Everett 1979: 76).

Gandhi believed that every man and woman had a duty to perform in the interest of self-realization and social well-being. While arguing that 'she should labour under no legal disability not suffered by men' and denouncing 'the sheer force of vicious circumstances' by means of which 'even the most ignorant and worthless men have been enjoying a super-iority over women which they do not deserve and ought not to have', he still thought that there was a particular sphere appropriate for women. This is most clearly illustrated in his ideas on female education. He was all in favour of educating women, but the emphasis must be different for men and for women. He said:

*The quotations from Gandhi, unless otherwise stated, are from *India of My Dreams* by M.K. Gandhi. Details in bibliography.

> In framing any scheme of women's education this cardinal truth must be kept in mind. Man is supreme in the outward activities of a married pair and, therefore, it is the fitness of things that he should have a greater knowledge thereof. On the other hand, home life is entirely the sphere of women and, therefore, in domestic affairs, in the upbringing and education of children, women ought to have more knowledge.

In this line of thought, he believed that courses of instruction for men and women should be based on 'a discriminating application of these basic principles' if 'the fullest life of man and woman is to be developed'.

Within this context, Gandhi in 1929 deplored the existing social evils which affected women, being, as he himself said, 'uncompromising in the matter of women's rights'. He was against the ban on widow remarriage, calling it 'this poison of enforced widowhood', though once again he based his arguments on religious and moral grounds. He argued (in 1926) that

> Voluntary widowhood consciously adopted by a woman who has felt the affection of a partner adds grace and dignity to life, sanctifies the home and uplifts religion itself. Widowhood imposed by religion or custom is an unbearable yoke and defiles the home by secret vice and degrades religion.

He had similar ideas on female morality and divorce, and in 1926 spoke against double standards for men and women: 'And why is there all this morbid anxiety about female purity? We hear nothing of women's anxiety about men's chastity. Why should men arrogate to themselves the right to regulate female purity?' To Gandhi, self-restraint in sexual matters was a great virtue, but it had to come from within the individual. Marriage was a sacrament; the dowry system should be abolished because it debased marriage, reducing it to an arrangement for money. Divorce was preferable to the continuance of a marriage which had ceased to be a vehicle for self-realization.

Gandhi's ideal woman was the mythical Sita, the self-sacrificing, monogamous wife of the Ramayana, who guarded her chastity and remained loyal to Rama in spite of many provocations. Sita was 'promoted' as the model for Indian women. 'Gandhi was perhaps hardly conscious of the fact that his ideal of womanhood, which he considered to be a revival of the Hindu ideal, contained in fact many traits of the puritan-Victorian ideal of woman, as it was preached by the English bourgeoisie.' Moreover, this image of woman had a 'strategic function in the political movement' (Mies 1980: 27).

Even though Gandhi appreciated the role of Indian peasant women, he still had no notion of economic equality for women. As Mies remarks:

> In Gandhi's idealised image of women her economic activity, especially the aspect of her economic independence, is not emphasised. As the most important activity he recommends to the women spinning and weaving, both of which he considers as religious acts and conforming to the 'nature' of woman. On the

economic independence of women he speaks evasively. The image of the modern independent career woman does not fit into Gandhi's conception of the ideal woman. (Mies 1980: 126)

Gandhi, however, was very conscious of the power that women could have in a struggle based on the concept of non-cooperation. He stressed the importance of their participation in political and social matters and exhorted them to join the nationalist struggle. 'In order to play her full and destined role in world affairs, in the solution of conflicts by non-violent means, women must extend their hearts and interests beyond the narrow confines of their homes and family and embrace the whole of humanity' (Mazumdar 1976: 56, 59).

Gandhi placed particular stress on the issue of non-violent struggle, claiming that women had great ability to endure suffering and could therefore play a key part in the movement. He claimed that the principle of 'non-violence' (*ahimsa*) and political non-violent resistance was suited to women as they were by nature non-violent. 'I do believe,' he wrote in 1938, 'that woman is more fitted than man to make *ahimsa*. For the courage of self-sacrifice woman is any way superior to man' (Mies 1980: 125). It was suggested that, being used to forms of passive resistance in their daily lives, they could the more effectively participate in socially organized passive resistance and non-cooperation.

Moreover, Indian women themselves were soon to take up the Gandhian ideology and to advocate *satyagraha* as a form of struggle particularly suitable for women. A women's journal, *Stri Dharma*, stated in 1930: 'Because the qualities which this new form of warfare is displaying are feminine rather than masculine, we may look on this life and death struggle of India to be free as the women's war' (Everett 1979: 76).

Nehru and Women's Rights

Jawaharlal Nehru's views on the status of women were more in keeping with those of the enlightened reformers of the time. Having sympathized, while in Britain, with the cause of the suffragists and having been exposed to the liberal and socialist debates on the 'woman question', he took what was at that time a 'progressive' stand on women's issues. He particularly emphasized the necessity for women to work outside the home, to be economically independent, and not to regard marriage as a profession. 'Freedom depends on economic conditions even more than political, and if a woman is not economically free and self-earning, she will have to depend on her husband or someone else and dependants are never free' (Luthra 1976: 5). He realized that this economic bondage was 'the root cause of the troubles of the Indian women', and clearly perceived that superficial reforms would not serve the cause of their emancipation. 'The joint family system of the Hindus, a relic of a feudal age utterly out of keeping with modern conditions, must go and so also many other customs and traditions. But the ultimate solution lies only in complete refashioning of our society' (*The Bombay Chronicle*, 25 April 1929).

In the same context, Nehru was rather suspicious of constant evocations of the past:

> I must confess to you that I am intensely dissatisfied with the lot of the Indian woman today. We hear a good deal about Sita and Savitri. They are revered names in India and rightly so, but I have a feeling that these echoes from the past are raised chiefly to hide our present deficiencies and to prevent us from attacking the root cause of women's degradation in India today. (Speech at Allahabad, 31 March 1928)

Nehru's more progressive attitude is also revealed in his ideas about female education. He did not agree that there was a fixed sphere for women and that education for women should therefore have a different emphasis. He took part in the foundation-laying ceremony for a women's college at Allahabad, but discovered that its prospectus laid down that woman's place was in the home, that her duty was to be a devoted wife, bringing up her children skilfully, and dutifully obedient to her elders. He was quite outspoken in his criticism of these ideals.

> May I say that I do not agree with this idea of women's life or education? What does it signify? It means that woman has one profession and one only, that is the profession of marriage and it is our chief business to train her for this profession. Even in this profession her lot is to be of secondary importance. She is always to be the devoted help-mate, the follower and the obedient slave of her husband and others. I wonder if any of you here have read Ibsen's 'Doll's House', if so, you will perhaps appreciate the word 'doll' when I use it in this connection. The future of India cannot consist of dolls and playthings and if you make half the population of a country the mere plaything of the other half, an encumbrance on others, how will you ever make progress? Therefore, I say that you must face the problem boldly and attack the roots of evil. (Speech at Allahabad, 31 March 1928)

Nehru also urged women to participate in the nationalist struggle. In 1931 he stated, 'In a national war, there is no question of either sex or community. Whoever is born in this country ought to be a soldier' (Luthra 1976: 3). Nehru spoke with great enthusiasm about the women who took part in the nationalist movement, of the thousands who braved police charges and prisons. However, he was quite conscious that women had to engage in a double struggle, against imperialism and against oppression by men and that these struggles were intimately linked. He wrote:

> They were mostly middle-class women, accustomed to a sheltered life, and suffering chiefly from the many repressions and customs produced by a society dominated to his own advantage by man. The call of freedom had always a double meaning for them, and the enthusiasm and energy with which they threw themselves into the struggle had no doubt their springs in the vague and

hardly conscious, but nevertheless intense, desire to rid themselves of domestic slavery also. (Nehru 1962)

Women in Political Action

Despite the many pronouncements of good intent by the male leaders, however, most of them still saw a woman's role basically as that of a housewife within a conservative family structure. Women activists became subsumed in the political struggle; women were lauded for being good *satyagrahis* (non-violent activists), but the real issues that concerned them as women were regarded by the men as of secondary importance. The agitation of the early social reformers about the social evils that affected women in the family were supplanted by nationalist issues, resulting in the neglect of women's unequal social and economic position. What is more, the few women's issues that were taken up were those that interested the middle-class women's organizations, such as the suffrage questions. In 1917, for example, Sarojini Naidu, Margaret Cousins and a deputation of women met the Viceroy and put forward demands for female franchise, and in 1919, Sarojini Naidu was part of a deputation of the Home Rule League who went to Britain to lobby for reforms and franchise rights. In 1918, the Indian National Congress supported the granting of the vote to women. The constitutional reforms of 1919 allowed provincial legislatures to decide on the issue; in 1921, Madras province, where the anti-Brahmin Justice Party had a majority, was the first to allow women to vote; other provinces followed, and in 1926, women were also given the right to enter the legislature, Dr S. Muthulakshmi Reddi becoming the first woman legislative councillor in Madras that year. Her struggle, however, to introduce social legislation such as the Devdasi Bill, banning temple prostitution of young girls, met with opposition and was unsuccessful (Lakshmi 1984: 22–3).

In the mass movements of the 1920s and 1930s, women's participation was much in evidence in certain acts such as the *khadi* campaigns (to wear homespun cloth), in the picketing of shops selling foreign goods, and in the Salt March of 1930 (when Gandhi urged the people to break the government's monopoly of salt manufacture by marching to the sea and making salt themselves), as well as in the general political demonstrations and mass agitation which resulted in the call by Congress for civil disobedience. Kamaladevi Chattopadhyaya, a militant Congress activist, was among the first to break the salt law and recalled that:

> Thousands of women strode down to the sea like proud warriors . . . they bore pitchers of clay, brass and copper . . . How had they broken their age-old shell of social seclusion and burst into this fierce light of open warfare? What had stirred them into militant rebels? (Basu 1976: 24)

Women all over India joined the struggle for independence and many thousands were jailed. Of the 80,000 arrested during the salt *satyagraha*, 17,000 were women. In 1931, the Congress delegates at the sessions held in Karachi congratulated the women 'who rose in their thousands and assisted the nation in the struggle for freedom' (Basu 1976: 29–30). Two women associated with this period of struggle were Sarojini Naidu and Kamaladevi Chattopadhyaya.

Sarojini Naidu

Sarojini Naidu (1879–1949) was the daughter of Aghorenath Chatto-padhyaya, a Bengali, who had studied chemistry at Calcutta University and had obtained a D.Sc. degree from Edinburgh in 1877. He was in the Brahmo Samaj movement for social reform as well as in Congress activities, and was the principal of a college in Hyderabad. Sarojini was educated in Madras and later studied in Cambridge, returning to India in 1898. She married a South Indian, Dr G. Naidu, that year, thereby breaking barriers of both province and caste. By 1904, Sarojini had made a mark as a poet and an orator and was influenced by G.K. Gokhale — the moderate nationalist leader. In 1914, she met Gandhi in England and in subsequent years was his devoted follower, also becoming one of the chief speakers of the Indian National Congress. In 1920, Sarojini joined Gandhi's non-cooperation movement and campaigned all over India on this issue. During the nationalist upsurge of the early 1930s, she worked with Gandhi and was with him on the Salt March of 1930, at the Round Table Conference in London in 1931, and during subsequent Congress agitation, being jailed in 1942 during the 'Quit India' movement.

Sarojini Naidu, during these years of political activity, also campaigned for women's rights (including franchise, education and divorce). In 1917, she was involved in the campaign for women's rights, lecturing on women's emancipation and petitioning the Secretary of State on women's franchise rights; but her views were conservative as she had a traditional view of the ideal woman. Moreover, 'Her emphasis was on harmony and comradely cooperation between man and woman in the common struggle for freedom and progress, not on confrontation' (Naravane 1980: 95). In 1926, she became the first woman president of the Congress, an event that received much publicity outside India. In her presidential address she evoked an idealized vision of the past, 'In electing me chief among you, through a period fraught with grave issues . . . you have reverted to an old tradition, and restored Indian women to the classic epoch of our country's history' (Naravane 1980: 96). In the 1930s, she was active in the All-India Women's Conference, and represented the moderate current of reformers who, while campaigning against discrimination against women, were more preoccupied with the nationalist political struggle, bypassing the issue of women's subordination within the family.

Kamaladevi Chattopadhyaya

More radical than Sarojini Naidu was her sister-in-law, Kamaladevi Chattopadhyaya, whose life reflected the many strands of activity in the women's movement of that time. She was born in South India in 1903, the daughter of a government official in a wealthy orthodox family; her husband died soon after their marriage and Kamaladevi, instead of adopting the secluded life of a Tamil widow, shocked conservative society by going to Madras to study and by marrying the Bengali playwright, Harindranath Chattopadhyaya. Through her marriage she became linked to a distinguished family; Chattopadhyaya's sister was Sarojini Naidu; and his brother Virendranath, who had grouped the Communist Indian political exiles in Berlin, was the common-law husband of Agnes Smedley (1892–1950) (the American feminist and Communist, later to achieve fame in China), whom Kamaladevi had met in the 1920s.

In 1926, Kamaladevi was the first woman in India to run for the Legislative Council, but she was defeated by 200 votes. Apart from her activities in the Indian national movement, which resulted in her being jailed for participating in the Salt March and *satyagraha*, Kamaladevi was also involved in the women's movement. She had been influenced by Margaret Cousins in Madras during her student years and had met feminists in Europe in the early 1920s. She joined the Congress Socialist Party in the 1930s and presided at the Meerut sessions of the party; in her presidential address she made the point that 'rather than running away from the Congress, calling it bourgeois', socialists should 'capture the Congress movement and prevent the leadership from converting it into a bourgeois party, thus stealing from us the Congress heritage' (Cobb 1975: 71).

Divorced in 1933, Kamaladevi travelled widely in Europe, China and Japan to propagate the cause of Indian independence. On returning to India in 1942 she was jailed, but used the occasion to write extensively. In 1946–47 she was on Nehru's Congress Working Committee, and in subsequent years concentrated her activities on developing a national theatre and reviving the handicrafts industry (Cobb 1975).

By this time, women had become active not only in nationalist and political bodies but also in organizations whose membership and direction were solely in their hands. One of the earliest of such organizations was the All-India Conference for Educational Reform, formed in Pune in 1927. This body laid emphasis on activities connected with the reform of education and of marriage law; it adopted resolutions demanding compulsory primary education, increased facilities for women in the education system, the abolition of child marriage and the fixing of the legal minimum age of marriage at 14 for females. The organization was composed of women from many strata of society — from feudal families and the middle classes, as well as women professionals and political activists. Its office-bearers reflected this diversity: the vice-presidents were the Rani of Sangli, Lady J.C. Bose and Sarojini Naidu; the chairperson was Margaret Cousins, and Kamaladevi Chattopadhyaya was its secretary. The president, however, was the Maharani of Baroda who had co-authored a book (published by Longmans in London in 1911) entitled *The Position of Women in Indian Life*, the views propounded in it being such as to provoke an attack by the socialist feminist, Rebecca West, who said 'she takes a step backwards; she actually recommends women to take up "genteel callings" ' (Marcus 1982: 12).

At the 1928 sessions of the conference in Delhi, Muslim women's participation was much in evidence; the name was changed to All-India Women's Conference (AIWC) and a Muslim president was appointed, the Begum mother of Bhopal, Maimoona Sultana. In 1929, the AIWC conference in Patna elected the Rani of Mandi as president and adopted a resolution that the scope of its activities should be widened to include 'the consideration of all social evils which hinder the progress of education'. Another change was seen at the 1930 conference when Sarojini Naidu was elected president and Kamaladevi Chattopadhyaya the secretary. These sessions passed resolutions on equal inheritance rights for women and also stressed the need to enquire into the conditions of life and work of working-class women and children, but no political resolutions were passed (Chakravartty 1980: 196–8).

As the nationalist movement developed in the 1930s, differences of opinion arose within the AIWC concerning its involvement in political issues. Some wished it to remain aloof from politics, but women of the Congress and Communist movements spearheaded the efforts to politicize the AIWC. The resulting dichotomy within the leadership of the association was described by a Communist militant as follows:

> One section . . . wanted to keep the organisation segregated from politics of any kind whether of a national nature or otherwise, while there were others, who saw that women's emancipation, social or economic, could not be achieved without national independence nor without struggling for social justice. Communist women activists tried their level best to work within the AIWC and turn it into a living mass organization in which broad sections of women of all classes could struggle for their rights and welfare. (Chakravartty 1980: 199)

Another left-wing Congress woman who was active during these years was Aruna Asaf Ali (née Ganguli), a Bengali Hindu teacher who had made an unconventional marriage to a Muslim lawyer. She joined Gandhi's Salt March agitation in the 1930s and was active in the Congress Socialist Party. During the 1942 'Quit India' movement she went underground and was involved in violent activity against the British throughout India. In 1945, she clashed with Gandhi over the issue of violence, and in 1952 joined the Communist Party of India.

Women and Revolutionary Nationalism

Although the Indian National Congress, which had adopted a policy of non-violence under the leadership of Gandhi, was the dominant nationalist organization, there were some Indian nationalist groups which followed a more militant policy of revolutionary and violent action. These groups were active within India (especially in Bengal, Punjab and Maharashtra) as well as abroad, where they were able to canvass and organize support. Several foreign women were linked with these revolutionaries and Communists, among them Evelyn Roy (wife of M.N. Roy) and Agnes Smedley, who worked with Indian revolutionaries in exile in New York and Berlin.

Bhikaiji Cama

The best-known Indian woman in revolutionary circles in Europe was Bhikaiji Cama (1861–1936), who came from a wealthy Bombay family of Parsee social reformers. In 1885, she married Rustomji Cama, a lawyer, who was pro-British. She left her husband at the age of 27 and became active in nationalist politics, attending the Congress sessions in Bombay. She went to Britain in 1901 for medical treatment; there she came under the influence of Indian revolutionary nationalist Krishnavarma. Her militant speeches attracted attention and she left for Paris to avoid being arrested, remaining there in exile (Nanavutty 1977: 78–9). In 1907, when the Indian nationalist Lala Lajpat Rai was arrested, she spoke at a protest meeting in Paris, and called for a boycott of the British:

> What is the good of talking about the glorious past of India . . . if you are living in slavery today? . . . what is it that makes you live in subjection? Come out and establish liberty and equality under Swaraj . . . Let us combine. If we all speak bravely like Lajpat Rai how many forts and prisons must they build before they can deport or confine us all? . . . Friends! show self-respect and stop the whole despotic administration by refusing to work for it in any capacity. (Srivastava 1983: 55–6)

In 1907, Cama was part of the British delegation to the International Socialist Congress at Stuttgart, where she spoke against British imperialism and unfurled the Indian national flag. She made an impassioned speech on this occasion:

> The continuance of British rule is positively disastrous and extremely injurious to the best interests of Indians. Lovers of freedom all over the world ought to cooperate in freeing from slavery one-fifth of the human race . . . I call upon you . . . to rise and salute the flag of Indian independence. (Srivastava 1983: 69)

In Paris, Cama became the focus of Indian revolutionary activity in Europe. She was also closely associated with the more radical and revolutionary Indians specially Krishnavarma and Vir Savarkar, both of whom the British regarded as anarchists and terrorists. When Savarkar swam ashore in Marseilles from the British ship in which he was being deported to India and was returned by the French police to the British authorities, Bhikaiji Cama organized the protests in France and mobilized the French left against this breach in international law. Cama was also responsible for two revolutionary papers (*Vandemataram* and *Talwar*) which were published in Geneva and smuggled into India. The British intelligence service was alert to Cama's influence, reporting in 1913 that she was 'one of the recognised leaders of the revolutionary movement in Paris', with contacts with revolutionary groups in exile from other countries (Kulke 1978: 210). It is hardly surprising, therefore, that having failed to get Cama extradited from France because of her contacts with Indian and foreign 'terrorists', the British confiscated her property in India; the French, however, interned her during World War I (Kulke 1978: 210–11). During these years several young Parsee women who were reported to have been under her influence were kept under police surveillance, one of her associates being Perin Captain (1888–1958), the granddaughter of the moderate nationalist, Dadabhai Naoroji. She had come to Paris in 1905 to study at the Sorbonne and in 1910, along with Cama, attended the first Egyptian National Congress held in Brussels (Nanavutty 1976: 89). In later years she was active in the Indian National Congress.

In India, too, women were involved in militant and violent activity during the various periods of agitation. For example, Saraladevi Chaudhurani, who worked with the Suhrid Samiti, supported the male revolutionaries, and another woman, Har Devi, collected funds for the revolutionaries in Lahore. In the late 1920s there was another phase of violent action in India in which women participated. In Delhi, Roopati Jain, aged 17, was in charge of a factory which produced chemicals for bombs. The Punjab revolutionary Bhagat Singh had several women collaborators including Sushila Devi, who had been jailed several times, and Durga Devi who had joined the freedom movement at 16 and had shot a policeman in Bombay. In Calcutta in 1928 a group of women students (Chhatri Sangha) recruited and trained women revolutionaries, organized study circles and gave lessons in cycling, driving and armed fighting. Some of them lived in a hostel where bombs were hidden and delivered to revolutionaries. The members of this group included Kalpana Dutt, who often put on male attire and was arrested and deported for life for her role in the Chittagong Armoury raid of 1930; and Preeti Waddedar who died in action after leading a raid on a Railway Officers' Club in 1932. The group also included two young girls, Santi and Suniti, who in 1931 shot the District Magistrate of Comilla and were sentenced to life imprisonment; there was also Bina Das who fired on the British governor of Bengal at a college convocation in 1932 and was imprisoned; and Kamala Das Gupta who acted as a courier, carrying bombs in Calcutta. Many members of the Chhatri Sangha were inspired by the Indian Congress leader, Subhas Chandra Bose, who was one of the principal

Congress socialist leaders of the 1930s and who, in Germany and later in south-east Asia, formed an Indian National Army to fight the British. Bose made a special appeal to women to join the struggle and formed a women's militia called the Rani of Jhansi Women's Regiment; this was led by Lakshmi (Swaminadhan) Saghal, who was given the title of captain.

Some of these women who were categorized as 'terrorists' were to join the Indian Communist Party (formed in 1921): one such was the heroine of the Chittagong Armoury raid, Kalpana Dutt, who later married P.C. Joshi, Communist Party General Secretary from 1935 to 1948. According to the Communist Party, 'these terrorist martyrs had turned from normal nationalist politics to terrorism only because of their frustrations in the Congress non-cooperation movements; their conversion to Communism . . . represented a still higher stage of political "maturity" ' (Overstreet and Windmiller 1959: 235). P.C. Joshi, commenting on his wife's reminiscences of the Chittagong raid, wrote, 'To read her own story is to understand a living phase of our national movement, how in the thirties the vast majority of the terrorist detainees and prisoners became Communists', adding that terrorism was the infant and Communism was 'the mature stage of their revolutionary lives' (Overstreet and Windmiller 1959: 235).

Women in the Communist Movement
Many other women were active in the Indian Communist Party in the 1920s and 1930s. One of them, Ushatai Dange, had been a child widow and had defied orthodox opinion against widow remarriage by marrying S.A. Dange, the Communist leader. She trained as a nurse from 1925 to 1927 in Bombay and participated in protest actions by nurses. In 1928 and 1929, when there was a wave of militant strikes in India, Ushatai Dange was involved in several textile-mill strikes, helping to organize the women workers. The strike at the British Textile Mills in particular, which lasted for eight months in 1929, was organized and led primarily by women; during this strike the employer was surrounded and detained by the women (Chakravartty 1980: 178–9), a tactic which was to become popular in later times as the *gherao*.

Another woman Communist militant active in the BTM strike was Parvatibai Bhore: she was of humble social origins and had earned her living as a tailor. In later years Bhore became a forceful public speaker and organizer of the textile workers (Chakravartty 1980: 180). Minakshi Sane was another Communist organizer who worked in Sholapur in Maharashtra among the textile and *bidi* (cheroot) workers. She was active during the economic depression of the early 1930s when several spontaneous strikes took place. Writing about the *bidi* workers' successful strike in 1936, Chakravartty says: 'The sight of women workers going on strike was a rarity in those days. This made such a sensation . . . that the famous Marathi novelist . . . N.S. Phadke came to see the striking women . . . [and] wrote a one-act play entitled Aagwali (the Firebrand).'

Minakshi Sane used the experience of the strike to organize women slum dwellers in Bhajan Mandals where *bhajans* (songs) were sung in between discussions about the week's events in India and elsewhere. Her group became popular and was invited to hold similar events in other slums (Chakravartty 1980: 182–3).

During the late 1930s and World War II (1939–45) Communist women were active in the nationalist struggle and in relief work during the Bengal famine, sometimes jointly with the All-India Women's Conference. Particularly active were the women of Bengal, a province that had been in the forefront of the nationalist agitation. In 1938, there was a strong movement in Bengal for the release of political prisoners who had been arrested by the British for 'terrorist' activities and imprisoned in the Andaman Islands. Women of various political groups in Bengal came together in this agitation: 'the first attempt at building a united women's organisation, in which political women were at the forefront' (Chakravartty 1980: 8).

At this time the All-India Student Federation set up a Girl Students Committee to mobilize militant young women in all parts of the country in a separate organization, support being the most enthusiastic in Bengal, Bombay and the Punjab. In 1940 the girl students held a conference in Lucknow which was presided over by Renu Chakravartty (born 1917), an active Communist who had recently returned after graduating in Cambridge (where she had been secretary of the Indian Students' Federation). As she recalls the Lucknow meeting:

> I told them of the menace of fascism which was but the extreme face of imperialism. I told them of the heroic battles being fought in Spain against Franco fascism . . . of that wonderful and courageous fighter and leader La Pasionaria — a glory to entire womanhood . . . but most important, the unparalleled united front being built from Europe to China to stem the tide of fascism. (Chakravartty 1980: 10)

The girl students' movement grew rapidly: its membership rose to 50,000 in 1941 and it became the source of inspiration for many young women. During this period of intense political activity many women left their homes in spite of parental objections to carry on their political activities, many running the risk of arrest by the British authorities. In 1940, the Girl Student Association leader, Kamala Das Gupta, was arrested; she was succeeded by Kalyani Mukherjee, who continued to be involved in political agitation and later married the Communist activist, Mohan Kumaramangalam (Chakravartty 1980: 13).

In 1942, some of the active women of the left, Kamala Chatterjee, Manikuntala Sen, Renu Chakaravartty and Ela Reid, formed the Mahila Atmaraksha Samiti (Women's Self-Defence League — MARS) which grew rapidly throughout Bengal. The Japanese bombings of Bengal helped to highlight the need for self-defence, both of the country and of its women. MARS put forward slogans for the defence of freedom, for the release from prison of Gandhi and other national leaders, and engaged in relief work during the famine: 'Humanitarian work and political work became one and indivisible. They taught women that the terrible sufferings of the people in famine or in war could never be solved unless they had a popular government' (Chakravartty 1980: 21–4).

The tragic events of the Bengal famine of 1942–44 brought women of all classes into relief work and political agitation. For example in 1943, the Calcutta MARS organized a hunger march of 5,000 Hindu and Muslim women to the Assembly to demand food and to protest about price rises.

> The demonstrators in their tattered rags and with babies in arms, famished and emaciated, marched before the eyes of Calcutta's public, telling them what words failed to do, of their pitiful plight. The march was unique, a model of orderly organisation. Neither police, nor Communist-baiters, could do anything. The impact of this demonstration was tremendous. It was one of the first militant actions of women which stirred the city of Calcutta. The demonstrators demanded "Open more shops, arrange proper supplies and bring down the price of rice." When they refused to move the Chief Minister distributed 100 bags of rice immediately to the women. (Chakravartty 1980: 29–30)

In May 1943, MARS held a provincial conference of women from the 21 districts of Bengal at which the secretary announced that they now had 22,000 members. When the second conference was held in 1944, membership had risen to 43,000. In that year the accent was on the rehabilitation of women who had been reduced to destitution and prostitution during the famine. Many homes for destitutes, and child-care and relief centres were begun; as Ela Reid reported in calling for expansion of the activities of the MARS, 'Women . . . suffered the most due to famine' (Chakravartty 1980: 67).

Conclusion

This study of the participation of women in the political struggles of India in the 19th century and first four decades of the 20th century, and in movements for the improvement of the status of women, provides much material for the historical understanding of some of the problems typically faced by women's movements in the Third World. The most revealing aspect has been the essential conservatism of what on the surface seemed like radical change. While highlighting and legally abolishing the worst excesses (like *sati*), emphasizing female education, and mobilizing women for *satyagraha*, the movement gave the illusion of change while women were kept within the structural confines of family and society. Revolutionary alternatives or radical social changes affecting women's lives did not become an essential part of the demands of the nationalist movement at any stage of the long struggle for independence, and a revolutionary feminist consciousness did not arise within the movement for national liberation. Women in the nationalist struggle did not use the occasion to raise issues that affected them as women. Rather than liberating themselves from traditional constraints and bondage, as Vina Mazumdar states, 'the woman's roles within the family as wives, daughters and mothers were re-emphasised or extended to be in tune with the requirements of the family in a changing society' (Mazumdar 1976: 63). Thus, while Indian women were to participate in all stages of the movement for national independence, they did so in a way that was acceptable to, and was dictated by, the male leaders and which conformed to the prevalent ideology on the position of women. As Mies has pointed out:

> To draw women into the political struggle is a tactical necessity of any anti-colonial or national liberation struggle. But it depends on the strategic goals of such a movement whether the patriarchal family is protected as the basic social unit or not. The fact that the women themselves accepted their limited tactical function within the independence movement made them excellent instruments in the struggle. But they did not work out a strategy for their own liberation struggle for their own interests. By subordinating these goals to the national cause they conformed to the traditional *pativrata* or *sati* ideal of the self-sacrificing woman. (Mies 1980: 121)

Nevertheless, the examples of women's militant participation in political struggles as well as their involvement in strikes and working-class protests and peasant rebellion (including the Telengana peasant struggles in the early 1950s) all show that Indian women have played a prominent part in anti-imperialist, anti-capitalist and democratic movements of protest over a long period. In contrast to the traditional ideal of womanhood, which even today is propagated in various ways, Indian women have another tradition of militancy and courageous activity in movements for social and political change.

7. Emancipation and Subordination of Women in Sri Lanka

> We went in the spirit of crusaders and answered the questions
> in an inspired manner. Lord Donoughmore asked if we wanted
> Indian Tamil women labourers on the estates to have the vote.
> I replied 'Certainly, they are women too. We want all women
> to have the vote'.
> *Agnes de Silva*, leader of the women's deputation to the Com-
> mission on Constitutional Reform, 1927 (Russell 1981: 58)

Sri Lanka attracted a great deal of attention in 1960 when Sirimavo
Bandaranaike became the world's first woman prime minister; this was
widely interpreted, both in Sri Lanka and outside, as an indicator of the
role and position of women in Sri Lankan society — a position of equality
and independence. To emphasize this interpretation, it was pointed out
that women in ancient society had enjoyed a position of importance, that
women in Sri Lanka have not had to suffer from many of the social evils
that affected women in neighbouring countries, such as *sati*, purdah, child
marriage and the ban on widow remarriage, and that women in modern
Sri Lanka enjoyed a better quality of life than in other countries of Asia
— a literacy rate among women of 83%, a maternal mortality rate of 1.2
per 1,000 live births, and a life expectancy of 67 years at today's levels,
which has been achieved in spite of a relatively low Gross National
Product. However, a closer look at the position of women in Sri Lankan
society, both ancient and modern, reveals that, in spite of conditions that
appear favourable to them, women have existed and continue to exist in a
situation of subordination.

The ancient history of Sri Lanka does show a number of examples of
women who made their own contribution to the religious and political
events of their times. Legend has it that 2,500 years ago, Sri Lanka was
ruled by a 'demon' queen, Kuveni; in later periods of history, women
ruled in their own right and there were queens like Anula Devi, Soma
Devi, Lilavati and Sugala who led the armies of her kingdom into battle.
However, such women were very often the mothers, wives or daughters
of kings and other important personages; such exceptional women did
not reflect the prevalent position of women in ancient Sri Lankan society.

The geographical location of Sri Lanka as an island at the tip of the Indian peninsula has influenced the country's demography, society and culture. The population is composed of two major ethnic groups — the Sinhalese and the Tamils — the result of successive waves of migration from all parts of India, mixing in various degrees among themselves and with the aboriginal inhabitants; during later periods Arab and Muslim traders as well as Europeans also established themselves in the island. The Sinhalese, who form the major ethnic group had, by the 5th century AD, developed an extensive irrigation system which enabled the cultivation of paddy over vast tracts of fields and the growth of a prosperous agrarian community. The surplus generated was appropriated by the monarchs, the bureaucracy and the Buddhist temples, and was sufficient to form the basis for an advanced civilization. The Sri Lankan state was, from about the 4th century BC onwards, a part of a regional polity comprising several monarchies in South India, with which it sometimes forged alliances and sometimes went to war. Close links have thus always existed between India and Sri Lanka and their social systems and ideology relating to women have been somewhat similar. As we pointed out in the chapter on India, women's primary role in the home, as mother, wife or daughter, was in subordination to the male members of the family. However, the one specific feature of Sri Lankan ideology has been the continuing presence of Buddhism, which has played a crucial role in forming Sri Lankan culture. Although the Buddha was born in India, the religion almost disappeared from the country of its birth, while continuing to flourish in Sri Lanka and in other countries of Asia. Buddhism was introduced into Sri Lanka in the 3rd century BC and quickly became the dominant religion. It was accepted by the kings, high officials and the people, and became the state religion, serving as the legitimizing ideology of the ruling system. In view of the central role of Buddhism in Sri Lanka (and some other parts of Asia), it may be appropriate at this point to discuss some aspects of its attitude to women.

Buddhism and Women

Buddhism came into being in the Gangetic plain in India at a time when settled agriculture had replaced the earlier pastoral economy, when trade in agricultural surpluses had become an important part of the economy and had brought into being an urban mercantile class, and when tribal social structures were giving way to absolute monarchies (Kosambi 1965: 144ff). The Brahmanic tradition associated with the earlier pastoral economy was no longer consonant with this rapidly evolving society, and Buddhism was the most important of a number of religions that emerged at this time. Buddhism, in this context, opposed many of the teachings and ritual practices of the Brahmins; the role of women in society was one of the areas on which the reforms of Buddhism had some immediate

110

impact. The Brahmanic social system, as we have indicated in the case study of India, was caste-based and strongly patriarchal. It denied to women any role other than the domestic. Buddhism opened up the social sphere for women, most importantly by admitting women into the ranks of its clergy, whereas in Brahmin practice the rituals had been a monopoly of men.

Many women from all strata of society, from royal families, from the households of rich urban merchants and from the common people, became Buddhist nuns. To the extent that women now had a culturally approved alternative style of life, the control of males over their social life and sexuality was diminished. The reasons that impelled women to enter the Buddhist order were many; some of them have been movingly enunciated in poems by the nuns themselves around 80 BC. Sumangalamata, the wife of a rush-weaver who became a nun, says:

O woman well set free! How free am I!
How thoroughly free from kitchen drudgery
Me stained and squalid among my cooking-pots
My brutal husband ranked as even less
Than the sunshades he sits and weaves.

(Rhys Davids 1909: 25)

Another nun, Mutta, speaks on the same theme:

O free, indeed! O gloriously free
Am I in freedom from three crooked things:—
From quern, from mortar, from my crookback'd lord!
Ay, but I'm free from rebirth and death,
And all that dragged me back is hurled away.

(Rhys Davids 1909: 15)

Relief from the degrading domestic sphere was thus one of the reasons for entering the monastic order. Another was probably the desire to combat the existing belief in woman's inherent incapacity in the spiritual field. The nun Soma is derided by Mara, the Lord of Death:

That vantage-ground the sages may attain is hard
To reach. With her two-finger consciousness
That no woman is competent to gain!

(Rhys Davids 1909: 45)

Here, Mara the 'evil one' makes a sneering reference to the accepted notion of female intelligence and consciousness. A woman boils rice from her young days but despite all this experience, never knows the precise moment when the rice is cooked; she must take some rice out and press it between her two fingers. Soma, the nun, challenges this view, stating:

111

How should the woman's nature hinder us?
When hearts are firmly set, who ever moves
With growing knowledge onward in the path? . . .
Am I a woman in these matters, or
Am I a man, or what am I then?

(Rhys Davids 1909: 45–6)

The other main reason for entering the order seems to have been the desire to move out of the reach of a male-dominated sexuality, as is evident in the verses attributed to Ambapali and Vimala, who had earlier been courtesans. The tribulations of the lay life and the obligations of marriage are described by Isidasi, the daughter of a rich merchant:

My salutation morn and eve I brought
To both the parents of my husband, low
Bowing my head and kneeling at their feet,
According to the training given to me.

My husband's sisters and his brothers too,
And all his kin, scarce were they entered when
I rose in timid zeal and gave them place.
And as to food, or boiled or dried, and drink,
That which was to be stored I set aside,
And served it out and gave to whom 'twas due.
Rising betimes, I went about the house
Then with my hands and feet well-cleansed I went
To bring respectful greeting to my lord.
And taking comb and mirror, unguents, soap
I dressed and groomed him as a handmaid might.
I boiled the rice; *I* washed the pots and pans
And, as a mother on her only child,
So did I minister to my good man.

(Rhys Davids 1909: 158)

Isidasi complains, however, that in spite of all her efforts, she was rejected by her husband.

For me, who with toil infinite thus worked
And rendered service with a humble mind,
Rose early, ever diligent and good,
For me he nothing felt save sore dislike.

(Rhys Davids 1909: 159)

Although admission to the order opened up more space for women, it was still a controlled space. The nuns had considerable autonomy in their internal organization and were specifically prohibited from rendering to monks any service of a personal nature such as washing their robes. Yet nuns as a whole were subordinate to male monks: all nuns, however senior in the order, should bow before any monk, however junior; in doctrinal and disciplinary matters they must obtain guidance from monks; monks could speak in a gathering of nuns, but no nun could speak in a gathering of monks. But even under such conditions, it was still a very considerable enlargement in the role of women.

In Sri Lanka, the introduction of Buddhism was quickly followed by the establishment of an order of nuns. We are told that women of all strata in society became nuns. While the more daring sought relief from orthodoxy in this manner, the old order reasserted itself quickly as far as the generality of women were concerned. The benign influence of Buddhism was also instrumental in reducing not only the rigours of the caste system, but also some of the glaring injustices practised against women such as *sati* and the ban on widow remarriage. However, in spite of the absence of such practices in Sri Lanka and the opening of some parts of the non-domestic spheres to women, the social structures were still patriarchal and gave women a subordinate role, typical of traditional societies.

The role and its reproduction are well illustrated in the following extract from the *Kavyasekeraya*, a Sinhalese narrative poem of the 15th century, still popular as a school text. The stanzas contain the advice given by a father to his daughter on marriage:

> Do not leave your house without your husband's permission;
> when you go out, do not walk fast and see that you are properly clad.
> Be like a servant to your husband, his parents and his kinsmen.

> Do not admit to your companionship the fickle courtesan,
> the thief, the servant, the actress, the dancer,
> the flower-seller or the washerwoman.

> Sweep your house and garden regularly and see that
> it is always clean. Make sure that you light the
> lamps to the gods both at dawn and dusk.

> When your husband returns home from a journey,
> receive him joyously and wash his feet;
> do not delegate this task to servants.

> Do not spend your time standing at your door,
> strolling about in gardens and parks and do not
> be lazy at your household duties.

> Protect the gods in your house. Do not give
> anything away even to your own children,
> without your husband's consent.

> If your husband's attention seems directed elsewhere,
> do not speak to him about it, let your tears be
> the only indication of your sorrow.

> Seek out your husband's desire in food and see that
> he is constantly satisfied, feed him and ensure his
> well-being like a mother.
>
> When you go to your husband let it be like a goddess,
> beautiful, clad in colourful silks, ornaments and sweet-smelling perfumes.
>
> Be the last to go to bed and the first to rise.
> When your husband wakes, see that you are by his side.
>
> Even if your husband appears angry and cold,
> do not speak roughly to him; be kind and forgiving
> Never think to look elsewhere for your comfort.

Such attitudes were common to both major ethnic groups inhabiting the island, the Sinhalese and the Tamils, and despite many changes which will be referred to later, they have persisted in Sri Lankan society to this day. The concept of female beauty prevalent in Sri Lanka is also reminiscent of Indian tradition. The much-quoted 15th-century Sinhala verses from *Salalihini Sandesaya* (influenced by Sanskrit poetry) describes the ideal beautiful woman who has blue-black hair reaching to the ground, eyes like lotuses, and teeth like pearls:

> A face like the full-moon,
> A waist that can be clasped with both hands,
> Hips as wide as a chariot wheel,
> Breasts like swans, golden-skinned,
> She is a celestial maiden but for the fluttering
> of her eyelids.

(Voice of Women 1980: 12)

The persistence of the attitudes illustrated in the *Kavyasekeraya* is attested to in later literature. In a popular play of the 1920s, *Ehelepola Natya*, a female character says, 'you know, my lord, that it is not the custom of Sinhala ladies of high birth to inquire from their husbands on their return home, where they have been or why they have been delayed', and then sings:

> I am the servant of my Lord . . .
> I am his servant.
> For my past sins
> I am limited to the home
> Matters outside the home
> Are not my concern.
> I am the servant of my Lord.

(Voice of Women 1980: 13)

The reference to past time arises from a concept common in Buddhism in Sri Lanka: the notion that being born a woman is a consequence of sins in previous lifetimes. Traditionally, a common aspiration among women was to be a man in a future birth, for only a man could become a Buddha.

Accepted ideology in traditional Sri Lanka thus required women to subordinate themselves at all times to the male, but there were some differences with the situation in adjoining countries. Although caste was an important factor in the hierarchical society, it was not as rigid as in India with its Brahmanic orthodoxy. Not only could women enter the Buddhist order of nuns, but men and women also participated together in religious rites. Among the peasantry, women worked alongside their men, although certain tasks in the cultivation cycle were forbidden to them. It was this traditional order which was affected and changed by the advent of imperialism.

Changes Under Imperialism

Foreign rule came to the coastal regions of Sri Lanka in 1505 through the Portuguese, who held some of the maritime areas for 150 years; the Dutch succeeded them, ruling these areas from 1656 to 1796, while British rule over the entire country dated from 1815 to 1948. Resistance to imperialism during Portuguese and Dutch occupation was continuous, from small-scale revolts to major uprisings that were able to hold the foreigners at bay for considerable periods. In the 19th century, after the fall of the Kingdom of Kandy in 1815, opposition to foreign rule took many forms. Apart from the 'great rebellion' of 1818, which lasted one and a half years and almost succeeded in ousting the British, the Kandyan provinces were in a state of continuous ferment, culminating in the rebellion of 1848, some of whose leaders drew their inspiration from the revolutionary movements then taking place in Europe.

The advent of imperialism brought basic changes to the political and social structures of the country. The Portuguese and Dutch occupiers suppressed the traditional religions and imposed new social, political and educational institutions on the people. One area of social practice which the foreign rulers tried to change forcibly was that of marriage. The marriage laws prevalent among the Sinhalese in the pre-colonial period were a reflection of the existing agrarian society. Women could be married in *diga* or *binna*. A *diga* marriage meant that the woman went to the husband's home and became a part of his family; she was given a dowry and had no further claims of inheritance. The *binna* marriage was uxorilocal with the husband taking up residence in the wife's home; in this form of marriage, the woman was entitled to an equal share of the inheritance when her father died, and her husband was subject to expulsion at will. Caste and other considerations entered into the marriage contract, which could be dissolved by mutual consent. In the Kandyan regions, polyandry, mainly fraternal polyandry (one woman marrying several brothers), was also practised, but was not very widespread.

115

The Dutch introduced the patriarchal Roman-Dutch legal system into the maritime areas under their control and enforced new marriage and inheritance laws. When the British captured Kandy, they attempted to change the marriage laws, basing themselves largely on a Victorian moral repugnance to polyandry; marriages should be monogamous and registration was necessary if the children were to be deemed legitimate and to share legally in the inheritance. Attempts to implement this law raised problems since the majority of the people in the Kandyan areas simply ignored the registration requirement. The government was thus forced to make some realistic compromise. Although inheritance problems remained intractable, the new laws 'liberalised the grounds on which marriage could be dissolved by inluding mutual consent and enabled the district and provincial administrators to grant divorce after inquiry, thus doing away with hearings in law courts' (Tambiah 1978: 277). Kandyans still enjoy this more liberal form of marriage contract.

The plantation form of economic organization (first coffee and later tea, rubber and coconut) was rapidly developed during the British occupation. It was the expansion of plantation capitalism that led to the rise of a Sri Lankan bourgeoisie and working class by the latter decades of the 19th century. From around 1900 onwards, the local bourgeoisie began to make demands for democratic rights, for equal opportunity and for political reforms. In the 19th century, they expressed their demands through religious and cultural movements, and in the early years of the 20th century, through political agitation for constitutional reforms. The working class too, from 1890 onwards, began to agitate for economic improvements and for the right to unionize, resorting to strikes on numerous occasions. These religious, nationalist and working-class movements were led by men from the Sri Lankan bourgeoisie and petty bourgeoisie, but there were always a few women who supported and joined them. In this respect, the situation in Sri Lanka was very similar to that of movements in other countries.

In order to assess the various forms of struggle in which women in Sri Lanka were involved in the 19th and early 20th centuries, it is necessary to distinguish between two classes: first, the working women in the plantation, urban and rural sectors who joined in the working-class struggles for economic and political rights; and second, the middle-class women, some of whom campaigned for equal status with middle-class men and others who demanded radical changes to the existing society. The ground was set for these advances by the growth of educational opportunities for girls, which even in the 18th century had advanced far enough to produce a school of women poets.

The Women Poets of the 18th Century

Education in pre-colonial Sri Lanka was largely a function of the Buddhist monks and was carried out in temples and monastic educational institutions known as *pirivenas*. In this context, it was open mainly to men.

There are recorded instances of women who were said to be well-versed in Sanskrit and Sinhala literature, but the very structure and form of education make it likely that such women from the upper strata were a rare exception; the generality of women were unlettered and uneducated.

The system of parish schools established by the Dutch in the regions under their control was also really a part of their ecclesiastical activities, education being regarded as 'a subtle vehicle of proselytism and a more efficacious weapon, perhaps, than the method of direct compulsion' (de Silva 1952: 241). These schools were also a means of educating the minor local cadres required by the Dutch administration. The most innovative fact about the schools, however, was that most of them were co-educational, thus providing women of a certain class with the opportunity of a lay education. Most of the women who were afforded this opportunity were the children of minor local functionaries and of teachers in the schools. To this situation we owe a remarkable instance of literary activity among Asian women in the late 18th century.

Sinhala literary activity had suffered, as all other forms of cultural expression, in the long period of foreign domination, but in the latter half of the 18th century, there was a revival of Sinhala literature in southern Sri Lanka, which was less in the classical tradition and more at the folk level. Prominent in this revival were a number of Buddhist monks and local-level officials, but it is of particular interest that women poets also took a leading part.

The best-known woman poet of the 'Matara school', as it was called, was Gajaman Nona. Born in 1758, the daugher of a minor Sinhala official and the granddaughter of a teacher at a parish school in Colombo where she is said to have been educated. She was subsequently married to an official working in the Matara district of southern Sri Lanka. Her real name was Dona Cornelia Perumal, the name itself being evocative of Western influence. She completed her Sinhala education under Buddhist monks and acquired fame as a poet. Her work combined the folk idiom of the era with traditional Sinhala poetic forms and was a true reflection of the changing times. Her poems dealt either with the harsh reality of contemporary society, poised as it was between an indigenous cultural revival and the growing impact of Western modernizing attitudes; or with erotic love, continuing one of the genres of ancient Indian and Sinhala poetry. Among her most famous compositions are a series of *risqué* love poems exchanged with Elapata Dissava, an official in charge of a district. Her own ambivalence is shown by the fact that she delighted in dressing herself in the fashion of a Dutch gentlewoman.

Other women poets of this period included Gajaman Nona's younger sister, Dona Arnolia Perumal; her daugher, Dona Katerina; Attaragama Kumarihamy, the daughter of a *dissava* (chief), and Dissanayake Lamatani. It is significant that all these poets came from families of local officials who worked for the Dutch administration. Runa Hamine and Ranchagoda Lamaya were two other women poets of the period, some of whose compositions survive. Little is known of their antecedents, but it is clear from a reading of their verses that they came from a lower social class. Runa Hamine was later commissioned by a Wesleyan missionary to put the Bible into popular Sinhala verse. Having done a large part of the work, she complained of the meagre reward and lack of recognition. She was astute enough to realize that both arose from the fact that she was a woman; in a complaint in verse, she wrote, 'If this work had been done by a man, he undoubtedly would have received both money and fame, but since it was done by a woman, she received no such reward' (Denham 1912: 425).

Female Education in the 19th Century*

Compared to other countries of Asia the women of Sri Lanka thus had a head start in the field of education. The British, who displaced the Dutch in Sri Lanka in 1796, inherited their system of education which included co-educational parish schools, although the single Dutch institution of secondary education, the Colombo Seminary, was for boys only. In the early British period, dominated by military and economic priorities, the colonial administration took little interest in the question of education. But Governor North founded the first English boys' school in Colombo in 1799, to train interpreters to meet the administration's needs; North also revived some of the old Dutch schools, and Lady Brownrigg, the wife of his successor, founded a girls' school in the early years of the 19th century.

The main educational activity of the period, however, was carried out by Christian missionaries who started their work in the second decade of the 19th century — Baptists, Methodists and missionaries from the American Mission and the Church Missionary Society. They opened schools using the local languages for the poor, and using English for the privileged. Since converts were lapsing back into their traditional religions after their marriage, English 'sister' schools were started to produce Christian wives for the converts. The first of these was Uduvil Girls' College, Jaffna, founded in 1824 by the American Mission, as a 'counterpart' to the Batticotta Seminary (later Jaffna College). According to Tennent, the pupils at first 'were of low caste and poor' but the school later attracted 'daughters of parents of property and influence in the district'. By 1841, the British Church Missionary Society started a girls' boarding school in Nallur (Jaffna), and found no necessity to canvass for pupils; there was a 'multitude of candidates' who applied to join the school (Emerson Tennent, quoted in Sivathamby 1979: 55).

After the 1833 Colebrooke-Cameron Report on constitutional and administrative reforms, the colonial government established a few English

---

*This section on female education is based mainly on material kindly provided by Professor Swarna Jayaweera.

schools: the Colombo Academy (later renamed Royal College) in 1835, and three central schools (for boys) in 1841. In response to a demand from parents, five girls' 'superior schools' were started in the 1840s — two in Colombo and the others in Kandy, Galle and Jaffna. These schools were staffed by British women from the Society for Promoting Female Education. The curriculum included English, British history, arithmetic, geography, ornamental needlework, drawing, music and Western cookery. The stress was on the acquisition of 'accomplishments', and C.A. Lorenz (a Sri Lankan liberal of the period) remarked of these schools that there was 'too much time and attention being bestowed on the ornamental rather than the useful'. By 1868, 87% of the girls at these élitist schools were Europeans and Burghers (mixed descendants of Europeans), the others being from rich Sinhala and Tamil families. The Central School Commission which had started the schools also opened some bilingual girls' schools in which half the girls were from Burgher families. By 1868, there were twelve Sinhalese or Tamil girls' schools known as vernacular schools. The Morgan Report (1869), which made recommendations on educational policy, proposed that girls' schools be opened wherever possible.

In the second half of the 19th century, the influence of the girls' high school movement in Britain was felt in Sri Lanka, but this was a period when the government withdrew from direct management of English education, preferring to leave it to the missionaries with state assistance wherever needed. The existing girls' 'superior schools' were closed down, and a petition in 1895, which called for the opening of a government girls' school parallel to the prestigious boys' school, Royal College, was refused. However, interest in female education led to more action by competing missionary societies, which seized the opportunity of subsidies offered by the government under the grant-in-aid system. Several English post-elementary, fee-levying girls' schools were opened for girls of bourgeois and petty-bourgeois families, and were often 'paired-off' with the existing boys' schools; for example the (Catholic) Good Shepherd Convent, Colombo (1869) with St Benedict's College, the (Methodist) Girls' High School, Colombo (1866) with Wesley College, and the (Anglican) Girls' High School, Kandy (1879) with Kingswood College. In other words, the policy of seeking to provide suitable wives of the correct denonimation for the products of the boys' schools was continued.

The children of the poor went to the vernacular schools (boys, girls or mixed). Education in these schools was free, but included only reading, writing, arithmetic and drawing. There were also Anglo-vernacular girls' boarding schools (seven in 1883), run by the missionaries for lower middle-class families. These offered a residential education for girls and were mostly agents of conversion and acculturation, one example being the Baptist Girls' School in Colombo.

There were also at this period a few private schools, one being Queen's College, Kandy, a 'ladies' school of the highest class, affording on terms suited to the times, all the educational advantages of the High Schools of England'. In many cases, however, daughters of rich Sri Lankan merchants and conservative landowning families did not go to school, but had governesses (sometimes foreign) to teach them English, arithmetic, needlework, music and drawing in their own homes. It may be noted in passing, that these women had adopted Victorian fashions by the 1850s, that in the 1860s, brides of this class wore imported gowns from London, and that up to the 1920s, when the Indian sari was introduced into Sri Lanka, the rich westernized Sinhalese women wore European dress.

The introduction of the Cambridge examinations was an important step in the development of secondary education in Sri Lanka; these examinations became the goal of both boys' and girls' schools, and the prestige of scholarships to English universities at a time when there was no university in Sri Lanka, awarded on the basis of the examination results, made them very popular. In 1881, for the first time, one girl sat for the Senior Cambridge and five for the Junior Cambridge examination. By 1900, the figures had risen to 15 and 77 respectively and in that same year, ten girls' schools sent candidates for the Senior Cambridge and 22 for the Junior Cambridge.

The curriculum was broadly the same in girls' and boys' schools and was borrowed almost wholesale from Britain. The subjects were English, British history, arithmetic, geography and two of the following: mathematics, Latin, mechanics, animal physiology, drawing, botany, physics, chemistry, sanitation, agriculture, book-keeping, shorthand, English literature, domestic economy (for girls), Pali, Sanskrit, French and German. It was a typical colonial education in which Sinhala and Tamil, the national languages, were not taught. The principals and many teachers of the prestigious girls' schools were British and the textbooks came from Britain. For example, botany lessons were about English plants and flowers; domestic science instruction was from Kelly's *Advanced Textbook of Domestic Economy*, and the cookery taught was Western. The only difference between the education of boys and girls was that certain 'accomplishments' such as domestic science and needlework were provided for the girls, and that whereas Greek and Latin were taught in élitist boys' schools, the leading girls' schools taught Latin only. Since knowledge of music enhanced a girls' dowry value, the music examinations of the Trinity College of Music, London, became very popular among the English-educated middle class.

However, the value of giving the same examination-orientated education to boys and to girls was the subject of spirited debate. Many colonial bureaucrats and influential women believed that girls needed only limited education, just enough to make them presentable housewives. As Hilda Pieris, the wife of Paul E. Pieris, a distinguished local civil servant of the time, said in 1912,

A good deal more might be done by devoting the time which is wasted in obtaining a valueless smattering of Latin, French, theory of music and trigonometry, to . . . music, drawing, dressmaking and fine needlework, subjects which will not only add to the charm of a girl's home life, but will also lead to a considerable saving in household expenditure. (Denham 1912: 426)

Nevertheless the demand for a 'Cambridge certificate' continued to increase among sections of the bourgeoisie; the Principal of the Wesleyan Girls School, in 1912, tried to reconcile these disparate views:

Apart from the practical value of those who want to go in for teaching, it improves girls' position especially to have passed a Cambridge examination, and this helps towards a better marriage settlement. That girls' education should have any higher or more lasting results than this is not, I think, a matter of general desire throughout Ceylon. (Denham 1912: 427)

The educational system was thus supportive of the prevailing class system and its ideology of women as housewives and mothers. But although the main aim of female education was to keep bourgeois women within the home as 'good' housewives, it was not long before demands arose from the women themselves to be able to use their education professionally, in the first instance as teachers. A Normal School was opened in 1870 but closed again in 1884: smaller vernacular schools for teachers were subsequently opened and an English Training College for teachers, which opened in 1902, started to admit women in 1908. The missionaries also had grant-in-aid training schools. The Cambridge examinations opened doors to other professions as well. The Ceylon Medical College was inaugurated in 1870; in 1892, the first female student was admitted and by the turn of the century, there were several Sri Lankan women doctors. Among these were Alice de Boer (born 1872), who qualified in Sri Lanka in 1899, and later at Edinburgh and Glasgow, and on her return worked at the Lady Havelock Hospital for Women until 1919; Winifred Nell, sister of Dr Andreas Nell (doctor and eminent antiquarian), also qualified in medicine at Edinburgh and Glasgow in 1900 and worked at the women's hospital in Colombo and later at the Leper Hospital, while Miss Rudd, also Edinburgh-qualified, became the Registrar of Deaths. These pioneer women doctors were from the Burgher ethnic minority, but they were soon followed by Sinhala and Tamil girls. But there were no girls in either the agricultural or technical schools during this period. Although 15 of the 31 industrial schools in 1900 were girls' schools, they were in fact schools for orphans and the destitute. There was, however, an Institute of Stenography and Typewriting, started in 1901 by Violet Muthukrishna, who along with her brother and sisters had studied in Madras and had introduced these skills to Sri Lanka. Since the demand for such office skills increased with the expansion of the colonial economy, a number of women followed the course and obtained employment (Wright 1907: 121).

121

It may be noted that the colonial structure also gave rise to the migration to the colonies of many British (and other foreign) women as missionaries, teachers, nurses and doctors, many of them the products of the expansion of higher educational opportunities for Western women in the late 19th century. To give only a few examples, Dr Mary Fysh (M.B. London), born in 1872, was appointed medical officer in charge of the Lady Havelock Hospital for women in Colombo in 1899 (Wright 1907: 131), while the Church Missionary Society, in 1900, began the Ladies College, a high school for girls, whose principal was Ruth Nixon, a graduate in modern literature from the Royal University, Ireland (Wright 1907: 117).

Although the majority of the female population at this time received no education at all, fairly quick progress in female education was made in the first decades of the 20th century. The number of girls in school rose from 50,000 in 1901 (27% of the total in school), to 135,000 in 1921 (33%) and 396,000 in 1946 (42%) (Jayaweera 1979: 266). By 1911, literacy rates for women had more than quadrupled from 3% in 1881 to 12% in 1911, while male literacy in the same period less than doubled. It is also interesting to note than in 1911, 21% of the women of the western province of the island were literate, reflecting the increase in education facilities and economic development in that area (Denham 1912: 401–4). Female literacy made dramatic strides in subsequent years, rising from 21% in 1921 to 44% in 1946 and 83% in 1981.

Women and the Buddhist Theosophical Movement

The political history of Sri Lanka in the latter half of the 19th century and the early 20th century is largely that of the attempt by the emerging bourgeoisie to obtain representative political rights. The population was multi-ethnic and multi-religious (composed of Sinhalese, Tamils, Moors and Burghers who were of the Buddhist, Hindu, Muslim or Christian faiths) but during these years, the nationalism that developed became identified with the Sinhala Buddhist majority, with the result that at certain times nationalism and chauvinism became synonymous. The Sinhala Buddhist section of the bourgeoisie and petty bourgeoisie, composed of merchants, monks, teachers and others, also launched a campaign against the local and foreign Christian élite who were economically and socially privileged, and against the missionaries who dominated in the field of education.

The first stage of the agitation was not directly political. It began in the form of Buddhist and Hindu revivalist movements, campaigns for temperance in 1904 and 1912 directed against the government's liquor policies and a drive for Buddhist education. One of the stimuli for the Buddhist educational movement was the arrival in Sri Lanka in 1880 of the founders of the Theosophical Society, Colonel Henry Olcott and Helena Blavatsky. Theosophy was an interesting mixtue of liberal views based on the 'universal Brotherhood of Humanity without distinction of

Theosophy

race, creed, sex, caste or colour', along with occultism and a faith in the 'Masters of Wisdom'. It was also an amalgam of various aspects of the world's religions, and a denial of the Christian, Eurocentric vision of the world; hence it was a rallying point for many European and American dissenters, as well as nationalists from Asia.

From its inception, the Theosophical Society also attracted many women, especially as the co-founder was a dynamic woman, Helena Petrovna Blavatsky (1831–91). Her origins were obscure and cloaked in legend; born in Russia, she travelled widely, developing an interest in the occult. Arriving in the USA in 1874, she moved among groups interested in spiritualism. With Olcott, she founded the Theosophical Society in New York in 1875 and, in 1877, wrote *Isis Unveiled* — 'a master key to the mysteries of ancient and modern science and theology', and until her death remained the main inspirer of the theosophical movement. Olcott referred to her as a 'wondrous woman, made the channel for great teachings, the agent for the doing of a mighty work' (Olcott 1954: vii).

Helena Blavatsky in other ways was typical of many of the liberated, independent women of the 19th century, who had renounced Christianity, did not conform to Victorian social norms and were attracted to Eastern mysticism. She had a strong personality and hypnotic qualities and 'was utterly unconventional . . . whether in religion or in social observances' (Jinarajadasa 1925: 125). Blavatsky travelled and lived at various periods in India, where theosophy was popular among a group of intellectuals and political leaders, and in 1880 she and Olcott visited Sri Lanka and gave an impetus to the Buddhist revival and educational movement. Another charismatic woman leader of the Theosophical Society was Annie Besant (1847–1933), freethinker, fearless critic of Christianity, champion of the famous strike of London match factory girls and a founder of the Fabian Society. As a theosophist activist she visited Sri Lanka in 1893 and 1908, making a deep impression on the Buddhist public by her advocacy of Buddhist education and national revival.

Many wealthy Buddhist women came forward to help in this challenge to foreign and missionary cultural domination, including Ms Wijeratne of Galle and Cecilia Ilangakoon of Matara. The latter entertained Olcott and Blavatsky at her home in 1880, where a meeting of 2,500 persons was organized; she also joined the local Theosophical Society and financed the first editions, in English and Sinhala, of Colonel Olcott's Buddhist catechism. This book, which spearheaded the Buddhist educational campaign, became a text in Buddhist schools and, according to Olcott, was very popular in Buddhist homes (Olcott 1954: 109–200).

By the late 1880s, the Women's Education Society had started the Sangamitta School for Buddhist girls, with an English principal, Louisa Roberts, and a local headmistress, Virajini Kumarasinghe. In 1889, Marie Museaus Higgins (1855–1926) joined the staff;* she was a German

*The details are from Museaus College, 75th Anniversary Souvenir, 1893–1968.

by birth, the daughter of Theodore Museaus, a high court judge. After graduating in Germany, Marie Museaus went to the USA where she studied, worked as a translator, became a theosophist and married an American theosophist, Anthony Higgins. After his death, she left for Sri Lanka; in 1893 she founded Museaus College, to provide an English secondary education for Buddhist girls, and in 1908, started the first Women's Teachers Training College, instructing in Sinhala. The funds were provided by wealthy Buddhists, who were keen that their women be educated, but did not want them to become 'Christianized'. Since Museaus College provided boarding facilities, many rural middle-class Buddhists sent their daughters to this school, there being 80 boarders in 1907. A student of the school (Elsie de Silva) passed the Junior Cambridge examination in 1897, and another student, Lucy de Abrew, became the first Sinhala girl to enter the Medical College (in 1902), and the first woman to win the Jeejeebhoy medical scholarship (Denham 1912: 426).

At the time that English secondary education for Buddhist girls was begun, the issue of further education was also discussed: the editorial of the *Buddhist Schools Magazine* of March 1895, entitled 'Higher Education for Females', stated;

> We see how successful the women of the Western countries are in their lives, and how energetically they work for the cause of suffering humanity. But we seldom or never see a blue-stocking in Ceylon . . . why should women who have means neglect education? And why should their attention be directed to household duties only? Their sole aim should be to reach the highest ladder of fame, to regenerate their sex and to distinguish themselves . . . It is . . . necessary . . . that a College should be established for the 'higher educatin' of the Ceylonese girls . . . If they receive proper education, women of the East will no doubt become as prominent as those of the Western countries.

It was, significantly, several foreign women who were the products of Western universities and were influenced by theosophy, who pioneered Buddhist female education, at a time when the demand for Buddhist girls' schools had grown with the development of a Sinhalese Buddhist middle class. Many such schools were begun including Maha Maya (Kandy), Sri Sumangala (Panadura), Visakha Vidyalaya (Colombo), Ananda Balika (Colombo) and Sujata Vidyalaya (Matara). The foreign principals of these schools included Hilda Kularatne, Doreen Wickremasinghe, Clara Motwani, and Lu Vinson, all of whom were university graduates. For example, Hilda Kularatne (1895–1956), née Westbook, was the daughter of an official in the British Foreign Office and his wife, Jessie Duncan Westbrook, a theosophist, who wrote on Sufism and translated Persian verses of Sufi mystics, including *The Diwan of Inayat Khan*, printed by the Women's Printing Society in London in 1915. After obtaining a modern languages degree in Cambridge, Hilda came to Sri Lanka in 1920, becoming the principal and founder of several Buddhist schools, from the 1920s to the 1940s. She married Patrick Kularatne, the principal of Ananda College, the leading Buddhist boys' school in the island and spent her life in the cause of Buddhist women's education. Clara Motwani, née Heath, an American, obtained a BA and MA respectively from the Universities of Louisville, Kentucky, and Iowa, married an Indian theosophist studying at Yale, and arrived in Sri Lanka in 1933, when she was 23; she, too, made her home in Sri Lanka and for over 50 years has been the principal and founder of several schools which provided a modern education for Buddhist girls.*

The content and purpose of education in these schools was the subject of much debate, the protagonists seeing in education the means of achieving goals relative to their conception of the role of women in society. A large group of Sinhala Buddhist leaders of the time argued that the education should be so geared as to produce good Buddhist wives, but with the modicum of modern knowledge necessary for the times. Others saw Buddhist women's education as an essential part of a national and political awakening and a means of emancipating women. Since the girls who attended Buddhist schools were given a more nationalist-biased education, which included stress not only on Sri Lankan and Indian history and culture, but on democratic and anti-colonial movements elsewhere, such students were also receptive to movements for social and political reform. It is not surprising that many of the women of the nationalist and leftist movements of later years had been teachers or students of these schools, and had been inspired by the foreign teachers with their background of anti-colonialism and religious dissent.

The foremost proponent of the more traditional view on female education was Anagarika Dharmapala (1864–1933), one of the main figures of the Buddhist revival movement. He was the son of a Sinhala furniture merchant and, in conformity with fashion, had been christened Don David and educated in English. Discarding both his Europeanized name and his job as a government clerk, he joined the theosophists in their work in Sri Lanka and India; he established Maha Bodhi societies in Calcutta and Colombo for the propagation of Buddhism and led semi-political campaigns against missionaries and foreign influences. Dharmapala's ideology was a mixed one; unlike other Asian reformers, he was against the Westernization and modernization of social life, holding that Europeanization meant barbarism and uncivilized behaviour. Influenced by his travels in Japan, however, and in contrast to the Indian leaders, Dharmapala rejected the spinning wheel and advocated industrialization and the adoption of the latest in scientific and technological knowledge, urging that 'What India and Ceylon need is more of technological and scientific education than Christian theology and European classics' (Guruge 1965: 716).

---

*I am grateful to Maya Senanayake and Goolbhai Gunasekera for material on their mothers, Hilda Kularatne and Clara Motwani respectively.

Dharmapala's attitude to the status of women was similarly mixed. He himself had been influenced by several independent foreign women; Helena Blavatsky (who had taken him to Madras in 1884), Annie Besant, the leading light of the Theosophical movement at the turn of the century, and Mary Foster (a rich American Buddhist living in Honolulu) who financed many of Dharmapala's projects with generous donations. Moreover, Dharmapala had travelled in Europe and the USA and was well aware of the struggles of suffragists and feminists. He wrote:

> Look at England today, watch . . . the strenuous efforts made by the women of England to gain their rights politically and on whose behalf some of the greatest men in England are willing to work. Mrs Besant . . . who is preaching to the people of India gentleness and obedience, yet in England, speaking on behalf of suffragettes says 'Europe looks on amazed as crowds of well-born, well-bred women go patiently to prison for the sake of their sex. The scandal caused is too great to be prolonged, there is only one way out — granting the vote . . .' (Guruge 1965: 513)

Dharmapala and others were at this time propagating the myth that the Sinhalese were descendants of Aryans from North India — a chosen people, who were defenders of the chosen faith (Buddhism); not surprisingly, their attitude to women reflected this basic chauvinism. Dharmapala was convinced that the subordination of women was a feature of other religious cultures — especially the Christian and Muslim — whereas Buddhism and the 'Aryan' way of life allegedly followed by the Sinhalese, gave freedom to women: 'Woman in ancient India was free . . . Indian woman lost her individuality after the Moslem invasion of India. Woman was not considered sacred by the Semitic races. The story of Adam and Eve made woman degraded forever' (Guruge 1965: 341). 'The 'freedom' of the ideal 'Aryan' Buddhist woman portrayed by Dharmapala was almost a reproduction of the stereotype in the verses from *Kavyasekeraya*:

> The Aryan husband trains his wife to take care of his parents, and attend on holy men, on his friends and relations. The glory of woman is in her chastity, in the performance of household duties and obedience to her husband. This is the Aryan ideal wife. (Guruge 1965: 345)

Dharmapala particularly deplored the effects of missionary activity on Buddhist girls who had adopted not only Western ideologies but also European dress. In the 1890s he warned that 'girls [are] being educated under western principles by Christian educationalists' and it was therefore 'impossible to expect that a race of true Buddhists could be produced in Ceylon' (Guruge 1965: 798). In his journal, Dharmapala frequently advocated the sari as a suitable garment for Sinhala women, opposed Western dress for girls as immodest, and ridiculed the Victorian hats and crinolines worn by the women of the bourgeoisie. Dharmapala's views were thus basically anti-foreign, but with a reversion to tradition in social structures, specifically regarding the role of women.

There was, however, another perspective on women's education. Some of the local Buddhist radicals, especially those who had been educated in Britain, were interested in women's emancipation and in promoting female education as a means of modernizing the traditional society. For example, A.E. Buultjens (1865–1916), a lawyer from South Sri Lanka of the Burgher community, had renounced Christianity as a student in Cambridge in 1887, and converted to Buddhism. He was also influenced by both British socialism and the trade union movement and became a critic of colonialism and missionary activities. In 1899 he wrote 'It seemed to one that practical Christianity was a mockery, for with the export of missionaries and bibles, there was a far larger export of bottles and bullets, the one to kill the mind, the other the body' (Buultjens 1899).

On returning to Sri Lanka, Buultjens became the principal of the leading Buddhist boys' school and led a campaign against the government and missionaries on the issue of Buddhist education. He was the first Sri Lankan to write about trade unions and to organize the Colombo workers, becoming the secretary of the country's first trade union, the Printers Union, and leading their first strike in 1893. Buultjens's liberal attitudes also extended to the support of female education, an issue much debated in Britain during his student years there. In Sri Lanka, he was active in the Women's Educational Society and encouraged the establishment of Buddhist schools for girls.

The impact of education, both Buddhist and Christian, was felt in the increasing participation of women in areas outside the domestic sphere to which they had traditionally been bound. Although education was designed primarily to fit women for the duties of housewife and mother in accordance with changing social values, education could not but open their eyes to the constraints of that traditional role. An article in the journal *Buddhist Companion*, published in Colombo in 1914, clearly illustrates this trend. Couched in the form of a dialogue between two women, it criticizes the traditional Buddhist view of women as depicted in old Sinhala writings, and goes on to say: 'Our Sinhala men are still trying to confine us to the kitchen. They are not interested in teaching us anything beyond that.' Men and their attitudes are thus seen as ultimately responsible for the subordination of women.

The Struggle for Political and Franchise Rights

With the expansion of education for women and the emergence of a group of professional middle-class women, especially teachers and doctors, political consciousness among women grew in the first decades of the 20th century, a few joining nationalist organizations. Associated with the earliest radical nationalist organization, the Young Lanka League (formed in 1915), was Nancy Wijekoon, a schoolteacher, who was well known for her stirring nationalist poetry. During the 1915 Buddhist-

Muslim riots, she came under suspicion and was kept under surveillance by the police. Reports by the Inspector-General of Police, H. Dowbiggin, mention her 'seditious' poetry, which reminded Sri Lankans of their past glory and urged them to rise up against the foreigner (Jayawardena 1972: 172). When the Ceylon National Congress was formed in 1919, several women delegates were present at the first sessions. They were Dr Nalamma Murugesan (who later married the estate trade union leader, Satyawagiswara Aiyar), I. Ganguli, a theosophist teacher from Bengal, and Maheswari Segarajasingham, daughter of the president of the Congress, Ponnambalam Arunachalam.

Sri Lanka was one of the first countries of Asia and Africa to achieve women's suffrage, this right being accorded to all women of over 21 years of age by the Donoughmore Constitutional Reforms of 1931. Middle-class men in Sri Lanka had received the vote in 1912, and from then on the campaign for suffrage rights for women was conducted by women's groups and male radicals. Beginning in 1923, the trade union leader, A.E. Goonesinha, raised the issue at the annual sessions of the Ceylon National Congress, but without success. Sarojini Naidu of the Indian National Congress, a campaigner for female suffrage who visited Sri Lanka in 1922, inspired the Sri Lankan middle-class women with her eloquent speeches. At the 1925 Congress Sessions, for example, a resolution of the Mallika Kulangana Samitiya (Women's Society), a women's organization affiliated to the Congress, that 'a limited suffrage be immediately extended to the women of this country' was unsuccessfully proposed by Aseline Thomas and seconded by Agnes de Silva.

Several middle-class and professional women, many of them wives of nationalist and labour leaders, formed the Women's Franchise Union in 1927 and in December of that year they organized a public meeting to demand voting rights for women. The meeting was presided over by Lady Dias Bandaranaike (mother of S.W.R.D. Bandaranaike, Sri Lanka's prime minister from 1956 to 1958) and was supported by many foreign women teachers and theosophists and by local professional women of different ethnic groups. When the Donoughmore Commission on Constitutional reform came to the country in 1928, a delegation from the Women's Franchise Union gave evidence before it and asked for the right of franchise for all women.

Leading the delegation was the secretary of the Women's Franchise Union Agnes de Silva, née Nell (1885–1961), niece of Winifred Nell, one of the pioneer women doctors, and daughter of Paul Nell, an engineer from Kandy, of the Burgher community. Nell was an 'extremely broad minded and liberal man, a humanist and rationalist who refused to countenance petty distinctions of social superiority which governed the principles of social life in late Victorian Ceylon' (Russell 1981: 16). His father, Louis Nell, was colonial Solicitor-General, as well as being a scholar 'and one of the earliest followers of Darwin in the East' (Russell 1981: 18). In 1908, Agnes made an unconventional marriage to a Sinhalese lawyer, George E. de Silva, who in later years became a leading liberal, nationalist politician, champion of the depressed classes and castes, and a campaigner for universal suffrage and social reform. Agnes de Silva became the foremost activist for female suffrage in Sri Lanka, and in 1928, when George de Silva went to Britain to campaign for reforms and universal suffrage, Agnes de Silva accompanied him. While in Britain she again raised the issue of female suffrage. The Donoughmore Commission had recommended a limited female franchise to women over 30, but when the reforms were implemented in 1931 all women over 21 were granted the franchise. Agnes de Silva also unsuccessfully contested the first general election under universal suffrage. At this election, Naysum Saravanamuttu, a Tamil doctor (who was elected to a Colombo constituency), and Adeline Molamure, a Sinhala woman from an aristocratic family (who won the Ruanwella seat), became the first women legislators.

After adult franchise was won in 1931, middle-class women formed several organizations, including the Lanka Mahila Samiti and the Women's Political Union, both inspired by Mary Rutnam, née Irvin, a doctor of Canadian origin (married to a Sri Lankan Tamil) who was active in the franchise and other movements. Together with a teacher, Annamah Muttiah, she also started the Tamil Women's Union in Colombo. Another influential Tamil woman of the 1930s was Maheswari Navaratnam, who had studied at Tagore's Shantiniketan and had been influenced by the Indian cultural and political movement. She edited *Tamil Mahal* ('Tamil Woman') which advocated the emancipation of women.

Although women in Sri Lanka, particularly the Westernized élite, fought and won the franchise much earlier than women in many other countries, their presence in the political structures has been marginal: representation in the national legislatures has never been more than 4% or so, and participation at local government levels has also been insignificant. The few women who have successfully contested and made a name for themselves in the political process have generally entered politics as the result of the death of a father or a husband, inheriting, as it were, the male's mantle of power, as did Sirimavo Bandaranaike, who entered politics after the assassination of her husband who was prime minister at the time.

The religious revivalist and nationalist movements also led to a cultural renaissance which had both positive and negative aspects. New forms of literature such as the novel entered the domain of Sinhala and Tamil literature. Some people used these new forms in order to propagate contemporary ideas. In 1914, Mangalanayagam Tambiah wrote a Tamil novel which criticized the system of arranged marriages; S. Sellammal was another Tamil woman writer who, in the early 1920s, wrote several novels on problems affecting women and the necessity for social reform. On the other hand, the novel was also used to revive traditional social values that were felt to be under attack by the new modernizing forces. The most popular Sinhala novelist at the time, Piyadasa Sirisena, extolled the conventional role of women in ancient Indian and Sri Lankan society and their subordinate status in the family; he was against education for women and harshly criticized their attempts to emancipate themselves.

The rise in women's consciousness brought about by education was channelled primarily into struggles for political and franchise rights. Women also concerned themselves with social welfare work but there were few social issues around which agitation could gather strength. Caste was an important aspect of social stratification but it was not rigid. Except for female circumcision practised by the Muslim minority of the country, there were no forms of torture or mutilation that could be highlighted. Female circumcision was a well-kept secret and never became a public issue; the only question provoking some discussion being that of dowry.

As in India, the dowry formed an essential part of the marriage ritual, among both Tamils and Sinhalese. The charge has often been made that while in traditional society the dowry was a means of maintaining the independence and integrity of the wife, it had become so commercialized in modern society that marriage had ceased to exist as a moral contract. In fact, the abolition of the dowry system never became a rallying cry of the women's movement in Sri Lanka. The first and (up to date) the last attempt to deal with this problem legally was made in October 1938, when Dr A.P. de Zoysa proposed in the legislature that 'it should be made illegal to give or receive dowries'. De Zoysa called the dowry system a social evil and drew attention to some of its obnoxious effects: 'there have been cases when young women have committed suicide because their parents were not rich enough to give them dowries . . . it is our duty to try and remove this evil.' He also tried to appeal to male pride: 'For a young man of character and ability to insist that the bride's parents should give him a dowry is not only immoral but it also shows that there is no character, no manliness.' The motion was dealt with facetiously by several members of the legislature and was defeated by one vote (Hansard, 27 October 1938).

In 1944, professional and other middle-class women formed the All-Ceylon Women's Conference (ACWC), inspired by the similar organization in India. This association took up many of the legal, economic and political demands of women, and organized several Asian women's conferences in Colombo. Its president for many years was Ezlynn Deraniyagala (1908–73), née Obeysekera, a member of the Bandaranaike family. She graduated from Oxford and was the first Sri Lankan woman to become a barrister (1933). Apart from her work in the ACWC, she was also on two occasions the president of the International Alliance of Women. The secretary of the ACWC for several years was Eleanor de Zoysa, née Hutton (1896–1981), from Durham. Her family was active in the labour and women's suffrage movements and she too was a Labour Party organizer in the north of England. She had also been interested in theosophy and Buddhism; in 1929, she married Dr A.P. de

Zoysa and came to Sri Lanka in 1934. Other office-bearers of the ACWC were Gladys Loos (principal, Methodist College), Sylvia Fernando (family planning organizer) and Leela Basnayaka (Buddhist activist). The ACWC over the years steered middle-class women away from purely charitable and social service activities and led the demands for the further emancipation of women.

Struggles of Working Women

While middle-class women were fighting for education, suffrage and equal political rights, the working women of the country were in the struggle for more material gains, for equal wages for men and women, and for more humane conditions of work. Not all the advocates came from the working class, however. As in many other countries, the trade union movement was first dominated by intellectuals and professionals from the middle classes, persons who were disillusioned with the reformist politics of the period and chose to ally themselves with the labour movement.

In the 19th century, the most exploited group of workers in Sri Lanka was the large semi-proletariat of women workers on the tea and rubber plantations. In 1881, there were 81,000 women in plantations out of 266,000 workers (30%); by 1911, this figure had risen to 234,000 women workers out of a total of 500,000 (47%) (Denham 1912: 493). Up to the early 1930s, wages on estates were 33 cents per day for men but 25 cents for women (5 cents = one UK penny of the period), although the women did the more important work of plucking the tea leaves. The wage rates for estate women were the lowest in the island, and their illiteracy, general mortality, maternal mortality and infant mortality rates were the highest in the island (in 1911, 98.5% of estate women were illiterate; today the figure is 52%). The general mortality, maternal and infant mortality rates on plantations are today the highest and the literacy and education rates the lowest in the country.

In the town, the poorest-paid workers in the 19th century were women employed in unskilled work in factories and other menial occupations. Many women in Colombo were employed in sorting and packing coffee; (there were 20,000 in the 1870s). From the 1880s onwards, women worked in coconut fibre mills as well as in tea packing and graphite sorting: their wage rates averaged around 50 cents per day. In 1908, the rates of pay for women and girls employed by the Public Works Department to break stones for road resurfacing were between 12 and 36 cents a day. There was also a large group of domestic servants (67,000 in 1911), mainly women, who worked as semi-slaves for board and lodging and a pittance of a few rupees a month; again, women servants received less than the men. Another group of women toilers were the peasants who worked as wage labour, sharecroppers or family labour in the countryside and were subjected to various forms of oppression and exploitation.

Despite the extreme exploitation on the plantations, trade unions did not appear there until 1931 — 100 years after the opening of the first coffee plantation in Sri Lanka. This was because the workers were kept as semi-serfs and had no opportunity to organize themselves. One of the early methods by which workers protested against oppressive conditions on plantations was to 'bolt' from their places of work. This was one of the numerous offences under the Labour Ordinance of 1865, under which many women were sentenced to terms of imprisonment with hard labour. In 1916, Ponnambalam Arunachalam referred to an advertisement in a newspaper which offered a reward of Rs 50 to any person who arrested half a dozen 'bolted coolies' including a woman described as 'sickly, with a baby in arms and two other children'. In 1915, the Social Service League protested against the imprisonment of women and children for labour offences, referring to two women who were sentenced by the Badulla magistrate on a charge of 'insolence'. The Attorney General in 1916 objected to exempting women from the provisions of the Labour Ordinance on the grounds that 'labourers employed on estates are very primitive and a woman may be quite as capable of giving trouble as a man.' However, the outcry continued until the law was repealed in 1922 (Jayawardena 1972: 209).

Early strikes among the urban wage workers were in trades that were purely male occupations: printers, carters, laundry men and railway and harbour workers. But during the general strike of 1923, led by A.E. Goonesinha and the Ceylon Labour Union, and followed by 20,000 workers of Colombo in both the private and public sectors, women factory workers joined in. This was the beginning of the staunch support that A.E. Goonesinha acquired among urban working-class women. The band of militant women dressed in red became an impressive feature of every subsequent strike, procession, demonstration and May Day rally organized by Goonesinha's Labour Union. Those who opposed him used to denounce them as 'fishwives', but these women, some of whom were factory workers and others itinerant hawkers, were militants who courageously came to the fore in all working-class struggles. Goonesinha's women's volunteer corps included Emaliya Hamy of Hunupitiya (an active fighter who is remembered for an incident that occurred during the famous tramway strike of 1929, when she garlanded the tram company owner, Cedric Boustead, with a snake), Pavistina Hamy, who worked at Hayleys, and Emmy Nona, a worker at Harrisons and Crossfield, both British firms.

The best-known of these working-class militants, however, was Isabella Hamy of Wanathamulla, Colombo, a woman who fought for the rights of the working class at the height of colonial rule, when trade unions were illegal, and exceptional courage was needed to join workers' agitations. Born in Colombo, Isabella was the youngest child of a family which earned its living by chopping wood. Both her parents died before she was seven years old and she was forced to work in a store, sorting graphite in order to exist. In the early 1920s, Isabella joined a militant labour union. She was a good speaker, had leadership qualities and became one of the keen supporters of labour leader, A.E. Goonesinha. During the 1929 tramcar strike, she organized demonstrations, participated in numerous meetings and processions, and was at the forefront of this famous struggle. Isabella Hamy was also active in politics; during municipal elections and the State Council elections of 1931, she led a house-to-house campaign on behalf of A.E. Goonesinha, who contested and won the Colombo Central seat. As a result of her militancy she came to be known popularly as 'Captain'.

By the early 1930s some middle-class women had become more ideologically and politically conscious and were prepared to join the urban and plantation workers in their struggles. In the plantation sector, the first trade union was formed by K. Natesa Aiyar and Satyawagiswara Aiyar in 1931. Both their wives were also activists: Nalamma Satyawagiswara Aiyar, who was a doctor, devoted her time to work on the plantations, while Kodandarama Natesa Aiyar created a sensation by appearing at public meetings and thrilling the crowds with her songs describing the sufferings of the estate workers. After 1945, many Tamil women from estates became active in the trade union movement, which grew in strength. Among them, Kokilam Subbiah is the best known for the novels she wrote on the degrading position of men and women on the plantations.

In the urban sector, many women were active in the labour movement after A.E. Goonesinha formed the Ceylon Labour Party in 1928. Agnes de Silva contested but lost the Galagedera seat as a Labour Party candidate in the 1931 elections. Other women who were on the executive committee of the Labour Party included Dr Satyawagiswara Aiyar, Anne Preston (an English theosophist), Caroline Goonesinha and Ms Richard de Silva (wives of the labour leaders), as well as Eva and Jennie Ferdinando and Madlin Jayawardena, a nurse by profession, who was one of the most active members and was also a member of the Dehiwela-Mt Lavinia Urban Council during World War II.

Women in the Left Movement

In the early 1930s, a Youth League of radical nationalists and socialists was formed with branches all over Sri Lanka to agitate for national independence. This movement attracted many radical women, especially teachers who had been inspired by the events in India. When the anti-imperialist Suriya Mal Movement was formed in 1933 in opposition to the sale of poppies (for British ex-servicemen on Armistice Day), its best-known members were women: the president was Doreen Wickremasinghe, née Young, an English woman born in Cheshire in 1907 of a family of Labour Party activists. She went to the school (St Christopher's at Letchworth) founded by Annie Besant and run by theosophists. On graduating from the London School of Economics in 1929, Doreen

Young was secretary to Krishna Menon in the India League in London; she came to Sri Lanka in 1930 and became the principal of Sujata Vidyalaya, Matara. She married Dr S.A. Wickremasinghe (who later became the chairman of the Communist Party) and was appointed the principal of Ananda Balika Vidyalaya in Colombo. While at this school she organized the teachers (Lilian Bandaranaike, Eva de Mel, Helen de Alwis, Shirani Gamage and others) in the Suriya Mal campaign. In a pamphlet on the importance of the movement, Eileen Wirasekera and Helen de Alwis wrote:

> Wear the Suriya flower on November 11th and demonstrate . . . your self-respect and independence . . . Register your refusal to encourage participation in Imperialist War. Every Suriya *mala* is a blow against Imperialism, Fascism and War. Wear the Suriya *mala* for freedom and peace. (Jayawardena 1974)

Many of these women teachers and their students not only made the yellow Suriya flower emblems but also sold them on the streets in the face of opposition from the colonial authorities. The money collected in this way was used to educate a girl from the most depressed caste in the island at a leading Buddhist school in Colombo, in order to show that the caste system could be challenged.

During the malaria epidemic which occurred in 1934 at a time of severe economic depression and caused around 100,000 deaths, all Suriya Mal organizers and other politically minded women like Selina Perera (wife of the socialist party leader Dr N.M. Perera) worked in the Kegalla and Ruanwella areas where the epidemic was at its worst. The activists of the Suriya Mal campaign and the malaria epidemic relief campaign had also led a militant strike of textile workers in 1933. In 1935 they formed the island's first socialist party, the Lanka Sama Samaja Party (LSSP), which had many women militant members including Susan de Silva, Doreen Wickremasinghe and Selina Perera. Contact was maintained continuously with the Indian political movement during the 1930s, and in 1931 and 1937 one of India's best-known women nationalists, Kamaladevi Chattopadhyaya, visited Sri Lanka. During her 1937 visit, she attracted the attention of the police and government as she made a speaking tour of the country together with the LSSP leaders.

In the late 1930s and early 1940s, a few young women graduates of the Colombo University were active in the left-wing movement, among them Vivienne Goonewardena and Sita Wickremasuriya who were prominent members of LSSP and the Communist Party respectively. The LSSP (which by then had become a Trotskyist party) was banned and its leaders arrested in 1940; they subsequently escaped to India with their wives. Women members of the LSSP who were in India during the war included Selina Perera, who became known for her trade union work in Calcutta, and Caroline Gunewardena who married trade union leader S.C. Antonypillai and stayed on in Madras. Other active women who escaped to India were Kusuma Gunewardena (wife of LSSP leader Philip

Gunewardena), who was arrested in India and deported to Sri Lanka, and Vivienne Goonewardena (wife of LSSP leader Leslie Goonewardena), who managed to evade arrest.

The activities of these and other radical women continued into the late 1940s. The leftist movement in Sri Lanka, as in most other countries, split into several groups, some of which supported the Soviet Union and others that were critical of it. Radical women believed that they had a role to play in unifying the left-wing movement and in January 1948, they formed the EKP (Eksath Kantha Peramuna — United Women's Front), dedicated to the achievement of socialism and the removal of all discrimination against women. The formation of the EKP was supported by the two main left-wing parties. It became active immediately, holding a public meeting in March 1948 to celebrate International Women's Day. It was representative of all ethnic groups in the island and included in its ranks women from the working class. The most active leader was Doreen Wickremasinghe; others were Edith Ludowyke (a Hungarian), Vimala Wijewardena, Helen Gunasekera, Parameshwari Kandiah, Vivienne Goonewardena, Noble Rajasingham and Ponsinahamy, a working-class leader. The EKP agitated for the removal of discrimination against the entry of women into the administrative and clerical services of the state, campaigned for the improvement of living conditions in the slums, and protested against the rising cost of living. The existence of the Front, however, was dependent on the active support of the two left-wing parties, and late in 1948, the Communist Party decided that it could no longer cooperate with the LSSP. This decision led to the CP's withdrawal from the EKP which had to be dissolved. Although it had been active for a year, received a great deal of press publicity, and had made an impact on the women's question, its dependence on political parties ultimately caused its dissolution. Some members tried to form an independent women's organization, but their efforts did not meet with success.

Conclusion

The women's movement in Sri Lanka, in its origins and development, was essentially a result of the movement for national independence and therefore reflected most of its characteristics. Independence was achieved through a process of peaceful negotiation and gradual advancement. In association with this movement, women were able to win rights to education, suffrage and juridical equality. Thus the case of Sri Lanka demonstrates the possibility of some advancement through a gradualist programme of reform. But this very ability also imposes certain limitations on the movement. It remained limited in involvement to bourgeois and petty bourgeois women; since it existed and worked within the social parameters, it did not question the patriarchal social structures, or the role of the family in the subordination of women. In these respects, it offers a contrast to countries like Japan where women were compelled to question the very basis of family and sexual morality. The other women to organize themselves and evolve their own methods of struggle were the urban working women. They sought to obtain some measure of change in the existing system of power relations, but they too were unable to push their understanding beyond economic relationships.

The processes of education for women also contributed to the socializing of women into roles that were only superficially different from those of traditional society. Sri Lanka is thus an interesting example of a society in which women were not subjected to harsh and overt forms of oppression, and therefore did not develop a movement for women's emancipation that went beyond the existing social parameters. It is precisely this background that has enabled Sri Lanka to produce a woman prime minister, as well as many women in the professions, but without disturbing the general patterns of subordination.

doesn't a woman prime minister go beyond social parameters?

8. The Movement for Equal Rights for Women in Indonesia

> I was still going to school when I heard of this courageous Indian woman for the first time. I remember it so well; I was very young, a child of ten or eleven, when, glowing with enthusiasm, I read of her in the paper. I trembled with excitement; *not alone for the white woman is it possible to attain an independent position, the brown Indian too can make herself free.* For days I thought of her, and I have never been able to forget her. See what one good example can do! It spreads its influence so far.
> *Kartini*, writing in 1902 on Pandita Ramabai. (Geertz 1976: 177–8; emphasis added)

The political entity that we know of as the Republic of Indonesia is a relatively late creation, which came into being in the aftermath of World War II. The Indonesian archipelago, consisting of a multitude of islands, inhabited by a large number of peoples speaking different languages, was brought into some kind of political unity by the Dutch colonialists; prior to that the islands had existed as independent principalities frequently at war with each other. Some of the islands of Indonesia, notably Sumatra, had figured as important entrepôts in the sea-borne trade between India and China from about 2,000 years ago. Relations with the Chinese were primarily economic; but those with India were deeper and resulted in the predominance of Indian religion and culture in the area. By the early 7th century, there were Hindu and Mahayana Buddhist kingdoms in Sumatra and Java. One of the most important was Sri Vijaya, which, at the height of its power in the 10th century, had spread its influence to South India and Sri Lanka. Palembang in Sri Vijaya was well known as a centre of Buddhist learning, attracting scholars from China and India.

With the decline of Indian power in the region, much of the trade in this area passed into foreign Muslim hands, and with the control of trade came political power. In the course of the next two centuries, Islam spread all over Sumatra and many of the other islands; in the 16th century, the Muslim kingdom of Atjeh in Sumatra was the principal state in the archipelago, overshadowing the decaying Hindu kingdoms of Java. The economy and social structures of this period were typical of self-sufficient agrarian communities; foreign trade in spices and other agricultural products was dominated by the state, and the surpluses generated contributed to the consumption of the princely classes and the erection and maintenance of huge religious monuments like Borobodur.

In this society, women had a defined role. Women of the ruling classes enjoyed a certain degree of autonomy and power. Just as in many other countries, women came to the throne when it was a question of preserving power within a dynastic group. Many kingdoms had women rulers including Atjeh, Sulawesi, Bali, Minangkabau and Java. The kingdom of Atjeh, for example, was ruled by women continuously from 1641 to 1699, and during the anti-colonial battles of the 19th century many women of Atjeh participated in the fighting. A princess of Atjeh, Tjut Nja Dien, is said to have fought by the side of her husband and to have continued to fight even after he had fallen in battle; she is still regarded as one of the heroines of Indonesian nationalism. Other king-doms too had their heroines, including the Minagkabau princesses Bundo Kandung, 'famous for the wisdom she showed in political affairs', and Sabai Nang Halus, who collected an army and went to war to avenge her father (Vreede-de Steurs 1960: 45).

The women of the peasantry participated fully in agricultural activi-ties as in a typical agrarian economy. The women of Java in the 19th century are described thus:

> It is the wife who has to take care of the paddy which she has planted, harvested, dried and will husk. It is she who prepares the rice and the spices . . . buys the household utensils . . . sells the products of her fields . . . dyes the cloth which she sells. (Poensen 1887, quoted in Vreede-de Steurs 1960: 42)

A missionary describes the women's activities:

> Further on is the clacking of a weaving loom worked by a woman . . . when we enter the house we find the women and the young girls busy making batik. We see them drying husks, preparing medicines and spices . . . In short we find women occupied with all kinds of home industries. (Kruijt 1908, quoted in Vreede-de Steurs 1960: 43)

No doubt these descriptions portray a situation which had existed even earlier. Agricultural occupations in traditional societies always pro-vide a specific place for the labour of women. Some have claimed that the women enjoyed a position of independence and were on terms of equality with the men; Vreede-de Steurs, for example, says that in traditional Indonesian society, a woman's duties and her rights were in no way inferior to those of the man (Vreede-de Steurs 1960: 42). This, however, ignores the strong patriarchal base of the social structure and the general subordination of women within it.

Although Islam came to be the dominant ideology, many Indian cultural patterns persisted in Indonesian society. Earlier Hindu and Buddhist beliefs retained their vitality, even though the trappings of religious ceremonial and kingship had disappeared. It is probably these factors which explain the absence of purdah and other similar practices in Indonesian society.

The Advent of Western Imperialism

The Portuguese arrived in the region in 1510 and were followed by the Spaniards, the Dutch and the British. They attempted to gain control of the spice trade by establishing their hegemony over the local kingdoms, while fighting each other as well. The Dutch were finally victorious and established their dominion over the islands of Indonesia by the end of the 17th century. Some of the islands were ruled directly by the Dutch; others were controlled through the agency of indigenous princes and rulers.

The Dutch objective was to exact maximum profits through the export of spices and other agricultural crops. Since free production for export was not sufficient, the Dutch introduced what was called the 'culture system'. In order to graft an export economy on to the economy of the existing self-sufficient village structures, they compelled the cultivators to devote a part of their lands to the cultivation of export crops like coffee, sugar, indigo and spices, and to deliver such products to the state in lieu of taxes. Although initially successful in expanding production and creating an exchange economy, this system of exploitation resulted in great discontent, and in 1870 it was replaced by large-scale cultivation with European and Chinese capital. This led to the formation of plantations with the use of compulsory labour and to a considerable expansion of export production. Private enterprise was encouraged and Dutch concerns were allowed to acquire land. Exports of coffee, sugar, tea, tobacco, rubber, tin and oil expanded rapidly; rail, road and shipping facilities were increased and, in the wave of European imperialist competition of the period, the Dutch empire in the 'Indies' was expanded and consolidated. Grimal states that the Dutch looked on their empire merely as a territory for mercantile exploitation, their policies being determined only by the need for efficient management. The Dutch had no philosophy of colonization, unlike the French who hoped for the ultimate assimilation of the colony into the metropolitan territory, or the British who hoped to prepare the 'natives' for the benefits of self-government (Grimal 1978: 75).

Armed resistance to Dutch aggression was widespread from the very beginning, the most notable resistance being the Java war of 1825–30, when Prince Diponegoro unsuccessfully challenged the Dutch in central Java. By the late 19th century, at a period when a sense of national identity and incipient nationalist feelings were developing among Indonesians, Dutch policies also underwent a change; liberal currents of opinion in the Netherlands envisaged a new colonial 'ethical policy' to create 'a multi-racial society, blending characteristics of East and West

. . . self-governing, but in some continuing relationship with the Nether-lands'. However, the measures adopted to reduce the harshness of Dutch rule and promote the welfare of the Indonesians, such as irrigation and public health, were meagre and the policy, 'far from earning the respon-sive gratitude of a dependent people positively accentuated the growth of Indonesian awareness of alien rule and of hostility towards it' (Legge 1972: 39–41).

The processes of economic change led to a certain degree of social differentiation. In addition to the rich and princely landowners from the previous era, there emerged a multitude of smallholders as well as a number of landless peasants. With the spread of education and the expansion of the bureaucracy, there also came into being a middle class, Western-educated and with a knowledge of the Dutch language. It was to satisfy the aspirations of such groups that the Dutch established a system of representative councils at the levels of the village, town and province: the system was enlarged in 1916 by the establishment of the Volksraad (People's Council); these bodies were chosen by an electorate limited in terms of income and education, with a heavy bias in favour of the Dutch settlers. 'The representative bodies had, in the eyes of the Dutch, the advantage of associating the Indonesian elite with the colonial adminis-tration and directing the elites' attention away from nationalist activities.' However, this aim was not realized; the Volksraad 'contributed to the development of a national consciousness by the mere fact that it brought together representatives from the various parts of the archipelago who were thus able to become better acquainted with each other and to discuss problems of common interest' (Grimal 1978: 77–8).

One consequence of the 'ethical policy' was the expansion of West-ern educational opportunities for some Indonesians, mainly from the urban middle classes and the landowners, among whose ranks discontent with colonial rule was to arise. In the early phase, education in Dutch produced both secular nationalists and Islamic revivalists. The influence of new currents of thinking in other Muslim countries, advocating a modernized Islam, free of obscurantism, linked to science and progress, and with an improved status for women, was evident in Indonesia; in fact, the principles of modern Islam, propagated from Cairo by Mohamed Abduh and his disciple Raschid Rida in the periodical *Al-Monar* had, between 1900 and 1930, a greater repercussion in Indonesia than in any other Muslim country (Grimal 1978: 83).

Kartini and the Issue of Female Education and Emancipation

During the early colonial period, there was little intervention by the Dutch in education, which remained mainly in the hands of the Muslim clergy, with the mosque as the centre of Islamic learning and cultural resistance to the Dutch. By the late 19th century, however, the need for trained local personnel to assist in the administration of the colonial economy led to the first educational reforms. In addition, with the economic deterioration in Java during this period, it was felt that a complete reform of the educational system would result in greater economic development of Indonesia. In 1901, the Queen's speech enunciated the new colonial 'ethical policy' of modernizing the country and spreading technical knowledge among the people. It was in this context that the issue of women's education arose. At that period, the educational status of women varied with their class position. The women of the peasantry had no schooling, whereas daughters of clerics had some religious-orientated instruction, and some of the daughters of the royal and aristocratic families and civil servants went to elementary schools or were educated at home.

One of the first Indonesian women to put forward ideas on women's emancipation was Raden Adjeng Kartini (1879–1904), whose writings reflected some of the problems faced by upper-class women and their desire for emancipation through education, their revulsion against polygamy, and their ambition to become independent through access to professions and through personal freedom.

Kartini was the daughter of the Regent of Jepara in North Java, who was a highly placed bureaucrat. In contrast to other girls from an aristocratic background, Kartini was educated along with her brothers at an elementary school for the children of Dutch planters and administrators, but kept up with her education even after she left school at the age of 12. Her great ambition was to study in the Netherlands, but her father refused her this opportunity. However, she had a window open to the West through J.H. Abendanon, a Dutch liberal (who as colonial Director of Education, tried to promote female education), and Ms Ovink-Soer, a Dutch socialist and feminist (the wife of a colonial official), who taught Kartini and exposed her to radical currents of Dutch thought. Kartini also corresponded with the editor of a socialist women's magazine, *De Hollandsche Lelie*, and with a penfriend in Holland, Stella Zeehandelaar, who was also a socialist and feminist.

This was a period during which the Dutch feminist movement had made considerable advances. In 1889, a Free Women's Society had been formed by radical women who demanded equal rights with men: 'This society consisted of ultra-radical elements, and its members were . . . by way of ridicule, termed "free women" . . . These women expressed themselves very strongly on the subjection of . . . woman and demanded for her the same rights as the man enjoyed' (Boissevain 1915: 7). This group also launched a Women's Suffrage Society in 1894. In 1898, the Groningen Women's League organized a Women's Labour Exhibition which created an impact by highlighting the exploitation of women in the Netherlands and the colonies. In the same year, another controversy arose over the publication of a sensational feminist novel, *Hilda Van Suylenberg* by Cecile Van Beek en Donk; it was the story of a single parent who tries 'to support herself alone in the face of social criticism'; the book also emphasizes the importance of women's education (Geertz 1976: 14). These developments had an echo in Java, and Kartini wrote to Stella Zeehandelaar that she considered this novel the finest book written on women's emancipation. 'I read HVS through in one sitting. I locked myself in our room, and forgot everything; I could not lay it down, it held me so' (Geertz 1976: 64).

> Oh, that we . . . had gone so far, that a book could cause such a violent controversy among us, as Hilda Van Suylenberg has in your country. I shall never rest till HVS appears in my own language to do good as well as harm to our Indian world . . . It is a matter of indifference whether good or harm, if it but makes an impression, for that it shows that one is no longer sleeping, and Java is in deep slumber. And how will her people ever be awakened, when those who should serve as examples, themselves love sleep so much. The greater number of European women in India care little or nothing for the work of their sisters in the fatherland. (Geertz 1976: 35)

Kartini who, while pregnant, visualized continuing teaching after the birth of the child, at the school that she had founded, wrote: 'We shall have something à la Hilda Van Suylenberg — a mother who with a suckling baby goes out to work' (Geertz 1976: 241). In 1899, Kartini asked her friend for news of Dutch feminism: 'Will you not tell me something of the woman of today in the Netherlands? *We take deep interest in all that concerns the Women's Movement*' (Geertz 1976: 35; emphasis added). And in 1900 she referred to a draft translation from English that she had done of an article, 'The Aim of the Women's Movement' (Geertz 1976: 64).

Kartini was constrained by the usual retrictions of high Javanese society, which made her all the more enthusiastic in advocating women's rights and condemning the prevalent practices of polygamy, female seclusion and forced marriage. Her own mother was one of several wives of the Regent and, living in such conditions, Kartini developed strong views on polygamy. 'The only dream we are permitted to have is to become wife number so much to one man or another . . . nearly every woman I know here curses this right of the men. But curses do not help, we must act' (Vreede-de Steurs 1960: 53). In spite of these criticisms, Kartini herself in 1903 married the Regent of Rembang who already had several wives. He was, however, progressive in outlook, encouraging Kartini in setting up a school. Since Kartini's ideas on the role of women were very advanced for her time, she carried her opposition to the practice of polygamy even to the extent of criticizing Islam and expressing strong views against marriage as sanctified in Islamic practices:

> The Moslem law allows a man to have four wives at the same time. And although it be a thousand times over no sin according to the Moslem law and doctrine, I shall forever call it a sin . . . And can you imagine what hell-pain a

woman must suffer when her husband comes home with another — a rival — whom she must recognize as his legal wife? He can torture her to death, mistreat her as he will; if he does not choose to give her back her freedom, then she can whistle to the moon for her rights. Everything for the man, and nothing for the woman, is our law and custom. Do you understand now the deep aversion I have for marriage? I would do the humblest work, thankfully and joyfully, if by it I could be independent. (Geertz 1976: 41–2)

Kartini's reflections on how she and her husband would treat a daughter show not only an awareness of women's oppression, but an unorthodox approach to the role of women: 'She will never be compelled to do anything abhorrent to her deepest feelings. What she does must be of her own free will. She will have . . . a father who will never force her in anything. It will make no difference to him if his daughter remains unmarried her whole life long' (Geertz 1976: 240).

Although she had close links with Dutch friends and was influenced by the feminist and socialist literature of the period, Kartini was also critical of European society. 'We do not expect the European world to make us happier. The time has long gone by when we seriously believed that the European is the only true civilisation, supreme and unsurpassed', she wrote in 1902, adding rather bitterly, but perceptively:

We know why *The Echo* is glad to publish our articles. It is because we are a novelty and make fine advertisement for that paper. The Dutch 'Lelie' placed its columns at my disposal and time and again the directress has asked for letters from me. Why? For the advertisement — letters from a true daughter of the Orient, from a real "Javanese girl", thoughts from such a half-wild creature written by herself in a European language, how interesting! (Geertz 1976: 203–4)

Kartini also developed a critical approach to rural poverty in Java and to colonial rule:

Why is it that the Javanese are so poor, they ask. And at the same time they are thinking how they will be able to get more money out of him . . . grass cutters who earn 10 or 12 cents a day are made to pay trade tax. A *sate* merchant who butchers two (goats) a day must pay . . . one hundred and forty-four florins in the course of a year. What is left for his profit? Barely enough to live on. (Geertz 1976: 243)

Kartini's reading was not confined to feminist literature, but included books which opened her horizons to the colonial reality. One example was the novel *Max Havelaar*, written in 1860 by a Dutch civil servant, Eduard Douwes Dekker, under the pseudonym Multatuli, in which he exposed Dutch economic exploitation of the poor of Indonesia. She often referred to this novel and in 1900 said, 'But an evil that does exist, is the taking of bribes, that I think as wrong and shameful as the forcible taking of goods belonging to the "little man" as in *Max Havelaar*.' Kartini was struck by a line in another Multatuli novel: 'Father said to her that to know, and to understand, and to desire, was a sin for a girl' (Geertz 1976: 53, 134).

Even more interesting is the way in which examples of other Asian women also influenced Kartini. In 1902, she asked her Dutch pen-friend whether there existed a Dutch translation of the life and writings of the unorthodox Indian woman, scholar and agitator, Pandita Ramabai. While Kartini admired the independent life of Ramabai, and was especially pleased to see that not only white women but also Asians could lead independent lives, she herself was unable to break away totally from family tradition and especially from the tutelage of her father. The denial of an opportunity to study in the Netherlands embittered her even more against orthodox society, yet she remained optimistic. In 1903, the year before her death, she wrote to her Dutch friend: 'We have not entirely given up the idea of going to Holland'. Even in her personal behaviour she was defiant: 'I am told that I must modestly (hypocritically) cast down my eyes. I will not do that. I will look men, as well as women, straight in the eye, not cast down my own before them' (Geertz 1976: 199).

Not surprisingly, Kartini was criticized by those in Javanese society who disapproved of her ideas: 'Oh if you only knew . . . the slander spread abroad about me! . . . we were the bearers of new ideas, which were incomprehensible to the great multitude, who scorned us because they could not understand', she wrote in the year of her death (Geertz 1976: 241). The criticism was to be expected as Kartini not only challenged and threatened the traditional patriarchal norms of male-dominated society but also went against the class traditions of the aristocracy. She spoke clearly and defiantly of her intentions: 'I have laid out for myself a full life, I have planned to be a pioneer in the struggle for the rights of the freedom of the Javanese woman' (Geertz 1976: 238).

Kartini herself was denied further education because she was female, and this led her to the conviction that education was an essential liberating force for Indonesian women. In 1901 she wrote to Nethe Van Kol, wife of one of the founders of the Dutch Socialist Party: 'It would be a blessing for Indonesian society if the women received a good education . . . The only road open to the Javanese girl . . . is marriage . . . teach them a trade so that they be no longer a defenceless prey . . . the only way to escape from such a life is for the girl to learn to be independent' (Vreede-de Steurs 1960: 53). Kartini thus had in her mind a vision of education for women, not merely as an end in itself, but as the basis for achieving some economic freedom which would in turn lead to their independence. However, she believed that education should serve not only personal escape but also social progress.

As in other countries of Asia, male and female reformers regarded female education as a necessary ingredient of progress for individuals and for society; Kartini wrote, 'We know that there are men who appreciate a thinking educated woman. I heard a man say (he was a highly placed native official) that the companionship of a woman who was educated and enlightened was a great comfort and support to a man' (Geertz 1976: 67). Kartini had a number of friends who had suffered the same difficulties — being denied the freedom to study, particularly to pursue higher education abroad, and being restricted by their society — and were therefore in revolt. She spoke of such friends with great sympathy:

> Many times have I talked with women, both with those of the nobles and those of the people, about the idea of an independent, free, self-supporting girl, who would earn her own living; and from each comes the answer, there must be someone who sets the example. We know a regent's daughter . . . who is also full of enthusiasm for the idea of freedom. She is crazy to study; she speaks excellent Dutch and has read a great deal . . . we know another . . . who is married; she speaks no Dutch, but she has gone further than the others. She has a great admiration for the free independent European woman; she would think it ideal if we could have the same conditions in our native world. (Geertz 1976: 137)

Kartini was an activist as well as a theorist. She tried to put her ideas into practice by going against conservative opinion and starting a school for the daughters of Javanese officials. She said: 'we ought to strike as quickly as possible and place before the public as an accomplished fact a school for native girls' (Geertz 1976: 220). By 1904, this school had enrolled 120 pupils, but Kartini was unfortunately not able to continue her plan of action as she died in childbirth at the age of 25.

In her short life, Kartini had expressed her views so forcefully that the posthumous publication of her letters was a source of inspiration for both the nationalist and the women's movement in Indonesia. Her letters (*Through Darkness into Light*) were edited and published in Holland and ran into four Dutch editions before being translated into the Indonesian language in 1923 (Geertz 1976: 24). A Kartini Foundation was set up and schools were established in her memory in Semarang, Jakarta and other towns, the Kartini school in Tegal being run by her sister Kardinah. The Indonesians also honoured Kartini by making her an important national heroine who is commemorated up to the present day. The nationalist Tjipto Mangunkusumo, describing Kartini's concern with the people, claimed that her ideal was to see the Indonesians 'rouse themselves from the lethargic sleep in which they have been lost for centuries'. Another nationalist, Sutomo, wrote in 1928, 'With respect and admiration I quote the name of R.A. Kartini . . . *who opened the way to Indonesian feminism*' (Vreede-de Steurs 1960: 54–9).

While in later years Kartini became a cult figure, used by many sections of Indonesian society, there is no doubt that the various facets of her views reflected the many currents of thought engendered by the clash of cultures. As Hildred Geertz has written:

> Kartini repeatedly swung back and forth between identifying herself with the Dutch liberal humanistic ethic as represented by Abendanon, with the radical

socialistic ideas of van Kol and Stella, with the cultivated noblesse oblige of her father as a Javanese aristocrat, and with the mystical spiritualism of her mother. At the same time that she felt attracted to each one, she also felt revulsion at the derogation she received from the Dutch who saw her as 'only a Javanese', at the crassness and uncouthness of so many Dutch people she met which jarred against the highly cultivated courtesy of the Javanese, at the wilful ignorance of her tradition-bound oldest brother, who in turn saw her as 'only a woman', and at the poverty and illness of the Javanese peasants who depended on prayer and spirit-offerings to improve their conditions of life. (Geertz 1976: 25)

Growth of Nationalism

The initial awareness of women's issues in Indonesia came in the late 19th century, as is evident from the writings of Kartini, the first woman openly to criticize polygamy and campaign for female education. The specific issues that occupied the attention of reformers of both sexes in the following period were, in the social sphere, polygamy and child marriage, and in the political sphere, democratic rights for women, especially the right to vote. Of these, the question of polygamy was to become the most persistent issue of the women's movement in Indonesia, even extending into the post-independence era. The eradication of polygamy and its substitution by the Western Christian model of monogamy became not only a symbol of the level of the progress and modernization of educated males, but also a touchstone of women's emancipation: this issue was the terrain for many conflicts since it ran counter to the views of traditional Muslims. However, this reform movement can be understood only in relation to the growth of nationalist consciousness in Indonesia in the late 19th and early 20th centuries. The women's movement was closely inter-linked with the Indonesian nationalist movement and also interacted in diverse ways with its main currents, namely nationalism, Islam and socialism.

As in other Asian countries, a movement for religious and cultural revival preceded the emergence of political organizations in Indonesia; at the turn of the century, there was a resurgence of Islam as the mobilizing and binding factor in struggles against 'infidel' rule, finding adherents among both the peasantry and the rising intelligentsia. In 1908, the Budi Utomo (Excellent Character) movement among middle-class intellectuals emphasized the reconciliation of traditional values and modernization. Its founders included several doctors, one of whom, Tjipto Mangunku-somo (born in 1885), had served the government and later became a strong critic of colonial rule, as well as an admirer of Kartini's views. In 1912, together with Ki Hadjar Dewantoro and Ernest Douwes Dekker, the Eurasian nephew of Multatuli, he founded the Indische Partij (Indies Party) which took a radical, non-racial stand and demanded full independence for Indonesia; the leaders of this party were soon after exiled to the Netherlands.

Ki Hadjar Dewantoro also began the Taman Siswa (Garden of Students), an educational reform movement intended to adapt Javanese culture to modern currents in education. Another group promoting cultural renaissance organized itself in 1918 as a new nationalist society called the Jong Java (Young Java). This group put forward the idea of a unified Javanese nation and advocated, as part of the movement towards this ideal, the use of the spoken 'low' Javanese language rather than either Dutch or 'high' Javanese. Many radical Javanese were active members of Young Java, and Sukarno, at that time a student, was president of its Bandung branch. Similar groups were set up in Sumatra and other areas. Many of them came together, in 1928, at a Youth Congress held in Jakarta, where young people took the pledge to work for national unity under the slogan: 'one land, one people and one language'.

The prominent Islamic component of the nationalist movement was Sarakat Islam, formed in 1912. This had developed from an association of Javanese merchants who wanted to resist Chinese trade expansion in Indonesia; it did not concern itself directly with political issues, but under the leadership of Tjokro Aminoto, it became the symbol of unity of a people dominated by foreign rulers. In 1914, it proclaimed itself as 'not just an economic or social movement, but also a movement in search of justice which the indigenous population has never experienced' (Grimal 1978: 86). The movement quickly spread among various strata of the population, including peasants, workers, traders and intellectuals, claiming a membership of 2.5 million by 1919. The aim of Sarekat Islam was to develop a modern, political Islamic movement based on 'non-cooperation with the Dutch and opposition to foreign capital' (Legge 1972: 45–6). Alarmed by the growth of Sarekat Islam, the Dutch authorities recognized its various local branches but refused such recognition to the central orgnization. This in effect permitted the entry of elements committed to Marxist and socialist ideals to the local branches.

The socialist strand in the nationalist movement came especially from the Indies Social Democratic Association, formed in 1914. This was originally composed mainly of Dutch Marxists, including its founder Hendrick Sneevliet, but later had Indonesian members. The members of the Association were admitted into the Sarekat Islam and, influenced by the events of the Russian Revolution, the policies of the movement became more radical and militant. Repression by the Dutch was harsh, leading to 'a clash of opinion within the Sarekat Islam between moderates who were afraid of the movement becoming too radical and the Marxists' (Grimal 1978: 87). The Marxists moved out of Sarekat Islam in 1920 and founded the Indonesian Communist Party (PKI). They quickly established their leadership over urban workers and the trade unions, and began to train personnel for militant activity. Disregarding advice from the international Communist movement, the party tried to stage a revolution in 1926. Communist units attacked the prison and the telephone exchange in Jakarta and there were uprisings in some of the other cities as well. They were, however, quickly suppressed; 13,000 were arrested and 831 deported to camps (Grimal 1978: 88). As Legge has pointed out: 'The decline of Sarekat Islam and the crushing of the PKI rebellion cleared the ground for a new type of movement based on more narrowly defined forms of nationalism . . . focussed simply on the goal of independence' (Legge 1972: 86).

The new organization included nationalists such as Sukarno who had been educated in Indonesia, as well as a new generation of politicized students who had studied in the Netherlands. Sukarno (1901–70) was the son of a Javanese school teacher and a Balinese mother. His father had been influenced by the theosophical movement, which was popular among Indian and Sri Lankan nationalist leaders of this period. Sukarno had his secondary education in Dutch in Surabaya, where he stayed at the home of Tjokro Aminoto, chairman of Sarekat Islam, a charismatic figure who influenced the young Sukarno. In this formative peroid, Sukarno used the Surabaya Theosophical Library: 'he became an omnivorous reader and . . . introduced himself with growing excitement to . . . Jeffersonian democracy, to the Fabianism of the Webbs, to Marxism . . . in his study of history he was attracted by two themes: national struggles for freedom and by the history of working-class organizations in Europe' (Legge 1972: 52–3). Starting in 1921, Sukarno studied engineering at the Bandung Technical College and was at the same time politically active among many nationalist groups. In 1926 he wrote an article, 'Nationalism, Islam and Marxism', in which he brought together the three strands of thought that influenced him.

In 1927, a group which included Sukarno formed the Indonesian Nationalist Association, which later became the Indonesian National Party (PNI). The PNI emerged as the leading nationalist group, bringing together all nationalist movements under one umbrella, and giving the movement a unity that had not been present earlier. Its Second Congress in Jakarta in 1929 was attended by 1,000 delegates and the discussions were held under Sukarno's chairmanship. 'Alarmed by the violent language and the anti-capitalist stance of the leader of the PNI the Dutch authorities chose to believe that a rebellion was being staged and took repressive measures' (Grimal 1978: 88). In the same year, the colonial authorities intervened and arrested Sukarno and three other nationalists, bringing them to trial in 1930. Sukarno was sentenced to prison but released in 1931. In the meantime the PNI had split and regrouped as the *Partindo*, which Sukarno joined. Events overtook the nationalists, however: Sukarno and other leaders were detained in 1934, and not released until the beginning of World War II.

Agitation by Women

In the years after Kartini's death, women's education expanded gradually, the numbers of girls in 'native schools' in Java and Madura rising from nearly 3,000 in 1908 to over 8,000 in 1911, with 5,745 girls attending private schools in 1912 and 6,000 attending 'village schools' — a total of about 20,000. On the other islands, the numbers of girl students had reached 32,280 by 1911 (Boissevain 1915: 26).

One of the pioneers of girls' schools in this period was Dewi Sartica (1884–1947), who started a school for girls in Bandung in 1904, and by 1912 had founded nine girls' schools; she also advocated vocational training for women. In 1912 she wrote,

> School instruction for our girls is lacking . . . It would be desirable at the same time to train midwives, office-girls, typists, housekeepers, horticulturalists, etc. in short, all the professions which, according to conservative ideas, do not belong to women and have been up to now reserved for men. Let us not forget that there is a considerable number of female laborers who have no professional training whatsoever and have at present to earn their 'bowl of rice' in the factories and on the plantations. (Vreede-de Steurs 1960: 58)

Although the process was slow, nevertheless the spread of education led to the emergence of women activists linked to various social, religious and political movements. For example, associated with the Budi Utomo movement was the first organization of women, the Putri Mardika (Independent Woman) formed in 1912. In the following years, as in other neighbouring countries, there was a quick growth of women's activities; these included numerous women's journals which highlighted issues such as polygamy and child marriage, and women's clubs such as 'The True Girl' and 'The Well-bred Woman'.

In the 1920s, women in many parts of the country began to organize on religious, regional and nationalist lines. The religious groups were Muslim, Catholic and Protestant, and regionally, women in the Moluccas, the Minangkabau and the Minahassa areas became organized. As Wieringa states, these organizations supported education, child care and skills such as sewing for women, to prepare them for the roles of good wife and mother. But the important issue dividing the women was that of polygamy:

> The Christian organizations, and the 'non-religious' organizations on the one hand, and the Islamic women's groups on the other hand, however, were deeply and decisively divided on a central issue: polygamy. The Christian and non-religious women's organizations saw polygamy as an unpardonable humiliation for women, against which they actively fought; the Islamic women's organizations only wanted to improve the conditions under which polygamy was allowed to occur, not to abolish the institution itself. (Wieringa 1985: 8–9)

149

The Indonesian women's movement as it developed in the 1930s was divided into two main strands which were both dominated by middle-class women and were concerned with issues of family law and education. The male nationalists supported both groups and attended their congresses. The reformist tendency was cautious, not only on issues of polygamy, but also regarding open political involvement in nationalist movements while the radical women were committed nationalists, some being influenced by socialism. They took a more uncompromising stand on social problems that affected women and extended their interests to include working-class women.

In 1928, several nationalist groups came together to form the Union of Indonesian Political and National Associations (PPPKI). As a corollary of this move to united action, the first Indonesian Women's Congress was held in Jakarta from 22 to 26 December, bringing together almost 30 women's organizations. Teachers seem to have taken the initiative, including Sukonto (sister of the nationalist Ali Sastroamidjojo), Sujatin and Suwardi (wife of Ki Hadjar Dewantoro); the issues discussed, as in earlier years, were those of importance to middle-class women, namely education and marriage laws. Two well-known nationalist lawyers, Sastroamidjojo and Suporno, addressed the conference on the legal position of women under customary law and Islam. The congress approved three resolutions: for an increase in the number of girls' schools, for the obligatory explanation to brides on marriage of prevailing divorce practices, and for the provision of assistance to widows and orphans of Indonesian civil servants. The congress also decreed that 22 December should be celebrated as Mothers' Day.

At the Second Women's Congress in December 1929, the Federation of Indonesian Women's Associations (PPII) was formed and the campaign for women's rights continued. The Federation sent delegates to the Congress of Asian Women held in Lahore (India) in January 1931, where a resolution was passed against polygamy. At the Third Congress in March 1932, the non-involvement of the PPII in politics was reaffirmed; however, issues of nationalism and politics were raised in the key speeches and Ki Hadjar Dewantoro 'impressed on his listeners the fact that feminist movements in Turkey, China, Persia and India had contributed largely to the success of the national movement in those countries' (Vreede-de Steurs 1960: 92). However, PPII activities remained class-bound and limited in their political commitment: 'nationalist ideas gained more prominence. Some attention was paid to women of the poorer classes, but membership was still recruited from the higher classes, and the demands voiced remained directed mainly to the interests of women of this group' (Wieringa 1985: 10).

The Second Congress of the PPII in Jakarta in July 1935 enumerated its fundamental principles as being nationalism, social action and neutralism on religious questions; Indonesian women were urged to inspire patriotism among children, since they had the duty to be 'mothers of the people'. It was decided that female employment should be promoted and that the status of Muslim women should be enquired into while endeavours were made 'to improve this position without depreciating religion'. The issue of female literacy was also discussed, especially since the 1930 census figures had revealed alarming rates of illiteracy among women. Total literacy among Indonesian women was only 17%, with regional variations — Java 7%, Sumatra 19%, Bali 5.7%, Sulawesi 31% (Vreede-de Steurs 1960: 93–4).

The main issue at the Third PPII Congress in Bandung in July 1938 was female franchise. This question had arisen in Indonesia in 1918 when the Dutch established a People's Council and several reformers unsuccessfully argued the case for female suffrage. In 1938, protests were voiced against a Dutch woman resident in Indonesia being elected to the People's Council, overlooking the claims of Maria Ulfah Santoso, a law graduate of Leiden, who was sponsored by the Indonesian women's associations. In 1941, further protests were made when Dutch women, but not local women, were given municipal voting rights. These protests led to the withdrawal of the proposal; the right to vote was eventually granted to Indonesian women during World War II (Vreede-de Steurs 1960: 96–7).

Isteri Sedar

A more radical current had emerged in October 1929 when Putri Indonesia, the women's section of Young Java, together with other women's groups organized a meeting in Bandung that was attended by 1,000 people of whom 600 were women. A radical, uncompromising approach was taken on issues such as polygamy, prostitution and women's education; the meeting had a political content and was addressed by Sukarno who urged women to join the nationalist cause. Suwarni (Jojoseputro) Pringgodigdo presided at the meeting; she was a member of the Youth Congress and in 1930 formed Isteri Sedar (The Alert Woman) in Bandung and started a journal, *Sedar* ('Alert') (Vreede-de Steurs 1960: 90–1).

By 1932, Isteri Sedar had become an open political movement; at its congress in Bandung in that year it urged Indonesian women to participate in politics, putting forward proposals to improve the conditions of working-class women and urging the adoption of a national education policy to serve the needs of the masses. On this occasion Suwarni Pringgodigdo said: 'Throughout the world, 90% of the population is made up of proletarians. In all countries, the lot of the children of the poor classes is a sad one, but in countries which have no liberty the children lack not only food and clothing but even schools' (Vreede-de Steurs 1960: 93).

At this conference, Sukarno was one of the speakers, taking as his theme 'The Political Movement and the Emancipation of Women'. It is interesting at this point to note the role of Sukarno in encouraging the

151

women's movement. Like many other Asian leaders of his generation, he had been influenced by socialist and liberal thought in politics and had been exposed to the debate on the role of women, which was one of the important issues for nationalists in the fight against imperialism. He supported the radical, nationalist Isteri Sedar and all through the nationalist struggle he raised the issue of women's rights. In 1947 he even wrote a feminist novel, *Sarinah*, which was 'a mixture of European socialist ideas of women and Indonesian elements'; he visualized the collectivization of housework so that women would be freed 'to go into production and thus assure equality with men' (Wieringa 1982: 41).

Many members of the Isteri Sedar belonged to the PNI (Partai National Indonesia) whose leaders had been arrested in 1929. Isteri Sedar was severely critical of Dutch colonialism and also opposed the positions taken by the Indonesian Women's Federation on religious, political and social questions, and refused to participate in the latter's congresses. In January 1931, Isteri Sedar participated at a congress of Asian women in Lahore and in June 1931, held its first congress in Jakarta at which a resolution was passed calling for the abolition of polygamy, quoting the policies of Mustapha Kemal in Turkey. During these years, the question of polygamy became a central issue for the women's movement and the subject of much debate and writing. The 1932 congress of Isteri Sedar also rejected all forms of polygamy and Suwarni Pringgodigdo, in an article on 'The Question of Polygamy' in 1934, replied to orthodox criticism and concluded that 'The Indonesian woman has a right to justice and independence and polygamy is the very denial of justice and independence' (Vreede-de Steurs 1960: 91, 107).

The campaign became caught up in the usual dilemma of attempting social reform in a colonial context. In view of the agitation and discussion in the 1930s regarding polygamy, the government drew up a draft Marriage Ordinance in 1937 which would have prohibited polygamy (where marriages were registered) and have given women divorce rights. All the Islamic associations opposed that draft as being against Islam, and the large nationalist parties and some nationalist women regarded it as 'intolerable interference of the colonial government'. Some women's groups, however, like Isteri Sedar supported the proposals, which were withdrawn by the government in the face of criticism. Nevertheless, the issue was kept alive by several women's organizations and the battles between traditional and reformist groups continued in the post-World War II period.

The War Years and After
The Japanese occupied Java and the other islands early in 1942. They did away with the representative organs set up by the Dutch, but wishing to run the local administration through nationals, encouraged the nationalists to join with them. The nationalist government broke up over this issue, some of them accepting office in the Japanese administration and

others setting up clandestine resistance organizations. The Japanese intention, however, was merely to obtain the cooperation of the people in their war effort.

On the defeat of the Japanese, the nationalists led by Sukarno proclaimed the independence of Indonesia on 17 August 1945. The Dutch tried to reassert their sovereignty through military and diplomatic means; they sought to persuade the nationalists to accept a federal union with Holland. After a great deal of fighting and intervention by the United Nations, sovereignty over Indonesia was finally transferred from the Dutch to the Indonesians in December 1949. All the islands agreed to a unitary form of government and the Republic of Indonesia came into being in 1950.

The Japanese occupation was a serious set-back to the women's movement. The only association permitted by them was the Fudjinkai; it engaged only in social work, running cooperative kitchens and anti-illiteracy centres. However, the movement broke out of these restraints with the declaration of independence in 1945. Women in large numbers came forward to support the guerrillas, forming themselves into groups of nurses, and organizing clinics and cooking centres. Many women's organizations joined together to form the Union of the Women of the Indonesian Republic, with a programme 'to form the rear-guard in defence of the countrys' liberty' (Vreede-de Steurs 1960: 114). This organization was later brought within the fold of a large umbrella grouping, the Kongres Wanita Indonesia (KOWANI). Forty-five groups were members of Kowani; some were women's groups associated with the political parties, and others were independent associations of women, including women in the various professions. Kowani agitated for equal legal rights for women and it was largely as a result of their efforts that the Indonesian Constitution, framed in 1949, gave equal voting rights to women.

Another area in which women's organizations were active was that of marriage laws. The agitation was for marriage laws, applicable to all Indonesians, that would recognize the equality of both parties in marriage and divorce and would also end polygamy. But orthodox Muslim groups firmly and successfully opposed the enactment of such legislation. The sense of frustration of Indonesian women is evident in a leading article in *Suara Perwari*, the organ of the Perwari women's movement, in October 1955:

> It is with envy that we read in the newspapers that Tunisia, a country which has only just obtained sovereignty and whose population, like ours, is chiefly Muslim, has passed a bill which aims at protecting the interests of the family by prohibiting polygamy, by depriving the husband of his power of repudiation, and by forbidding child marriage. (Vreede-de Steurs 1960: 137)

It was only in 1975 that a uniform marriage law was enacted. Even this, however, permits polygamy. If his religion permits it and his wife gives her consent and if he proves that he can support two families and promises fair treatment, a man can enter into a polygamous marriage under this law.

Conclusion

The early women's movement of Indonesia developed within the framework of a nationalist movement whose ideology was conditioned, at first, primarily by ideals of liberal democracy and by the values of a resurgent Islam. Socialism later became a strand in the nationalist movement, growing more important as time went on. Thus the early efforts of the women's movement were restricted to advocating suffrage and to fighting practices like polygamy. It did not develop to the point of evaluating or criticizing the patriarchal structure of traditional society, even though some of Kartini's writings indicate an understanding of the importance of man-woman relationships.

Women's movements played a significant role in the fight for Indonesian independence and in the struggle to stabilize the independent state in the face of foreign intervention. Women received the right of suffrage, but they were unable to obtain desired reforms in the marriage laws, polygamy still being permitted under certain conditions. In spite of provisions in the Constitution which guarantee equality to men and women, the juridical position of women remains insecure.

9. Women's Struggles for Democratic Rights in The Philippines

> 'My chauffeur, my cook and my man servant who are all under me can vote; why can't the government allow me and Filipino women in general the privilege of going to the polls?'
> *Dr Maria Paz Mendoza-Guazon* in the 1920s (Mendoza-Guazon 1951: 3)

The Philippines have a history and culture that is rather different from that of other Asian countries, for the islands came under the suzerainty of two colonial powers that were otherwise absent in Asia, namely Spain and the United States of America. The cultures of these two countries left their impact on the Philippines, moulding forms of struggle and of political action which are significantly different from other examples in Asia. Another important differentiating factor is that of religion; with the exception of the Muslims in Mindanao, the great majority of the people adopted the religion of the colonizer, so that the Philippines became and remain Roman Catholic. The ways in which these factors affected the course of the feminist movement in the Philippines will be discussed below.

The Philippine archipelago consists of three main regions, Luzon, the Visayan Islands and Mindanao, and its population is made up of a number of ethnic groups, the results of various historical connections. People of Malay origin came from South-East Asia, bringing the culture of Islam, and established themselves in the southern islands of the Philippine group. Chinese and Arab traders added another strain, as did Indian merchants who introduce some elements of Hindu culture. Manila developed into an important trade entrepôt between India, Japan and China. The advent of the Spanish with Magellan's arrival in 1521 stopped the northward expansion of Islam in the Philippines and profoundly influenced the subsequent development of the Filipino people.

The pre-Spanish society and, in particular, the place of women in that society, are now seen rather idyllically by the Filipinos. Women were said to be the equal of men. This was demonstrated by the myth about their creation: the original ancestors were said to have come from different segments of a bamboo, and upon seeing each other for the first time, the man bowed before the woman. Marriage and divorce were by mutual consent; marriage, except among the Muslims, being monogamous. After marriage, a woman retained her maiden name and certain rights; for instance, she shared equally in the inheritance from her parents and, if she was the eldest, was even eligible to succeed her father in a chieftaincy. Reference is also made to such legendary rulers as Queen Sima and Princess Urduja, who had women counsellors and commanded armies in the field. Writing in 1934 and summarizing the position of women in pre-Hispanic society, Encarnacion Alzona paints an idealized picture:

> Filipino women occupied a high social position which could only be possible in a civilized community. Women enjoyed a large measure of freedom which was unknown to women of other oriental countries. As they were free, they were able to participate in social, economic and political activities to the advantage of both individual and society. They commanded the respect of men; they were amply protected by the native laws and they possessed civil and political rights. (Alzona 1934: 20)

The Spanish Conquest and Struggles for National Independence

After Magellan's landing in 1521, the Spanish mounted a number of expeditions to the Philippines and by 1574 had conquered the greater part of the country, even though the Moro Muslims entrenched themselves in some of the southern islands and offered resistance until 1880. Initially, the Portuguese and the Dutch unsuccessfully attempted to contest the Spanish occupation, the Portuguese withdrawing after the union of Spain with Portugal and the Dutch after heavy naval defeats. Although traders of other nationalities were allowed into the country, internal trade was monopolized by the Spanish. The Spanish incursions were accompanied by friars who set up churches and started their very successful campaigns of proselytization. In time they acquired much power and land, and resisted all efforts to set up parishes that would be controlled by regular local parish priests. Resistance to their power later became a focal point of struggle among the Filipino nationalists.

Spain was thus earlier than the other Western European nations in acquiring a colonial empire. Even though it was able to draw on the resources of the Americas, however, it remained basically a poor country; the Spanish nobility invested their money in land instead of in productive enterprises, but did not add to it the productive capacity. Spain's outdated social structures and economic vulnerability proved too fragile a base for holding on to its far-flung empire. By 1824, it retained only the islands of Cuba, Puerto Rico and the Philippines out of its once extensive colonies, but even these were to be lost by the end of the century.

The diversity of the Filipino population, broken up into numerous ethnic and linguistic groups, at first militated against the rise of nationalism; but the spread of education and the training of Filipinos abroad, particularly in Spain, led to the growth of a nationalist movement, and the emergence of an élite group of *illustrados* whose economic base was the commercial cultivation of coconuts, tobacco and other tropical produce for an export market. The first daily newspaper, *La Esperanza*, appeared in 1847. Of greater impotance to the growth of the movement was the publication in Barcelona of a journal called *La Solidaridad*, founded by the Filipino nationalist Graciano Lopez-Jaena. This journal which was published from 1889 to 1895 became an organ of Philippine propaganda, arguing for reforms in both government and church. A principal contributor to this journal, Dr José Rizal, ultimately became one of the prime proponents of Philippine nationalism. Born in 1861 of a wealthy family of sugar cane growers, educated in the Philippines and in Madrid university (where he qualified in medicine), Rizal lived in Europe between 1882 and 1892. He and other early nationalists were influenced by the ideals of the French Revolution, especially by the writings of Voltaire, the slogans of liberty, equality and fraternity, the prevailing liberal currents of opinion in Madrid, the Spanish Liberal Party and the anti-clericalism of the time. Similarly Freemasonry appealed to these nationalist *illustrados*, especially since the 'Masonic spirit of egalitarian fraternity', as well as its secrecy and comradeship, seemed relevant to the struggle (Fast and Richardson 1983: 57, 83).

Rizal wrote numerous articles, putting forward the view that the Filipinos were the intellectual and moral equals of the Spanish rulers. He also wrote two novels in which he portrayed the harshness and cruelty of Spanish rule, but at the same time indicated that the Filipinos were a moral people who had absorbed the doctrines of the Catholic Church. Rizal and a few fellow nationalists including Lopez-Jaena and Marcelo del Pilar (also both Freemasons) founded the Young Filipino Party, which protested against the severity of the Spanish rulers and the domination of the Catholic Church by Spanish friars. In the 1880s and early 1890s, the concern of the nationalists was with 'mismanagement of the economy, bad government, lack of civil liberties, clerical conservatism and deficient education' (Fast and Richardson 1983: 61).

A new and active stage of Philippine nationalism began in 1891. Rizal founded a political organization, the *Liga Filipino*, in Hongkong and then moved on to Manila where a branch of the Liga was also established. The reformist viewpoint changed from demands for assimilation and equality with Spain, to demands for separation and independence. In 1891, del Pilar, speaking to politically active Filipinos in Madrid, called for 'the abolition in the Philippines of every obstacle to our liberties, and in due time and by the proper method, the abolition of the flag of Spain as well (Fast and Richardson 1983: 63). Festering discontent had now become open and in August 1896 the Katipunan insurrection against the Spanish broke out, starting in the Cavite province where it was led by Emilio Aguinaldo, but soon spreading through the islands. The Spanish brought in reinforcements and inflicted a military defeat on the nationalists after a hard campaign of nearly two months. Rizal was arrested and tried for complicity in the insurrection; a military tribunal found him guilty and he was shot in December 1896.

Rizal's execution incited a further upsurge in insurrectionary action which was even more extensive. Unable to suppress it through military means, the Spanish authorities opened negotiations with Aguinaldo in the hope of reaching a compromise. But these efforts were overtaken by the outbreak of the Spanish-American War in February 1898. The insurrection gathered strength and the Philippine nationalists declared their independence from Spain on 12 June 1898, establishing a provisional republic with Aguinaldo as President. This provisional republic proceeded to call a Revolutionary Assembly and to establish local tribunals.

In December 1898, however, the Filipinos found themselves with a new set of masters. Under the Treaty of Paris, concluded at the end of the Spanish-American War, which had originated in the Cuban struggle for independence from Spain, and had seen a major naval battle in Manila Bay, the Philippines were ceded to the United States. Nevertheless the Filipinos proceeded on the basis of their newly declared independence and Aguinaldo was formally elected President. The course was set for a bloody confrontation with the USA which was bent on taking over the Philippines from their Spanish predecessors. Fighting broke out between the Filipinos and the American army, and on 31 March 1899 US forces captured Malolos, the temporary capital of the Philippine government. Although organized resistance was quickly subdued, the Filipinos resorted to guerrilla tactics and continued to harass the US forces until the capture of Aguinaldo in March 1901 brought armed resistance to a virtual end.

The Impact of Spanish Colonization

Spanish colonization, coming as it did in the 16th century, brought the Filipinos under the influence of Western culture much earlier than other countries of Asia; the closure of the Philippines to other influences, both economic and cultural, also ensured that the country remained isolated from the rest of Asia and Europe. The Spaniards imposed their religion, customs, language, laws and other institutions upon the Filipinos, and these were to have a profound effect on the development of Filipino women.

Unlike the other colonial powers of the time, the Spaniards were vitally concerned with the moral problems of conquest, an attitude which perhaps originated in Spain's own history. It had been the only multi-racial and multi-religious country in Western Europe, but in the process of centralization under an absolutist rule it had resorted to the forcible conversion or massacre of its non-Catholic groups, mainly the Jews and the Moors. The Spanish Inquisition had been an infamous instrument in this process which was now repeated in Spain's colonies. The majority of the *conquistadores* were doubtlessly impelled by the lure of wealth and power, but they were always accompanied by the Dominican friars who set themselves the task of converting the heathens to Catholicism by any means.

This also applied to the Philippines. Unlike other countries of Asia, and with the exception of the Muslim Moros, the Filipinos had no developed religious system which could offer any resistance to this onslaught. Some of the priestesses of the earlier tribal faiths offered some resistance, refusing to give up their idols, but they were soon forced to surrender or to retreat into the interior. As is customary, the new faith was first adopted by the higher strata of society and then by the majority of the people.

The new converts were zealous both in the observation of the new faith and in winning more converts. Alzona gives many examples of early converts, including a number of Filipino women who were raised by church authorities to the rank of Venerable, a first step towards sainthood. The converts were also attracted to the monastic orders; many became Sisters of Charity, or Companions of Jesus, an order founded by a Filipino woman, Ignacia del Espiritu Santo (1688–1748) under supervision of the Jesuits. These organizations were also active in social welfare work and education (Alzona 1934: 24).

Women's Education

In addition to proselytization, the church undertook the task of education. The first boarding school for girls was founded in Manila in 1591, the Colegio del Santa Potenciana; several others were set up later. At first these schools were reserved for Spanish girls and for *mestizos*, the offspring of marriages between Spaniards and Filipinos, but later they were thrown open to girls from wealthy and influential Filipino families. Schools for Filipino girls were established in the early 17th century. By 1863, each town had two elementary schools, one for boys and one for girls.

The curriculum followed in these girls' schools was restricted. Alzona describes it as follows:

> The instruction in these boarding schools at the beginning consisted of the teaching of the Christian doctrine, reading, writing and needlework. Arithmetic was sometimes taught . . . the Spanish language was also taught indifferently, for the aim of these institutions was not to turn out learned women, but *devout, chaste, modest and diligent women who would become good wives and mothers.* The greater part of the girls' time was devoted to religious practices, long prayers and frequent visits to the chapel which was to be found in each school; music, for which Filipino girls had shown marked aptitude, was an elective study. (Alzona 1934: 27; emphasis added)

The attitude of the church authorities towards teaching the Spanish language was quite pragmatic. They feared that knowledge of Spanish would provide the divided peoples of the Philippine archipelago with a common language which would facilitate communication among them and therefore make the spread of subversive nationalist ideas all the easier. The general training in schools imparted 'correct behaviour in the classroom, in the presence of old people, and in the church . . . so that the public schools turned out polite and god-fearing girls and boys' (Alzona 1934: 29–30)

Teaching in school was the one avenue of employment that was kept open for Filipino women by the Spanish rulers. In 1875, a special school was established for women teachers with a three-year programme of instruction, to be followed by several others towards the end of Spanish domination. These were the highest academic institutions open to Filipino women during this era, for they were not admitted to the university which had been opened in 1611. Restricted though it was, education opened up new horizons for women. In the 19th century, several women writers and novelists had published their works: Leona Florentina (born 1849), who had been educated privately, wrote poems (in Spanish and in the local language) which were of a high quality. Alzona makes an interesting reference to Florentina:

> In recognition of her literary work, her name was included in the *International Encyclopaedia of Women's Works* edited in 1889 by Madame Andzia Wolska. Although many of her literary productions have been lost, some may still be found in the public libraries in Manila, Madrid, Paris and London, (Alzona 1934: 33)

Other women writers were Florentina Arellano who wrote highly praised articles for the nationalist press; Marta Jalandoni, a writer of poems and dramas in the Visayan languages, and Magdalena Jalandoni, an important novelist.

Another phenomenon noted in other Asian countries also made its appearance in the Philippines. Education, however limited by the secular or religious authorities, sets its own momentum for expanding and deepening. In 1887, for example, the women of Malolos petitioned the authorities to grant equal educational opportunities to women. Their attempts were supported by such nationalists as Rizal and Marcelo del Pilar. Rizal wrote to this women's group in 1888; Alzona summarizes this letter as follows: 'he wrote that women had the mistaken notion that piety consisted of kissing the friars' hands, going to confession frequently, repeating long prayers, burning candles, wearing scapularies, counting beads and believing in false miracles.' Complaining that women allowed friars to mislead them, he said: 'Let us be reasonable and open our eyes, above all you women, because you are the first ones to influence the minds of men' (Alzona 1934: 35).

The Spanish also introduced their Civil Code into the Philippines, with enormous consequences for women. The rights of married women were severely restricted: they had no rights of disposal over property brought into their marriages, could not engage in any outside economic activity without the formal consent of their husbands, and could hold no public office except that of teacher. A noteworthy aspect of this Civil Code was the emphasis placed on the unity and stability of the family, by giving all power within the family to the husband. Catholicism and canon law also ensured that no divorce was possible.

The almost wholehearted acceptance of the religion and culture of the Spanish moulded the values and attitudes of Filipino women, making it possible for them to internalize these values. Catholicism inculcated in them the notion of male superiority and endowed it with the strength of religious dogma. Relationships between males and females were regulated by an elaborate set of conventions, which effectively made the female the passive object of male attention. Women were segregated into the domestic sphere; although women of the peasantry still laboured by the side of males in the field, the dominant ethos was one in which they were economically non-active and socially non-initiating. Maria Clara, the chief character of Rizal's novel, *Noli Me Tangere*, epitomized this prevailing view of women. As pointed out earlier, Rizal was one of the leaders and ideologists of the nationalist movement and had advanced ideas regarding the education of women, yet he too shared this general view of the place of women in a society in which the family was held sacrosanct, and which depended on concepts of female chastity and faithfulness.

Even against this background, however, Filipino women were not entirely immune to the rising tide of nationalism and did contribute to its success. A few women even took an active part in the insurrections against Spanish rule in the 1890s. They included Trinidad Tecson, who fought in twelve battles between 1896 and 1899 and was responsible for organizing a group of women nurses; Agueda Kahabagan, who actively fought the Spanish, leading a group of revolutionary fighters; Gloria de Jesus, who was one of the leading organizers of the movement; Melchora Aquino, better known as Tandang Sera and as the 'Mother of the Revolution' for her role in organizing food and shelter for the revolutionary fighters (Alzona 1934: 49). While the leaders of the Katipunan struggle did not put forward views on women's equality, they emphasized the deplorable consequences of a 'disorderly life'. One of the leaders, Bonifacio, emphasized the need for showing love to 'thyself, thy wife and children [and] for thine countrymen' and condemned 'gambling, drunkenness, laziness, concubinage, and ill-treatment of wives' (Fast and Richardson 1983: 82).

The Period of American Rule

The United States consolidated its occupation of the Philippines after crushing the independence struggle which had originally been launched against the Spanish. The occupation was justified, of course, in the 'civilizing' rhetoric of all imperialists. President McKinley declared that the government that was being established was 'designed not for our satisfaction nor for the expression of our theoretical views but for the happiness, peace and prosperity of the people of the Philippine Islands'.

The Americans established a Philippine legislature in 1907 and proceeded to govern the country with a fair amount of local autonomy. It was quickly realized that the Philippines were valuable as a source of tropical products and minerals and of cheap labour. American investments began to come in on a large scale to exploit these resources. Philippine national sentiment was still strong, however, and the people continued to agitate for independence, although peacefully and along constitutional lines.

The campaign for Philippine independence was supported in the United States by liberal forces and also by American producers of sugar, tobacco, etc., who did not favour the duty free entry into the USA of Philippine products, and by trade unions that were averse to the competition posed by Filipino immigrants. The congruence of these various forces resulted in the establishment of the Philippines as a Commonwealth within the United States in 1934, with Quezon as first President and with the promise of full independence in 1946. Commonwealth status was accompanied by the abolition of duty free exports into the USA. Filipino immigration into the USA was also controlled. World War II and the Japanese occupation intervened, and the Philippines became an independent sovereign state in July 1946.

The Social Impact of the American Regime

The transition from Spanish to American dominance caused changes in methods of administration and in the prevailing ideology. From the women's point of view American influence tended to erode the general ideas of female subservience that had been inculcated by the Spanish.

The educational system in the Spanish period, as we have seen earlier, was organized by the religious authorities and orientated towards instilling Christian values. The Americans set about introducing a secular educational system; 1,000 American teachers were brought to the country in 1901 and English was established as the medium of instruction. Links were also established with American colleges and universities, to which many Filipinos were sent to study; these scholars included women, the first of whom went to the USA to study medicine in 1904. The spread of education was such that in 1918, 'of a total of 3,138,634 literate Filipinos, 1,457,068 were women' (Alzona 1934: 54).

Several universities and institutes of higher learning were established and opened to women. The Spanish law that had restricted women to the teaching profession was repealed; women of the wealthier classes in particular took advantage of the new opportunities, enrolling in the new institutes as they were opened. By 1928, women could be found in almost all the professions: 40 physicians, 53 dentists, 562 pharmacists, 30 lawyers and 1,700 nurses (Mendoza-Guazon 1951: 50). The process was not an easy one, however. As Alzona says:

> the question as to whether it was advisable for women to enter the various professions became a lively topic of public discussion. As in other countries, there were men, and women too who were tacitly opposed to this innovation, alleging that it would be detrimental to the home, to femininity and to other supposedly sacred Filipino traditions. Some courageous women, however, despite this contrary attitude, invaded the professional schools here and in America. (Alzana 1934: 58)

Despite the various difficulties, others were quick to follow and by 1931 there were 3,064 Filipino women graduates. This spread of education had an inevitable result: the desire of Filipino women for full participation in the civil and political life of the country was stimulated. On the civil side, they agitated successfully for the removal of some of the restrictions that the Spanish Civil Code had imposed on women. They were given full control of their inherited property, but their efforts to achieve the legalization of divorce were not successful until 1938. Attempts to revise family law so that a married woman would have full civil rights without having to seek the husband's permission for all her activities were also unsuccessful, being opposed on the grounds that the stability of the family would be affected. American influence did serve to liberalize relations between men and women in general, however, releasing women from the grip of the *machismo* creed which had earlier circumscribed their existence.

The Struggle for the Franchise

The struggle to obtain voting rights for women was long drawn out, lasting until 1937, three decades after the male franchise. This campaign was also one of the issues around which women organized themselves; it is also important as revealing many of the characteristics of Filipino women's struggles.

Women's organizations, composed mainly of bourgeois women and dedicated to social work, came into existence very soon after the American occupation. Their involvement with wider issues like the franchise dates back to 1905, when Concepción Felix formed the Asociación Feminista Filipino. Concepción had taken part in a public debate in Manila, speaking on the place of women in Philippine society; she argued against speakers who advocated that education and training for women should be confined to making them fit for the occupations of stenographer, nurse and teacher. She attracted the attention of Fiske Warren of the Anti-Imperialist League of Boston who tried to persuade her to form a women's political party. Concepción Felix considered this premature and formed her own association which took up the question of suffrage in addition to other social services (Subido 1955: 17).

Other women were also stimulated into activity. In 1906, Pura

Villanueva Kalaw founded the Asociación Feminista Ilonga, whose main aim was women's suffrage. Their activities were sufficient to win some male support for the issue; a bill seeking to give women voting rights was introduced in the House of Representatives in 1907 but did not succeed. The association continued its efforts, however, receiving fresh impetus from two sources. The first of these was a magazine called *Filipinas* (1909), the first local magazine to be devoted entirely to issues and matters affecting women. It agitated for the greater political participation of women and for women's suffrage, stating its aims clearly in its first issue:

> To fulfil our duty towards the members of our sex, at the same time to revindicate the rights of women not only socially but politically as well.
> To consecrate ourselves completely to the education and culture of the Filipina, to work with courage to achieve their equality with the members of the stronger sex, and to take an active part in matters affecting the management of the government of our country. (Subido 1955: 18)

The second impetus came from the visit to Manila in 1912 of two suffragists: Carrie Chapman Catt, an American, and Dr Aletta Jacobs, who was Dutch. They did their best to establish a broad-based women's suffrage organization but failed to persuade the individual organizations to come together for this purpose. On their initiative, an organization called the Society for the Advancement of Women was formed; this was later renamed the Women's Club of Manila, and although it failed to mobilize women behind the fight for suffrage on a country-wide basis, it was successful in giving new momentum to the movement. As a result, four bills seeking the vote for women were introduced in the Philippine House of Representatives between 1912 and 1918. The agitation was not sufficient to ensure their passage, however, even though the 1918 bill was supported by Francis Harrison, who was then the American Governor-General, and although notable women such as Felix and Kalaw appeared before the Legislature to argue the case (Subido 1955: 19).

Until that time, the women's organizations had largely been confined to Manila and their members had belonged mainly to the middle classes. In 1920, realizing that this did not give the movement sufficient strength, Concepción Felix and other members of the Women's Club of Manila summoned a general convention of women's organizations throughout the country, after which the National League of Filipino Women was formed, one of its chief resolutions being to petition the legislature for women's suffrage (Subido 1955: 31). As a result of these activities, the issue came up before the legislature again in 1921. The Governor-General in his message to the sixth Philippine Legislature said: 'I earnestly invite . . . the extension of the suffrage to the women of the Philippine Islands under the same conditions and to the same extent that you have extended it to the men', but the all-male House of Representatives was not yet willing to extend the vote to women (Subido 1955: 21).

As education spread among women, the numbers joining the struggle increased. The Women Citizens League, organized in 1928 by Dr Maria Paz Mendoza-Guazon, was a principal instrument of their agitation. Maria had been the first Filipino woman to graduate as doctor of medicine in 1912 and was also the first woman to be awarded a Chair at the University of the Philippines. Thereafter, she became very active in the suffrage movement.

The fight for the vote was begun by bourgeois women, working and thinking along class lines. However, the Women Citizens League was able to carry the struggle to broader strata of Filipino women. It organized public meetings and rallies throughout the country and launched a propaganda campaign to win the support of the press. This campaign was so successful that by 1931 the greater part of the press was supportive of the suffrage movement (Subido 1955: 32).

The long struggle appeared to come to a triumphant conclusion in December 1933 when the House of Representatives finally passed a bill giving women the right to vote, subject to the same literacy qualifications as applied to men. This right was to be effective from January 1935, but the victorious feelings of the women were short-lived. In 1934, the Philippines were given a new status, that of a Commonwealth within the United States, and the Constitutional Convention which drafted the new Constitution did not favour granting women the vote. The suffragist organizations together formed a General Council of Women with members from the different groups, who then appeared before the Convention. They were unable to win immediate acceptance of their demand, however, the Convention deferring this issue to a future plebiscite. It was decreed that this plebiscite should be held within two years of adoption of the Constitution, and that women should then have the vote if no less than 300,000 women voted affirmatively.

The suffragist organizations immediately started a new campaign, first winning the right to appoint women watchers at each polling place and then the right for speedy registration and for an early plebiscite. Proclaiming the plebiscite, President Quezon supported women's suffrage; speaking *extempore*, he said: 'Once more I ask our men: Are you going to deprive our women of the opportunity to say how their lives are going to be regulated and is it fair for us to presume that men can always speak in this country for women?' (Subido 1955: 38). Even though the plebiscite only concerned the women, the President's appeal to men is revealing of the masculine domination over women which still prevailed.

The General Council of Women then undertook a country-wide propaganda campaign, exhorting women to register and to vote 'yes' to women's suffrage. They held rallies in schools and community centres, organized lectures and house-to-house visits, and also used the press, radio and posters. Concepción Felix, Kalaw and other feminists toured the country mobilizing the women, with over 500,000 women registered for the plebiscite. When 447,725 voted 'yes', the result was hailed as revealing 'the true and real sentiment of the women towards the question of woman suffrage'. Finally, in September 1937, a law giving women voting rights on the same basis as men was enacted (Subido 1955: 41).

Conclusion

The national struggles against Spanish domination had aroused and involved women who played a significant part, both actively and supportively. Nevertheless, their involvement did not induce them to question the general pattern of family and social structures which relegated them to a secondary role; it seems reasonable to assume that the attitudes imposed on them by the Catholic Spanish culture had been completely internalized by the Filipino women.

With the substitution of American for Spanish rule, the liberation movement flowed into purely constitutional channels; simultaneously, the women's movement became largely confined to such issues as suffrage. Women eventually won the right to vote and also succeeded in getting rid of most of the social disabilities that had been imposed on them by the Spanish. It is significant that even during this period, the women's movement was primarily orientated towards achieving legal equality. They do not appear to have questioned the subordinate position of women in society, as in most other Asian countries, perhaps because of the character of the nationalist movement and the strength of the prevailing ideology. In the Philippines, education served as usual to bring women out of their homes, but did not awaken their consciousness to their subordinate role within the family and society; again, this was due to the strong religious bias of the educational system.

After three years of Japanese occupation during World War II, the Philippines achieved independence as a republic in July 1946 but remained within the American sphere of influence, economically and militarily. The social structures and cultural patterns of the people also continued to be influenced by developments in America. Thus Filipino women have achieved the legal and social appearance of freedom, but they remain in the subservience characteristic of patriarchal capitalist societies.

10. Feminism and Revolutionary Struggles in China

> Women indeed are human beings, but they are of a lower state than men and can never attain to full equality with them.
> *Confucius*

> Women must get educated and strive for their own independence, they can't just go on asking the men for everything. The young intellectuals are all chanting 'Revolution, Revolution' but I say the revolution will have to start in our homes, by achieving equal rights for women.
> *Jiu Jin* (1875–1907) (Spence 1982: 57)

China provides perhaps the best case study of the links between feminism and socialism during periods of social upheaval and revolutionary change. A study of the development of feminism and feminist activity in China and of the ways in which the Chinese experience contrasts with that of other countries provides many useful lessons and insights to those interested in the analysis of such issues as the limitations of bourgeois feminism, the role of feminist struggles during periods of anti-imperialist activity, and the interlinking of reformist and revolutionary feminism in certain periods. A brief survey of the impact of imperialism on China and of Chinese resistance to it will supply the background to such an understanding.

By the beginning of the 19th century, the Manchu dynasty which had ruled China since 1644 was in a process of decline. Revolts had broken out between 1796 and 1804 and again in 1813, and the Manchus were losing their control over the vast territory. The trade in Indian opium, the importation of which was prohibited in 1800, continued to grow with foreign connivance. French, Dutch, British and American ships, using Macao as a base, penetrated as far as Canton where specie (coinage) and opium (which formed 57% of Chinese imports in 1838) were exchanged for tea, porcelain, silk and cotton goods. This limited trade, however, could not satisfy imperialist interests. The Industrial Revolution had inaugurated a period of expansion and Western countries demanded that China be opened up as a market for the goods of its factories and as a source of raw materials. Seizing on attempts by the

167

Chinese to enforce the prohibition on the import of opium, the British waged their first war of aggression on China in 1839–42, the conflict which became known as the First Opium War. Chinese forces were defeated and in 1842 British troops occupied Shanghai. Under the Treaty of Nanking, signed in 1842, China ceded Hong Kong to the British, opened up five ports to foreign trade and residence, and agreed to a large indemnity and to the establishment of a 'fair and regular tariff'. Foreigners were declared exempt from Chinese law, and the Chinese government was forbidden to charge more than 5% tax on imports of foreign goods. Following the British victory, many other Western states, including the USA, France, Belgium and Russia, obtained similar concessions.

But these concessions were not sufficient to satisfy the imperial powers. Seizing on a trivial incident, namely the violation of the British flag in the seizure of a ship, Britain again attacked China, this time together with the French. This was the Second Opium War (1856–60), during which the Chinese were again defeated and forced to make further concessions by the Treaty of Tientsin. More ports were opened up for foreign residence and trade, the importation of opium was legalized, and traders were given internal navigation rights on the Yangtze River, thus enabling the penetration of the vast hinterland of China. In spite of these concessions, even further inroads were made into China in the early 1860s; it was in one of these forays that British forces burned the Summer Palace of the Chinese emperors in Beijing.

The basis for this new type of aggression was the doctrine of extra-territoriality, which imposed imperialist control and ensured the presence of traders, missionaries and foreign agents in China, facilitating the exploitaiton of the country through 'spheres of influence' and unequal treaties. By the 1890s, the foreign nations interested in China included Britain, France, USA, Germany, Italy, Japan and Russia. Taking advantage of the weakness of the Manchu regime, the foreign powers began to exercise further control over the disintegrating empire. In 1898, the Russians obtained a 25-year lease on the Liaotung Peninsula and Port Arthur, and in 1900 annexed Manchuria, thereby challenging the expansionist ambitions of the Japanese. The resulting conflict led to the victory of Japan over Russia in the 1904–5 war and Russia was forced to give up its earlier gains.

Within the country, the Manchu dynasty was unable to combat the inroads of foreign powers on the one hand and the local rebellions on the other. Foreign aggression aggravated the problems of the dynasty:

> It demonstrated their weakness and helped to shatter the dynasty's prestige and image of military invincibility. Economic conditions deteriorated, exacerbated partly by the opium trade, growing Western economic inroads, the payment of the indemnity, and the breakdown of the monetary systems. (Nee and Peck 1975: 6)

In fact, the treaties that were forced on China weakened its sovereignty and threatened the very existence of the Chinese state. It was probably only the squabbling that was rife among the imperialist powers which prevented China's total partition and annexation.

Resistance to foreign aggression and local tyranny took many forms. Between 1850 and 1870, many revolts occurred in various parts of China, the chief among them being the Taiping rebellion. This peasants' revolt was directed not only against landlords and officials, but also against the Confucian gentry and the Manchu regime. Faced with external threats and internal revolt, the Manchus gave further concessions to the foreigners who then helped them to defeat the Taiping rebels. This surrender by the Manchu government to Western interests gave rise to the beginnings of a national consciousness among sections of the Chinese: for example, certain Confucian scholar-officials advocated a 'self-strengthening movement' including the building up of military power with which to combat Western aggression; others advocated confronting the West through 'wealth and power', i.e. by developing China's industries. Many reforms were envisaged, including new schools at which Western as well as Chinese subjects would be taught, the introduction of Western military equipment and methods and the conscription of a national army, in addition to the reform of courts of law and a new principle of recruitment for the civil service.

Conservative reaction set in, however, even before many of these reforms could be implemented. The Dowager Empress took control, attempting to restore the earlier government and make it strong enough to resist foreign invasion. In 1900, this conservative reaction unleashed a popular attempt to rid China of the foreigners once and for all. This was the Boxer Rebellion, the motto of which was 'protect the country, destroy the foreigner'. 'Foreigners' were deemed to include Chinese Christians who were known as 'secondary foreign devils'. The foreign quarter in Beijing was occupied, many legations sacked, and foreigners killed. This led to the occupation of Beijing by British, American and Japanese forces, who ruthlessly crushed the uprising, exacted reparations and enforced an 'open door' policy of free trade.

An internal threat to the feudal regime was also demonstrated by the newly emergent Chinese bourgeoisie. The impact of foreign trade had led to the development of a local class of merchants with linkages to foreign capital. But in addition there was a group of indigenous industrialists and entrepreneurs who had interests in textiles, mining and other manufactures, and were more 'national' in their outlook; they advocated a strong central government conducive to the growth of a national market and were against both the feudal overlords and the foreign aggressors. In such a situation, it was hardly surprising that members of the bourgeoisie, together with intellectuals and other nationalists, led reform movements for the creation of a modern nation state which could resist imperialism and promote China's economic, political and social advance. It was some of these elements who also raised the issue of women's emancipation and women's position in society.

Confucianism and Women

Traditionally, China's dominant ideology had been Confucianism, a body of thought first enunciated by Confucius in the 5th century BC. Confucian ideas were based on the principles of humanity and love. They taught moral self-cultivation and the improvement of the social and political order through moral effort. Confucianists wanted the family to be harmonious, the state to be well ordered and the world to be at peace. In the early centuries AD, Confucianism suffered some decline as Buddhism and Taoism, with their deeper philosophical and metaphysical bases, made headway. In the 11th century, however, the body of Confucian thought was reframed, absorbing in the process some of the philosophical tenets of the other systems.

According to Confucianism, the most important social institution is the family: first because it provides the natural ground for training, and second, because it forms the bridge between the individual and society. Society is seen as comprising five relationships, the characters of which were enumerated as follows:

> between father and son there should be affection, between ruler and minister there should be righteousness, *between husband and wife there should be attention to their separate functions*, between elder and younger brothers there should be order, between friends there should be good faith.

Significantly, three of these relationships were within the sphere of the family and it was these relationships that conditioned the role of women in Chinese society. The 'attention to their separate functions' meant that the husband's responsibility was outside the home and the wife's within it. While Confucianists argued that this envisaged the equality of man and woman, each being supreme in his or her separate area of activity, in reality it hid the existence of double standards for men and women. It meant that the public sphere was for the men and that women were restricted to strictly domestic functions.

The five relationships also stressed the hierarchical order of human society, which in turn meant that each person had to recognize his or her proper position in society. As far as women were concerned, this meant that the male had precedence over the female. This concept was also sanctioned in cosmological terms: as heaven (yang) dominates earth (yin), so does man prevail over woman. It was in order to preserve this hierarchical relationship that Confucianists drew a sharp distinction between the public and domestic spheres. They considered that this asymmetrical relationship was necessary in order to 'restrain sexual indulgence and selfishness which would lead to social disorder, and to establish the different functions of husband and wife' (Deuchler 1977: 4).

The inferiority of women was thus seen as part of the law of nature, and social practice was developed on this basis. The woman was subject to 'Three Obediences': males were always her superiors to whom obedience was due — to her father when unmarried, to her husband when married, and to her son when widowed. This was the subordination of the domestic sphere to the outer public sphere. However, the woman was expected to exert her authority and to assume leadership in the domestic sphere. 'The Confucian image of woman was thus a double one: she had to be modest and submissive, but also strong and responsible. On the level of Confucian idealism, the image was considered virtuous; on the level of daily life, it often meant bondage' (Deuchler 1977: 4).

A man could thus have more than one wife, could divorce her and remarry, but similar rights were denied to women. Rigid codes were laid down for women in the name of moral integrity; they were required to protect their chastity under all circumstances and to swear loyalty to their husbands. A woman also had to accept the 'Four Virtues', which included the general virtue of knowing her place in society, as well as the specific virtues of reticence in speech, attractiveness in person and diligence in housework. These concepts were institutionalized in the form of precise patterns of conduct and behaviour, and became part of the orthodox wisdom on women (Croll 1980: 13–14).

As in many Asian societies, however, there was often a gap between the accepted ideology and the reality; for example, as Croll points out, the class position of the women — divided in traditional society into scholar-gentry, merchants, peasants, artisans and those considered 'lumpen' — often determined their status. Each class was

> associated with a distinctive occupation and life-style which affected the lives of their women by modifying the division of labour, the amount of seclusion and their particular positions in the household. It was the interaction of economic with ideological and physical mechanisms of subordination which finally determined the degree of subjugation and control experienced by women in society and in the household. (Croll 1980: 14–15)

The Challenge to Tradition

While Confucian ideology exercised some dominance over thought in China, it was challenged from time to time, sometimes in controversies within the broad parameters of the movement itself. There had been frequent debates on the subject of women between scholar-officials, reflecting changing opinions on the issue. In the 11th century, reformers like Fan Chung-Yen advocated giving money incentives for widows to remarry; Chu Hsi (1150–1200), on the other hand, opposed their re-marriage (Handlin 1975: 14). Again, during the late Ming period of expanding urban culture in the 16th century, when women were increasingly literate, the debate on women was continued and they were sympathetically portrayed in popular fiction. In 1590, for example, an official, Lu K'un, wrote *Kuei Fan* ('Regulations for the Women's Quarters'), a widely read handbook of moral behaviour for women. Lu K'un showed a sympathetic middle-path attitude to women: he reflected an uneasiness that upper-class women might forget their correct place in society, but at the same time was liberal in his views. Although he based his opinions on the assumption of women's inferiority, he called for due respect to be shown to them and condemned widow suicides, female infanticide and large dowries. He also urged women to master practical knowledge, especially of medicine, and to circulate this among themselves (Handlin 1975: 35–6).

During the Ching dynasty too, scholars continued the debate about the role of women, and the question of their education became an issue in the 18th century (as in Europe). Writing before Mary Wollstonecraft, but in similar vein, Ch'en Hung-mou (1696–1771), a scholar who compiled a book for the education of women, claimed that whatever their social class women could be educated:

> There is no one in the world who is not educable; and there is no one whom we can afford not to educate, why be neglectful only in regard to girls? Just after leaving infancy, they are raised and protected deep in the women's quarters. They are not like the boys who go out to follow an outside teacher; who benefit from the encouragement of teachers and friends . . . when girls grow older, they are taught to embroider to prepare their dowries and that is all. (Handlin 1975: 37)

The creative art of that period also portrays some aspects of the debate on women's education. The novel entitled *The Scholars* by Wu Ching-tzu, published in the 1740s, sympathetically depicted relations between husbands and educated wives. Dealing with a woman who had been trained by her father to write the famous 'eight-legged essays' set for the mandarin examinations, and who ultimately married a talented poet with no interest in studying for examinations, the novel highlights the consequences that follow on divergent types of education (Rankin 1975: 42). At the end of the 18th century the debate on education was continued between Chang Hsueh-ch'eng (who, in an essay 'Women's Education', stated that women should be taught to be modest in behaviour and decorous in speech and not be encouraged to study poetry) and Yuan Mei, who challenged many of the Confucian views on women: he advocated freer contact between men and women, opposed foot-binding and helped women to publish their poetry (Rankin 1975: 42).

In spite of many restrictions imposed by Chinese society on women, the 'usually accepted dark picture', as Rankin has said, needs modification. 'The actual lives of gentry women often deviated markedly from the restrictive Confucian ideal.' There were also women who were active in the 'outer sphere' and participated in warfare and rebellion: Ch'in Liang-yu (d. 1668) sent troops to support the Ming dynasty in time of trouble and K'ung Ssu-chen was active in politics in the period of rebellion in the 1670s. In addition, women poets, artists and writers flourished in the 17th and 18th centuries, especially in those regions of China where there were high levels of education (Rankin 1975: 40–1).

Although Confucianism imposed many constraints on women, an alternative status was visualized in some novels and poetry and was sometimes achieved in reality. One of the most popular stories set in the 6th century was that of the female warrior Mulan, who dressed as a man, replaced her father (who had been a general) and led the imperial troops for twelve years, fighting heroically in many battles and being finally rewarded, without her identity being discovered. In another popular novel, *The Dream of the Red Chamber*, written in the 1790s by Tsao Hsueh-Chin, two of the heroines renounced traditional family life to join a convent of Buddhist nuns, this being another alternative to the rigours of housebound lives. Women also joined some of the secret societies that were a feature of Chinese society, especially in the south: 'Women played a large part in secret societies and those who became leaders were known as "female polished sticks". Many were sworn members . . . they spied out the land, hid the booty and screened the guilty. Women often split off to form autonomous all-female associations as at the time of the White Lotus Rebellion in the 1790s' (Croll 1980: 36).

In the 19th century, when there were major external and internal challenges to the established order, writers began to question Confucian orthodoxy, particularly its tenets on women, and intellectuals and social reformers took up the issue of women's rights. A well-known scholar, Kung Tzu-chen (1792–1841), was opposed to foot-binding and concubinage and proposed an equal standard of virtue for men and women (Rankin 1978: 43). Another sharp challenge came from Li Ruzhen who, in a novel *Flowers in the Mirror* (1825), reversed the sex roles in his 'kingdom of women' where men wore dresses, had bound feet and were ruled by women, who alone were educated and had official positions. This novel, which questioned the basic inequality between the sexes, was later regarded as the first declaration of women's rights and the author himself made the point that 'the essence of heaven and earth is never endowed exclusively in any one sex in particular' (Croll 1980: 38).

Women's associations also appeared during periods of unrest and rebellion. For example, during the White Lotus Rebellion of the 1790s there were autonomous associations of women. The presence of women was also notable in the Taiping Rebellion of the mid-19th century. This great political-religious uprising, based on the accretion of pseudo-Christian notions on traditional Chinese thinking, proclaimed the total equality of men and women; its programme included monogamy, the equal distribution of land, and the prohibition of prostitution, foot-binding and slavery. Influenced by the Hakka women, who had relatively more freedom, women were not only freed from such restrictions, but were allowed to sit for official examinations and take high positions. For fighting purposes, women were organized into a separate army corps under the leadership of Hong Xuanjiao, who was active in battle, 'By the time the capital was established in Nanking there numbered forty women's armies each with 2,500 soldiers. The early women followers, mainly from minority nationalities, had been augmented by numerous village women. Sometimes whole families joined the Taiping force' (Croll 1980: 40). A folk poem of the period describes the phenomenon:

> Women able to follow Hong Xuanjiao
> able to use fire arms, do sword play;
> At Niu Bai Ling, Hong Xuanjiao prepared
> her defences, throwing the enemy with
> broken backs down the hillside.

> (Quoted in Croll 1980: 40)

Many of the Taiping leaders, however, were ambiguous about women's participation and tried to reinforce the Confucian ideal. But even after the defeat of the rebellion itself,

> the military exploits of the women members passed into the folklore of the villages and the experience of the Taipings clearly indicated that women formed one of a number of oppressed groups in the social structure which could potentially contribute to a movement to improve both their sexual and class position. (Croll 1980: 41)

Women's units joined in the uprisings during the Boxer Rebellion of 1900, there being an organization for girls between 12 and 18 and another for widows, known as the Blue Lanterns; married women were not recruited into these groups (Davin 1977: 9)

In this period of change and upheaval, other negative forms of protest were devised by Chinese women to express their rejection of traditional oppressive customs. One was the 19th-century marriage resistance movement in Cantonese areas, where women workers were grouped together in silk production. The movement, which lasted for around a hundred years up to the early 20th century, took the form of women organizing sisterhoods and taking vows against marriage or, if they were married, refusing to live with their husbands. The 'anti-marriage associations' were composed of girls and women who lived together in groups (Topley 1975: 67).

> The rebellious spirit and alternative lifestyle of these primitive feminist associations constituted a consciously deviant form of behaviour. The anti-marriage associations were an expression of opposition to the traditional forces of 'fate' but they remained at the level of rejection and furnished a form of escapism rather than a significant force for change. (Croll 1980: 44)

Another such negative form of protest against family oppression was that of suicide by young women, and by widows in particular. The high rate of female suicides in China became widely known. 'The dramatic public suicides of young Chinese widows in the last century became almost as well known in the West as the Hindu custom of suttee . . . like suttee it made a strong statement about the status of women' (Wolf 1975: 111). The issue of female suicide was also to become an issue among

Chinese radicals and feminists in the early 20th century.

The Reformist Movement

Apart from rebellion, the reaction to foreign aggression took several other forms which had a bearing on the situation of women and attitudes towards them. One was the attempt to establish bourgeois democratic institutions and to develop capitalism within the framework of a monarchical system. Many such reformers were influenced by the West and by the experience of Meiji Japan. The European impact on China led to the appearance of 'Westernized mandarins' and other bourgeois reformers who were interested in saving China from 'national humiliation'. In the 1860s, Western writings became available, especially after the establishment of a school for translators. In 1887, the Christian Literature Society began translating books on religion, political science, law and history. Yung Wing, the first Chinese student to study in the United States in the 1860s, stated that his aim was to 'bring in Western knowledge and turn China gradually into a *civilised, prosperous and strong country*' (*Reform Movement of 1898*; emphasis added).

The leading intellectual of the reformist movement of the 1890s to support women's rights was Kang Yuwei (1859–1927), a scholar from a landlord-bureaucrat family who had absorbed European ideas and in 1891 established the Wanmu Academy which developed into a centre of ideas of political reform. Kang Yuwei travelled widely in Europe, North America and Asia, and in 1895 started a daily paper which expressed the views of the reformists. He wrote a book (which was banned) on the need for re-examining the Confucian texts, showing that some versions of the classics were false, and he advocated the structural reform of Chinese society within a framework of tradition. 'Kang Yuwei did strike at the superstructure of China's feudal society, but he (attempted) to adapt Confucius to the needs of bourgeois reformism, using this ancient "sage" as a stepping stone for the bourgeois reformists to mount the political stage' (*Reform Movement of 1898*: 19). Kang Yuwei frequently sent petitions to the monarch on the need for reform. He also started many societies to propagate his views on the need for China to launch a 'self-strengthening programme' by modernizing the tax structure and currency system, developing industry and mining, creating efficient railway, shipping and postal services, reforming education, and building schools for agricultural and industrial training (Spence 1982: 9–11).

Kang Yuwei's major work was the *Book of the Great Community*, a Utopian vision where the world is described as a sea of bitterness in which all, whether poor or rich, are victims of sorrow. This could be changed to a paradise with 'no state boundaries, no kings . . . where people would be friendly and equal', an equality which includes women. Instead of achieving this through the 'bitterness of iron and blood', he suggested that the 'spirit of compassion' would help to achieve harmony between classes and groups. Although Kang Yuwei's ideas were anti-feudal and expressed the views of the bourgeoisie, like many such intellectuals, he ended by supporting the traditional hierarchies and, in the words of Lu Xun, became 'a protagonist of restoration' (*Reform Movement of 1898*: 18–20). Nevertheless, Kang Yuwei became famous in his time for his champion-ing of women's rights. In his *Book of the Great Community* (1903) he describes women's oppression with great eloquence and indignation. Kang's vision of the future was one where everyone has equal rights, where the traditional family system is abolished, where marriage is a renewable contract, and where men and women dress identically. He wrote with emotion and idealism, not merely of the oppression of Chinese women, but on behalf of all women.

> I now have a task: to cry out the natural grievances of the incalculable number of women of the past. I now have one great desire: to save eight hundred million women of my own time from drowning in the sea of suffering. I now have a great longing: to bring the incalculable inconceivable numbers of women of the future the happiness of equality, of the Great Community and of independence. (Spence 1982: 40–1)

It was during this period of intellectual debate and exposure to Western culture that the Chinese bourgeoisie began to adopt European dress both as a gesture of modernization and as a protest against the feudal Manchu regime which, for example, had imposed the queue (pigtail) as the hairstyle for men. In the late 19th century,

> it became a symbol of shame to Chinese nationalists, especially to those who travelled abroad. Lu Xun mocked those Chinese students in Japan who kept their queues coiled up on their heads 'so that their hats stood up like Mount Fuji' though he knew . . . they would be pinpointed as potential revolutionaries if they returned to China without them. (Spence 1982: 63)

While the reformist and revolutionary men cut off their 'pigtails', women too began to cut their hair short and to wear Western clothes as a symbol of emancipation, gestures which (as in other Asian countries) caused great resentment among the traditionalists.

Women's Education

Due to the separation between public and domestic spheres, women's education had been severely restricted in early China; they were taught only domestic duties and the rules of social behaviour. As in many other countries, however, the issue of women's education as a means of intellectual and social advancement became an integral part of the reformist movement.

The earliest schools in China to impart a Western-style education to girls were started by missionaries of various denominations, after the forcible opening up of ports to foreigners after the Opium War. The first two schools were opened in Ningpo in 1844 and 1847, by Miss Aldersley of the Church of England and the Presbyterian Mission respectively. Other girls' schools were started in Shanghai (1849), Foochow (1851), Canton (1853) and Tientsin (1864); by 1877, there were about 38 girls' schools. In these first years, the pupils were 'slave-girls, foundlings and beggar girls picked up off the streets. Only the very poorest families pressed by the bribes of the missionaries in the form of a cash payment and the promise of food . . . risked sending their daughters to the schools.' The schools were part of the Christian missionary effort, but the missionaries' attempts not only to convert but also to campaign against bound feet led to hostility towards the schools, and in 1877 the Chinese government condemned their activities (Croll 1980: 42–3). Between 1910 and 1919, the number of girls' schools in China increased from 42,000 to 134,000 and students increased from 1.6 million to 4.5 million; in 1920, women were admitted to the universities. Some women, like the writer Ding Ling and five other girls, entered a boys' school in Changsa, thereby causing a scandal. Many Chinese students of both sexes went to Japan for their education during this period, Japan being admired by other countries of Asia for its scientific advances and policies of modernizing and strengthening the country.

In the major cities, girls' schools became centres of social and political agitation; they strengthened their position by forming alliances of girls' schools which then affiliated to the National Union of Students. The new attitude of the girls can be seen in a speech made by a leader of a Girls' Normal School in Tientsin: 'First we bind our feet; second, our minds are bound, third, we are inferiors and servants of our husbands. Today, in the amalgamation of our Women's Society with the Students Union, we are unbinding ancient restrictions' (Croll 1980: 92, 93).

The advantages of access to education, including higher education, were best appreciated by the women themselves. Women writers often experienced a desperate struggle for advanced schooling which was

> a prerequisite for becoming a writer . . . it meant access to ideas, to higher literacy and above all it meant physical and psychological liberation from the confines of home. The elders resisted hard, because they understood, more clearly perhaps even than the rebellious young themselves, that the women's struggle for education marked the end of the old order. (Feuerwerker 1975: 156)

Employment opportunities for women expanded with education and women began to enter the teaching and nursing professions and to become doctors, business women and bankers, a Chinese bank being formed in 1922 in Shanghai. With the development of industries by foreigners and by the Chinese bourgeoisie, women also became the cheapest source of wage labour, being used especially in the textile and silk factories.

Revolt Against the Old Order

The question of women's emancipation and feminism in China was linked intrinsically with the political movements for change that arose as a challenge to imperialism and local reaction. But although such challenges had existed in the 19th century, 'it was in the twentieth century that the real defiance took place'. As Croll has remarked:

> Three embryonic forms of challenge or forces for change, the intellectual questioning of the traditional social institutions, the formation of feminist associations and the linking of the fortunes of women to those of other oppressed groups, combined to give rise to a women's movement in which women began to widely and collectively protest against the traditional role and status assigned to them in the family and in society. (Croll 1980: 44)

As in other countries which were directly colonized, the reformers began to analyze the source of their 'backwardness' and to link this with the low status of women in their societies. The bourgeoisie and intellectuals felt the need to give their country a progressive 'image' abroad and this led to an attack on degrading social practices. In the case of China, this was mainly against foot-binding, an old custom especially prevalent among the gentry, whereby girls' feet were bound and crippled in order to keep them small. This was supposed to be a sign of beauty, but in effect it prevented the mobility of women and reinforced their subordination. The reform leader Kang Yuwei, who had organized the first 'Unbound-Feet Society' in 1892 in Canton, wrote, 'There is nothing which makes us objects of ridicule as much as foot-binding'. He described the harmful physical effects of foot-binding, and in 1898 called for its prohibition. In addition, it was argued that crippled women with bound feet would produce weak children and be unsatisfactory mothers.

Societies against foot-binding were formed which were supported by local reformers and officials and encouraged by foreign women resident in China. In 1902, the Empress issued a decree against foot-binding; incentives were given to promote the campaign, and many men joined societies against the practice and took oaths not to marry women with bound feet. Notwithstanding the fact that the practice was again officially prohibited in 1911, it still persisted especially among the upper classes and in areas where women did not traditionally work outside the home. The issue became an important one not only for male reformers but also for feminists and other women who were breaking with tradition. The revolutionary woman leader Jiu Jin lectured on the subject, showing its links with women's subjection; and, as Davin has shown, many famous women of the upper classes, in refusing to allow their feet to be bound, made the first step in a long struggle to escape a traditional style of life' (Davin 1979: 11).

The nationalist, republican and anti-foreign movements of this period drew women into political activity, in particular after eight powers combined in war against China in 1900. In 1908 women joined the movement to boycott Japanese goods and demonstrated in the streets. As anti-Manchu republican feeling grew, women also joined the revolutionary groups which later became Sun Yat-Sen's Revolutionary Alliance, the best-known women in this movement being his wife, Song Qinling (Soong Ching Ling), He Xiangning, Sophia Chang, Soumay Cheng and Jiu Jin.

Jiu Jin

The most remarkable of the revolutionary feminists of the period was Jiu Jin (Quiu Jin) (1875–1907). Her grandfather and father were officials of the gentry class; her mother was educated, and Jiu Jin was given a traditional education. She was well-versed in the classics, in history and poetry, and also benefited from exposure to books on European, American and Russian history and translations of foreign literature, which were popular among Chinese intellectuals of the period. Living in a period of China's political humiliation by foreign powers and the corruption and decadence of the Manchu regime, Jiu Jin became committed to nationalist and republican politics. Unlike other women, she had the advantage of travel within China when her father was posted to remote parts, enabling her to see the economic and social conditions of Chinese men and women. After marrying a merchant's son, she lived in Beijing where she was exposed to cosmopolitan influences. Deciding to break with the constraints of her way of life and encouraged by her women friends, she left her husband and children, sold her jewellery and went alone to Japan in 1904. In a poem written *en route* to Japan she stated:

> Sun and moon have no light left, earth is dark;
> Our women's world is sunk so deep, who can help us?
> Jewellery sold to pay this trip across the seas,
> Cut off from my family I leave my native land.
> Unbinding my feet I clean out a thousand years of poison,
> With heated heart arouses all women's spirits.
> Alas, this delicate kerchief here
> Is half stained with blood, and half with tears.

(Spence 1982: 52)

By that time Japan had become a centre not only for young intellectuals from China and Vietnam, but also for revolutionaries from neighbouring countries. Many Chinese women who went to Japan for studies in the early 20th century were at the forefront of early revolutionary agitation. Jiu Jin studied for two years in Japan, engaging in political activities among Chinese revolutionary students and becoming one of the best known of Chinese activists. She also formed the first association of Chinese women revolutionaries in Japan, with the aim of agitating against the Manchu dynasty and also liberating the women of China. Jiu Jin wrote in revolutionary journals, became the first woman member of Sun Yat-Sen's group in Japan, and learned riding, fencing and sword play.

One of Jiu Jin's best-known writings is *Stones of the Jingwei Bird*, written in the form of *tanci*, a traditional prose-poetry epic which could be sung or recited. This style of writing was popular among the illiterate and among women in particular. It had existed from the 17th century onwards, becoming a 'truly feminine literature, written by women for women and about women' (translated from Gipoulon 1976: 19). Jiu Jin's book, which was autobiographical, was intended as political propaganda, highlighting both the subordination of China to foreign and Manchu domination and the oppression and slavery of women within the patriarchal system. These themes were presented through the lives of five girls of gentry families, their escape from the constraints of traditional society, their epic journey to Japan, and their involvement in political activities. Returning to China in 1906, Jiu Jin became a teacher in a girls' school and was made the representative of Sun Yat-Sen's party for the province of Chekiang. During this year her activities included the publication of the *Chinese Women's Journal*, the transformation of the girls' school into a centre of revolutionary activity and the organization of a women's army. In 1907, she was implicated in a plot to overthrow the government and was arrested and executed.

Jiu Jin's intense patriotism and feminism were expressed both in her writings and her independent style of life; she caused scandal not only by leaving her family to involve herself in political struggle, but also by riding on horseback, drinking wine and frequently making daring appearances in Western male attire, thereby challenging the traditional Confucian image of a woman. In her writings she stressed the theme of heroic women who could save the country from slavery and also break the chains of their own slavery as women. She was influenced by French heroines of the Revolution, and by the Russian revolutionary, Sofia Perovskaya, a woman from a wealthy family of officials who was executed at the age of 27 for her part in the assassination plot against the Tsar, and who became a 'spell-binding model for Chinese proto-revolutionaries' (Spence 1982: 45). The Chinese influences on Jiu Jin included woman warriors such as Mulan as well as 'heroic figures from Chinese history, fiction and Taoist mythology, and the Buddhist Bodisattvas' (Rankin 1975: 52).

> Every day I express the ardent desire that women be freed from their subjection so that they can become heroines of a free world and can follow the paths taken by Madame Roland, Sofya Perovskaya, Harriet Beecher Stowe and Joan of Arc. I am ready to go to all lengths to achieve this aim. I hope that our two hundred million women do not turn their backs on their responsibilities as citizens. Hurry, hurry, women, save yourselves. (Gipoulon 1976: 27; translation)

Her feminism was linked to her revolutionary politics and to the struggle to rid China of imperialist influence and Manchu domination. To Jiu Jin,

The darkness pervading the world of women appeared to be a particularly painful manifestation of that greater blackness which enveloped the whole Chinese nation. She differed from those reformers who believed women's problems could be solved by correcting the specific abuses that they condemned. Feminism was not an isolated matter . . . but an integral part of the political problems to which she sought solutions. (Rankin 1975: 57)

She wrote in a poem:

> We want our emancipation!
> For our liberty we'll drink a cup,
> Men and women are born equal,
> Why should we let men hold sway?
> We will rise and save ourselves,
> Ridding the nation of all her shame
> In the steps of Joan of Arc
> With our own hands we will regain our land.
>
> (Croll 1980: 68–9)

Jiu Jin was to become a legendary heroine and model for future generations of revolutionary Chinese women, providing the necessary inspiration through her politics, feminism, unconventional life and strong commitment. Soong Ching Ling (Madame Sun Yat-Sen) in later years referred to Jiu Jin as 'one of the noblest martyrs of the revolution' (Soong Ching Ling 1953: 157), and as Rankin has written,

> Women's armies invoked her spirit during the 1911 Revolution, and Sun Yat-Sen attended a memorial service . . . to her in 1912. Under the Republic she was admired by advocates of female independence — Kuo Mo-Jo praised her as the incarnation of Ibsen's Nora — and her determination, valor and self-sacrifice inspired subsequent women revolutionaries. (Rankin 1975: 63)

Women in the Bourgeois Democratic Revolution

The first decade of the 20th century saw an increase in the popular influence of the more radical elements among the Chinese reformers who had grouped under Sun Yat-Sen (1866–1924). Born of a peasant family, he joined a brother who had migrated to Hawaii, and successfully completed his studies abroad, but his life was devoted to political agitation to overthrow the Manchu regime. Sun Yat-Sen organized revolutionary groups and secret societies in China and abroad and after many years of political activity, fund-raising and unsuccessful uprisings, his Revolutionary Alliance finally came to power in 1911.

Sun Yat-Sen's group had been associated with support for women's rights. 'They backed feminist causes, sponsored plays written by and for Chinese women and invoked the powerful image of Qui Jin in their cause' (Spence 1982: 78). Sun Yat-Sen's 'People's Principles' (nationalism,

181

democracy and improving the people's livelihood) were eagerly taken up by women, especially activist teachers and students. For example, the Patriotic Girls' Schools in Chekiang were centres of anti-government activities by teachers and students. Feminism also expressed itself through women's journals which proliferated in the first decade of the 20th century. Among them the *Chinese Women's Journal* was a radical venture started in 1906 by Jiu Jin and Xu Zihua (teachers in Shanghai) and consisted of articles on politics and women's emancipation. Jiu Jin wrote, 'We want to unite our sisters into a solid whole . . . we Chinese women should become the vanguard in arousing women to welcome enlightenment.' Many women's papers were produced, including the first women's daily paper published in Beijing between 1906 and 1908. They were 'a radical departure in the history of the women's movement in China' and although they did not last long and their circulation was limited mainly to students and urban women, 'their appearance marked the first significant expression of a collective feminist consciousness' (Croll 1980: 59).

In the 1911 uprisings against the Manchu dynasty, women were fighters, couriers, nurses and arms smugglers. Many were arrested and some were executed, including actress Jin Jilan for her part in purchasing arms and fomenting rebellion. In 1911, a Japanese journalist claimed that compared with 'modern Chinese women, the militant London suffragette is nothing. Daily she supplies arms and ammunition to her brother revolutionaries and is occasionally arrested with her tunic lined with dynamite' (quoted in Croll 1980: 63). In spite of male opposition, women organized themselves into separate battalions to fight on the republican side, some of their exploits becoming legendary. When the 1911 revolution resulted in the final collapse of the Manchu dynasty and the inauguration of the republic with Sun Yat-Sen as its President, the feminists who had fought against the old order now formed associations for equal rights and the franchise. The militant British suffragist movement seems to have been a source of inspiration. In Beijing, several women's organizations added 'suffragette' to their names; the Chinese Suffragette Society was formed by Tang Junying (who had studied in Japan) with the aim of abolishing foot-binding, concubinage, child marriage and prostitution and of promoting political rights and education for women, the main area of agitation being the right to vote (Croll 1980: 70).

The revolution of 1911, however, failed to realize the expectations of the women; the National Assembly (which had drafted a new Constitution) and the Provincial Assemblies, denied them the right to vote. In response, another organization, the Women's Suffrage Union, led an attack on the assembly which lasted three days. In the onslaught windows were smashed and property damaged, with the result that troops were summoned for protection. The women were also active in besieging the Provincial Assemblies in Beijing and Canton. It is interesting to note that in Canton the men had changed their opinion on the women's franchise issue. Earlier there had been agreement not only on women's franchise but also on allowing them to be members of the Assembly. The Provincial Assembly had been formed in Canton; 'subsequently, however, the men seemed to have regretted their momentary enthusiasm, for soon it was announced that women would have no part in the establishment or running of the Provincial Assembly' (Croll 1980: 72). This led to protests by the women, including deputations, meetings and an invasion of the legislature. But they had little success, and the assembly elected in 1913 was composed only of men.

In 1913, a political shift of power that marked a new phase in China's history occurred when Yuan Shikai, a reactionary war-lord, became President. The laws which banned political and social associations included a ban on suffrage groups and women's journals, and a Chinese newspaper boasted that 'China had shown the way in dealing with suffragettes' (Croll 1980: 78). The new President was able to get a loan from a consortium of great powers to bolster his regime and set about dismantling democratic institutions and trying to make himself emperor. His death in 1916 changed the situation and the war-lords took over power in the provinces. There was no effective central government in China from then until 1927. Sun Yat-Sen, who had withdrawn to regroup his political party, the Guomindang (Kuomintang), came under the influence of Soviet Russia and was in contact with Lenin. Declaring that Russia was 'the only ally and brother' of the Chinese, he sent Chiang Kai-shek to Moscow for military training and in 1924, the Guomindang Congress admitted Communists to the party. Although Sun Yat-Sen died in 1924, the new Nationalist-Communist Alliance began its military moves to sweep the country of war-lords.

The great powers were eager to take advantage of the internal turmoil in China. During World War I, the British, in return for Japanese support against the Germans, had connived at Japanese attempts to reduce China to the status of a Japanese protectorate through unequal treaties:

> The history of Sino-Japanese relations from 1915 to the declaration of war between the countries twenty-one years later is . . . an attempt by Japan to put into effect the paramountcy she claimed to have acquired by treaties . . . and an equally determined effort by China to resist all such claims by every means in her power. (Panikkar 1955: 281–2)

Women and the May 4th Movement

It is in this context that the growth of revolutionary awareness, militant nationalism and feminism in China should be understood. In the years after 1916, a cultural renaissance occurred among Chinese youth and intellectuals, who began to question the basic structures and traditional ideology of Chinese society, including the status of women. The literary and cultural ferment is indicated by the fact that in 1919, 400 new periodicals appeared. The new ideas were expressed most effectively in radical journals like *New Youth*, and *The Renaissance* and in women's magazines such as *The New Woman, Women's Bell, Girls' Daily of Canton* and *The Women's Monthly*. These journals raised all the issues of women's subordination and attacked the old customs regarding marriage; in addition, they publicized the militant activities of British suffragists, translated their articles and, influenced by the visit to China of feminists and birth control pioneers like Margaret Sanger (of the USA) and Ellen Key (of Sweden), published articles on birth control and motherhood. In 1921, the *China Weekly Review* remarked that in that year, the press had 'devoted more space to matters concerning women than in any previous year' (Croll 1980: 81, 87).

In this period, the whole issue of women's subordination, female chastity and traditional marriage structures were questioned by young intellectuals, both men and women. Lu Xun (Lu Hsun, 1881–1936) who was China's leading writer at the time, was also involved in the contemporary debate on women. In his famous article, 'My Views on Chastity' (1918), he was severely critical of Confucian morality, claiming that arguments based on the male and female principles of *yin* and *yang* were 'absolute gibberish', adding that

> Even if there are dual principles, there is no way of proving that *yang* is nobler than *yin*, the male superior to the female. Besides, society and the state are not built by men only. Hence we must accept the truth that the two sexes are equal. (Lu Xun (1918) in *Selected Works* 1980: 18)

Condemning the age-old oppression of Chinese women, he wrote

> These women are to be pitied. Trapped for no good reason by tradition and numbers, they are sacrificed to no purpose. We should hold a great memorial service for them. After mourning for the dead, we must swear to be more intelligent, brave, aspiring and progressive. We must tear off every mask. We must do away with all the stupidity and tyranny in the world which injure others as well as ourselves. (Lu Xun (1918) in *Selected Works* 1980: 24–5)

Lu Xun criticized double standards on the question of chastity and made fun of the allegation that unchaste women were ruining society:

> In what way do unchaste women injure the country? . . . There is no end to the dastardly crimes committed, and war, banditry, famine and flood and drought follow one after the other . . . Besides all government, army, academic and business posts are filled by men, not by unchaste women. And it seems unlikely that the men in power have been so bewitched by such women that they lose all sense of right and wrong and plunge into dissipation. (Lu Xun (1918) in *Selected Works* 1980: 15–16)

Significantly, Ibsen's *Doll's House*, translated in 1918, was very popular in China. Nora's action in leaving her family was keenly debated, even involving a lecture by Lu Xun at the Beijing Women's Normal College in 1923 entitled 'What Happens after Nora Leaves Home?', in which he concluded that without economic independence, her only choice in that society was to starve, to go back or to become a prostitute.

> After leaving, though, she can hardly avoid going to the bad or returning. Otherwise the question arises: What has she taken away with her apart from her awakened heart? If she has nothing but a crimson woolen scarf of the kind you young ladies are wearing, even if two or three feet wide it will prove completely useless. She needs more than that, needs something in her purse. To put it bluntly, what she needs is money. (Lu Xun (1923) in *Selected Works* 1980: 87–8)

Davin has noted, however, that the 'doll's house' for Chinese women was not so much married life but the family into which they were born: 'Successful Chinese Noras avoided arranged marriages, obtained their education, and sometimes even began an independent life in some profession, in most cases as a teacher' (Davin 1976: 13).

The increase in feminist activists during the post-World War I period was also inspired by political ferment. As in other dependent countries, the terms of the 1919 peace treaty ignored China's legitimate demands for the return of its sovereignty. The rights of the Germans in Shandong were transferred to the Japanese, and the concessions obtained by the other powers were left unchanged. The news of this betrayal led to patriotic agitation throughout China, beginning with anti-Japanese student demonstrations and a call for a boycott of Japanese goods on 4 May 1919. The movement spread to students in all parts of the country as well as to intellectuals, sections of the bourgeoisie, and industrial workers in Shanghai who went on strike. The agitation was directed against external and internal forces of imperialism and reaction, the slogans being 'externally, struggle for sovereignty' and 'internally throw out the traitors'. The leaders of the May 4th Movement, who also directed their attacks against the politics and old cultural values of Chinese society, were influenced by nationalist movements abroad (in Turkey, Egypt and India) by the writings of Marx, Kropotkin and Tolstoy and by the visits to China of Dewey, Tagore and Bertrand Russell (Chesneaux *et al*. 1977: 70–1). The outcome of the agitation that began on 4 May was that the Chinese government refused to sign the 1919 peace treaty; however, it succeeded in crushing the popular movement by June 1919. The movement was one of great historical significance, giving a further impetus to nationalism and feminism, as well as being a training ground for future leaders of the Communist Party (formed in 1921), such as Mao Zedong (Mao Tse-tung) and Zhou Enlai (Chou En-lai).

Mao Zedong

It was during this period that Mao Zedong became active on issues affecting women's position in Chinese society. Born to a peasant family of

Hunan in 1893, Mao went to Changsha and studied under the philosopher Yang Chanji, whose daughter Yang Kaihui was to become his first wife. In 1915, Yang Chanji had written an article in which he contrasted the oppression of the Chinese system of arranged marriage with the free choice of spouses in the West. Even before Mao had become fully policitized, he had begun to take a strong stand on issues affecting women (Spence 1982: 131).

Mao was particularly impressed by the student movement in Hunan and the 'unprecedented participation of girl students in Hunan's internal political struggles awakened Mao to the revolutionary potential of women'. In 1918, Mao Zedong and Cai Hesen (Tsai He Sheng) organized the New People's Study Society, which by 1919 had around 80 revolutionary students, many of whom joined the Communist Party in later years. The group included many women students and teachers of the leading Changsha schools, among them Cai Chang (Tsai Chang) who later became an active women's leader. They were explicitly concerned with the woman problem and particularly with instilling in women a consciousness of their potential social and political roles (Witke 1967: 131). Another organization which Mao helped to launch was the 'Society for Work and Study in France'; a girls' branch of this society was formed in the early 1920s to encourage Chinese revolutionary women to study and undergo political training in France. By 1920, there were eleven women students in France, including Cai Chang and Xiang Jingyu. In May 1919, Mao was in the forefront of the agitation, helping to form the students' co-ordinating body; this included the militant girl students who took part in numerous political activities.

The issue which inspired Mao's early political writings was the case of a certain Miss Chao who, on being forced into marriage by her parents, committed suicide on her wedding day in November 1919.

> While in ordinary times this incident might have passed unnoticed, during the . . . May Fourth period it was blown up to become one of Changsha's biggest news stories of the year. Miss Chao's suicide was the subject of at least nine impassioned articles by Mao Zedong which set the style of the "case study", a new genre of May Fourth polemical literature. (Witke 1967: 128)

Mao used the case of Miss Chao to attack the Chinese patriarchal marriage system and blamed the girl's death on society.

> A person's suicide is entirely determined by circumstances. Was Miss Chao's original idea to seek death? On the contrary, it was to seek life. If Miss Chao ended up by seeking death instead, it is because circumstances drove her to this. The circumstances in which Miss Chao found herself were the following:
> (1) Chinese society; (2) the Chao family; (3) the Wu family, the family of the husband she did not want. These three factors constituted three iron nets, composing a kind of triangular cage. Once caught in these three nets, it was in vain that she sought life in every way possible. There was no way for her to go

on living; the contrary of life is death, and Miss Chao thus felt compelled to die . . . It happened because of the shameful system of arranged marriages, because of the darkness of the social system, the negation of the individual will, and the absence of the freedom to choose one's own mate. It is to be hoped that interested persons . . . will defend the honour of a girl who died a martyr's death for the cause of the freedom to choose her own love . . .

If we conduct a campaign in favour of marriage reform, it is first of all the superstitions about marriage that must be demolished, above all the belief that marriages are predestined by fate. Once these beliefs are demolished, the pretext behind which the arrangement of marriages by parents hides itself will disappear at the same time . . . the army of the family revolution will arise in countless numbers and the great wave of the freedom of marriage and of the freedom to love will sweep over China. (Schram 1969: 334–6)

Mao Zedong's concluding article in the series, called 'Against Suicide' was not merely a rejection of suicide as a solution to social problems, but also an appeal to people to resist tyranny and oppression and to die in struggle rather than by resorting to suicide.

My attitude toward suicide is to reject it . . . Man's goal is to seek life. Although suicide results from the fact that society deprives people of all hope . . . we should struggle against society in order to regain the hope that we have lost. It is so much better to be killed in fighting than to take one's life . . . The goal of struggle is not "to be killed by others" but "to aspire toward the emergence of a true personality". If a person does not attain this despite all his efforts, if he fights to the death and sacrifices himself, then he will be the most courageous of all on earth, and his tragedy will make a great impression on men's minds. (Schram 1969: 336)

Agitation by Women

In the 1919 agitation, girls' schools had formed patriotic organizations and groups of girls went out to lecture to women and distribute leaflets; women participated in the mass demonstrations held in the cities during May and June; 1,000 girl students from 15 schools in Beijing protested in front of the President's Palace against the arrest of their colleagues and a special demonstration of 10,000 women was held in Canton to support the cause. The events of 1919 led to the formation of women's associations in the leading cities. In 1921, the press reported that in Canton over 1,000 'militant suffragettes' had held a meeting on equal rights, in a hall decorated with banners demanding 'Equality of the sexes' and 'Give us the vote'. Seven hundred women who marched to the Canton Provincial Assembly to demand suffrage rights were roughly treated (Cousins 1922: 9).

In Changsha, the Hunan Women's Association, formed in 1921 and known as the 'five proposals movement', demanded suffrage, inheritance rights, education, equal rights to work, and free marriage for women. The agitation for the vote was successful and Hunan became the first province to grant women's suffrage, to be followed by Guandong and

Zhejiang (Croll 1980: 96–7). But when a National Congress met in 1924 in Beijing to prepare a Constitution for the whole country, the suffrage proposed was limited to educated men over 25 years. The resulting demonstrations by women in Beijing against their exclusion were broken up by the armed forces.

Sun Yat-Sen's call for a national convention 'to give leadership' to the country received the enthusiastic support of the women's movement. A document entitled 'Proclamation of the Wives and Daughters of Tientsin', issued in December 1924, is a good example of the commitment of women both to national liberation and to their own emancipation. It summarized the current position of women vividly: 'We are still almost a kind of merchandise, we are still slaves. We are not yet human beings. We must still, as in 1915, call for equal rights for the two sexes and for suffrage and employment for women . . .'

It went on to demand 'for the good of all the people', the abolition of unequal treaties, the removal of laws discriminating against workers, improvements in their living and working conditions, including an eight-hour working day, endowment of schools and the promotion of education. The proclamation then proceeded to make demands specific to women, which was almost a litany of women's oppression:

> For the good of women in particular — Let their legal, financial, and 'educational' situation be equal to that of men. They must have dignity and equal rights. From the lowest through the highest grades of elementary school, let boys and girls receive the same instruction and let the special classes "for girls" be eliminated. Let all careers be open to girls, for them to choose. Let daughters inherit as well as sons. Let the old educational system which produced "good wives and tender mothers" (Confucius) be abolished and one created which turns girls into real human beings. Let very severe penalties be imposed upon those who drown little girls, who mistreat their wives or daughters-in-law, who bind their daughters' feet or pierce their ears. Provisions will be made in workshops and in the teaching profession for the necessary rest period for women who are carrying children, without loss of salary or with special financial aid. Let the enslavement of girls, concubinage, the practice of raising a fiancee along with her future husband, and prostitution be abolished. Let the patriarchal family system be replaced by that of the "small family", each married couple constituting a separate household. Let the ridiculous honors formerly given to chaste women — including commemorative arches, etc. — be abolished. Let a man who is contemplating marriage with a young woman or with a widow first be able to enter into a social relationship with her which will allow him to get to know her. Let the right to divorce be granted to women who are unhappy in their marriages. Let the freedom of young women who do not want to marry be respected. (Chesneaux *et al.* 1977: 179–81)

While the agitation for the suffrage and women's rights had been an urban middle-class phenomenon, led by students, teachers and intellectuals, the working-class women were also militant during this period of industrial unrest and strikes. In 1922, a period of many strikes including that of 50,000 Tangshan coal miners, women workers struck in the silk mills of Shanghai, the first important industrial strike by Chinese women (Chesneaux 1977: 144). Organized by the Society for Promoting the Welfare of Working Women, the strike called out women, estimated at between 20,000 and 60,000, in 70 silk factories. The immediate cause was an increase in working hours; the demonstration of women strikers had banners calling for a ten-hour day, increased wages and a day of rest every two weeks. The strike was crushed, many strikers were arrested and the women's union office was closed down; as a contemporary journal noted, however, the women's strike indicated 'that a new phase of the women's rights movement is opening in China' (quoted in Croll 1980: 106).

Women and the Revolutionary Struggles of the 1920s and 1930s

For an understanding of the strong currents of feminism and the backlash against feminism that emerged during the years of revolution and reaction, it is necessary to recall the turbulent historical events in China. By 1926, the nationalist armies of the Guomindang-Communist Alliance had succeeded in ridding part of the country of war-lords, but the revolutionary successes in town and country produced a change in policy by the right-wing Guomindang and the Chinese bourgeoisie, who turned upon their Communist allies. A bitterly fought struggle resulted in a victory for the right wing and the severe repression of Communists in 1927. 'The unions were dissolved, strikes were banned, the peasant unions were liquidated, the Communists were hunted down and militant workers were fired' (Chesneaux *et al.* 1977: 147).

In the following period, a government under Chiang Kai-shek was set up at Nanjing (Nanking) based on collaboration with the West. After the failure of the strategy of urban uprising, the Communists regrouped and changed their tactics to armed peasant struggles led from 'red bases'. When these red bases in South China were defeated, the Communists organized the Long March of 1934 under the leadership of Mao Zedong, and established liberated areas in the north-west. The Japanese invasions of Manchuria in 1931 and of North China between 1933 and 1935, and the general Japanese aggression against China in 1937, caused the political situation to change, and in 1937 a tacit alliance against the Japanese was reached between the Nanjing government and the Communists.

From its inception in 1921, the Communist Party had championed equality of rights of men and women and the right of female suffrage, protective measures for women workers and the abolition of discriminatory legislation. A women's section of the party was started in 1923, under the leadership of Xiang Jingyu, a teacher who had been a May 4th activist and had lived in France from 1919 to 1922, where she had joined a

Marxist study group. In 1923 she was a Central Committee member of the Chinese Communist Party and was also involved in organizing women working in Shanghai silk and cigarette factories (Spence 1982: 142). Croll has stated of Xiang Jingyu that she 'saw no future in a movement which conceived of the struggle as primarily that of women versus men or the pursuit of individual happiness within a monogamous family and had for its platform the "vote", "individual liberty" and "free love".' She further stated that women's rights without social change was without meaning. Criticizing the suffragists, Xiang Jingyu wrote that they did not have 'the courage to take part in the real political movement — the national revolutionary movement — the prerequisite to the movement for women's rights and suffrage and emphasised the need for intellectual women to combine with working women' (Croll 1980: 120–1).

From 1925 to 1926, Xiang Jingyu followed a course in Moscow at the Communist University of the Toilers of the East, which had opened in 1921. The Chinese Communist Party attached great importance to the training of women cadres and regularly sent women to this course. One hundred Chinese students were enrolled in 1924 and 10% of these are estimated to have been women. The programme of studies included Marxism, the world revolutionary movements, the Soviet Communist Party, the history of the labour movement and the women's movement; some military training was given during the vacations. Many of the best known of the Chinese women students who attended this course worked on women's issues on their return. In addition to Xiang Jingyu, they included Tsai Chang, who returned to organize women workers and later joined the political department of the Revolutionary Army, and Chen Pi-lan, who edited *Chinese Women* in the mid-1920s (Price 1975: 19). From 1926 to 1930, the Sun Yat-Sen University in the Soviet Union gave a similar training course and several Chinese women participated; of these, Meng Ch'ing-shu and Tu Tso-hsiang were successively heads of the party's women's department in 1931 and Chang Ch'in-ch'iu was in charge of work among women in the Oyuwan Soviet in 1931 (Price 1975: 20).

The nationalist Guomindang Party also had an active women's section led by Soong Ching Ling and He Xiangning, who headed the party's women's department formed in 1923. At the first party congress in 1924, resolutions were passed on equal rights for women and female employment, education and labour laws. When the historic alliance took place in 1923 between the Guomindang and Communist parties in the hope of achieving national unity and independence, it gave a great impetus to the women's movement. Activists from both parties worked together in the Women's Department to train leaders to mobilize women. Women's Day on 8 March was celebrated in Canton each year from 1924 to 1927, in which year 25,000 women participated (Croll 1980: 124).

As a result of this activity, important women's associations grew up in the provinces, especially in Guangdong, Hunan and Hubei. The nationalist armies, which were liberating the country from the regional war-lords in the northern and central parts of China, had teams of women who travelled with the armies to mobilize and politicize the women of the area. In the liberated areas, many reforms concerning women were carried out, especially after 1926 in Hankou where divorce rights, protection of servants and prostitutes, and women's right of inheritance were proclaimed and women's working hours were reduced (Croll 1980: 135, 143).

The women's movement was an important casualty of the rupture in 1927 between the Guomindang of Chiang Kai-shek and the Communist Party, and the consequent civil war. Not only was the Women's Department disbanded, but the short-haired activist women became targets and thousands were killed, including the Communist, Xiang Jingyu.

Two Policies

In the period following these events, two distinct policies towards women were followed in the Guomindang-controlled areas under Chiang Kai-shek on the one hand, and the Communist bases on the other. In 1931, the Guomindang government introduced a civil code which again prohibited foot-binding, and allowed freedom of choice in marriage and divorce by mutual consent (with the children's custody going to the father) and political, civil and property rights to women. These reforms were mainly to benefit the urban bourgeoisie and the wealthy. But the reactionary, sexist features of the Guomindang regime were to show up in the ideology of patriarchy and male supremacy promulgated in 1934 in the New Life Movement of Chiang Kai-shek, 'a neo-Confucian revival which emphasised ascetic self-discipline and obedience to the leader'. The early Guomindang policies of the 1920s were replaced by conventional programmes under the leadership of Soong Mei Ling (Mme Chiang Kai-shek): these emphasized welfare activities, hygiene, child care and relief work (Davin 1979: 16).

One of the sharpest critics of Mme Chiang Kai-shek's movement was her sister Soong Ching Ling, who joined the Left Guomindang after Sun Yat-Sen's death and remained active in Chinese politics even after the 1949 revolution. In the 1920s and 1930s, she travelled widely and spoke on many platforms on subjects which included the issue of women's role in the revolution. In 1927 while in Moscow she wrote:

> One of the principal tasks of the Revolution in China is the emancipation of over two hundred million women from the bondage of semi-feudal and mediaeval social ideas and customs. As long as this great human mass is not liberated, a real revolutionary change, not only in the institutions of the country, but in the general life and thought of the people will not be effected. (Soong Ching Ling 1953: 22)

In her denunciation of the New Life Movement which sought to

191

restore Confucian morality, Soong Ching Ling was very outspoken:

> Instead of reviving anachronistic Confucianism, it is of utmost importance for us to eradicate all remnants of feudalism in rural as well as urban life. We must cleanse the Chinese mentality and free it from the cobwebs of Confucianism ideology which block our cultural development. Revival of Confucianism is pure reaction disguised as concern for social order . . . In the 'New Life Movement' there is nothing new to be found. (Soong Ching Ling 1953: 97, 103)

In the 20 years of revolutionary activity of the Chinese Communist movement after 1927, the question of mobilizing women for the struggle and simultaneously improving their position in the liberated areas was the strategy followed. In 1927, Mao Zedong described the forms of oppression (the 'four thick ropes') that bound the peasant women of China. This much-quoted statement was a forthright declaration of women's subordination, recognizing the 'feudal-patriarchal' ideology of the oppression of women:

> A man in China is usually subjected to the domination of three systems of authority (political authority, clan authority and religious authority) . . . As for women, in addition to being dominated by these three systems of authority, they are also dominated by the men (the authority of the husband). These four authorities — political, clan, religious and masculine — are the embodiment of the whole feudal-patriarchal ideology and system, and are the four thick ropes binding the Chinese people, particularly the peasants. As to the authority of the husband, this has always been weaker among the poor peasants because, out of economic necessity, their womenfolk have to do more manual labour than the women of the richer classes and therefore have more say and greater power of decision in family matters. With the increasing bankruptcy of the rural economy in recent years, the basis for men's domination over women has already been undermined . . . With the rise of the peasant movement, the women in many places have now begun to organize rural women's associations; the opportunity has come for them to lift up their heads, and the authority of the husband is getting shakier every day. In a word, the whole feudal-patriarchal ideology and system is tottering with the growth of the peasant's power. (Mao Tse-tung 1967: 44)

The mobilization of both peasant and urban working-class women was attempted in subsequent years. Women propagandists travelled with the Red Army, explaining Communist policies to the villagers, as they moved across the country and formed women's associations. In the Red Army School in the Jiangxi (Kiangsi) province, which trained 2,000 cadres between 1931 and 1933, there was a special women's detachment; led by a woman, Kang K'o-Ching, it was made up of peasant women who received six months' training before being sent to the rural areas (Price 1975: 20, 23).

In the Jiangxi Soviet, which existed from 1931 to 1934, laws were formulated that recognized equal status for women and their freedom in marriage; women's departments were formed in all party organizations for the implementation of the new laws. The Decree Regarding Marriage issued by Mao Zedong in 1931, epitomizes the spirit of the new laws:

> Under feudal domination, marriage is a barbaric and inhuman institution. The oppression and suffering borne by woman is far greater than that of man. Only the victory of the workers' and peasants' revolution, followed by the first step toward the economic emancipation of men and women, brings with it a change in the marriage relationship and makes it free. In the Soviet districts, marriages now are contracted on a free basis. Free choice must be the basic principle of every marriage. The whole feudal system of marriage, including the power of parents to arrange marriages for their children, to exercise compulsion, and all purchase and sale in marriage contracts shall henceforth be abolished.
>
> Although women have obtained freedom from the feudal yoke, they are still laboring under tremendous physical handicaps (for example, the binding of the feet) and have not obtained complete economic independence. Therefore on questions concerning divorce, it becomes necessary to protect the interests of women and place the greater part of the obligations and responsibilites entailed by divorce upon men. (Schram 1969: 337)

Women were also encouraged to participate in political work and to join the city and village soviets, the number of women in many of these organizations rising to 24% of the representatives in 1934:

> women were encouraged to attend schools and in some evening courses more than two-thirds of the pupils were women. Efforts were made to explain the policies behind the popular slogans. 'Extinguish the feudal forces', 'Struggle for the freedom of marriage' . . . 'Cut the hair short and unbind the feet' and 'Oppose the Three Commands of Obedience and Four Virtues'. (Croll 1980: 192–3)

In 1934 when the Jiangxi base had to be abandoned after encirclement by the Guomindang, the Red Army broke out of the region and embarked on the Long March of over 6,000 miles. The marchers included 50 women who, 'despite the arduous route . . . undertook political and educational work, nursing duties and collected provisions from the peasants' (Croll 1980: 198). On finally reaching Yenan in Northern Shanxi and expanding its base from there, the Communist Party formed peasants', workers' and women's organizations in the liberated areas, and began to build up the women's movement in areas that were poor and backward (where bound feet and female infanticide still prevailed) and which showed initial resistance to the Red Army's women in uniform. Separate associations of women and women's co-operatives drew the peasant women into political activity, into social production and into the war effort against the Japanese. A women's militia trained them in guerrilla activity, espionage and sabotage. Women were also urged to join class organizations of peasants and workers and in the liberated areas were given suffrage rights.

During the Yenan period, several institutions trained women leaders and activists, including the K'ang-ta (Anti-Japanese Military and Political University), the North Shensi Public School, Yenan University and the Chinese Women's University. At the K'ang-ta for example, 'women . . . prepared for mobilization work through military drill, physical labour in production campaigns and course work on the united front and problems of the Chinese revolution.' The Chinese Women's University which opened on Women's Day 1939 lasted for two years under the direction of Wang Ming and his wife, Meng Ch'ing-shu, who had studied in Moscow. The students were women from peasant and middle-class backgrounds. The curriculum included Marxism, problems of the Chinese revolution and the Communist Party, military education, hygiene and the women's movement. According to Price, 'feminist concerns were subordinated to general revolutionary objectives', but nevertheless, women made remarkable progress during this period:

> Women were exposed to educational experiences that were largely identical to those of men. Women were recognized as a potential leadership resource and during their training at Chinese communist schools, prepared for the same roles as men. In theory women were expected to perform functions far removed from household duties: to anticipate work assignments abroad or far from their homes; to see themselves as a part of the vanguard of a vast social, economic and political movement attacking traditional values and division of labour. (Price 1975: 21)

Even though new laws were promulgated and propaganda carried out among both men and women, sexism still prevailed and Chinese women criticized the prevailing attitudes. In 1942, the famous writer Ding Ling (Ting Ling), who was editor of the literary page of the *Liberation Daily* in Yenan, wrote a critical essay on 'Reflections on March 8 Women's Day', in which she admitted that although women in Yenan were better off than elsewhere in China, they were still subjected to the double standards of the men. Ding Ling's independent critical writing on this and other issues led to her being deprived of her positions and exiled to work in the countryside (Spence 1982: 289–95).

In the subsequent years of war and revolutionary struggles which culminated in the victory of the Chinese revolution and the proclamation of the People's Republic of China in 1949, women continued to be in the forefront of the movement. Many debates were held on the theme of women's liberation and revolutionary struggles, and on the role of women in a liberated society.

Conclusion

A study of the early years of the revolutionary movement in China serves to show the importance of the women's struggle as an essential component of the political struggle. As Jiu Jin asserted in 1906, women's slavery and the slave status in which China found itself could not be separated. The remarkable and continuous struggles of Chinese women in the years before 1911, in the uprisings led by Sun Yat-Sen against the Manchu government in 1911, and in the revolutionary struggles for liberation from the war-lords, the Japanese aggressors and the right-wing forces of Chiang Kai-shek (from the 1920s to 1949), serve to show that the issue of women's liberation *was an issue of the revolution* and not a side issue to be tackled after the revolution. One could not cut off three of the thick ropes binding the Chinese people, described by Mao Zedong in 1927, and leave uncut the rope that bound women. Nor could a woman wait until after the revolution before breaking what Mao Zedong referred to as the three iron nets forming a triangular cage that imprisoned women (i.e. Chinese society, a woman's own family and her husband's family). Feminist consciousness, far from being a diversionary matter, became part of the revolutionary consciousness and this may clearly be seen from a study of Chinese experiences in the years of revolutionary struggle.

11. Women Reformists and Revolutionaries in Vietnam

> I only want to ride the wind and walk the waves, slay the big whale of the Eastern sea, clean up the frontiers and save the people from drowning. Why should I imitate others, bow my head, stoop over and be a slave? Why resign myself to menial housework?
>
> *Trieu Thi Trinh*, peasant woman leader of a rebellion in AD 245 (Marr 1981: 99)

The history of the nationalist movement in Vietnam, in which women participated to a significant extent, presents certain dissimilarities with the other countries we have dealt with; it is one of the few movements that was able to move from a nationalist, anti-imperialist struggle straight into an anti-capitalist, socialist struggle. It also reveals some specific characteristics linked to French imperialism. French colonial policy veered between two viewpoints: first, the doctrine of assimilation based on the idea of union between the colonies and the metropolis and on the concept that the colonies should be brought within the cultural sphere of France and adopt its language, customs and values; second was a doctrine of association which implied indirect rule and economic development as well as respect for indigenous customs and traditions (Grimal 1978: 59). These two tendencies vied with each other in French Indo-China; the offer of union with France, made to the Indo-Chinese after World War II, was the culmination of the policy of assimilation. The two concepts of assimilation and association were to influence the specific character of the Vietnamese nationalist movement. It absorbed, on the one hand, some of the liberal and internationalist ideals of the French Revolution and, on the other, it developed a distinct sense of the national identity of the Vietnamese people. The women's movement that developed alongside the nationalist movements also shows, more than in other countries, the impact of libertarian ideals.

The northern part of Vietnam — the Red River delta which was then known as Tonkin — came within the orbit of Chinese imperial power from the first century before Christ. The small, rice-growing river basins to the south were loosely associated during the late Han period, becoming known as Annam, 'the dominion of the South'. The southern coastal area and the delta of the Mekong, known as the kingdom of Champa, were inhabited by the Chams, a sea-going people who worked as traders and fishermen; they also cultivated rice, using an ingenious irrigation system. The kingdom of Champa was an outpost of Hindu civilization; the literary medium was Sanskrit, and Saivism with elements of Hinanyana and Mahayana Buddhism formed its religion. The Chams were under continuous pressure from the Chinese and from Annam, but they maintained a precarious independence until finally being overrun and subjugated by the Chinese in the 15th century.

Cham society was both matrilocal and matrilinear, and Cham culture played an important part in forming the culture of Vietnam, mitigating the effects of the Confucian ideology which had come with Chinese suzerainty. Such aspects of female oppression as foot-binding were therefore not practised in Vietnam. Nevertheless, the general tenets of Confucianism that impose a subordinate status on women became dominant in social practice: while never completely successful, particularly among peasant women, such sustained indoctrination did have a major impact; women internalized submissive norms almost to the point of believing them to be natural law (Marr 1981: 191).

Chinese overlordship of the area was neither continuous nor stable. Popular uprisings occurred frequently, bringing military action by the Chinese to retore the area to subject status. It is a significant fact of Vietnamese history that women played an important role in these uprisings, sometimes even leading them. These early heroines of the resistance have figured prominently in Vietnamese consciousness. Among the most outstanding were the famous Trung sisters, Trung Trac and Trung Nhi who, in 43 BC, led an army of 80,000 with women generals, and successfully drove the Chinese from the country. Trung Trac ruled the country for three years until defeated by the returning Chinese, which caused the sisters to choose the traditional way of keeping their dignity by committing suicide. The Trung sisters became national heroines: 'a popular cult developed around the spirits of these two women, and individual villages also kept alive the names and exploits of their twenty or more female lieutenants' (Marr 1981: 198).

Similarly honoured was Trieu Thi Trinh, a 19-year-old peasant girl who, in AD 248, led a rebellion against the Chinese and succeeded in achieving a short-lived independence for Vietnam; on being defeated, she too committed suicide. Trieu later became a legend: 'The stories that grew up about her tell us much about both the dreams of Vietnamese women and of the fears of the men who fought, followed, or heard of such women in subsequent centuries. According to a late eighteenth-century account, for example, Trieu . . . was nine feet tall . . . and was able . . . to walk five hundred leagues in a single day' (Marr 1981: 198).

Despite the adoption of Confucianist ideology, a perusal of Vietnamese history shows that the position of women there tended to be better than in China. During the Le dynasty, which spanned the 15th to 18th centuries, women had equal inheritance rights, could own property and, if there was no son, could keep the extra land allocated by law for ancestor worship. These rights were enumerated in the Hong Duc Code which was promulgated in 1483 and remained in force till the end of the 18th century. The Code also contained provisions that sought to secure the personal rights of women, who were protected from abuse, abduction or sale by members or servants of powerful families. Women were also given the right to divorce for neglect or abandonment by the husband. The basis for granting such rights to women has been attributed to an attempt by the Vietnamese leaders, after the defeat of the Chinese, 'to separate its identity from China's by incorporating traditional laws and customary practices in their legal and political framework' (Truong 1984: 5).

The Tay-Son peasant uprisings took place between 1788 and 1802 and the leader of the rebellion ascended the throne for a short period. Women were prominent in this struggle. Bui Thi Zuan, the wife of a Tay-Son leader, joined in the armed struggle against the ruling lords and continued the battle even after the other leaders had fallen; she was eventually captured, tortured and killed. Under the Nguyen dynasty, which succeeded to power after the Tay-Son rebellion was crushed, 'the country was pushed back to its feudal age suppressing all voices protesting against the prevailing oppressive social conditions including those of women'. All the clauses pertaining to women's rights under the Hong Duc Code were withdrawn (Truong 1954: 7). There was a reassertion of the Confucian Code with its rigid patriarchal rights.

Criticism Through Poetry

Opposition to the Confucian ideology regarding women and their inferior status was often expressed in literary work. For example, at the end of the 18th century, Nguyen Du (1765–1820) wrote an epic poem, *The Tale of Kieu*, which became nationally popular and was regarded as a Vietnamese masterpiece. It recounts the misfortunes of women in the person of a rich and talented woman, Kieu, who was bound by Confucian constraints and was forced by circumstances to become a prostitute, concubine, servant and nun, before she found happiness with her first lover. *The Tale of Kieu* was written in the people's language, *nom*: 'It became so popular that after only a few decades it had become widely known by all social strata . . . Illiterate people knew long passages of it by heart and recited it during evening gatherings.' The work was also popular for its content: 'the denunciation of oppressive and corrupt feudalism, of greedy and wily mandarins, of unscrupulous "traders in human flesh" is most incisive' (Vien 1977: 61). What is most remarkable about the poem is its unorthodox and non-Confucian approach to sexuality. The heroine freely chooses.

her lover and even falls in love a second time, whereas 'the puritanical society of that time demanded that a woman remain absolutely faithful to one man until her death' (Vien 1977: 62). Moreover, in a society where the Confucian principle of chastity (*trinh*) was the predominant ideology governing the conduct of women, Nguyen Du's *Tale of Kieu* 'created a scholarly storm for over a century with, among other things, his revisionist interpretation of chastity' (Marr 1976: 374). The poem highlights the suffering of women and also attacks the traditions of decaying feudal society. 'How tragic is women's fate', wrote Nguyen Du, and it is interesting that his poem was used in later years as an allegory of the tragic fate of Vietnam under colonial rule.

A well-known woman poet of the early 19th century was Ho Xuan Huong, who had access to education because her father was of the scholar gentry. She adopted the classical forms, but used a popular language that could be understood by the people. Her feminist poetry on free love, unmarried mothers and equality of the sexes, and her bold attacks on polygamy and double standards of morality, caused such a scandal that her works were forbidden; this was hardly surprising since her poems challenged all the norms of Confucian patriarchy: 'To marry and have a child, how banal! But to be pregnant without the help of a husband, what merit!' (Bergman 1975: 35).

Vietnam and French Imperialism

By the time the European powers came to Vietnam in the 16th century, two powerful feudal families — the Trinh and the Nguyen — effectively controlled the northern and southern parts of the country. The monarchy established by the Le dynasty two centuries earlier had been gradually reduced in power due to a succession of weak rulers and was by this time merely nominal. The Dutch and English merchants set up trading posts in Hanoi early in the 17th century. The French followed soon after and became very active in the area, though their presence in the initial stages was largely confined to Catholic missionaries; it was actually a French missionary who first Romanized the Vietnamese script.

In 1773, the two brothers Tay-Son led a successful peasant uprising, heavily defeating the ruling families. But one of these families, the Nguyen, was able to re-establish itself in power with French assistance. In 1802, Gia Long of this family crowned himself Emperor of Annam; the concept of Chinese suzerainty still held such sway, however, that he received his formal investiture from the Emperor of China.

French influence in Vietnam thereafter increased. In 1858, as other European powers were carving out spheres of interest for themselves in the East, the French decided that they should tighten their hold over Vietnam. A French naval expedition captured Saigon in 1859. The campaign was concluded by the Franco-Annamite Treaty of 1862, which ceded the southern area — the Mekong River delta and its hinterlands — to the French, opened up ports in Annam and Tonkin to French trade, and gave the French an indemnity of 20 million francs. Not satisfied with the economic potential of the Mekong delta, the French later aspired to control the northern, more populous and more prosperous Red River delta. They attacked and took Hanoi in 1873 and, after a gruelling campaign, forced the Emperor Tu Duc (1848–83) into another unequal treaty in 1874 (the Treaty of Saigon) under which he accepted French direction of his policies and conceded trading rights, particularly in tin. The French thus acquired protector status over Vietnam.

Following further campaigns designed to consolidate their control, the French virtually annexed Vietnam in 1883, installing a puppet of their choosing, Dong Khanh, as emperor. The subjection of the country to French imperialism was thus ensured by the monarchy and the court, which had initially used French assistance in their internal struggles. Tu Duc, for example, even dismissed from office those mandarins who had advised resistance; other sections of the people, however resisted the French. As Vien says:

> While the royal troops offered only weak resistance, that of the popular forces was powerful and protracted, and compelled French imperialism to wage a long and costly war. But the defection of the monarchy undermined the efforts of the Vietnamese patriots. The king and high dignitaries . . . gradually became agents of the foreigners and put themselves at the latter's service by repressing the people's patriotic movement. (Vien 1978: 10)

Many women were active in these resistance movements against the French. For example, one of the leaders of a nationalist organization near Hanoi between 1883 and 1885 was a woman named Nher, wife of a patriot Tu-So who had been executed. Nher led attacks on the French and local pro-French forces and organized a resistance base; on being defeated she exiled herself in China; Commander Khuy, daughter of the leader of an insurrection in 1880, took over leadership of her father's forces on his death, and two peasant women, Co Bac and Co Giang, were active leaders of peasant resistance against the French, beginning in 1873.

After establishing control, France brought the three territories of Tonkin, Annam and Cochin China into one administrative unit, although the three areas had different modes of political control. French law applied throughout Vietnam and members of the higher judiciary were all French. Attempts were also made to spread French culture and to win over sections of intellectuals. However, a nationalism that unified all the people emerged and became a force that the French were never able to suppress. In Tonkin in particular, nationalism had a revolutionary character; an excessive rural population exerting great pressure on land was its base. In Cochin China, where agricultural expansion under French aegis had eliminated the remnants of the feudal aristocracy, nationalism was more reformist and channelled itself into normal political activity.

Many young people supported the anti-feudal measures which they hoped would lead the country in the direction of needed reforms. However, the French were so severely repressive of opposition that most nationalist parties and groups were compelled to work underground.

Resistance of the Intellectuals and the Issue of Women

Resistance of an anti-colonial nature also came from liberal scholars and other middle-class intellectuals. In 1907, Luong Van Can and Nguyen Quyen started the Dong Nghia Thuc (Tonkin Study Institute) in Hanoi which was supported by many intellectuals. The organization held study programmes and conferences and became a forum for debate on contemporary problems. Its journal, *Dang Co Tung Bao*, was critical of traditional society and those with conservative views; it called for reforms and industrial development, and published books and translations of Rousseau and Montesquieu. These activities had a clear anti-colonial bias and it was hardly surprising that after a year the French colonial authorities closed down the institute and deported the activists. While radicals were penalized, the more moderate scholars also suffered harassment. For example, Pan Chu Trinh, a scholar who advocated reform and called for the abolition of the monarchy and the mandarin system, was arrested in 1909 (Vien 1978: 47). Women also had a significant share in the work of the institute. Several women attended lectures on history and politics, and two of them taught languages there. On the cultural level, a dramatic presentation of the exploits of the Trung sisters was attempted (Marr 1981: 200).

Women were also among those imprisoned for nationalist activities. One of them recorded her views on French atrocities against prisoners in a poem written in blood on a prison wall; the poem ended with the lines: 'All women should be united in the struggle against the French colonialists in order to survive' (Bergman 1975: 48).

As in many Asian colonies of the period, the question of the status of women became an issue in Vietnam, particularly in the first decade of the 20th century when Vietnamese intellectuals were questioning colonial rule and the subordination of the Vietnamese people, including its women. Many Vietnamese had been influenced by the protest movements in China, by the activities of Sun Yat-Sen, and by the historic victory of Japan in 1905 over Tsarist Russia. This event, together with the Russian revolution of 1905, influenced nationalists in India, China, Iran and Vietnam: they saw the Japanese victory as the first important triumph over European aggression, and the Russian revolution as a victory over tyranny.

The best known of the Vietnamese intellectuals of the period was Phan Boi Chau (1867–1940). Already in the 19th century there were movements of patriotic scholars who opposed colonialism; these included the Can Vuong, a movement of scholars against French colonialism, formed in 1886, which supported the monarchy and aimed at restoring traditional values. Phan organized the reformers of the Can Vuong movement into a new group, the Duy Tan (Renovation), the aim of which was the 'reorganizing of forces within the country coupled with the sending of men abroad to study new military and political techniques and the preparation for armed struggle' (Vien 1978: 45–6). Japan was then considered to be the most advanced nation of Asia and many men and women from other Asian countries went there to study. Together with a Vietnamese prince, Cuong De, Phan Boi Chau promoted a Dong Du (Go East) movement and organized Vietnamese students to study in Japan. By 1908, several hundred students whose fathers had been in resistance movements against the French had been sent to Japan. The Japanese, however, betrayed the Vietnamese; they recognized French conquests in Vietnam in return for monetary advantages and expelled the Vietnamese from Japan. The French authorities arrested members of the Duy Tan, and Phan Boi Chau and Cuong De escaped to China (Vien 1978: 46).

The Chinese revolution of 1911 and the proclamation of the republic was to influence Phan Boi Chau, who in 1912 formed a new group, Viet Nam Quang Phuc (Association for the Restoration of Vietnam). This organization was anti-imperialist and republican, and advocated violent acts to alert public opinion, such as the assassination of high French officials and the organizing of armed resistance on the Vietnam-Chinese frontier. These attempts failed and the group was disbanded in 1914. Phan was subsequently arrested and sentenced to life imprisonment, which was later commuted to house arrest.

Phan Boi Chau also concerned himself with the status of Vietnamese women; he wrote a drama about the Trung sisters, making the characters in the drama 'colonial and anti-colonial archetypes in first-century AD costume'. His aim was:

> to focus on the role of Vietnamese women in the forthcoming anti-colonial struggle. He posed a situation where women were expected to act more according to the same patriotic principles that motivated their fathers, husbands and brothers than from deference to Confucian concepts of female servitude and obligation. (Marr 1976: 376)

Education for women was another issue raised by these intellectuals. During the earlier periods, Confucian tenets had guided educational practice and the situation was broadly the same as in China. Now, as in other Asian countries, the need was felt for a limited amount of education for middle-class women: an education that would make them 'presentable' without exposing them to 'false' doctrines of emancipation. In 1917, for example, Pham Quynh (1892–1945), editor of a monthly journal, *Nam Phong*, catering to Vietnamese literati, wrote an essay on 'The Education of Women and Girls', attacking the 'medieval mentality' which kept women illiterate, but warning of the danger of losing traditional values. With the approval of the French colonial bureaucrats, he formulated a curriculum in Vietnamese for women of the upper bourgeoisie, which included appropriate Vietnamese literature, history, natural sciences and some Chinese and French literature, and another for girls of the middle class which included sewing, arithmetic and some basic French. The courses were clearly designed to produce suitable wives for the men of these classes. However, even these modest proposals met with opposition. A well-known writer, Nguyen Ba Hoc, commented that 'The higher that women are able to study, the more income they will squander, the more their sexual desires will be inflamed, the more destitute they will end up' (Marr 1981: 202–3).

Pham Quynh continued the debate in his journal, and persuaded Suong Nguyet Anh (1864–1921), a poet, to take up the issue of women's education. She was the daughter of Nguyen Dinh Chieu, an independent scholar who had refused to collaborate with the French and in the 1850s had written *Luc Van Tien*, a story of the fluctuating fortunes of a young scholar which, in effect, was a critique of colonial society and an assertion of traditional pre-colonial values. Suong Nguyet Anh became the editor of *Nu Gioi Chung* ('Women's Bell'), a journal published in Saigon in 1918 with French financial backing. The journal was very cautious in attitude and non-political in content, and only lasted a year. As Marr has pointed out, however: 'Nevertheless, the fact that a woman had taken editorship of a major periodical, however briefly, provided concrete impetus for other upper-class matrons to venture beyond the family' (Marr 1981: 205).

Despite these endeavours, women's education in Vietnam made slow progress. Even as late as 1924, only 72,000 of a total school age population of 600,000 children were in the educational system; of these, girls numbered only 10,000, that is 3% of female children (Bergman 1975: 47). Under these circumstances, the structures of informal education became important. Informal classes for girls sprang up, providing an increasing market for textbooks intended primarily for them. Some of these texts merely taught the 'three obediences' and 'four virtues' of Confucian ethics; others emphasized nutrition, health, hygiene and other accomplishments appropriate for future housewives. There were also notable exceptions, however. A textbook for girls, published in 1926 by Trinh Dinh Ru, had a strong patriotic and anti-colonial content, including a story of a Japanese girl who contributed her savings to the war against the Russians in 1905. It was also very emphatic on the necessity for female education: 'A country that really wants to overcome ignorance must not only have boys studying, but also girls . . . we are born in Viet Nam and that makes Viet Nam our motherland. Those who keep on referring to France as the motherland are really wrong' (Marr 1981: 209). Trinh Dinh Ru also advised women teachers to circumvent the restrictions of the colonial regime and to inculcate a greater awareness of the country's concrete situation among their students (Marr 1981).

In 1927, Phan Boi Chau wrote a text intended for use in schools on the subject of women's role in society; the book was cautiously worded, the message to young women being that they should be 'mothers to the nation'. But while encouraging obedience to parents and responsibility to children, Phan urged that husband and wife should share all tasks, whether in the home or in society. He referred to the life of Madame Roland and her republican role during the French Revolution and to the example of Chen Yu-hsiu, a Chinese woman who had studied law in Paris and had taken part in the 1911 Chinese revolution. If asked 'Do you have a husband?', girls were urged to say, 'Yes, his surname is Viet and his given name is Nam' (Marr 1981: 210–11).

Phan Boi Chau's clearest call to action came in 1929 when he published *Van De Phu Nu* ('The Women's Question'), in which he strongly criticized traditional attitudes to women and attacked the moderates who wanted to limit women's rights to the use of cosmetics and a smattering of French:

> He bluntly advised young women to stop putting so much time and energy into trying to alter the sexist attitudes of their elders — especially the men — and instead put themselves into women's collectives, teach each other, share the labour . . . Women should not feel an absolute obligation to marry. But for a woman who did prefer marriage, he urged her to select . . . a man who was in the first instance a dear "inner" friend and comrade, and only secondly a husband in the "outer" or formal sense. (Marr 1976: 389)

In the conclusion of this remarkable book, Phan Boi Chau appealed to women not to put their hopes in changes through the educational system and not to depend for support on the family system or on officials, but to involve themselves in action — a message that was a call for women to join movements that would change the course of history. He wrote:

> Talking about swimming and being scared to jump in the river, or wishing to climb and being afraid of mountains will never get you anywhere . . . Sisters, don't put hope in today's educational system; it is completely rotten. Don't depend on the family; its future is uncertain. Don't look to the officials; they are in the dark and want to keep you there too. The real and only way to strengthen your intellect is through practical execution (thuc-banh), relying on your intuitive knowledge and on perception of the new wind and tides about in the world. (Marr 1976: 378)

Women's Organizations and Publications

A remarkable feature of the late 1920s was the upsurge of women's associations and books and journals concerned with women's issues. In 1926, Dam Phuong and other women of Hue formed the Women's Labour Study Association (WLSA). In making the opening speech, Phan Boi Chau cited examples of women's movements in Japan, China, Britain and the USA, and urged Vietnamese women not to spend their time only in the kitchen and on playing cards, but to join the wider struggles. During these years, a spate of books appeared which dealt with famous

Vietnamese heroines and women in Korea and China who had resisted foreign aggression; a Chinese book on *Three Brave Heroines of Russia* was translated into Vietnamese. The objective of the WLSA was 'to build for women a sense of self-development by means of new occupational skills and within the parameters of both Eastern and Western virtue and independence'. It started classes for girls in Hue, imparting some income-generating skills such as raising silkworms and weaving. Dam Phuong toured the country speaking on the status of women and helping small groups of women to organize. For example, a women's press (Nu Luu Tho Quan) was active in Go Cong, and by 1929, 16 books on women's issues had been published (Marr 1981: 217).

The moderate stance of Dam Phuong came under attack from women who had begun to be more articulate on the issue of women's rights and were critical of the emphasis on handicraft production. In the association's journal, *Phu Nu Tung San* ('Women's Review') in 1929, its woman editor, Tran Thi Nhu Man, condemned the traditional family and social structure. As Marr has noted: 'She and others were coming to the opinion that one-sided chastity, arranged marriages and female occupational and educational restrictions would have to be tossed out of the window along with the more obvious "three submissions" and "four virtues" ' (Marr 1981: 218). Tran Thi Nhu Man also wrote a historical analysis of women's oppression from primitive society to the present, which had a Marxist content. She claimed that capitalism, while turning women into factory workers, had also raised their consciousness; while exposing the exploitation and oppression of Vietnamese women, she advocated 'socialising the family' and stated that 'in contemporary Vietnamese social conditions, woman must live not only for the family, but also for herself and for society' (Marr 1981: 231).

The political situation of 1929 and 1930, a period of nationalist agitation and increasing Communist activities, made the French very wary of any type of criticism. Women's groups came under suspicion as the authorities were alert to their possible spreading of subversive ideas. In Annam, about 20 books on women were banned and five books published by the Go Cong women's press were banned in 1929, its woman editor Phan Thi Bach Van was fined, and the publishing house closed down for 'disrupting peace and security in the region by means of literature and ideas'. Tran Thi Nhu Man's writings were also banned and the Women's Labour Study Association ceased its activities. When the WLSA was allowed to resume in 1930, Dam Phuong was replaced by a conservative, the journal ceased its social criticisms, and published 91 recipes in place of the normal lead essay of social commentary; by 1931 the WLSA was organizing a handicrafts fair with official French patronage (Marr 1981: 218–20).

In 1929, radical women regrouped around a new journal, *Phu Nu Tan Van* ('Women's News'), published by a woman, Nguyen Duc Nhuan, with the financial backing of sections of the local bourgeoisie, among whom were successful women entrepreneurs. The journal, which lasted five and a half years, dealt with a wide variety of topics and provoked controversy; at the height of its popularity it had a circulation of 8,500 a week and was read by both men and women. Apart from giving news of Vietnamese nationalists and revolutionaries and their trials and imprisonment, it was 'at once catalyst, conceptual testing ground, and disseminator of new ideas . . . the attacks on sexual segregation, polygamy, wife-beating, religious escapism and superstition . . . had the most effect' (Marr 1981: 226). In 1933, the editorial policy shifted further to the left under the guidance of a woman poet, Nguyen Thi Kiem, and a Trotskyist philosophy teacher, Phan Van Hum, before the journal was banned in 1934.

Kiem had made a successful tour of Central and North Vietnam in 1934 speaking in public on women's issues, including the attitude of men to progressive women; this resulted in smears about her 'loose behaviour'. Marr describes the way such criticism was tackled:

> Public oratory was one test of female nerve that *Phu Nu Tan Van* encouraged . . . Reaction to these new, energetic, publicly involved females was not all positive . . . *Phu Nu Tan Van* . . . was accused of encouraging women to abandon their families, and a caricature of the liberated Vietnamese woman emphasized her alleged desire to be equal with men in gambling, extra-marital sex, and conspicuous consumption. Eventually the editors responded in detail to articles . . . that condemned or mocked female activism, and when rumour campaigns occurred, they brought the matter out into the open for all to judge. (Marr 1981: 227)

Women and Revolution

The high level of participation of Vietnamese women in revolutionary activity and the left political movement was the result of several historical factors. The country had a long tradition of heroines who had led armed resistance movements against foreign and local oppression; thus from its beginning, the Vietnamese left movement utilized this tradition to highlight the role of women in revolutionary activity, linking the issues of colonial oppression and women's oppression. In addition, during the 1920s and 1930s the Vietnamese were in close contact with the Chinese Communists, and the example of Chinese women revolutionaries in nationalist and revolutionary movements was a source of constant inspiration. The Vietnamese revolutionary leaders, especially Ho Chi Minh, were particularly concerned to mobilize Vietnamese women in the revolutionary movement.

Ho Chi Minh (1880–1969), the son of a self-taught scholar, studied at several French schools in Vietnam before leaving the country in 1911, as a cook's assistant on a ship. He travelled widely for several years, visiting many parts of the world; in 1914 he arrived in London and worked for a short time at the Carlton Hotel as assistant pastrycook, before going to France in 1917. Under the name of Nguyen Ai Quoc, he was active in the French left and became a member of the Communist Party. While ekeing out a living in Paris, he consistently highlighted the colonial question in the Communist Party and mobilized Vietnamese abroad in the agitation for national liberation. In Paris, he helped to produce a journal, *Le Paria*, which claimed to be a 'forum of colonial workers' and presented the 'colonial rebellion in global terms' (Lacouture 1968: 36). In 1919, after the end of World War I, Ho became part of a delegation that pleaded the cause of Vietnam at the peace conference.

Ho Chi Minh's years in America and Europe coincided with periods of militant suffragist activity and the emergence of outstanding women in the Communist movements of China, France, Germany and the Soviet Union, whose points of view he would have encountered at Communist Party and Comintern meetings of the 1920s. One of his early articles, written in Paris in 1922, was on the rape of Vietnamese women by the French; in it he appealed to women in France to mount a campaign in support of the oppressed women of Vietnam (Bergman 1975: 47). Ho left France in 1923 for Moscow where he attended the Comintern Conference in 1924. He went to China in 1925, but after the attacks on Communists he escaped in 1927 to Moscow. Returning to Asia he lived in Thailand in 1928 in the guise of a Buddhist monk (Lacouture 1968: 44–9).

In June 1925, Ho and other revolutionaries organized the Association of Vietnamese Revolutionary Youth, publishing a news sheet *Thanh Nien* by which name the group was to become known. Their policies were nationalistic but within a Marxist framework. The first stage of activity was mobilization of the traditional peasantry and conscious elements of other classes in a bourgeois-democratic programme. In 1926, however, Ho wrote a more obviously Marxist document, *The Road to Revolution*, which emphasized the need for a Marxist party to lead the revolution (Lacouture 1968: 45–6). In Vietnam, as in India, Sri Lanka and Indonesia, the late 1920s was a period of increased nationalist agitation and working-class unrest. Although small in numbers, the Vietnamese workers were both militant and politically active, and in 1928 and 1929, a wave of strikes occurred in the petroleum, cement, railway, rubber, textile and other industries (Lacouture 1968: 50).

There was also a link-up between the revolutionary Vietnamese groups abroad and at home, which resulted in the formation of the Communist Party in 1930. A ten-point programme put forward by the party on its formation included the realization of equality between men and women. In 1930, the party, holding that a separate organization was needed to mobilize women and to promote the battle for equal rights, formed the Vietnam Women's Union which was affiliated to the party. The demands were for reduced rents, equal pay, two months' paid maternity leave, an end to dangerous work for women, and an end to forced marriage, polygamy and the practice of holding women in contempt (Bergman 1975: 52). The Communist Party's interest in the question of women is apparent from the Programme of Action that was adopted at its first plenary meeting:

> The Party must free women from bourgeois ideas, eliminate the illusion of "equality between the sexes" expounded in bourgeois theories. At the same time, it must enable women to participate in the revolutionary struggles of the workers and peasants; this is an important task. For if women do not take part in these struggles, they can never emancipate themselves. So it is necessary to fight the feudal or religious customs and superstitions in their way, give women workers and peasants intensive political education, arouse their class consciousness and enable them to join the organizations of the working class. Political work must be carried out not only in towns but also in the countryside, among the poor peasants and all working women. (Mollander 1981: 14–15)

The late 1920s saw an upsurge of militant activity by various groups in all parts of the country. In 1927, a nationalist group (Viet Nam Quoc Dan Dang) was formed by Nguyen Thai Hoc, a teacher who had been inspired by the Guomindang of China. The garrison at Yen Bay was infiltrated by this group and in February 1930, a mutiny broke out, but it did not result in a widespread uprising. The rebels were crushed; the events caused a stir in Vietnam, however, and led the Vietnamese Communist Party to meet and analyze the mistakes of the uprising. In mid-1930, a more spectacular uprising took place in the densely populated, impoverished area of North Annam where the peasants seized large estates, shared out the land among the people and established soviets in the Nghe Tinh region. The movement was crushed by the French and many of the leaders were killed or imprisoned. Ho Chi Minh was sentenced to death in his absence, but escaped to Hongkong and from there to Shanghai and later to Moscow (Lacouture 1968: 55–60). In 1932 the Communist Party's Programme of Action condemned the French for reinforcing the feudal oppression of women. It stated that 'the most advanced sisters in Indochina have already engaged themselves in the heroic struggle', and claimed that 'the most numerically oppressed group' in the country were the women workers in plantations and in industry (Marr 1981: 237).

Many women were active in the party in the early 1930s, the most notable of them being Nguyen Thi Nghia and Nguyen Thi Minh Khai. The former had received a primary education and, though from a well-off family, had taken up political activity among the factory workers in the Nghe Tinh region; this was the area in which peasant uprising had occurred during which, 'for the first time in Vietnamese history, lands were distributed to women, and women took part in public meetings and political education classes' (Bergman 1975: 52). The French finally recaptured power and brutally repressed the people of the area. Nguyen Thi Nghia, who, together with many other women, had been active in the soviets, was arrested and tortured. Before her execution at the age of 23, she wrote 'I'm going to die and I wish all the sisters who remain will continue the struggle until the revolution succeeds and women gain equal rights with men' (Bergman 1975: 52).

The participation of women in this revolutionary upsurge in Nghe Tinh was important. Many poorer women joined the Communist movement and a leaflet entitled *To Our Women Compatriots* stated that sexual equality was inevitably bound up with revolutionary success; French officials also commented on women's involvement in this uprising. Marr reports that during this period 'colonial soldiers tried to break up a demonstration by tearing off the clothes of one female activist . . . other women proceeded to strip off their clothing in solidarity, then marched to jail with the first activist, chanting Communist Party slogans en route' (Marr 1981: 245).

Nguyen Thi Minh Khai

The other heroine of this epoch was Minh Khai (1910–41), whose father was a railway clerk and mother a petty trader. In her youth, Minh Khai had been influenced by Phan Boi Chau's writings and, leaving home at the age of 15, she became an active revolutionary. In 1931, she went with Ho Chi Minh to the Hong Kong office of the Comintern for training. The British authorities detained her, but she evaded deportation and escaped to China. She was arrested and jailed there for three years and on her release in 1934 was smuggled to Moscow where she continued her studies. In 1935, she addressed the seventh Congress of the Comintern and used the opportunity 'both to stress the greater oppression of women workers and peasants in colonial . . . societies and to chide the congress for not having more female delegates from advanced Western parties' (Marr 1981: 244; Molander 1981: 17). Minh Khai was well received by the delegates, including Lenin's widow Krupskaya. On her return to Vietnam via Berlin and Paris, she worked for the Communist Party among women and peasants, and was made secretary of the Saigon-Cholon party branch. She became the leading woman Communist Party official during this period and married the head of the party's Overseas Leadership Bureau, Le Hong Phong. Both were to die in the 1940s: Minh Khai was arrested for being involved in a revolt in Nam Bo and executed in 1941 by the French, and Le Hong Phong died under torture in 1942 (Marr 1981: 244). She is still commemorated as one of the country's leading heroines and her picture hangs on the walls of many homes (Molander 1981: 17).

The Debates on Women

The united front against Fascism put forward by the Comintern in 1935, and the assumption of political power in France by the Popular Front coalition of Socialists and Communists from 1935 to 1939, made for changes in the political climate in Vietnam. In 1936 the French Popular Front government granted amnesties to several Vietnamese Communists in jail, and gave the party the right to work legally. During this period Communist activity increased: there were three Communist municipal councillors in Saigon by 1937; several left-wing journals were published, and on May Day 1938, Socialists and Communists had a joint demonstration which included 'tens of thousands of workers together, French and Vietnamese standing side by side' (Lacouture 1968: 63).

This era of open action saw an increase in the activities and influence of the Vietnamese Communist Party, which extended into the area of women's rights. Demands put forward by the Communists for working women included equal pay, two months' paid maternity leave, legal protection for domestic servants and wet nurses, and the implementation of laws against women working in mines or at night; for middle-class women, demands were made for equal inheritance rights, access to jobs in the service sector; and on behalf of all women, demands were made for better education and training opportunities, freedom of marriage and divorce, the right to vote and the abolition of polygamy (Marr 1981: 237).

In 1937 and 1938, the Communist Party passed resolutions emphasizing the importance of female participation in politics, and ordered party branches to form special women's committees and to organize working women in textile and other factories where they predominated. The party had a journal for young people with a women's column in which young women were urged to be daring and 'to have the courage to liberate themselves'. It was during this active period that the large May Day rally in Hanoi in 1938 included many thousands of militant women marching in paramilitary fashion; this rally was addressed by a young woman, Bao Tam, who demanded the 'progressive eradication of barriers differentiating men and women' (Marr 1981: 246).

The debate on women by Marxists was also much in evidence during the years of the Popular Front. In 1938, Nguyen Thi Kim Anh wrote *The Question of Women* in which she analyzed the role of women under earlier modes of production, contrasted the limited goals of bourgeois feminists in Europe with socialist feminists such as Clara Zetkin, Alexandra Kollontai and Krupskaya, and praised the initiatives of the Third International. In Vietnam, women were 'the most exploited group of all in family and in society', and revolutionaries were urged therefore to give more attention to the feudal and capitalist forms of women's oppression (Marr 1981: 238).

Again in 1938, a two-volume study was published on the role of women (*Sisters' Life* and *Sisters, What Is To Be Done?*) by Cuu Kim Son and Van Hue. The first volume contained a detailed account of the conditions of various categories of working-class, petty-bourgeois and upper-class women and the social questions that affected all women, such as marriage, divorce, prostitution, polygamy, lack of education and sexual repression. A quotation from Lenin that housewives should be able to manage affairs of state was also used in the text. It is interesting to note these authors' suggestions for adapting the Confucian 'four virtues' for women to modern circumstances: 'labour' (*cong*) would include factory work and political work; 'physical appearance' (*dung*) included strong physical movements (as opposed to the required languid postures) and expressions of eagerness and anger; 'appropriate speech' (*ngon*), instead of meaning a 'sweet' manner of talking, should include bold talk, whether in convincing people to join the liberation struggle or in firmly telling husbands that they were wrong; the fourth virtue of 'proper behaviour' (*hanh*) was not subservience, but commitment to the freedom struggle and resistance to exploitation (Marr 1981: 240).

In the second volume, Cuu Kim Son and Van Hue linked women's liberation to that of the working masses. They gave credit to the efforts of bourgeois and petty-bourgeois women of the earlier phase, but said that these had placed more importance on changing customs than on economic and political transformation. But even changes in customs such as riding bicycles, wearing European clothes and refusing to blacken their teeth (as custom demanded) had been pioneered by 'lower class wives or mistresses of Frenchmen' (Marr 1981: 241). The authors reflected the 'united front' tactic of the period in suggesting that women of all classes should pool their resources (theoretical knowledge, skills in speaking, writing and organizing demonstrations) to join in a united front on issues such as anti-Fascism, female literacy, anti-superstition campaigns, occupational training and social service (Marr 1981: 241).

At the end of 1939, the political climate changed drastically. World War II broke out, France was occupied by the Germans and a collaborating government was installed at Vichy. In the colonies, the period was one of repression of nationalist and revolutionary movements, and this was particularly so in Vietnam where the revolutionaries had been active. The Communist leaders were arrested; some of them, including Pham Van Dong and Vo Nguyen Giap, escaped to China where they linked up with Ho Chi Minh. The armed struggle within Vietnam continued and in 1940, the Zone of Bac Bo (Tonkin) was declared liberated; Ho Chi Minh, after 30 years, was able to return to his country to organize further resistance and to build up the Viet Minh. In 1942, while on a mission to China, Ho was captured and imprisoned for 15 months; he was then released by the Chinese to head the struggle in Vietnam against the Japanese, who had occupied the country. The Vietnamese revolutionary movement thereafter fought against the Japanese, the French and the USA. Women participated at all stages of this struggle with distinction and contributed to its success at various levels.

Conclusion

In Vietnam, as in other countries, the women's movement was able to carve out a specific role within the nationalist movement; more forcefully in a sense, because it was able to assert itself equally in the subsequent phase of socialist revolution. However, the process of modernization — the spread of education, literacy, expansion of humanist and socialist thinking at one level and the creation of new classes with their own economic interests — contributed to the development of new ideas on the role of women; in the process, the traditional Confucianist ideals were shattered and Vietnamese women were enabled to fight as equals with men for national liberation. Many outstanding women, including Madame Binh, came to the forefront during these years of struggle.

The tasks of reconstructing the Vietnamese economy and society occupy the energies of the people today. Within this process, women have achieved equality with men in education and in the economic and social spheres. The obvious discriminations against women in education, in employment and in marriage are no more. In this sense the struggle of the Vietnamese women has succeeded in its objectives. However, this equality is not reflected in an adequate presence of women in the Vietnamese economic and political structures. Moreover, the ideology of the women's movement in Vietnam has not developed to the point of questioning the family structures or the notions of female sexuality that perpetuate the subordination of women.

12. Women and Resistance in Korea

> Should we only use the word civilisation and not adopt its content; . . . should we only be intoxicated by the beautiful words of male and female equality and not cultivate our capacity for equality . . . should we only adopt Western hair styles . . . and dress and not create the situation that requires it . . . should we only be proud that we do not do sewing and not learn more important skills; and should we only be proud of escaping from ordinary kitchen work and not learn more important work?
>
> Editorial in *Puin* ('Woman') 1922 (Park 1977: 109–10)

The history of feminism in Korea forms an interesting exception to developments that have been discussed in other chapters in this volume. Korea was not colonized by any Western imperialist power, but at various times in its history it came under the suzerainty of its more powerful neighbours, China and Japan. The people of Korea had to struggle in order to assert their national identity, and feminist agitation formed an important part of that history.

Until the beginning of the Christian era, Korea was an assemblage of tribal groups who practised a *shamanist* faith and believed in the virtue of venerating tribal ancestors. Women were as free as in other tribal societies; there were numerous female *shamans* who performed the roles of priestess, healer and diviner. About 2,000 years ago, however, the tribal groups found it necessary to organize themselves into larger and stronger political organizations, partly in order to resist Chinese aggression. The three kingdoms of Silla, Paekche and Koguryo were the results of these processes, with Silla ultimately establishing its hegemony over the entire Korean peninsula in the 7th century AD.

An important event that influenced the development of Korean society was the introduction of Buddhism in the 4th century, first into the kingdom of Paekche and subsequently into the other kingdoms. It appears that ruling groups first embraced Buddhism, believing that it would function as a force to unify the various tribes. Buddhism did not really diminish the role of women, although the power of the *shamans* was reduced; the tribal gods were absorbed into the Buddhist pantheon and faith in the powers of *shamans* continued, particularly among the lower classes. Women enjoyed equal status with men in Buddhist practices, but did not play a leading role as under *shamanism*; many became nuns and donated large tracts of land to the new temples that were established.

Kinship still continued to be the dominant factor in social relationships, as is evident from the fact that queens were chosen to reign over the Silla kingdom when the male line of the royal family had died out. Queen Sondok reigned over Silla in the beginning of the 7th century. She is spoken of in the Korean annals with great respect and was succeeded by another woman, her cousin, Chindok. It is obvious that family lineage mattered more than sex. Even in the 9th century, a king who died without an heir was able to nominate as his successor his sister, who reigned as Queen Chinsong (Kim 1976: 26–8).

However, Confucian ideas had begun to infiltrate into Korea in the 6th century; the ruling groups found that its system of values was more useful than Buddhism in organizing a hierarchic and authoritarian kingdom. By this time the Buddhist monasteries had become wealthy landowners and entered into a period of degeneration. Temples had become centres of debauchery, so much so that in 1009, women were prohibited from becoming nuns; a later edict prevented women from even visiting temples (Kim 1976: 83).

With the decay of Buddhism, Confucian ideology assumed complete dominance over Korean society, including the women. Society became rigid and stratified along hierarchical lines with a woman deriving her status only from that of her father, husband or son. As in all Confucian societies, women were restricted to the domestic sphere and the role in public life that they had previously enjoyed was severely curtailed (Deuchler 1977: 4). There were, of course, certain modifications dictated by Korean culture: both patrilineal and matrilineal descent was recognized; women had equal inheritance rights and widow remarriage was not frowned upon; divorce was possible, although it was easier for a man than for a woman to obtain one; and a wife was totally subservient to her husband. The list of offences for which a wife could be sent away (the seven evils) is an interesting illustration of Confucian values: disobedience to parents-in-law, bearing no son, adultery, jealousy, hereditary disease, garrulity and larceny. A manual enumerated the various rules of conduct for women according to strict Confucian values (Kim 1976: 35).

We may note here an apparent contradiction within this structure. This period saw the beginning of the tradition of Kisaeng — the women entertainers. These were beautiful women mainly from the lower classes, who were trained in a special institute, the Kyobang, to be professional entertainers who could sing, dance, play instruments and engage in lively and witty conversation. Their duty was to entertain at court and at the houses of the nobility; no feast or party was complete without them. These entertainers very often also became victims of sexual oppression, but they existed outside the boundaries for women fixed by the Confucian system. Some of them became strong forces in the polity acting from 'behind the screen', as is said in Korea (Kim 1976: 54).

The Mongols, who had established themselves in China as the Yuan dynasty, invaded Korea in 1231 and gained a degree of suzerainty over the country. Peace was concluded only on condition that the Korean kingdom would pay a heavy tribute, Korean princes would marry Mongol princesses (one actually married Kublai Khan's daughter), and artisans, eunuchs and women would be sent to Beijing as demanded. Numerous stories of this period describe the various stratagems adopted by parents to prevent their daughters being sent off to Beijing. With the fall of the Yuans in China, the Mongol grip on Korea also became looser; after a period of civil confusion, a Korean general named Yi asserted himself in 1392 and founded the Yi dynasty which reigned till 1912.

The new dynasty introduced certain economic reforms including some redistribution of land which gave rise to a new class of landowner — officials who used Confucian values to maintain and reproduce an ideology that sustained their economic status. Confucian texts were widely propagated, using movable-type printing processes that were brought into use in the 13th century (Kim 1976: 82).

An inevitable consequence of the reinforcement of Confucian values was a tightening of control over women. It was widely felt that the Buddhist influence and the chaos of the Mongol invasion had helped to loosen women's morality, and action was quickly taken to counteract this. In 1432 the *Samgang haengsil-to* (*The Three Principles of Virtuous Conduct*) was compiled and published. This laid down guidelines for female behaviour, illustrating them with stories of 'virtuous women' (Kim 1976: 84). A woman of true Confucian virtue had to follow certain rules of conduct. A woman of noble birth could not play outdoor games nor enjoy the mountains or the riverside. A woman could not participate in any social activity without the permission of her husband or the head of the family. A woman could not walk in her garden or go out except under specific circumstances. When she went out her face had to be veiled. Women did not have names, being identified only by their relationship to their menfolk. When married, she belonged to the family of her husband. If widowed, she could not remarry. Marriage was a matter to be arranged by the family and the woman had no voice in the selection of her husband. She was totally confined to the domestic sphere; in fact, *anae* ('inside person') was one of the words for wife. This restriction was manifested even in the architecture of Korean houses, which were divided into two parts: an outer part reserved for men and for receiving visitors, and an inner part for the female members of the household, which they seldom left. This segregation was to be seen in the houses of all classes, although there was some laxity of the rules among women of the poor classes (Kim 1976: 85–6). This Confucian family system with its emphasis on domination by the male persisted in Korean society until modern times.

Changes in the Yi Period

Education played a great part in initiating and maintaining women in the Confucian ethic. By the 17th century, Korea had developed a rather elaborate system of education with schools at the national, district and village levels. These were exclusively for boys, however, designed to prepare them for the mandatory examinations and with curricula that were restricted to the Chinese classics. The general view of education for women was reflected by Yi-Ik, a Confucian scholar of the 18th century, who said: 'Reading and learning are the domains of men. For a woman it is enough if she shows the Confucian virtues of diligence, frugality and chastity' (Kim 1976: 154). It was felt that these virtues could best be inculcated by informal family-centred education at home, but even this process was regulated by the state. In the cities, responsibility for educating the women of the family was placed on the chief householder; in rural settlements, a respected elder was appointed to visit homes and talk to the girls. While the general subjugation of women to male authority was thus buttressed by ideological and state authority, three classes of women still managed to retain some freedom, i.e. the *shamans*, healers and Kisaeng.

Shamans, of whom about 70% were women, continued to tell fortunes or placate the spirit of nature, areas in which Confucian ethics played no role (Kim 1976: 133). Women healers formed a similar category, as it was deemed immoral for a male physician to examine women patients; they were generally recruited from the lower classes and given a training in acupuncture and midwifery. Their professional skills gave them a degree of autonomy not enjoyed by other women.

The Kisaeng were also able to survive, though becoming subject to tighter regulation by the state. By virtue of their skill in the arts of entertainment, they too enjoyed a degree of independence denied to the ordinary women of traditional society. It is also noteworthy that a large proportion of Korean women poets and novelists came from among the Kisaeng (Kim 1976: 139).

The Struggle Against Foreign Intervention

Due to its geographical position, Korea had always been prone to intervention from China and by the Mongols, but from about the 18th century intervention from other sources began with the flow of Western influences. The first reaction of the Korean kingdom was to try to resist these influences and to adopt a policy of isolationism. Two factors prevented this, however: the first was the strength of the Western powers; the second was the growth of a movement among young Korean intellectuals for a programme of modernization along Japanese lines. These elements were impatient with the delaying processes of the Korean state and tried to take power into their own hands with an attempted *coup d'état* in 1884; even though there was Japanese support for this attempt, it failed.

Nevertheless, the impetus for modernization was too strong to be denied. Korea entered into commercial treaties with Japan, the USA, England, Germany, Russia and France by 1886, and opened up the ports of Pusan, Inchon and Wonsan to foreign commerce. Their growth was rapid: by 1893, for example, Pusan had a foreign population of over 5,000, the majority of whom were Japanese. Korea also sent out missions and trainees to other countries in order to modernize its society.

The important Tonghak Peasant Rebellion which occurred in 1894 was externally against Japanese and Western aggression and internally against Confucian social norms. When the government asked for Chinese assistance in suppressing the rebellion, the Japanese intervened against the Chinese and the result was the Sino-Japanese war of 1894–95. Japan emerged as the victor with paramount influence over Korea. A section of the government tried to counter this influence by making overtures to the Russians, and Korea became a cockpit in which foreign interests contended with each other. The Russo-Japanese War of 1904 grew out of these conflicts and Russia's defeat brought Korea under the direct control of the Japanese. For a short period Korea had some internal autonomy with all foreign relations in the hands of the Japanese, but by 1910 it had become totally a Japanese colony. This process was not without internal opposition. A group of intellectuals who aroused the people against the take-over of Korea by foreign interests established a new political organization, the Independence Club led by Dr So Chae-p'il, who had studied in Japan in 1883 and qualified as a doctor in the USA, returning to Korea in 1896. The membership of the club grew from 30 to 10,000 in three months.

The Japanese policy over Korea was classically colonial. The country was treated as a source of raw materials and as a market for Japan's growing industrial sector. The military regime inflicted on Korea was both harsh and oppressive. Korean intellectuals again tried to shake off the Japanese at the end of World War I; in 1919, they formed the Independence Declaration Movement and appealed to the allies for independence, but once again without success. Japan continued its exploitation of Korea which, in the war against China, became Japan's advance logistical base. At that time too, Japan modified its policy and initiated an unsuccessful programme that was designed to assimilate all Koreans. Japanese was made the national language and Koreans were forbidden to use their own language; Koreans were also ordered to change their names to Japanese ones and to swear allegiance to the Emperor. At this stage, Japan also set out to industrialize Korea as a complementary base for its campaign to dominate Asia. Korea finally regained its independence at the end of World War II — following the defeat of Japan — later to be divided into North and South Korea.

The Impact of Christianity
Christianity came to Korea indirectly from neighbouring countries
because the Korean authorities had forbidden the Western trade missions
from bringing in missionaries. However, internal conditions in Korea
provided a stage for Christian penetration. The group of scholars known
as Silhak (Practical Learning), influenced by Western scientific developments, were interested in Christianity; for them Christianity was as much
part of learning as science. The Confucian structures were also by this
time in a state of decay: the fact that both Buddhism and Confucianism
had been seen as religions from abroad supported by the ruling élites
created a favourable situation for Christianity.

Since foreign missionaries had tried and failed to enter Korea,
proselytization in Korea had to wait for Koreans themselves. In the latter
part of the 18th century, many Koreans who had been to China and Japan
adopted the Christian faith and had tried to spread the religion. Though
the state persecuted them, these early Christians were successful in laying
the foundations for later missionary work. The first Korean Roman
Catholic priest, trained and ordained in Macao, entered the country in
1845. Catholicism spread fast, particularly among people of the lower
social strata; it was seen as going against class barriers. The fact that it
permitted common worship for both sexes was also seen as a desirable
innovation by many Korean women. Despite state persecution, such as
the massacre of about 8,000 converts and priests in 1866, the church
continued to grow and to appeal to both men and women; 'Women
Believers Associations' were an early form of organization for converted
women. Protestant missionaries followed towards the end of the 19th
century and were equally successful in attracting converts.

A fair percentage of the foreign missionaries who subsequently
entered Korea were women who were specially concerned with female
education. Their influence on the growth of a women's movement will be
considered later. However, Christianity also brought in new attitudes
with regard to sexual morality; it spoke against a double morality for men
and women, and denied church membership to non-monogamous males.
The social status of women was also advanced by the propagation of the
idea of equality between husband and wife in marriage.

Reforms and the Role of Women
As in other Asian societies, Western influences, together with internal
struggles, helped to emancipate Korean women from their traditional
subordinate roles. Koreans who travelled to the West formed one such
influence. Yu Kil-Chun had been sent to the United States as a member
of a mission in 1883. In 1892, he published an account of his experiences,
Soyu Kyonmun ('An Account of Travels in the West'), in which he
examined the position of women in the USA; he discussed their status in
society and also the marriage pattern which ideally permitted women to
choose their own partners on the basis of love. The author also noted

American women's activities outside their homes, and stated that some women endeavoured as much as men to become doctors, lawyers and nurses. Having thus pointed out the great differences between the roles of women in American and Korean society, he 'advocated the equality of men and women not out of esteem for human rights but because he recognized its merit in promoting the welfare of children, home and country' (Kim 1976: 188).

The group of modernizers in Korea generally accepted this view-point and argued for a degree of liberalization in the role and status of women. Korean male reformers, like their other Asian counterparts, were concerned with women's emancipation in an instrumental way: not because it was right on its own terms, but because it was useful in establishing Korean society's claim to modernity and to economic and social development. This reflected the influence of Western thought on their minds; not only developments in science and technology, but also the social structures which had given rise to such developments, were seen as worthy of emulation.

The spread of Christianity, particularly of Catholicism, helped this process. The early missionaries' great stress on the education of women was due to their anxiety to advance the cause of Catholicism by drawing in the women. A significant element in women's resistance to their subordinate role in Confucianism was the defiance shown by the Catholic women in the early 19th century. Since these converts had rejected traditional domestic life, they were seen as a threat to the social order. Repression and persecution were the result. In 1801, for example, Kang Wan-suk was tried for treason for leaving her family to become a missionary and in the 1839 massacre of Catholics, two-thirds of the victims were women: 'Their martyrdom marked the beginning of the change in the Korean woman's traditional status — the symbolic beginning of the women's modernization movement' (Park 1977: 99).

From 1885 onwards, foreign women missionaries were active in Korea, Mary Fitch Scranton of the Methodist Women's Foreign Missionary Society being the first. These missionaries devoted themselves mainly to female education and their success was such that associations of Catholic women called 'Women Believers Associations' soon sprang up. The enthusiasm of women for the church is explained thus: 'Catholicism helped break down class barriers and essentially the barrier between the sexes. This was one of the most important factors that motivated Korean women to step into the church' (Kim 1976: 197). The old attitudes of subordination broke down to such an extent that women began to insist that they should participate in church matters on an equal basis with the men. A real loosening of the beliefs that had traditionally held Korean women in a situation of general subordination thus took place under the influence of modernizing elements in the society.

The Tonghak rebellion of 1894 also served to highlight the women's issue. The ideology of the rebellion, described as a 'harmonious mixture of Oriental religions' and ideas on equality 'similar to that of Christianity', rejected Confucian views on women, especially on widows, and urged that 'equal treatment for all humans and a respect for women was very important'. Several women were among both the leadership and the ranks of the rebels, and in the subsequent peace treaty, the Tonghak leaders, in their twelve reforms, demanded that widows should legally be permitted to remarry (Park 1977: 100).

Modern Education and Nationalism

Christianity was one of the influences behind the spread of modern education, together with certain Korean state policies of modernization. In 1880, for example, the government sent 58 specialists in various fields to Japan for a tour, and in 1881, 69 students went to China. In 1883, the government also set up a special Ministry for Education; its first Minister, Min Yong-Ik, went on an observation tour to the United States, met the dean of Goucher Women's College in Baltimore, and showed some interest in women's education (Kim 1976: 213–14).

At the time there was a great deal of public discussion on the issue. Pak Yong-hyo, for example, while in exile in Japan in 1888, wrote a memorandum to the King in which he mentioned women's rights and demanded prohibition of the mistreatment of women by their husbands, the legalization of widow remarriage, the abolition of concubinage, and the granting of equal education for girls (Park 1977: 100–1). The modernizing liberals also advocated women's rights. Their views found expression in *Tongnip Sinmun*, a liberal journal started by Dr So Chae-p'il, which was the first non-governmental paper in Korea; in 1896 this paper stated: 'Women are not inferior to men; men are so uncivilised that they mistreat women without any humane considerations or just cause. Isn't it a sign of primitiveness that they oppress women merely by their physical superiority?' (Kim 1976: 214). This paper was at the forefront of the campaign for women's education. In 1896, it stated that the task of educating girls was a most urgent one, adding that 'girls are always forgotten beings in Korea' and that it was 'a pity to waste half the human resources available':

> If women are educated and develop interests in society, they would realise that their rights as human beings are equal to men's. They would also find a way to stop the brutality of men. We ask, therefore, that women be educated even better than men in order to educate other women and become an example of behaviour to men. (Kim 1976: 215)

In the public debate on women's education, however, the motives were varied: some wanted education to provide them with 'good wives and wise mothers' who would be compatible with an era of modernization. Others were inclined to see education as a process whereby women could emerge as educated citizens, hold public office, and even become leaders.

The impact of these liberalizing tendencies resulted in the Kabo reforms of 1894, which were Japanese-inspired. Child marriage was abolished and the remarriage of widows legalized. The wearing of Western clothes and short hair was allowed, Yun Chi'i-o (a prominent liberal who had returned to Korea after study abroad) and his wife becoming the first to wear Western dress (Kim 1976: 215).

Considerable opposition to these tendencies was voiced by the conservative, Confucianist factions, however, and government policy often vacillated. For example, the Minister of Education was a die-hard conservative, who preferred to resign rather than to carry out reforms; in a memorandum presented to the King in 1896, he wrote:

> To cut the hair and wear Western clothes is to become savages, and using the Korean Alphabet instead of Chinese characters is not desirable. That is equivalent to making men beasts and destroying Confucian society. Under these circumstances, I plead to be relieved of my duty. (Quoted in Kim 1976: 217)

The process of women's education could not be thwarted by such men, even though their influence caused the role of the state to be rather negligible. The pioneer of women's education in Korea was the missionary, Mary Fitch Scranton, who founded the first school for women, Ewha Haktang, in 1886. It started with an attendance of seven, women being still under the domination of Confucian thought, but ten years later had 174 pupils. These included the wives and daughters of leaders of the modernization movement, who were encouraged to go into the countryside during their holidays and teach other women. This school later developed into the Ewha Women's University. Esther Pak, a student of the school, became the first Korean woman to study medicine in the USA in 1896; her sisters were also pioneers — entering the teaching and nursing professions (Kim 1976: 229).

The first non-religious school for girls was the result of the awakening women's movement. In 1898, an organization linked with the *Tongnip Sinmun* and called the Ch'anyang-hoe, made up of women of all classes, but led by upper-class widows, began the Sunsong Girls' School. The founding statement of this school was in fact a declaration of women's rights, the first such statement in Korea. It called for women's education, not only as an end in itself but also as a means of achieving for women the same civil rights as were enjoyed by men. This school was entirely privately funded, with no assistance from the government (Kim 1976: 249–50).

The success of the Sunsong Girls' School led to the formation, in 1906, of the Society for Women's Education, which founded a number of private girls' schools throughout the country. This society conducted meetings and debates on issues concerning women and was also responsible for the first women's journal in Korea, *Yoja Chinam*, which came out in 1908. Most of the articles in this journal dealt with women's education and with the necessity for women to change their role in Korean society in the context of the struggle for national liberation. An exception was an article by Yi Kang-ja who emphasized the rights of women as free human individuals. She agreed that women had lost this right through their dependence upon men and that it would only be regained by the achievement of economic independence (Kim 1976: 245–6).

The Ewha Haktang continued to be an important centre of feminist activity, its students playing a leading role in forming an underground society called the Patriotic Women's League, and meeting secretly with other women activists. They also planned but failed to send a woman as a member of the delegation which attended the Versailles Peace Conference in 1919, in an attempt to highlight Korean struggles against Japanese aggression and to obtain Korean independence.

Ewha students also played a prominent role in the agitation organized by the March First Movement in 1919 against Japanese occupation. On this day when an Independence ceremony was held and the Korean flag raised, women marched at the head of demonstrations and processions and many were wounded or killed. One of the most prominent of these protestors was Yu Kwang-Sun, a secondary student at Ewha. She was arrested and imprisoned for a short time after demonstrating in Seoul. When all schools were closed by the Japanese, she returned to her home town in Ch'ung-Ch'ong province and, assisted by her brother and other friends, organized similar demonstrations. Her parents were killed in the course of these struggles; she herself was arrested and died in 1920, aged 16, after long months of torture (Kim 1976: 260). The Korean events influenced other Asian nationalist movements. Commenting on the 1919 struggle, Nehru in a letter to his daughter wrote: 'The suppression of the Koreans by the Japanese is a very sad and dark chapter in history. You will be interested to know that young Korean girls . . . played a prominent part in the struggle' (quoted in Park 1977: 106).

Women Writers and Poets

The spread of education among women gave rise to a number of journals, mainly devoted to issues affecting women, and also a number of women writers who contributed to the development of a modern literature in Korea. The magazine *Puin* ('Woman'), published in 1922, reflected the debate on women that prevailed and raised important issues arising from the concept of female equality.

The first prominent Korean woman writer was Kim Myong-sun (born in 1896), who published her work under the pen-name T'ansil. She was educated first at Ewha and then in Tokyo, where she associated with Korean writers. Her first work in 1917 was a short story, 'A Girl with Suspicion'; it was cast in a realist mode and revolutionized Korean writing. She wrote a great deal thereafter, but her later works were 'romantic, aesthetic and sentimental', partaking of the general nature of literary activity of that period (Kim 1976: 281).

The second important woman writer was Kim Won-ju (1896–1971), who used the pen-name Ilyop. She too had studied at Ewha and Tokyo, and began her literary career as the editor of a journal *Sin Yoja* ('New Woman'), which was sponsored by Ewha. She was thus more concerned with the issue of women's emancipation and this was an important theme in many of her creative writings. An article by her, 'First Break Through the Status Quo', published in 1921, is an example of her feelings. She believed that women's liberation from men was essential for their development and growth. A novel called *Awakening*, published in 1926, also adopts this same view, namely, that women should liberate themselves from men, and even children, in order to achieve self-awakening. It is a comment on the state of Korean society that she ended up a disillusioned Buddhist nun.

Another women's journal, *Yojagye* ('Women's World'), served as a stepping-stone for a woman writer, Na Hye-Sok (1885–1946). She was educated in Tokyo and Paris, and began her writing career in 1918. Her poem 'Nora', celebrating Ibsen's heroine, was indicative of her interest in poetry and women's liberation (Kim 1976: 283). Significantly, all the three women writers referred to had studied in Tokyo, which at that time had also attracted many radical women students from China. The three writers also all belonged to a group which founded the literary magazine *P'yeho* in 1920: 'They printed their works in the magazines, held literary meetings, and made personal contacts with the men in the group. In conservative Korean society such free associations with men made women the objects of social disapproval and criticism' (Kim 1976: 279).

These pioneer women writers were to pave the way for many others in later years, when the further spread of education widened the market for literary products. Among the prominent women writers of the 1930s were novelists Pak Hwa-Song and Kang Kyong-ae; both wrote realistic novels dealing with the harsh conditions of life of the average Korean during the period of Japanese occupation. They also wrote novels and short stories dealing specially with women's problems, but the standpoint implicit in their writings was not by any means feminist. One writer who adopted a more radical viewpoint was Paek Sin-ae (1908–39); she was a committee member of the Young Women's League and her creative writings portray her commitment to feminism. She wrote many short stories and novels; in *Chokbin* ('Poverty Stricken'), she deals with the problems of a widow in Korean society, and in her other stories she writes of women faced with particular problems. Her women are said to be strong-willed characters who fight in order to overcome their problems and ensure their survival, not passively accepting society as it is, but actively striving against it. Im Ok-in was another woman novelist skilled in portraying female characters, showing an understanding of their psychology. There were also a number of women poets, working in the traditional forms of Korean poetry, as well as in more modern forms (Kim 1976: 287–91).

Although a significant number of women writers thus came into being and were recognized as an important part of the literary life of the country, they worked within the parameters of the society they lived in. They portrayed the harshness of life for both men and women, and implicit in their works are ideals of justice and love. But they lacked an ideological framework in which the plight of their female characters could be understood and traced back to their social subordination.

Women During the Period of Japanese Repression

After the failure of the nationalist movement to obtain independence in 1919, resistance against Japanese occupation continued sporadically, both politically and militarily, and women participated in these struggles. As Park Yong-Ock has said: 'The women's movement after 1919 became more systematic in its stand against the Japanese.' A provisional government in exile was formed in China and its Constitution included the equality of men and women as one of its principles. Park's analysis of women's organizations is illuminating in showing the impact on women of education and of religious and modernizing influences: 'All of the members were Christians and the leaders were women who had gained leadership experience in the Church by the time of the March First movement' (Park 1977: 106). Most of the women participants were students, teachers, missionary workers, nurses and bank clerks; they not only joined actively in demonstrations, but also organized other supportive activities.

During these years of Japanese occupation and repression, women continued to resist on several fronts. First through education they challenged Confucian orthodoxy and tried to modernize society. The need for female education was increasingly accepted in the 1920s. The numbers of girls in elementary schools increased from 1,146 in 1910 to 105,000 in 1930, and in secondary schools from 283 in 1912 to 5,800 in 1931 (Park 1977: 108). Second, Korean women continued to be active in the democratic anti-Japanese struggle: 'she was no longer a secluded pawn in Korea's history, but an active participant — a patriot equal in stature to men' (Park 1977: 110). Third, was the participation of women in the socialist movement. A new agitational base developed among women workers who were harshly exploited in industries and other enterprises owned by the Japanese. They set up the Chosan Women's Co-operative Society which had a socialist orientation and was mainly concerned with the problems of working women. By 1924, such organizations were widespread, with about 40 branches in various areas of the country; meetings and lectures were organized to increase popular awareness of the women's movement (Park 1977: 108).

Because of the specific characteristics of the Korean situation, the leaders of the women's movement decided that their focus of activity should be on the economic conditions of Korean women. The editorial in the first issue of a new women's journal called *Sin-sahoe* ('New Society') was entitled 'The Viewpoint of the Korean Woman in the Transition Period' and reflected the tensions of the movement:

> Although freedom of vocation is emphasised, the low industrial development in Korea limits the fields in which the educated woman can work. Consequently, the day women's economic independence can be achieved is still very distant. In addition to that, our country has lost its sovereignty; we cannot even imagine something like women's voting rights. (Quoted in Park 1977: 110)

It was on the basis of this realistic assessment that the women's movement continued its work until the end of World War II and the end of Japanese occupation.

Conclusion

Korea is yet another example of a traditional society with a strong Confucian value system in which the subordination of women to men was a central feature, which attempted to modernize itself and, in the process, accepted in theory if not in practice that the equality of women is an essential facet of modernity. Part of the impetus for this change came from the West; but the spread of scientific knowledge and technology, and the growing awareness that Korean national independence lay in the country's ability to absorb this knowledge, led to the belief that the nation's social structures should also be transformed. Changes in the relationship between men and women was a basic element in this transformation.

The process was not without its contradictions. *Sohak* (Western knowledge) was admired and one school of thought advocated its total acceptance; another school, designated as *Tonghak* (Eastern knowledge), attempted to combine the material benefits of Western knowledge with a value system that derived from Eastern philosophies. This movement gave the Tonghak Peasant Rebellion an ideological character that was somewhat similar to the Taiping movement in China. The development of Korean society and of women within it was undoubtedly affected by the specifics of Korean culture, but it is obvious that the spread of scientific knowledge was in itself the basis on which those aspects of Korean culture which kept women in a subordinate position began to be questioned.

13. The Challenge of Feminism in Japan

> The mountain-moving day is coming
> I say so, yet others doubt.
> Only a while the mountain sleeps
> In the past
> All mountains moved in fire,
> Yet you may not believe it.
> Oh man, this alone believe,
> All sleeping women now awake and move.
> *Yosano Akiko* (1878–1942)

The growth of feminist consciousness in Japan in the late 19th and early 20th centuries was interwoven with the external challenge faced by the country and the basic internal transformations that took place during those years. Japan successfully resisted all efforts at direct colonization but still had to contend with the economic power of Western imperialism. This Japan sought to do by adopting a policy of rapid industrialization and economic growth and by reforming its internal structures to suit such a policy. These transformations laid the foundation for the emergence of democratic and feminist movements.

The Japanese had contact with both Portuguese and Dutch traders from the 16th century onwards. The Portuguese arrived in Japan in 1542 and established trading and missionary centres, but were expelled by the Japanese government in 1639. The Dutch, who were more concerned with trade than religion, were permitted to have a trading station. They succeeded in interesting several Japanese scholars in European learning and the orthodox Confucian scholar, Shibano Ritsuzan (1734–1807), stated of the Dutch that 'even barbarians incapable of reading Chinese books might possess the ability to make deductions from their personal experience that were valid for all mankind' (Keene 1969: 29). The study of Dutch medicine became the most accepted form of 'barbarian learning', and some who had studied medicine turned to other branches of knowledge. For example, the scholar Otsuki Gentaku (1757–1827), who became a doctor, wrote a textbook on Dutch studies in 1783, and in 1789 opened the first Dutch-language school in Japan, which had 94 pupils (mainly those interested in medical studies) between 1789 and 1826 (Keene 1969: 25, 30).

The rulers (Shoguns) made deliberate efforts to restrict foreign influence and activities to trading ports such as Nagasaki, as well as to control foreign missionary activities. This effort was successful until 1853, when an American expedition forcibly entered the country; the monopolies in trade held by the Portuguese, Spanish and Dutch were then ended and the country was opened up to commerce by other European powers. Public opinion against foreigners, and dissatisfaction with the Shogun increased, leading to his deposition and the assumption of power by the Emperor Meiji, who ruled from 1868 to 1912 ('the Meiji restoration'). The policies followed thereafter aimed at building a modern state based on industrial development and involved military and naval reorganization, educational changes and scientific and technological borrowing from the West. All these changes were introduced carefully and gradually so that essential aspects of traditional society could be preserved. In a Charter Oath of 1868, which expressed the desire for modernization within the existing hierarchical structures, the new Emperor urged the population to abandon 'all absurd usages' and commanded that 'knowledge shall be sought for all over the world and thus shall be strengthened the foundation of our imperial polity'. In following these strategies of rapid Westernization in selected areas, Japan emerged 'from feudal isolation to a position of unprecedented authority and strength' (Panikkar 1955: 208).

In his study of Japanese capitalism, Halliday has shown how 'the dialectic of the internal and external' worked in 19th-century Japan, referring to the forcible opening of the country to Western traders and the breaking of its previous policy of seclusion, as well as the internal responses in Japan to this external pressure which resulted in the Meiji restoration.

> When the Western bourgeoisie broke into Japan by force, they provoked a crisis that was both political and economic . . . This involved . . . not simply building defences against the rest of the world but also mobilising and transforming the domestic society — which in turn meant promoting the capitalist mode of production and the ascendancy of the bourgeoisie. (Halliday 1975: 22-3)

These developments occurred within a hierarchical framework of social organization, within which the Emperor was held sacrosanct and no dissent was tolerated. The state ideology was one of promoting the concept of the 'family state' (*kazoku kokka*): 'The Confucian-type familistic ethic provided the real foundation for the society, and . . . Japanese ideologists spoke of the nation as an "extended family" sanctified by the Emperor above as head of the family "sacred and inviolable".' This ideology was the basis of the educational system which emphasized filial piety and obedience and sought 'to transfer familial loyalty towards

227

the Emperor by identifying Emperor-loyalty with filial piety' (Halliday 1975: 41–2). Linked to this were expressions of patriotism and chauvinism which were to characterize Japanese politics up to the first decades of the 20th century.

A liberal reformist current of opinion also emerged during the Meiji era which reflected the opinion of intellectuals, the urban middle classes and businessmen. Organized as the Liberty and Popular Rights Movement, in 1874 it demanded a written Constitution and a National Assembly. However, it was not until 1889 that the Meiji Constitution was adopted, providing for an elected House of Representatives with limited male franchise and a cabinet system; the office of emperor, however, continued to be sacred and inviolable. The succeeding governments were based on a consensus between parties representing the interests of capitalism, linked to a conservative ideology that was founded on authoritarianism, hierarchically organized institutions, extreme nationalism and patriarchy.

Position of Women

It is in the context of these historical changes that the expression of Japanese feminism in the late 19th and early 20th centuries must be understood. The position of women in Japan had changed over the centuries. In the legends of Japan's mythical creator-goddess Izanami and the supreme deity, the sun goddess Amaterasu, there are perhaps vestiges of a matrilineal society. The chronicles record many early women rulers; from AD 147 to 190 there is said to have been civil war and anarchy until Queen Pimiko restored law and order. She was succeeded by her relative, a girl of 13. Six empresses ruled Japan in the two centuries after AD 592, but in the 8th century, the rule of the Empress Koken, who was unmarried, ended female rule and women were debarred from succession to the throne, a practice that prevails to the present day (Paulson 1976: 2–3).

The Heian period (794–1185) saw the strengthening of the state apparatus and the rise of such great families as the Fujiwara. It was during this period that the capital was established at Kyoto; this was also a time of great excellence in art and literature. Women played a significant role in the politics and aesthetics of the aristocratic classes; though physically limited in their contacts with the outside world, they were educated and accomplished. Some of the best-known literary works of the period were produced by ladies of the court; they generally wrote in Japanese as distinct from the literary Chinese which was considered the appropriate style for men. Lady Murasaki Shikibu (970–1040), the author of *The Tale of Genji* which achieved fame as the world's earliest (as well as an outstanding) novel, reveals in her diaries that although she had a fairly comprehensive education, she was not taught Chinese; however, she was resourceful enough to learn it by eavesdropping on her brothers' lessons. Another famous woman writer of this period was Sei-Shonagon, who wrote the *Pillow Book* in the 10th century, a witty and sensitive chronicle of court life that was to inspire much creative writing in Japan.

It was during the 8th century, however, that social laws based on the Chinese family system were introduced into Japan through the adoption of the Taiho Code. These laws established the patrilineal family system and adopted the Confucian beliefs regarding the natural inferiority of women; they also embodied discriminatory attitudes towards the rights of women with regard to property, marriage and divorce. In the Kamakura period (1185–1333), women regained some property rights and continued to hold an important place in society, but the growth of feudalism in the Muromachi period (1338–1500) and the emergence of the masculine *samurai* ethic caused them to lose their position, including inheritance and property rights (Paulson 1976: 8–10).

Feudalism flourished in Japan between 1600 and 1868 (the Tokugawa era). Writers of the period, such as Kaibara Ekken (1631–1714), author of *Greater Learning for Women*, a popular book of 'wisdom', laid down the philosophical basis for women's subservience to the male:

> Woman has the quality of yin (passiveness). Yin is of the nature of the night and is dark. Hence, because compared to a man, she is foolish, she does not understand her obvious duties . . . She has five blemishes in her nature. She is disobedient, inclined to anger, slanderous, envious, stupid. Of every ten women, seven or eight will have these failings . . . In everything, she must submit to her husband. (Quoted in Sievers 1983: 5)

Proceeding on this basis, the 'book of wisdom' placed restrictions on women's activities: 'To temples and other places where there is a great concourse of people, she should go but sparingly till she has reached the age of forty' (Paulson 1976: 11). The traditional Confucian concept of woman's role was advocated in this period: 'the family being all important, woman's function as "heir provider" in the context of Confucianism, feudalism and ancestor worship had rendered her, on the eve of the Meiji Restoration, virtually devoid of legal rights' (Paulson 1976: 13). The growth of feudal institutions was thus related to a decline in the position of women; during the period when feudalism was at its highest, woman's subordination to man was unquestioned; she was merely a 'borrowed womb' (Sievers 1983: 4). The ideal woman was depicted as follows: 'A woman should never disfigure her face with anger. She should be diffident in speech, never presuming to be familiar with her husband . . . she must endure without complaint' (quoted in Vavich 1967: 404).

The Reformist Phase
Women's subservience in Japan began to be questioned in the latter decades of the 19th century, when strategies of capitalist growth and policies of modernization were adopted. During the more liberal phase of

the Meiji period, some interest was shown in democratic rights and in women's emancipation. In the newly established prefectural assembly of Hamamatsu, the issue of female suffrage was unsuccessfully raised in 1876. The Liberty and Popular Rights Movement of the 1870s and 1880s not only included some liberal elements that supported women's suffrage, but also produced the first women activists.

Another issue taken up during this period affecting the status of women was that of prostitution. Japanese and foreign reformers had spoken out against prostitution; their agitation received dramatic support from an incident in 1872 when the *Maria Luz*, a Peruvian ship engaged in the recruitment of men as workers and women as prostitutes for America, stopped over in Yokohama and one of the prostitutes escaped. In the aftermath of this incident, the government declared itself against prostitution and cancelled the contracts and outstanding debts of prostitutes to the houses they served; all prostitutes were freed but prostitution was not made illegal. This duality of attitude had been earlier demonstrated by the government's decision regarding concubines when in 1870, concubines had been given the same rights as legal wives (Sievers 1983: 13).

Support for women's rights was expressed openly by several male reformers, especially those who believed in modernizing and 'civilizing' the country. For instance, in 1885, Iwamoto Zenji published a journal, *Women's Education*, in which he made the point that the West equated the degree of civilization with the status of women:

> In present-day Japan, the condition of women is such that Japan cannot be considered a civilised or cultured country . . . we must exert ourselves to the improvement of the condition of women; by combining Western women's rights with traditional virtues of our women, we will produce models of perfection. (Vavich 1967: 406–7)

The traditional Japanese family system was also criticized during the Meiji era, but the aim of the reformers was to replace the feudal, extended family by the nuclear family, which was held to be more in keeping with capitalist development and liberal values. Tokutomi Soho (1863–1957), one of the most influential liberal writers of the period (who later became a strong conservative), deplored the tyrannical, traditional family system as 'a breeding ground of every abuse, servility, double-dealing, jealousy, alienation and treachery'. He stressed the lack of freedom for women, who were treated as 'natural slaves' of the other members of the family and had no independent life or identity of their own, adding that 'women are not recognised as human beings'. Soho believed strongly in individualism and criticized the family system for emphasizing the support of relatives and elders ('youth must sacrifice itself for today's elders'); he argued that society could not develop unless the basic family structures were reformed through the establishment of nuclear family units, with married children living apart from their parents, and with property belonging to individuals and not to the family as a whole (Pierson 1980: 208–9).

Many of these male reformers banded together in the Merokusha (Meiji Six Society) in 1873. Through a journal *Meiroku Zasshi* (the 'Meiji Six Journal') and public lectures, they attempted to interpret and adapt Western ideas and practices to Japanese society. They agreed with Western criticism of the status of Japanese women and accepted that 'the low regard for women in Japan was a major contributor to its backwardness . . . If there was to be real reform in Japanese society, it must begin with the family — and women must be at the centre of change' (Sievers 1983: 18).

The Minister of Education, Mori Arinori (1847–89), a member of the Meiji Six Society, attacked concubinage and double standards of morality and advocated egalitarian, contractual marriage; he supported women's education and was responsible, in 1871, for sending five girls to the USA to be educated, 'an action stirring such wonder in Japan that one contemporary Japanese writer compares it to man's arrival on the moon' (Pharr 1981: 17). It is, however, indicative of the confused nature of state policies regarding women that these girls were not to be trained in any specific skills, but were to be merely 'students of American home life' for ten years. One of these, Tsuda Umeko, subsequently became a campaigner for higher education for women (Sievers 1983: 12).

The leading intellectual reformist to challenge the Confucian attitude towards women was Fukuzawa Yukichi (1833–1901), another member of the Meiji Six group; he had travelled on the first Japanese ship to America in 1859 and joined the first official Japanese mission to Europe in 1861–62 as interpreter. His book, *Seiyo Jijo* ('Things Western'), written in 1866, became a popular success and gave detailed descriptions of all aspects of Western society. In 1872, Fukuzawa made his plea for equal rights, individual independence and self-respect. He caused a sensation by the opening lines of his book *The Encouragement of Learning*, which said: 'Heaven never created a man above another nor a man below another' — a denial of traditional, hierarchical structures and relationships. He applied some of these ideas in his writings on women, including the *Essay on Japanese Women* (1879) and *The New Greater Learning for Women* (1897) which was a critique (on the lines of John Stuart Mill) of the status of women in traditional Japanese society. His views naturally gave rise to much opposition in conservative circles.

Fukuzawa also expressed the new attitude to marriage, stressing the concepts of freedom of choice and of monogamy, advocating equality in marriage, the acceptance of second marriages for women, separate households as opposed to joint families, and opportunities for women to make profitable use of their education (Paulson 1976: 14). He was particularly concerned with promoting the nuclear family and with denouncing polygamous practices. In his autobiography he states:

There are people who hold that it is ridiculous to advocate abolishing polygamy . . . I am sure that the majority of people in Japan are on my side. So I intend to work as long as I live for the abolition of the unhealthy custom . . . I shall attempt to make our society more presentable if only on the surface. (Fukuzawa 1968: 306)

Although he condemned Confucianism and proposed equal rights and education for women, there was a contradiction between his liberalism in the early Meiji era and his subsequent conservatism. In his later writings, he not only attacked China but also emphasized woman's role as wife and mother and took a conservative approach to women's education.

The debate by the intellectuals of this group raised important questions on the family and the role of women in society. Although the central issue of women's equality was not touched upon, the debate emphasized the need to change the accepted notions of Tokugawa society on the 'spheres' of women. It is very significant that very soon after this debate by male reformers, women began to speak for themselves and to participate in movements for social and political rights. This debate was also stimulated by translations from English writers: Sheldon Amos's *Differences of Sex* appeared in Japanese in 1878 and John Stuart Mill's *On the Subjection of Women* in 1879 (Sievers 1983: 16).

The liberal-democratic journals of the period also frequently discussed the issue of women's emancipation. One of the most influential newspapers, *Kokumin no tomo*, started in 1887 by Tokutomi Soho, became a forum for debate and intellectual discussion during the Meiji era, and dealt with 'practically every aspect of modern society and culture, from politics, economics, and social problems, to literature, art and science' (Pierson 1980: 165). The status of Japanese women was a frequent subject of debate in the journal, and in his editorials, Tokutomi stated that concern for social reform was meaningless unless the deplorable condition of Japanese women was taken into consideration:

In human life we pity the poor, the ignorant, the blind, but we have not yet been able to feel compassion for our Japanese women. In themselves they combine all the characteristics of those with whom we ordinarily sympathise. Who is poorer than they? For even if they live in splendid houses they have not the right to own property. Who is ignorant in the way they are? What have they to occupy their minds? With their eyes they cannot see the happenings in society. With their ears they cannot hear of conditions in the world. Their obligations do not extend beyond the kitchen. (Sievers 1983: 182–3)

Even though such a liberal current favouring reform existed during the early Meiji era, when it came to the actual drafting of legislation on issues that affected the status of women, a strong conservative bias showed itself, and what had looked like a step forward in general terms (legislatively) proved to be two steps backwards for women. In order to follow a Western model of parliamentary democracy, for example, a

Constitution was adopted in 1889 which provided for a National Assembly and elections on a party basis. In 1890, however, a Peace Preservation Law was passed to regulate and suppress subversive activities. Article 5 of the Police Security Regulations was revised to include women among those ineligible to participate in politics. Women were thus prevented not only from joining political parties or associations but also from sponsoring political meetings or even attending them. This meant that only such activities as the Women's Christian Temperance Union (formed in 1886) were open to them.

Similarly, the Meiji Code of 1898 was drafted to protect the existing family system and to uphold traditional Japanese concepts of morality and filial piety. Parental consent was needed for the registration of a marriage; adultery by women was made a civil and criminal offence; divorce rights were given to women, but the husband had custody of the children; a woman had property rights, but the control of that property remained with the husband. Nevertheless, the issue of women's rights was discussed during this period and male champions of women's rights were able to express their views in public.

Dress Reform in Japan

With Westernization, dress reform occurred all over Asia, both men and women of the middle class discarding their traditional clothes and hairstyles for the current fashions of Europe. From the early years of the Meiji era, the government tried to interfere in this private domain, but with different policies for men and women. The Emperor himself led the way with a Western-style haircut, and the long-haired *samurai* were urged to cut off their hair by the government, which linked short hair with 'progressive attitudes and individual willingness to embrace drastic change for the sake of the country' (Sievers 1983: 14). These changes were for men only, and when in 1871 an organization arose to advocate short hair for women, the government (in 1872) made the new fashion for women illegal and even women who cut their hair for health reasons had first to obtain government approval. To stress the point, in 1873, the Empress appeared in public with the approved look for women, namely long hair, unblackened teeth and natural (instead of shaved) eyebrows. Many women in the equal rights movement, however, not only defied the ban by cutting their hair, but also abandoned the traditional kimonos and adopted Western clothes. As Sievers remarks:

> The banning of short hair for women . . . is one of the most important and revealing policies on women in the early Meiji period. To the extent that women cutting their hair can be viewed as a real, if spontaneous, attempt to join the progressive forces trying to create a new Japan, the government denial of their right to do so was also a denial of their right to participate and contribute

actively to that change. In fact, it can be seen as a symbolic message to Japan's women to become repositories of the past rather than pioneers, with men, of some unknown future. (Sievers 1983: 15)

Apart from the dissenters, men and women of the bourgeoisie, in their desire to be fashionable, also adopted Western dress, and by the late 19th century a Westernized social life existed among those belonging to 'high society'. Criticism of the slavish imitation of the West, however, came from some reformers. For example:

The writer Tokutomi Soho criticised the emphasis the Meiji leaders gave to impressing foreigners by adopting the outward forms and material products of Western societies, and their neglect of the more important spiritual and ethical aspects of Western civilisation. He deplored their pre-occupation with copying such trappings as styles of dress, diet and social graces, and their indulging in such superficialities as dancing, masked balls and horse-racing . . . he complained that the nation's leaders were providing them with examples of frivolity and extravagance . . . importing western luxury goods . . . liquor, tobacco, top hats and ladies' lace. (Pierson 1980: 161)

Women of the bourgeoisie also adopted both the fashions and social graces of contemporary Europe. Even Tokutomi Soho and his wife, despite theoretical objections, felt compelled to follow the prevailing fashion. Pierson describes the scene:

On a few occasions she was taken out by her husband to attend the large, formal, Western-style banquets and "fancy balls" that were held to celebrate important state events, such as the one given by the Prime Minister at the time of the promulgation of the constitution in February 1889. Dressed in a high-collared Victorian gown, complete with parasol and high-top lace boots, she was able to meet the ladies of "high society", the wives of government officials and of the resident foreign community, for whose pleasure many of these functions were held. (Pierson 1980: 161)

Education and Westernization

The Meiji leaders believed that modernization strategies necessitated education for women, but the education they visualized was intended to prop up the traditional family by producing what was popularly known as *ryosai kembo*, 'good wives and wise mothers'. In 1872, an Education Ordinance was introduced with the goal of achieving universal literacy. It was stated that: 'throughout the nation — peers . . . farmers, craftsmen, merchants, women and children — there shall henceforward be no un-educated families in a community, no uneducated members in a family' (Koyama 1961: 21–3). This Ordinance was geared to the creation of a national system of education for boys and girls, but secondary education for girls was of lower quality and emphasized the 'development of national

234

morality and the cultivation of womanly virtues' (Paulson 1976: 15). The government set up, in 1872, the Tokyo Girls' School which had a broad curriculum; the girls in the school were also set to study Fukuzawa's 'Conditions in the West' and other Japanese works, but the school was abruptly closed in 1877 (Sievers 1983: 12). Though the Ordinance appeared to provide for female education, there was no organized attempt either to establish sufficient places for girls or to persuade parents that girls needed to be educated. In fact, from the 1880s onwards, educational policies in general changed from the earlier liberal reformism to conservatism: 'Close supervision was maintained over texts and materials to eliminate undesirable western influence. Instead of functioning as independent scholar-educators, teachers were made public officials . . . education was not for the sake of the student but for the sake of the country' (Pierson 1980: 210).

The missionaries who were also active began from 1870 onwards to open schools for girls which were popular because of their more advanced curriculum. In 1876, the Tokyo Women's Normal School was established to train teachers for primary schools, and by 1900, women formed 15% of co-educational elementary school teachers, rising to 33% by 1927. By 1910, universal primary education had almost been achieved. Whereas 40% of boys and 15% of girls had attended primary school in 1873, by 1910 these figures had reached nearly 99% for boys and just over 97% for girls. The need for girls' education beyond primary levels became an issue, and in 1899 middle-grade education for girls was established by a Girls' High School Ordinance. Again the statistics are impressive. In 1872, of 1,779 students who received middle-level education, only 36 or 2% were girls; by 1910, however, the figure was 26% and rose to 37% by 1920. A women's college with ten students was started in 1900 by Tsuda Umeko (one of the women who had been sent to the USA for studies in 1871), and a woman doctor, Yoshioka Yayoi, started the first women's medical college in 1900. In 1901 the Japan Women's University was founded by Naruse Jinzo, and by 1913 a few women had been given places in some of the imperial universities, but women were still debarred from the leading universities of Tokyo and Kyoto. Even by World War II, there were only 40 women in the imperial universities compared to nearly 30,000 men (Paulson 1976: 16).

Japan aimed at achieving universal primary education for girls, but with a heavy emphasis on producing good wives and mothers, and these policies were reinforced under the growth of conservative nationalism during the Russo-Japanese War of 1904–5 and later (Mouer 1976: 164). The teaching in girls' schools served to encourage traditional views on women's inferior status and perpetuated feudal values, thereby providing an example of how education, *while seeming to be a liberating factor for women, actually proved to be the opposite.* Koyama makes an important point about the adverse effects on poorer women who lost their earlier power as a result of the patriarchal ideas that became more widespread:

Side by side with the authority of the patriarch, his wife had an authority conferred on her by the patriarch . . . "housewife's authority" based on custom and on the power exercised by her in . . . family consumption . . . Among the common people, the wife's role was . . . also in regard to (family) production . . . and constituted a kind of social convention . . . it may be said that *common people became deferent to the authoritative patriarchal concept of the family in the Meiji era when education spread and when moral and legal norms penetrated all parts of Japanese society.* (Koyama 1961: 34; emphasis added)

The expansion of education, however, brought about some employment opportunities for women. Women teachers appeared on the scene in 1875, followed by women doctors and nurses (1885), telephone operators and stenographers (1889), bank and office workers (1900), and the increase of industries in the early 20th century brought large numbers of women workers into factory employment (Koyama 1961: 98ff).

Women in the Workforce

The establishment of a modern industrial sector was one of the key elements of the Meiji government's drive to modernize Japan. It was realized very early that light industries, particularly spinning and weaving, could be made competitive in world markets if they were able to utilize cheap female labour. Besides, these industries required little capital and could in fact generate the resources for the development of capital-intensive heavy industries. The government set up the first technologically advanced spinning and weaving mill in 1883 and private entrepreneurs quickly followed suit. The new policies of the government had already created dislocations in the traditional agrarian patterns of the countryside; the daughters of impoverished rural families were thus available for mobilization as mill workers.

The enticement of women into factory work was so quick that by 1876, women constituted 60% of the entire workforce; this ratio continued until 1912 and even up to the beginning of World War II. In 1894, for example, there were nearly 6,000 factories employing 239,000 women (62% of the total labour force in factories) while in 1907, there were 11,400 factories with 400,000 women (60%) (Sievers 1983: 50, 206). The greater part of this female workforce was in the textile industry, though sizeable numbers of women also worked in the coal mines and match factories. Young unmarried women from poor families in the countryside constituted the bulk of this workforce. They were housed in dormitories that resembled prisons and condemned to work 15 hours a day for a contracted period. The working conditions and work regimes were exceedingly harsh. The health and vitality of women workers were drained away so fast that the typical rate of annual turnover of labour in Meiji mills was 50 per cent (Sievers 1983: 65).

236

The system of contracting with the family for female labour with housing in factory dormitories replicated traditional family structures, with the factory management assuming the role of parent. It was also understood that work for women was only temporary, an opportunity to add to a family's resources before marriage. However, behind this paternalist façade lay extremely harsh forms of exploitation. Most workers chose to run away from these conditions and some were even driven to suicide. But those that remained in the industry quickly learned to organize themselves and to use the ultimate weapon of the worker — the withdrawal of labour. Thus Japan's first strike took place in June 1886, at the Amamiya Silk Mill in Kofu, when 100 women walked out in protest at the owner's proposal to increase working hours while reducing wages. The strike was settled after four days, with the owner withdrawing his proposal. The partial success of this strike encouraged other women workers and there were at least four other strikes in 1886 and an increasing number in subsequent years. These female mill workers, although stigmatized as 'ignorant farm girls', were, as Sievers maintains, 'the pioneers of Japan's modern labour movement' (Sievers 1983: 79). In fact, the social costs of Japan's rapid industrialization were borne by Japanese women.

The entry of women into the workforce, however, even in such large numbers did not contribute in any significant way to changes in the traditional role or status of women. One of the reasons may have been the lack of contact between the working women, who were experiencing the harshest possible oppression and the feminist activists who worked through the Liberal Party. In addition, while women represented more than half the industrial workforce, there was hardly any trade unionism among these workers and even in the period of rapid trade union development after 1918 women union members represented only 1% of all female workers (Koyama 1961: 121).

Women in the Popular Rights Movement

The nature of the Meiji reforms and the character of the modernization movement (which was modern in some respects, conservative in others) led to the development of a nationwide political opposition to the oligarchy that was ruling Japan. The movement was called *Jiyu minken undo* (Movement for Freedom and Popular Rights); it demanded that political power be shared among all the strata of the population, objected to taxation without political representation and called for a Constitution that would establish representative political institutions. The movement based itself on the natural rights theory and appealed to the *samurai* who had lost their privileged position, and to the farmers and merchants who were trying to establish themselves within the framework of modernization policies (Sievers 1983: 26–7).

The early leaders of the popular rights movement were not interested in women's rights, nor indeed in involving women in their activities. Yet, by 1878, the need arose to expand the movement into new social strata and new areas. A consequence of this initiative was a new attitude towards women, regarding them as a force to be mobilized. Concurrently, however, women themselves began to see that popular rights theory was applicable to their own condition and that principles like 'no taxation without representation' should apply to women as well as men.

The issue was dramatically raised in 1872 by Kusunose Kita, a woman of 45, who had been compelled to assume the property and tax liabilities of her husband at his death. Her questions linked property rights, voting rights and gender inequalities. In a protest letter to the authorities that was later to become a much publicized document, she wrote:

> We women who are heads of households must respond to the demands of the government just as other ordinary heads of households, but because we are women, we do not enjoy equal rights. We have the right neither to vote for district council representatives nor to act as legal guarantors in matters of property, even though we hold legal instruments for that purpose . . . My rights, compared with those of male heads of households, are totally ignored. Most reprehensible of all, the only equality I share with men who are heads of their households is the onerous duty of paying taxes. (Sievers 1983: 29)

Kusunose's protest had a widespread impact. She became a symbol of the Japanese woman's efforts to speak out on questions that affected her and indeed forced the leadership of the popular rights movement to rethink their attitude to women's issues.

Kishida Toshiko

One of the striking aspects of the growth of the popular rights movement and its successor, the Liberal Party, was in the numbers of women who became politically active, the most prominent of them being Kishida Toshiko. Coming from an affluent merchant family in Kyoto, she had been selected as a lady-in-waiting to the Meiji empress on the basis of her reputation for beauty and intelligence; she found the atmosphere at court uncongenial and left after two years, pleading ill health. Kishida, at 20, has been described as 'an idealist with the optimistic belief in the possibility of social reform based on enlightened public opinion'. She had been influenced by Western liberal thinkers like Spencer and the French socialist, Jean Jaurès, and was aware of the campaign for women's suffrage in the West; she felt that 'the exclusion of women from the tasks of nation-building was irrational, and to the extent that such exclusion meant a continuation of "respecting men and despising women", unethical as well' (Sievers 1983: 35).

Kishida first spoke on a Liberal Party platform in 1882 in Osaka and thereafter appeared at public meetings all over Japan. She spoke on women's issues and on the problems of Japanese women. A speech she made at the town of Okayama was entitled 'The Government Lords it over the People; Men Lord it over Women'. The issues that Kishida emphasized were the same as the questions raised by women in other Asian countries. She demanded that women have equal opportunities in education and that they be trained in practical skills that would enable them to be economically independent. She argued for sexual codes that would apply equally to men and women and for equality in law as regards civil and property rights. The impact made by Kishida on other women has been recorded by Fukuda Hideko, later an outstanding feminist herself:

> Listening to her speech, delivered in that marvellous oratorical style, I was unable to suppress my resentment and indignation . . . and began immediately to organise women and their daughters . . . to take the initiative in explaining and advocating natural rights, liberty and equality . . . summoning those of high purpose to the cause, so that somehow we might muster the passion to smash the corrupt customs of former days relating to women. (Sievers 1983: 36)

Many women's groups were formed under Kishida's inspiration, such as the Kyoto Women's Lecture Society. She was particularly skilful in meeting the traditional arguments about women's 'inherent inferiority'. Kishida argued that 'accepting the right of those with superior force to dominate those who were weaker, whether man over woman or western nation over Asian nation, was an argument for savagery, not civilisation.' She also commented sarcastically that if this notion of the superiority of physical strength was to be accepted, then *sumo* wrestlers should occupy the highest positions of state. Faced with arguments of women's mental inferiority, she cited the examples not only of Japanese women like the Lady Murasaki but also of Western women like Madame de Staël and Elizabeth Barrett Browning, and stated that any present inferiority was merely the product of a system that prevented women from benefiting from education (Sievers 1983: 39).

Kishida was arrested and jailed for a week for a speech made at Otsu in October 1883; her lecture there, entitled 'Daughters Confined in Boxes', has been described by Sievers as 'one of the earliest attacks on Japan's family system by a woman' (Sievers 1983: 41). It was in the course of this speech that she compared the Japanese unfavourable attitude to daughters to growing flowers in salt. During this period there was widespread political activity by women. The increasing popularity of the opposition movement, however, caused the government to intensify its persecution of the Liberal Party and its leaders. The party itself became prey to internal dissension and in 1884 the leaders announced its dissolution. This was a big disappointment for the women who had used its platforms to articulate women's issues, but it did not mean the total cessation of their activities. Kishida, for example, turned to journalism and wrote frequently for the many women's magazines. Women's participation in the popular rights movement was very important for subsequent developments. It had demonstrated the capacity of Japanese women to formulate, articulate and fight for their demands and it had raised the consciousness of women to their plight and the reasons behind it.

Through Social Reform to Feminism

Two groups of women thus had shown their opposition to the established order: those who articulated women's issues through the political rights movement and those who made their protest at the workplace. The potential for women's power being thus demonstrated, the state took steps to curb its further development. It was made illegal in 1890, through an amendment of the Police Security Regulations, for women to join a political party, to form a political association or group, or to attend a meeting defined as political by the relevant authorities. A Japanese scholar, Maruoka Hideo, sees 'a clear relationship between these events and the revised law, particularly between the labour strikes and the new restrictions' (Sievers 1983: 206).

Thus the intervention of the state in guiding and restraining the pace of social change became more intense. Although the basis of such restrictions, particularly as regards women, was often couched in terms of traditional Confucian values, the structures that were developed were modelled after authoritarian political structures. As restrictions on political expression had tightened, some women drawn from the middle class — teachers, journalists and intellectuals, most with a Christian educational background — had banded together in 1886 to form the Tokyo Women's Reform Society. The principal issues raised by this society centred on the system of concubinage and prostitution, which were seen as social evils in need of reform. It is to the credit of the reformers that they saw these two evils as interconnected with sexual oppression by the male. As Sievers says, they were arguing that 'any household where the concubinage system was still in place was not just a household that fostered prostitution: it was a centre of prostitution' (Sievers 1983: 97). The society took up these two themes on a country-wide basis in 1887, conducting their campaign through lectures and articles.

After the law forbidding women's participation in politics was passed in 1890, forums like the Reform Society were the only organizations through which women's issues could be articulated. In arguing against concubinage and prostitution, in challenging women's inferior status, the Reform Society was undertaking a task that was broadly political; but this aspect of its work could not be fully developed in the conservative mood that dominated Japan during this period. As time went on, the Reform Society began to shift its emphasis to social welfare work, particularly relief in times of disasters like earthquakes and typhoons. The war with China in 1894 was another factor that strengthened conservative tendencies and served to shift the emphasis away from internal divisions. One example of this phenomenon was the formation of the Japan Women's Patriotic Association in 1901. Its ostensible purpose was to 'console the families of the war dead and impress on women their patriotic responsibilities' (Sievers 1983: 114), but it quickly became an instrument of the government for keeping women in their traditional role.

Some women who had been active in the popular rights movement found the Reform Society activities totally inadequate, and were drawn to the socialist and anarchist groups. Fukuda Hideko, along with other women like Sugaya Iwako and Masuoka Fumiko, joined the Socialist Association. They were interested in socialism from a woman's point of view and were successful in getting women's issues to figure in the association's journals.

The beginning of the war against Russia in 1904 created some difficulties for the socialists, and government repression was a constant factor in their work. The socialist women led by Fukuda nevertheless persisted in their activities, the most important of which was the launching, in 1905, of a campaign to remove the restrictions on women imposed by Article 5 of the Police Security Regulations of 1890. This campaign was described by Sievers as 'the Japanese woman's equivalent of the suffrage movement' (Sievers 1983: 122). However, the socialist group was split by personal and ideological differences; its various factions were also subject to police harassment, the leaders of the groups being jailed and their journals frequently shut down. It was in this context that Fukuda decided, in 1907, to launch her own journal, *Sekai Fujin* ('Women of the World'). The editorial in the first issue, appearing on 1 January 1907, set out the objectives:

> What are our reasons for publishing *Women of the World*? In a word, to determine the real vocation of women by extracting it from the tangled web of law, custom and morality that are a part of woman's experience . . . when I look at the conditions currently prevailing in society, I see that as far as women are concerned, virtually everything is coercive and oppressive, making it imperative that we women rise up and forcefully develop our own social movement. This truly is an endless enterprise . . . our hope is that this magazine will inspire you to become a champion of this movement. (Sievers 1983: 127)

The journal covered not only issues specific to women in Japan, but also the international women's movement; it published reports of suffragist movements elsewhere, as well as pictures and articles about prominent European and American women. Madame de Staël and Madame Roland were featured in many of the early issues. It appears that Fukuda wrote much of the journal, but it also became a forum where socialist men and women debated the question of the relationship between socialism and women's issues. An article by the socialist leader Kotoku Shusui said: 'If I were asked what the first requirement of the women's movement is, I would reply that it is for women to learn about socialism.' For Kotoku, the liberation of women could come only through socialism. Fukuda contested his point of view and put her case strongly; she argued that the priority was wrong and that the liberation of women should come first:

> There is a general call for economic liberation, which is a good thing for us to be aware of . . . but calling for economic liberation fails to go beyond sloganeering in advocating women's liberation. As always, we must strike down today's classist discriminatory attitudes between men and women; without carrying out such a revolution in attitudes, is it likely that economic liberation can be accomplished? (Sievers 1983: 132)

Fukuda was perceptive when she declared, as early as 1908, that without such a change of attitude, economic independence might make women even worse off. She published her journal for two and a half years, but met with increasing economic difficulties as well as state repression. She tried to meet these threats by making the journal more literary, but it was finally closed down by the state in 1909.

Revolutionary Women: Kanno Suga

Opposition to the government in Japan came from several groups on the left including the socialists, communists and anarchists; women were prominent in all these formations, several of them achieving notoriety in Japanese society. The best known is Kanno Suga (1881–1910), who is remembered for her revolutionary commitment and her advanced feminism. She had an unhappy childhood in Osaka and did not proceed beyond elementary school level. Returning to Osaka after two years of unsuccessful marriage to a merchant in Tokyo, she became a reporter on a newspaper and was active in the Osaka Women's Reform Society; in the course of her work, she met socialist groups in Osaka as well as visiting socialists from Tokyo. Kanno took over the editorship of another newspaper, *Muro Shimpo*. At this time, Kanno was also burdened with the task of looking after her consumptive younger sister. This experience led her to 'a new conviction that the kind words of the Reform Society were not adequate to deal with poverty: charity was not the answer to tuberculosis among the poor or abandoned, mistreated children; only drastic social change could make a difference' (Sievers 1983: 147).

Kanno's writings of this period reveal her growing feminism, her anger as well as her impatience with the pace of change. She discusses the question of female chastity in an article in 1906 entitled 'Rebuff':

> Among the many annoying things in the world, I think men are the most annoying . . . when I hear them carrying on interminably about female chastity I burst out laughing.
>   . . . I greet with utmost cynicism and unbridled hatred the debauched male of today who rattles on about good wives and wise mothers. Where do all of these depraved men get the right to emphasize chastity? Before they begin stressing women's chastity, they ought to perfect their own male chastity, and concentrate on becoming wise fathers and good husbands! . . .

Rise up, women! Wake up! Though of course the root of the problem must await a socialist revolution, we women must struggle not only against husbands, but against the entire self-serving world of men

Rise up, women! Wake up! As in the struggle workers are engaged in against capitalists to break down the class system, our demands for freedom and equality with men will not be won easily just because we will it; they will not be won if we do not raise our voices, if no blood is shed. (Sievers 1983: 149)

Kanno's articles became more aggressive because of her conflicts with socialist men. In an article 'A Perspective on Men', written in 1906, she argued that most men were motivated by conceit and preferred therefore to associate with weaker persons, shunning women who were independent. Such men, she wrote, were 'like people shut up in castles under siege whose provisions have been exhausted. On first inspection, one thinks the outer walls are strong enough, but the gate is vulnerable and easily forced, producing immediate surrender.' Women, however, continued to revere such men merely because of the illusion of security they provided (Sievers 1983: 150). Kanno's writings also included articles on prostitution and on male hypocrisy, an anti-war novel *Breaking Off* (1903), and a semi-autobiographical novel *Tsuyuko*.

It is thus not surprising that she moved to the radical faction of the socialists and was arrested in the Red Flag incident in 1908, when a group raised banners reading 'Anarchism' and 'Anarcho-Communism'. After her release from jail, she and other socialists started a new journal in 1909 under her editorship (*Free Thought*) but this was suppressed after two issues. It was this blow and the conviction that she would no longer enjoy the right to express her ideas in print that turned Kanno Suga towards violent activity. In 1909, Kanno became involved with a group who planned to assassinate the Emperor, 'thereby demonstrating to the country and the world that he was not a god, but a human being who would bleed and die like everyone else' (Sievers 1983: 157). Twenty-six people, including Kanno and Kotoku Shusui, were arrested for treason in 1910, and 24 were sentenced to death. Protests all over the world led to reduced sentences for many, but Kanno and Kotoku were executed. As Sievers comments, 'The most obvious target of the trial was Kotoku Shusui, the ideologist with the vitriolic pen, who was found guilty largely because others were demonstrably influenced by his ideas' (Sievers 1983: 159). Similarly, Kanno Suga's fearless and spirited defence at her trial, the revolutionary sentiments she expressed and her bitter denunciations of the government and the former prime minister, Yamagata Aritomo, account for the keenness of the government to execute her.

Kanno: I thought that though we might not be able to start a fullscale revolution, we should at least begin on a small scale. I think the Emperor as an individual may be deserving of sympathy, but he heads the system that oppresses us and . . . is politically responsible. That is, it is unavoidable because he is chief of the exploiters . . . The person I consider most abominable as an individual is Yamagata. I think, given the opportunity, I would try to throw a bomb at him.

Prosecutor: For what reason?

Kanno: . . . Yamagata's ideas are the most antiquated. He has consistently persecuted us for our proletarian ideology. (Sievers 1983: 160–1)

Sievers, commenting on Kanno Suga's evidence at the trial, compares it to the famous trials of Russian women:

In testimony reminiscent of the famous trial testimony of the Russian terrorist Vera Figner, she ascribed her actions to a government that made anything short of violence an ineffective mechanism of change. She had concluded, as Figner had, that unusual measures were required to dismantle social institutions and topple the corrupt and powerful personalities who oppressed the entire society. (Sievers 1983: 159)

In the following years, in spite of the repression, many women came forward as activists in the trade union and left-wing movements. Examples of action by women include the Rice Riots of 1918, which occurred when the soaring price of rice caused a group of women workers at the port of Ootsu to refuse to load rice on to ships; this sparked off widespread demonstrations, strikes and uprisings in other areas among port workers, miners and peasants, which lasted several months and led to violence against the people and the fall of the government (Halliday 1975: 70–1).

Seitosha and Feminism

The revival of a literary tradition among women had begun in the early part of the Meiji era. There was a flowering of women writers and many of those who had benefited from the expansion of female education took to literary activity. Women published their work in various journals, but a significant development occurred in 1907, when a group of women writers got together to organize the Lady Writers Society (Keisho Bungakukai); they held meetings of writers and discussions on subjects of literary interest both local and foreign, particularly the works of Ibsen. A member of this group, Hiratsuka Raicho (1886–1971), launched a new phase of feminist activity in 1911, by forming a group called Seitosha (Bluestockings) and publishing a journal called *Seito*. Hiratsuka stated 'women should awaken now. We must get up and develop the natural abilities God has given us . . . Our magazine *Seito* is for use by the unknown writer. It shall be an organ for the dissemination of women's philosophy, literature and culture' (Vavich 1967: 408–9). Referring to the sun goddess of Japanese mythology, she also wrote:

In the beginning woman was the sun.

An authentic person.

Today she is the moon.

Living through others

Reflecting the brilliance of others . . .   (Sievers 1983: 163)

Seito was thus a rallying point for the creative talents of women. Initially it did not concern itself with the economic or political emancipation of women. However, the reaction to their work soon forced Raicho and others of the group to realize that the obstacles to the development of women's creativity in literature lay in the social structures that subordinated women. Raicho voiced this experience: 'That our literary activities would put us in direct opposition to the ideology of "good-wife, wise-mother" was not totally unexpected. What we did not expect was to have to stand and fight immediately all of the traditions of feudalism in the society' (Sievers 1983: 164–5).

A debate in the early issues of *Seito* on Ibsen's *Hedda Gabler* and *A Doll's House* illustrates this tendency. The Japanese feminists, just like the Chinese women, not only saw the parallel between the house-bound bourgeois women of their society and Ibsen's confined heroines, but also debated the fate of Nora after she had slammed the door and left the 'Doll's House' (Paulson 1976: 17). 'The women of the Seitosha were worried over Nora's fate after leaving home, while the public was more concerned over the fact that she had left home . . . The public coined the expression "Japanese Noras"! Newspapers . . . attacked them for being the "New Women" or the "Awakened Women" and considered them fickle and frivolous' (Vavich 1967: 409).

Such reactions compelled the journal to consider issues other than literary ones. Prostitution, abortion, women's suffrage and other similar issues began to be debated, and the 'journal became a vehicle for feminist criticism and issues ranging from the meaning of motherhood to women's suffrage were discussed' (Pharr 1981: 18). The women writers of *Seito* also established links with the surviving members of the earlier popular rights movement. While writers like Yosano Akiko had appeared in the journal from its very beginnings, new activists such as Fukuda began to write for it. In an essay called 'A Solution to the Woman's Problem', Fukuda traced the development of the women's movement in Japan and, according to Sievers, argued that 'both men and women should be free in absolute liberation, freed from the tyranny of artificial, irrational economic and social systems created by self-interested elites' (Sievers 1983: 178).

The expanding interests of *Seito* are also seen in the diversity of foreign feminists held up as sources of inspiration. The interest in Ibsen had led Raicho to Ellen Key, parts of whose book *Love and Marriage* appeared in her translation in *Seito*. Ellen Key (1849–1926) was a Swedish feminist of liberal opinions who had explained the relevance of Ibsen for women, on the ground that he portrays the masculine soul as 'inorganic, definitive, finished, determined' and the feminine as 'organic, growing, in evolution' (Sievers 1983: 226). Key also claimed for women a biological and creative superiority over men. Emma Goldman was another influence; parts of her 'The Tragedy of Women's Liberation' were translated and several of her other articles appeared in *Seito*. Two works by the South

African, Olive Schreiner (1855–1920), were also translated into Japanese. She had made a sensation by her novel *Story of an African Farm* (1883), where the heroine, who expresses strong views on women's equality, has a child but refuses to marry; in later years, Schreiner championed women's rights, advocated pacifism during World War I, and became famous for her unconventional views.

The interests of the Bluestockings thus expanded to cover all the issues which had been the concern of the feminists of the popular rights movement, namely social reform, economic independence for women, the right of women to full participation in politics, and education for women. But the significant contribution of the Bluestockings to the feminist movement in Japan stemmed from their early emphasis on the creative talents of women, an emphasis on the female self and on female sexuality; this is evident in the many articles in *Seito* on the subjects of abortion, prostitution and motherhood. The result was the creation of a stronger and fuller feminist consciousness. This amalgam of concerns is well illustrated in a statement by Raicho:

> The new woman; I am a new woman
> . . .
> The new woman curses yesterday.
> The new woman is not satisfied with the life of the
> kind of woman who is made ignorant, made a slave,
> made a piece of meat by male selfishness.
> The new woman seeks to destroy the old morality and
> laws created for male advantage.
> The new woman does not merely destroy the old morality
> and laws constructed out of male selfishness, but day by day
> attempts to create a new kingdom, where a new religion,
> a new morality and new laws are carried out . . .
> Truly the creation of this new kingdom is the mission
> of women.
>
> (Sievers 1983: 176)

Another influence on the development of the Bluestocking group was the entry in 1912 of Ito Noe, who became the journal's administrator as well as principal writer, taking over full responsibility in 1915. However, the increasingly feminist line pursued by Ito alienated many middle-of-the-road women who dropped out of the group. During the period of Ito's editorship, *Seito* became bolder in handling issues like abortion and prostitution. Even earlier, several issues of the journal had been banned by the state authorities on the grounds that articles had 'seemed corruptive of the virtues traditionally associated with Japanese women' (Sievers 1983: 180). Now, faced with increasing state interference and economic difficulties, Ito also gave up the struggle; the last issue of *Seito* appeared in February 1916. The Bluestocking group gradually disintegrated, but not before it had pushed feminist consciousness in Japan to a higher level.

Seito was seen as a threat by the government since the anti-traditional views expressed, and the discussion of freedom and equal rights for women, went against the government's policies of perpetuating hier-archical structures and patriarchal authority. The Bluestockings' aims were clearly more than literary, as was seen in the pronouncements of the journal: 'The new woman is neither satisfied with life as an ignoramus nor as a slave to the male ego. The new woman is eager to destroy traditions and laws established solely for the convenience of the male.' It is not surprising that *Seito* was accused of propagating 'revolutionary ideas' and was frequently censored and banned. Although *Seito* ceased to publish, as Vavich says: 'Nevertheless, the intense desire for, and belief in, freedom and emancipation for women which had found lively expression in *Seito* could not be abandoned overnight . . . it raised the issue of emancipation among Japanese intellectuals — both men and women.' Moreover, the movement had 'given the world a glimpse of the "new woman" that was at last breaking feudal bonds, thereby setting in motion a chain of events that spanned well over a quarter century' (Vavich 1967: 409–10). Ito Noe continued with her work, helping her common-law husband, Osugi Sakoe, with his writings. Their life was one of economic distress and police harassment. Osugi and Ito were arrested by the police in 1923, and were killed by a policeman on the pretext that they were 'enemies of the state' (Sievers 1983: 180).

Young Poets and Writers

Linked to the Bluestockings was an important feminist woman writer of the period, Yosano Akiko (1878–1942), a member of the Shinshisha literary group of Japanese poets, who revolutionized poetry in the early 20th century. Akiko was a very advanced feminist for the time, who critically analyzed patriarchy and the family as an institution, advocated women's economic independence, and was also active in anti-militaristic and revolutionary political activities. The themes of her poetry and her unconventional lifestyle made her a notorious and controversial figure. Her collection of poems, *Tangled Hair* (1901), was concerned with 'the passion and sensuality of love from a woman's point of view' (Sievers 1983: 169). At a political level, her stand against militarism during the Russo-Japanese War of 1904–5 went counter to the prevalent war hysteria. She wrote an anti-war poem, 'Ode to My Younger Brother who Was Drafted by the Army', which began 'Do not die a purposeless death on the battlefield'. This created a sensation and led not only to Yosano being branded a traitor, but also to suggestions from politicians that she be prosecuted. By 1911, her poems had become more feminist and *Seito* published her famous poem 'Sozorogoto' (translated as 'Mountain-moving Day') which uses the metaphor of 'a rumbling volcano, long dormant in a mountain, for the power of women' (Sievers 1983: 224), and ends with the challenge 'All sleeping women now awake and move' (quoted at the head of this chapter).

In the years after World War I, the leftist movement also produced several well-known women writers who were political activists, including Miyamoto Yuriko (1899–1951), a Communist militant who was frequently arrested for her activities during periods of repression. She was a member of the women's committee of the Japan Proletarian Writers' League and also edited a journal called *Working Women*. In the 1920s, she helped to found the Women's Democratic Club. Also in the leftist movement was Sata Ineko (born in 1904), who as a child worked in a factory and later became a waitress in a literary café that was frequented by young 'proletarian' writers. Influenced by this group, she wrote a novel based on her factory life. She was involved in political activity and joined Miyamoto Yuriko in the Proletarian Writers' League, becoming well known as a writer and poet. Another woman anarchist was Yagi Akiko (b. 1896) who, leaving home and child when she was 27, worked as a teacher and reporter. She helped to edit two militant women's magazines, *Nyonin Geijutsu* ('Women and Art') and *Fujin Sensen* ('Women's Front'), and was imprisoned many times for her links with the anarchist movement (Feminist International 1980: 35, 2, 87).

Women's Rights Agitation

Feminist activities continued in the post-World War I period, when the dominant concepts in the intellectual atmosphere were those of democracy and socialism. It was in this period that Japanese women began to have closer contacts with European and American suffragists, and other women's groups. Ishimoto Shizue, for example, studied the birth control movement pioneered by Margaret Sanger in New York and launched a similar campaign in Japan; but when Sanger visited Japan in 1922, the Tokyo police prevented her from lecturing. This provoked an interest in her writings, which were translated into Japanese, and sparked off a debate on birth control.

Another long and interesting debate, between Hiratsuka Raicho and Yosano Akiko, on whether women should agitate for and accept government assistance, took place in a popular magazine and served to highlight the question of women's emancipation. While Hiratsuka strongly supported allowances, pre-natal facilities and aid to dependent children, Yosano opposed such schemes, believing that they merely perpetuated women's subordinate position in the family. Although they disagreed on many such issues, both feminists 'were struggling with the problem of how to extricate women from the role obligations imposed by the traditional family against the background of the changing economic realities of Taisho Japan' (Bethel 1980: 92–4).

In 1919, Hiratsuka Raicho, Ichikawa Fusae and others of the Seitosha group formed the Association of New Women, which campaigned for equal rights, women's suffrage, a labour union for women workers and the repeal of repressive legislation such as Article 5 of the Police Security Regulations passed in 1890, which had prohibited women from joining political associations and attending political meetings and had, in effect, legally restricted their activities to charitable or religious organizations. Women, who were legally deprived of direct participation in the election campaign in 1920, supported, by other means, those candidates who favoured women's issues, particularly suffrage. As a result, the law was revised in 1921, allowing women to attend and organize political meetings, but prohibiting them from joining or organizing political parties. After this success, however, the Association of New Women was disbanded because it had become weakened by criticism and opposition.

Ichikawa Fusae was in the USA between 1920 and 1924 (when American women had just obtained suffrage rights) and had contact with Carrie Chapman Catt who had founded the League of Women Voters, and Alice Paul, the organizer of the National Women's Party. Ichikawa and Yamataka together organized a new group, Fusen Kakutoku Domei (Women's Suffrage Alliance). They campaigned for three reform bills: for women's suffrage, for civil rights for women, and for the lifting of the ban on women joining political parties. At this stage, however, the women's movement broke up, after the disintegration of the left into four parties. Each party organized its own women's group, even though they all campaigned on such issues as equal opportunities for women and equal pay. Ichikawa and the Women's Suffrage Alliance announced in 1928 that they would adopt a position of political neutrality, hoping in this way to mobilize all forces in support of women's suffrage. This position did not win the support of the women's groups affiliated to the left-wing parties, which attacked Ichikawa and the Alliance as being uninterested in any women's issues other than that of suffrage. As Ichikawa herself said:

> Their reasons were based on their belief that the cause of women's low social status was capitalism which protects personal property. They also believed that if a communist society was established, women's status would rise simultaneously. For them to aid or support our suffrage movement meant the acceptance of a capitalist society. (Vavich 1967: 417)

The campaign met with little support, even from the generality of women. Ichikawa became a target for attack: 'a tall woman who smoked and wore her hair short, she was an object of ridicule in the Japanese press for her manner as well as her convictions' (Pharr 1981: 20).

In 1928, the Seiyukai, a leading political party, adopted the female suffrage issue and the Japanese press changed its critical position to one of support. But hopes of an early reform bill were soon dashed. The Home Minister, Mochizuki Keisuke, opposed any move towards reform, saying unequivocally to the women: 'Go back to your homes and wash your baby's clothes! This is the job given to you and there is the place in which you are entitled to sit!' (Vavich 1967: 418). But hopes rose once again when Mochizuki was replaced by a minister who was more sympathetic to women's issues. In 1930, approximately 500 women were present at the first national meeting for women's suffrage; it was, as Ichikawa has said, a 'period of hope', especially after the Lower House of the Imperial Diet passed a modified bill on women's civil rights in 1931. However, the Upper House rejected the bill by 184 to 62, after bitter controversy on the issue in the press and among political groups. Emotions were aroused, for example in 1931, when a women's rally supporting female suffrage resulted not only in controversial debate but also in violence, when a man attempted to pull Ichikawa off the platform (Vavich 1967: 419).

Takamure Itsue (1894–1964)*

Of the early feminists, Takamure Itsue is particularly important as regards the development of women's studies in Japan. The daughter of an elementary school principal on the island of Kyushu, after graduation she became an assistant teacher in an elementary school, and in 1919 married Hashimoto Kenzo, also a teacher. They then moved to Tokyo, aspiring to take part in intellectual and feminist activities. Kenzo was a nihilist and his home became a gathering place for nihilist friends and poets. Itsue was reduced to playing the traditional role of a housewife, and found herself too busy to engage in any literary work. In 1925, unable to bear this situation any longer, she left her husband. This made Kenzo realize what an unjust burden he had put on her; they were reconciled and thereafter contrived to build a home life that enabled her to give full play to her talents.

Itsue's main preoccupation with the conditions of women is reflected in her book *Renai Sosei* ('Genesis of Love') published in 1926, and according to which, concern for the condition of women passes through four stages: (i) the women's rights movement, exemplified by such women as Mary Wollstonecraft, centred in the UK, and concerned with the removal of sexual inequality; (ii) feminism, exemplified by such writers as Ellen Key of Sweden who contended that love should be the foundation of marriage; (iii) the new women's rights movement, centred in the Soviet Union, which argued that the question of women's subordination would be solved only with their economic emancipation; and (iv) new feminism, which combined economic freedom with the freedom of love and the abolition of the marriage system. Her specific contribution aimed at transcending the patriarchal and monogamous marriage systems and was obviously 'located within anarchism, and sought liberation from all manner of state power'.

---

*The section on Takamure Itsue is from an article by Kano Masanao, 'Pioneer in the Study of Women's History', *Feminist International* No. 2, Tokyo 1980.

But it is Itsue's post-1931 work that is important. In that year she withdrew from all other activities to devote herself to uncovering the history of women in Japan. As in all other countries, this was submerged history. There were a few biographies of women which concentrated on their feminine virtues, but there was no understanding or awareness of women in history. Itsue set herself to remedy this situation and the results of her research were published in 14 volumes. The earlier books, *Research on the Matriarchal System* and *Research on the Adoption of Sons-in-Law*, uncovered the existence of a matrilineal line in ancient Japan, and its subsequent suppression by the patriarchal system. Itsue demonstrated that the male-dominated system was a product of history and not pre-ordained; it was therefore changeable. These researches were subsequently embodied in her *History of Marriage in Japan* in 1963. The other massive contribution made by Itsue was *The History of Women*, published in four volumes between 1954 and 1958.

During her lifetime, Itsue's work was almost totally ignored by Japanese male historians, but it is now being increasingly recognized for its fundamental value. More than anyone else, she has convinced people that the subjugation of women is rooted in specific historical circumstances and that it was therefore open to change.

Militarism and the Women's Movement

The repression in the 1920s of all leftist organizations, including the Japanese Communist Party which had been formed in 1922, led to their women militants being hounded and also to the suppression of feminist activities. Even in the 1920s, the army and conservative business interests had a stranglehold on Japanese political life and joined together to prevent the growth of democratic institutions. All these developments had an impact on the women's movement. The rise of totalitarianism and militaristic expansionist policies in the following decade further weakened the movement. By the early 1930s, Japan had embarked on policies of aggression. The great economic depression of the period had plunged the country into crisis, leading the government to launch expansionist policies. Moreover, the racist immigration policies of the USA and Australia and the Naval Agreements of 1931 (which fixed the ratio of ships for the USA, Britain and Japan at 10:10:7 respectively) caused resentment. This period also saw the growing power of the Japanese armed forces and an increase of militarism which later led to the spread of Japanese imperialism in Asia.

In 1931, the occupation of Manchuria by the Japanese army caused an international crisis. The Japanese had made large investments over the years in Manchuria, which was part of Chinese territory. The League of Nations condemned the aggression. As a result, Japan withdrew from the League in 1933 and continued her aggression into North China; after

251

1937, this developed into a full-scale war which lasted until 1945. With the outbreak of World War II in 1939, Japanese expansionism rapidly extended to the rest of Asia, and the war in Europe enabled the Japanese to occupy several colonial territories, including Vietnam, Indonesia, Singapore and Malaysia.

The growth of militarism in politics resulted in major shifts on the women's issue. As Pharr has remarked:

> The Manchurian Incident in 1931 led to the increased ascendancy of a highly anti-feminist military in civilian affairs and a reordering of national priorities that left women's suffrage a dead issue. In an increasingly repressive society, those advocating women's rights causes were harassed and their publications rigorously censored. (Pharr 1981: 21)

In spite of the adverse situation, women continued to be involved in political resistance. For example, the Third National Women's Suffrage Conference held in 1932 condemned the Japanese government's policies, declaring that 'From the standpoint of women, we firmly oppose the present rise of fascism' (Sano 1980: 77). But by 1937, when Japan had plunged into war with China, many women, including liberal women, turned to collaboration with the government and support of the war effort. The Women's Suffrage Conference of 1937 was the last to be held and the name of the organization was changed to 'Provisional Women's Conference'. It proclaimed 'patriotic' and militaristic slogans, expressing gratitude to the 'Emperor's soldiers, who continue to achieve such a brilliant record abroad' and asserted a desire 'to be strong in our duty; protection of the home front' (Sano 1980: 77). Like the Fascist regimes of Germany and Italy, the Japanese rulers also manipulated women in furthering their political and military goals.

During this period, emphasis was given to the tasks of women in production and reproduction. They were urged to give labour service to the nation by working in industry, and laws restricting their work were relaxed. The militarists, formerly staunch supporters of 'women in the home', now advocated 'women in the factories' (Paulson 1976: 19). Women were also urged to give birth to more 'subjects of the Emperor', and under a Motherhood Protection Law of 1937 benefits were given to poor mothers: 'Women were told that their children were not their own property but the Emperor's, and so their sons must later be sent away joyfully, as the Emperor's soldiers. In short, mothers were being made to produce the means for aggressive war' (Sano 1980: 78).

The government used the occasion of war to appoint leading Japanese women to fill posts on various committees involving the war effort; significantly, these women, 'having turned sharply to the right . . . were already prepared to go along with government requests for cooperation' (Sano 1980: 78). The early women's movement was subsumed in the Greater Japanese Women's Association formed in 1942.

It was only after Japan's defeat and American occupation in 1945 that the earlier political prohibitions on women were lifted and they achieved the right to vote; they first went to the polls in 1946 and elected 39 women deputies. The winning of the suffrage was thus long delayed, but it is important to remember that the groundwork for this victory had been laid during almost 20 years of struggle.

Conclusion

To sum up, just as policies of modernization and industrial development in the Meiji era were achieved within the traditional structures, those regarding women, including in particular universal primary education for girls and changes in private laws, were devised to reinforce and not overthrow hierarchical family relationships. From the beginning of the 'reform era', feminism was kept well under control through judicial killings, as in the case of Kanno and others, through laws prohibiting women from political activity, through the patriarchal Meiji family code, through censorship and prohibition of feminist journals like *Seito*, and through restricting foreign women's influence, such as banning Margaret Sanger's lectures on birth control. Dissenting voices on the issue of women's liberation and other issues were silenced by repressive governments which followed militaristic policies. Hence Japan, while emerging dramatically as an advanced capitalist nation, economically ahead of other countries of Asia and Africa, proved to be one of the most backward where women's rights were concerned.

Two areas of women's demands (namely education and employ-. ment) were, however, readily granted. Women were encouraged to come out and work and they provided the bulk of the cheap labour that enabled Japan to achieve rapid growth rates. The education system was also expanded to include almost all females of school-going age, but this spectacular achievement also served to spread the ideology of submission and subordination. Japan thus presents an interesting study of how certain demands for women's emancipation can be granted by governments concerned with capitalist growth, while undesired changes which would have raised the real issues of women's liberation are blocked. Nevertheless, among all the countries under discussion in this book, feminist consciousness developed to its highest level in Japan, to encompass not only demands at a political and economic level, but also concerns arising from the traditional perceptions of man-woman relationships and woman's role in the family. The material base for this advanced development probably lay in Japan's rapid and successful industrial growth, which in spite of all the constraints imposed by the rulers, gave women the necessary conditions for developing feminist consciousness.

Conclusion

The existence of early feminism in Asia, which has generally been over-looked, was an important force for social change in the late 19th and early 20th centuries. The extent of women's participation in the social and political movements of that period, in nationalist and patriotic struggles, working-class agitations and peasant rebellions, as well as the formation of autonomous women's organizations, has so far not been adequately recognized. It is hoped that these country studies will be of some use in revealing the role played by women in these processes and in locating it in specific economic, social and political contexts. In this conclusion I look at some of the problems encountered when trying to rescue women's history, and to comment on the forces that have shaped women's activities.

The country studies, while dealing mainly with women in the colonial period, mention women only briefly in the pre-capitalist or traditional societies before the intrusion of Western imperialism. It will be observed, however, that many such descriptions emanate either from foreign missionaries and travellers, or from local nationalists, male reformers, and women who were active in feminist struggles. This has had some unfortunate effects. In the first instance, such descriptions or analyses fall into the category that has earlier been defined as 'Orientalism', that is, reflecting Asian reality through the prism of certain Western attitudes; in the second instance, those who were trying to establish a nationalist identity, found it useful to romanticize the past, to paint a picture of an idyllic society where women were said to have been free. Yet another factor sometimes distorts our understanding of the role of women in these traditional societies, namely, the recourse to and defence of indigenous religious traditions as part of the process of constructing a national identity. Women activists and scholars who support women's emancipation sometimes refer to religious texts and, by a very literal reading, attempt to imply that their idealist statements about women accurately reflect society at some time in the past, and that, unlike the 'false' beliefs of neighbouring countries, their particular brand of 'true' religion advocates the liberation of women.

In this context, some objective research into the condition of women in these early societies is needed. The economic and social organizations of the countries selected for this study were very diverse. Some, like Japan, were feudal societies; others were at varying stages of development which had been atrophied by Western intervention. While the general statement may be made that women were an object of oppression in all these societies, the specific forms of oppression and the ideologies which supported it differed. The country studies have made use of available material, but a more intensive examination of the area is needed, particularly because, given the relative autonomy of cultural forms, pre-capitalist social concepts, structures and practices have persisted to this day and continue to influence and shape the role of women in various ways.

Whatever their state of development, these traditional societies became transformed by the growth of capitalism and the emergence of nationalism. There can be no doubt that the feminist movements in those societies were the products of economic and social changes set in motion by the forces of capitalism and nationalism. In most cases, capitalism was not an organic product of indigenous historical forces active in traditional societies, but was imposed on them by imperialism with the active intervention of the state. There is much debate on the nature of this imposition, on the kind of capitalism that developed in the countries in question, on the relationships between local and metropolitan capital, and on the nature of the classes that grew up in the process. Without entering into controversy on these matters, we can conclude that some form of capitalism developed, that a local bourgeoisie emerged and that sections of that bourgeoisie sometimes developed to a point where their interests conflicted with those of the imperial power. As a consequence, such bourgeoisies embarked upon struggles for national independence in which they were able to involve the broad masses, leading to the establishment of states with a strong sense of national identity. In other countries, the bourgeoisies were more dependent and in such cases, national identities were only half-formed and rarely progressed beyond the cultural level.

But whatever the type of capitalist growth and the nature of the bourgeoisie, the process had a significant effect on the role and position of women, affecting women of various classes in varying ways. It freed the women of the bourgeoisie from certain pre-capitalist constraints and traditions, making them literate and educated, even though the content of their education was limited; it brought them out into society, into employment and into social work. The state also took measures to introduce changes in social customs and to force certain superstructural features of Western capitalism upon pre-capitalist societies. Such reforms were most often at the surface level, for example, the adoption of European clothes and the discarding of traditional costumes, as well as the imitation of European social etiquette, lifestyles and recreation.

The content of social reform, although progressive, was also class-determined; issues such as female education, property rights, polygamy, *sati*, and widow remarriage principally affected the privileged classes and castes, and were raised as 'burning social issues' by members of these groups. Reformist demands for the abolition of social evils that affected women were also intended to strengthen family structures and to perpetuate the subordination of women and, in some cases, had that effect. In many parts of Asia, campaigns to eliminate the worst forms of female oppression were supported both by moderate and radical male reformers who were concerned about the deleterious effects of these malpractices on middle-class family life. In supporting the prohibition of obvious social evils and in promoting the ideal of the bourgeois nuclear family and monogamous marriage, the reformers helped to promote stable family life as a cornerstone of capitalist development and modernization.

The basic reforms that involved the freeing of women from pre-capitalist social constraints of various kinds, giving them freedom of mobility, bringing them out of seclusion and facilitating their work outside the home, were in keeping with strategies of capitalist forms of economic production and capitalist ideology. In many countries, the periods of reform coincided with attempts to develop capitalism and to harness the supply of cheap female labour into factory production and the service sector of the economy.

It may be argued that many reforms did not affect the masses of women but only those of the bourgeoisie and petty-bourgeoisie; nevertheless, an ideology which supported the freeing of women from traditional constraints and allowed their 'freedom' to be exploited economically was one that the bourgeoisie encouraged. This, perhaps, was because many of the upper-classes' 'restrictive' practices, which became accepted ideology sometimes filter down to other classes. Examples of such practices include the veiling of women or their seclusion in the home, which may occur when a rise in income permits a man to bring the women of his family out of the fields and into the home. Hence, any decrees or legislation intended to free women from traditional types of bondage were generally in the interests of capitalist ideology, and particularly in the interests of creating a potential, if not actual, labour supply.

As regards the women of the peasantry, the need was to bring them out of their homes and to make them available for work on the plantations, in the textile mills, and various other enterprises being opened up by metropolitan and local capital. But this gave them only comparative freedom. As in the case of the Japanese textile workers, women thrown together in such working conditions developed some degree of independence, even to the point of forming autonomous organizations. After work, however, they were still encapsulated in their homes, bound by the traditional ideologies of male domination; even at their work places, the structures of control were male-dominated and replicated the domestic situation.

Capitalist growth in these countries was thus able to loosen some of the traditional bonds of subordination among women of all classes, to give women some mobility and education, and to bring them out of the domestic sphere into the social sphere. However, it continued to constrain them in a system of overall male domination, even though some of the specific features of domination changed. The concept of the 'new woman' enunciated by the ideologues of many countries, exemplifies the situation. It can actually be argued that, for certain categories of women, capitalism and bourgeois ideology actually intensified their subordination. It was this limitation that stimulated a few women to question the role of capitalism itself, for example, women anarchists in Japan and women revolutionaries in China and Vietnam. If capitalism brought women into the social sphere and into economic production, nationalism pushed them into participating in the political life of their communities. Nationalism in these countries was both the product of, and a reaction to, imperialism. As the country studies show, resulting from education and exposure to European domination on the one hand, and European political thought on the other, sections of the bourgeoisie imbibed ideals of humanism, liberalism and nationalism, and were motivated to launch struggles for self-government and national independence.

It is important to note, however, that these struggles were devoted to the establishment of modern nation states based on the European model — secular, democratic, capitalist states. This motivation generated two impulses that were sometimes contradictory: on the one hand, to modernize their societies along Western lines, using borrowed concepts of science, technology and social organization; and on the other hand to assert national identities based on their own past histories in antithesis to Western influences. Both these impulses had their effect on women. The first brought them into the open: having seen the relative social freedom of women in Western societies and noting it as one of their strengths, many nationalist leaders, from Kemal Atatürk to Fukuzawa, sought to bring about similar changes for their own women. To educate them, to dress them in Western clothes, to shed symbols of barbarity like foot-binding, to bring them out into society, to teach them 'social graces', to involve them in the nationalist struggle — these men tried to accomplish a series of superficial and less superficial changes.

The impulse to assert a national identity, however, worked at a rather deeper level. It was necessary to go back to cultural or religious roots, to modify or reinterpret them in accordance with the needs of the times, and thus to evolve a national identity which could serve as the basis for national aspirations. This ideal circumscribed the freedom generated by the impulse to modernize. It was claimed that the women of the East were more spiritual; that they were heirs to the wisdom of centuries; that although they might be educated and take part in political struggles, they were still the custodians and transmitters of national culture. Examples of these diverse trends can be found in almost all the country studies. Ultimately, however, the net effect of all these tendencies was to keep women within the boundaries prescribed by the male reformers and leaders.

Women's participation in nationalist struggles was, however, a direct result of the modernization trend. The ancient East had its share of exceptional women — rulers and warrior queens — but these were isolated examples of women who stepped into the breach when male successors were not available. The first arena in which women as a group began to be involved in political action was that of nationalist struggles. While these were mainly directed towards national independence, there was a specific women's agenda which included not only the abolition of social evils and feudal practices, but also the struggle for such bourgeois democratic rights for women as the franchise. We have shown that in most of the countries concerned, an important part of women's struggles was for the vote — the symbol of modernity and of women's emancipation, and an area of militant action that was dramatically highlighted by the British suffragists. In granting suffrage and other democratic rights to women, including the right to education, property, employment and political representation, the interests served were mainly those of bourgeois women, some of whom reverted to their basically subordinate role in society once the single-issue struggle had been won, having been appeased by the mirage of 'equal rights'.

However, while certain issues such as the right to education were also class-determined, they were vitally important areas of struggle. Education for women was supported for various reasons: by women, as a democratic right to knowledge, employment and mobility, and as an important factor in self-reliance and independence; by men, as a buttress to family stability through the production of suitably 'civilized' wives and mothers, as a vehicle for conversion to a given ideology — such as Christianity in the case of missionaries — or as a means to perpetuate a reactionary political ideology of subservience to the male hierarchy which, as in Japan, ranged from the Emperor, the ruling class, and the employer, to the husband. But the democratic rights gained in this way also helped create a greater awareness of feminist issues among women. This motivated some of them to take the struggle further by participating in women's movements organized as wings or subsidiaries of male-dominated political organizations. With rare exceptions, autonomous women's organizations did not exist. It was made quite clear that women's struggles were subordinate to the political struggle and to the male groupings in political parties. Thus, when alliances were formed, the women's group also became allied; when the alliances broke, the women were fragmented. In 1946, for example, in Sri Lanka, women of the various left-wing parties grouped together, but had to disband when the political parties disapproved. Such experiences have led many women to consider the necessity for autonomous women's organizations: one need look only at the history of women' groupings in the Japanese left to understand the origins of such an attitude. But in spite of the need for autonomous activity, only a few independent women's movements arose during the period.

The lack of autonomy of women's organizations, and the concentration of all efforts on the achievement of national independence, also explains the relative decline of women's movements after the period covered by this study. With the attainment of independence, the establishment of nation states and the winning of the suffrage, women's movements in most of the countries under study either faded away or degenerated into social welfare organizations concerned with women's education, handicrafts and home care. The seeds of this decay were inherent in the nature and organization of the women's movements during the period of nationalist struggle. This struggle was a necessary factor in pulling women out of the traditional domestic sphere into the public and political sphere; but equally, it placed limits on the movement, limits that contributed to the decline of women's movements in the aftermath of the success of nationalist struggles. Once independence had been achieved, male politicians, who had consciously mobilized women in the struggle, pushed them back into their 'accustomed place'.

The subsequent experiences of women in these countries is also of interest, although it can only be touched upon very briefly here. Most countries of the region, with the exception of China and Vietnam, followed one of two paths — which have now almost converged — towards development. Some opted for a capitalist path, inviting technology and capital from the advanced countries of the West and manufacturing mainly for export markets. Others preferred to experiment with the concept of a mixed economy — a blend of state capitalism together with a private sector. Their objectives were the satisfaction of domestic needs and the establishment of a more egalitarian society, but domestic crises forced most of these countries — Indonesia, Sri Lanka, and so on — to abandon these strategies and to relink with the world capitalist system.

This kind of development has continued to draw in Asian women as workers in new sectors of employment, especially in the garments and electronics industries that have been established in the industrial trade zones of Asia, in tourism, and as housemaids in the oil-producing states of the Middle East. The absorption of women into the labour force is a common factor in all Asian countries, but as many studies of such employment have revealed, entry into the workforce has not served to break through the bonds of male domination. Even economically active and independent women find themselves constrained, both at home and at the workplace, in structures that emphasize and perpetuate female subordination.

Women workers had begun to participate in trade union activities during the period covered by this study. With the increased numbers of women employed, the tendency to organize themselves had grown, but it did not lead to increased assertion of their situation as women. This has also been owing to the fact that, in many cases, the left parties leading the trade union movement did not consider the 'woman question' to be part of the class struggle against employers. In fact, the 'woman question' has barely figured in the consciousness of trade union and left-wing leaders: if it did so at all, it was considered a subordinate problem that would be solved with the achievement of socialism. This attitude still lingers, even today; some Asian leftists consider emphasis on feminism to be a divisive tactic, one that draws attention away from the class struggle and therefore indirectly benefits the bourgeoisie.

All these factors meant that, after World War II, the question of women's emancipation became a non-issue in many Asian countries. There were few women's organizations other than those devoted to social welfare; there was no movement that sought to question women's subordination, because consciousness among women had sunk to a low level. But this was only a temporary pause in the years after independence and liberation. The increased exploitation of these countries' economies by local and foreign capital had made some women workers aware of the double oppression to which they are subjected. The exposure of Asian societies to Western influences also made women of all classes aware of the feminist movement in the West and of the theoretical and practical impulses that were behind it. Born out of these influences, women's movements are now active in all Asian countries, extending into all classes, active in social and political agitation, and aiming to make all women conscious of their subordination within the prevailing family structures. These growing movements have taken up many issues that affect women: dowry deaths, rape, abortion, prostitution and general violence. In doing so, they expose the male domination that underlies all Asian social practice. It should be noted, however, that these movements also draw upon the strengths of earlier ones and rely on the memories and experiences of an earlier stage of feminist struggle; it is as if, after a long period of dormancy, women's consciousness has suddenly come alive again.

Since this study has been concerned with uncovering the role played by women in nationalist and other struggles, it is necessary to make some brief comments on the writing of women's history. Over the last twenty years or so, there has been a great deal of academic activity in Europe and the USA, especially by women, that has been aimed at demonstrating the participation of women in all areas of social production and reproduction and placing it in a correct perspective. The analysis of pre-capitalist societies by anthropologists and other social scientists has brought an understanding of the major role that women have played in such societies. Numerous studies have shown the fundamental role of women, not only in social reproduction but also in the very task of capital accumulation.

However, this generally signifies an addition of women into the framework of conventional history. The country studies in this book have indicated that, in the period of nationalist struggles, men were the main movers of history. They organized nationalist movements and political parties, set the parameters for the struggle, even determined the role that women should play. In this sense, with a few exceptions, the women worked within the boundaries laid down by men. The history uncovered in this way is a 'contributive' history. This in itself is important, asserting that women have played a role that has been consistently ignored, and correcting the picture of men as the only historical actors. It is to be hoped that the women in these countries will be moved to delve more deeply into their archives and to expand on those aspects of women's participation that have only been touched upon in these country studies.

To complete a history of Asian women during this or any other period would require examining the precise ways in which the sexual division of labour in production and reproduction have been transformed into a relation of subordination and oppression within the social structure. For, as Elizabeth Fox-Genovese has said: 'The domination of women by men figures at the core of the domination of specific classes, races, ethnic groups and peoples. It intersects with all forms of subordination . . . and cannot be understood apart from them' (Fox-Genovese 1982: 14).

This is the history that remains to be written.

Bibliography

Abadan-Unat, Nermin (ed.) *Women in Turkish Society* (E.J. Brill, Leiden, 1981).
————— 'Social Changes and Turkish Women', in *Women in Turkish Society* (E.J. Brill, Leiden, 1981).
Abdel Kader, Soha *The Status of Egyptian Women 1900–1973* (The American University of Cairo, Social Research Centre, September 1973).
Agayev, S.L. and Plastun, V.N. 'The Communist and National Liberation Movement in Iran in the 1920s', in R.A. Ulyanovsky (ed.) *The Comintern and the East: A Critique of the Critique* (Progress Publishers, Moscow, 1978).
Ahmed, Leila 'Feminism and Feminist Movements in the Middle East', in *Women's Studies International Forum*, vol. 5, no. 2, 1982.
Aksan, Akil *Citations de Mustapha Kemal* (Ankara, 1981).
Altiok, Fusun 'The Image of Women in Turkish Literature', in Abadan-Unat (ed.), *Women in Turkish Society* (E.J. Brill, Leiden, 1981).
Alzona, Encarnaçion *The Filipino Woman, Her Social, Economic and Political Status 1565–1933* (University of the Philippines Press, Manila, 1934).
Asthana, Pratima *The Women's Movement in India* (Delhi, 1974).
Ataturk, Kemal Mustapha *The Turkish Woman – Speeches of Kemal Mustapha Ataturk* (Ankara, undated).
Basham A.L. *The Wonder that was India* (London, 1954).
Basu, Aparna 'The Role of Women in the Indian Struggle for Freedom', in B.R. Nanda (ed.) *Indian Women from Purdah to Modernity* (New Delhi, 1976).
Basu, Krishna 'Movement for Emancipation of Women in the 19th Century', in R. Ray *et al. Role and Status of Women in Indian Society* (Calcutta, 1978).
Bayat-Philipp, Mangol 'Women and Revolution in Iran 1905–1911', in Lois Beck and Nikki Keddie (eds), *Women in the Muslim World* (Harvard University Press, Cambridge, Mass., 1980. First edition 1978).
Beck, Lois and Keddie, Nikki (eds) *Women in the Muslim World* (Harvard University Press, Cambridge, Mass., 1980. First edition 1978).
Bergman, Arlene Eisen *Women of Vietnam* (People's Press, California, 1975).
Bethel, Diana 'Visions of a Humane Society, Feminist Thought in Taisho Japan', *Feminist International*, no. 2, Tokyo, 1980.
Bhatty, Zarina 'Status of Muslim Women and Social Change', in B.R. Nanda (ed.) *Indian Women from Purdah to Modernity* (Delhi, 1976).
Bisbee, Eleanor *The New Turks — Pioneers of the Republic, 1920–1950* (Pennsylvania, 1951).
Boissevain, Mia *The Women's Movement in the Netherlands* (Amsterdam, 1915).
Buultjens, A.E. 'How I Became a Buddhist' (Colombo, 1899).
Chakravartty, Renu *Communists in Indian Women's Movement* (People's Publishing House, New Delhi, 1980).

Chesneaux, Jean, Bergere, Marie-Claire, le Barbier, Françoise *China from the 1911 Revolution to Liberation* (The Harvester Press, Sussex, 1977).

Cobb, Betsey 'Kamaladevi Chattopadhyaya', *Bulletin of Asian Scholars*, vol. 7, no. 1, January–March 1975.

Cosar, Fatma Mansur 'Women in Turkish Society', in Lois Beck and Nikki Keddie (eds), *Women in the Muslim World* (Cambridge, Mass., 1980).

Cousins, Margaret *The Awakening of Asian Womanhood* (Madras, 1922).

Croll, Elizabeth *Feminism and Socialism in China* (Schocken Books, New York, 1980. First edition 1978).

Das, Harihar *The Life and Letters of Toru Dutt* (Oxford University Press, 1921).

Davin, Delia *Woman-Work, Woman and the Party in Revolutionary China* (Oxford, 1979).

Denham, D.B. *Ceylon at the Census of 1911* (Government Printer, Colombo, 1912).

Desai, Neera *Women in Modern India* (Bombay, 1957).

De Silva, Colvin R. *Ceylon under British Occupation* (Colombo Apothecaries, Colombo, 1952).

Deuchler, Martina 'The Tradition: Women in the Yi Dynasty', in Sandra Mattielli (ed.) *Virtues in Conflict* (Seoul, 1977).

El-Saadawi, Nawal *The Hidden Face of Eve — Women in the Arab World* (Zed Press, London, 1980).

Elwell-Sutton, L.P. *Persian Oil. A Study in Power Politics* (London, 1955).

———— 'Reza Shah the Great: Founder of the Pahlavi Dynasty', in G. Lenczowski (ed.) *Iran Under the Pahlavis* (California, 1978).

Everett, J.M. *Women and Social Change in India* (Delhi, 1979).

Fast, Jonathan and Richardson, Jim *Roots of Dependency, Political and Economic Revolution in 19th Century Philippines* (Foundation for Nationalist Studies, Quezon City, 1983).

Feminist International no. 2, 'Asian Women '80', Tokyo, 1980.

Fernea, Elizabeth W. and Bezirgan, Basima Qattan (eds) *Middle Eastern Muslim Women Speak* (Austin University Press, Texas, 1977).

Feuerwerker, Yi-Ysi 'Women as Writers in the 1920s and 1930s', in M. Wolf and R. Witke (eds) *Women in Chinese Society* (Stanford, 1978. First edition 1975).

Fischer, Michael M.J. 'On Changing the Concept and Position of Persian Women', in Lois Beck and Nikki Keddie (eds) *Women in the Muslim World* (Cambridge, Mass., 1980. First edition 1978).

Fox-Genovese, Elizabeth 'Placing Women's History in History', *New Left Review* no. 133, May–June 1982.

Fraser-Tytler, W.K. *Afghanistan. A Study of Political Developments of Central and South Asia* (Oxford, 1953).

Fukuzawa, Yukichi *The Autobiography of Yukichi Fukuzawa* (Columbia University Press, New York, 1968).

Gandhi, M.K. *India of my Dreams*, compiled by R.K. Prabhu (Navajivan Publishing House, Ahmedabad, 1962).

Geertz, Hildred (ed.) *Letters of a Javanese Princess. Raden Adjeng Kartini* (Heinemann, Hong Kong, 1976).

Gipoulon, Catherine *Qiu Jin, Femme et Révolutionnaire en Chine au XIXème Siècle* (Editions des Femmes, Paris, 1976).

Gopal, S. *Jawaharlal Nehru. A Biography* (London, 1975).

Grimal, Henri *Decolonisation: the British, Dutch and Belgian Empires* (Routledge & Kegan Paul, London, 1978).

Guruge, Ananda (ed.) *Return to Righteousness, a Collection of Speeches, Essays and Letters of the Anagarika Dharmapala* (Government Press, Colombo, 1965).

Haldar, Gopal *Vidyasagar — A Reassessment* (People's Publishing House, New Delhi, 1972).

Halliday, Fred 'Revolution in Afghanistan', *New Left Review*, no. 112, November–December 1978.

Halliday, J. *A Political History of Japanese Capitalism* (New York, 1975).

Handlin, Joanna F. 'Lu Kun's New Audience. The Influence of Women's Literacy on Sixteenth Century Thought', in M. Wolf and R. Witke (eds) *Women in Chinese Society* (Stanford, 1978. First published 1975).

Heimsath, Charles H. *Indian Nationalism and Hindu Social Reform* (Princeton University Press, 1964).

Hibbert, Christopher *The Great Mutiny, India 1857* (London, 1980).

Hitti, Philip K. *The Near East in History* (Princeton, 1961).

Jayawardena, Kumari *The Rise of the Labour Movement in Ceylon* (Duke University Press, North Carolina, 1972).

———— 'The Participation of Women in the Social Reform, Political and Labour Movements of Sri Lanka', in *Woman in Asia* (Logos, Colombo, August 1974).

———— and Mies, Maria *Feminism in Europe. Liberal and Socialist Strategies, 1789–1919* (Institute of Social Studies, The Hague, 1981).

Jayaweera, Swarna 'Women and Education', in *Status of Women — Sri Lanka* (University of Colombo, 1979).

Jazani, Bizhan *Capitalism and Revolution in Iran* (Zed Press, London, 1980).

Jinarajadasa, C. *The Golden Book of the Theosophical Society* (The Theosophical Publishing Society, Adyar, Madras, 1925).

Kaur, Manmohan *Women in India's Freedom Struggle* (Sterling Publishers Private Ltd, New Delhi, 1985).

Keddie, Nikki *Roots of Revolution. An Interpretative History of Modern Iran* (Yale, 1981).

Keene, Donald *The Japanese Discovery of Europe, 1720–1830* (California, 1969).

Keyder, Caglar 'The Political Economy of Turkish Democracy', *New Left Review*, no. 115, May–June 1979.

Kommunistische Fraueninternationale (in German), journal of the Communist Women's International 1921–5, Stuttgart. Available at the Institute for Social History, Amsterdam.

Kim, Yung-Chung (ed.) *Women of Korea, A History from Ancient Times to 1945* (Ewha Women's University Press, Seoul, 1976).

Kosambi, D.D. *The Culture and Civilisation of Ancient India* (London, 1965).

Koyama, Takashi *The Changing Social Position of Women in Japan* (UNESCO, 1961).

Kulke, Eckehard *The Parsees in India, A Minority as Agent of Social Change* (Vikas Publishing House, New Delhi, 1978).

Lacouture, Jean *Ho Chi Minh* (Pelican Books, London, 1968).

Laqueur, Walter *Communism and Nationalism in the Middle East* (London, 1956).

Lakshmi, C.S. *The Face Behind the Mask. Women in Tamil Literature* (Vikas Publishing House, New Delhi, 1984).

Lebra, Joyce, Paulson, Joy and Powers, Elizabeth (eds) *Women in Changing Japan* (Stanford University Press, California, 1978).

Legge, J.D. *Sukarno. A Political Biography* (Penguin Books, London, 1972).

Lenczowski, George *Iran under the Pahlavis* (California, 1978).

Lewis, Bernard *The Emergence of Modern Turkey* (Oxford University Press, 1965).

———— *The Muslim Discovery of Europe* (Weidenfeld and Nicolson, London, 1982).

Little, Tom *Modern Egypt* (London, 1967).

Luthra, Bimla 'Nehru and the Place of Women in Indian Society', in B.R. Nanda (ed.) *Indian Women from Purdah to Modernity* (New Delhi, 1976).

Lu Xun 'My Views on Chastity' (1918) in *Lu Xun Selected Works* volume 2 (trans.) Yang Xianyi and Gladys Yang (Foreign Languages Press, Beijing, third edition 1980).

———— 'What Happens after Nora Leaves Home?' (ibidem).

Madhavananda, Swami and Majumadar, Ramesh Chandra *Great Women of India* (Advaita Ashrama, Calcutta, 1953).

Mao Zedong *Selected Works of Mao Tse-tung*, Vol. 1 (Foreign Languages Press, Peking, 1967).

Marcus, Jane *The Young Rebecca: Writings of Rebecca West 1911–1917* (Macmillan London Ltd in association with Virago Press, London, 1982).

Marr, David 'The 1920s Women's Rights Debates in Vietnam', *Journal of Asian Studies*, May 1976.

———— *Vietnamese Tradition on Trial, 1920–1945* (University of California Press, Calif., 1981).

Marsot, Afaf Lutfi al-Sayyid 'The Revolutionary Gentlewomen in Egypt', in Lois Beck and Nikki Keddie (eds) *Women in the Muslim World* (Harvard University Press, Cambridge, Mass., 1980. First edition 1978).

Mattielli, Sandra (ed.) *Virtues in Conflict, Tradition and the Korean Woman Today* (Royal Asiatic Society, Seoul, 1977).

Mazumdar, Vina 'The Social Reform Movement in India from Ranade to Nehru', in B.R. Nanda (ed.) *Indian Women from Purdah to Modernity* (New Delhi, 1976).

Mehta, H.B. *Women's Emancipation in India 1813–1966* (Delhi, 1973).

Mendoza-Guazon, Maria Paz *The Development and Progress of Filipino Women* (Manila, 1951).

Menon, Chandu *Indulekha* (Calicut, 1965).

Mies, Maria *Indian Women and Patriarchy* (Vikas, New Delhi, 1980).

———— 'Indian Women and Leadership' in *Bulletin of Concerned Asian Scholars*, vol. 7, no. 1, 1975.

———— and Kumari Jayawardena *Feminism in Europe. Liberal and Socialist Strategies, 1789–1919* (Institute of Social Studies, The Hague, 1981).

Minai, Naila *Women in Islam. Tradition and Transition in the Middle East* (Seaview Books, New York, 1981).

Mollander, Cecilia *Women in Viet Nam* (Upsala, 1981, translated from Swedish).

Mouer, Elizabeth Knipe 'Women in Teaching' in J. Lebra *et al.* (eds) *Women in Changing Japan* (Stanford, 1978. First edition 1976).

Mukherjee, Radhakamal 'Great Indian Women of the Nineteenth Century', in S. Madhavananda and R. Majumadar *Great Women of India* (Calcutta, 1953).

Mukherjee, S.N. 'Raja Rammohun Roy and the Debate on the Status of Women in Bengal' in Michael Allen and S.N. Mukherjee (eds) *Women in India and Nepal* (Australian National University, Canberra, 1982).

Nag, Kalidas and Burman, Debajyoti (eds) *Selected Works of Raja Rammohun Roy* (Government of India Publications, New Delhi, 1977).

Nanda, B.R. (ed.) *Indian Women from Purdah to Modernity* (New Delhi, 1976).

Nanavutty, Piloo *The Parsis* (National Book Trust, India, New Delhi, 1977).

Naravane, V.S. *Sarojini Naidu — An Introduction to her Life, Work and Poetry* (Orient Longmans, New Delhi, 1980).

Nee, Victor and Peck, James *China's Uninterrupted Revolution — from 1940 to the Present* (New York, 1975).

Nehru, Jawaharlal *Glimpses of World History* (4th edn) (Lindsay Drummond Ltd, London, 1949).

———— *An Autobiography* (Asia Publishing House, Bombay, 1962).

Olcott, Henry Steele *Old Diary Leaves* (2nd Series, 1878–83) (The Theosophical Publishing House, Madras, 1954).

Omvedt, Gail 'Caste, Class and Women's Liberation in India', *Bulletin of Concerned Asian Scholars*, vol. 7, no. 1, 1975.

Öncü, Ayşe 'Turkish Women in the Professions: Why so Many?' in N. Abadan-Unat (ed.) *Women in Turkish Society* (E.J. Brill, Leiden 1981).

Overstreet, G.D. and Windmiller, M. *Communism in India* (University of California Press, Berkeley, 1960).

Panikkar, K.M. *Asia and Western Dominance* (London, 1953).

Park, Yong-Ock 'The Women's Modernization Movement in Korea' in S. Mattielli (ed.) *Virtues in Conflict* (Seoul, 1977).

Paulson, Joy 'Evolution of the Feminine Ideal' in J. Lebra *et al.* (eds) *Women in Changing Japan* (Stanford, 1978. First edition 1976).

Pharr, Susan J. *Political Women in Japan. The Search for a Place in Political Life* (University of California, 1981).

Philipp, Thomas 'Feminism and Nationalism in Egypt', in Lois Beck and Nikki Keddie (eds) *Women in the Muslim World* (Harvard University Press, Cambridge, Mass., 1980. First edition 1978).

Pierson, John D. *Tokutomi Soho 1863–1957. A Journalist from Modern Japan* (Princeton, 1980).

Potts, E. Daniel *British Baptist Missionaries in India, 1793–1837* (Cambridge University Press, 1967).

Price, Janet 'Women and Leadership in the Chinese Communist Movement 1921–1945', *Bulletin of Concerned Asian Scholars*, January–March 1975.

Ram, N. 'The Dravidian Movement in its Pre-independence Phases', *Economic and Political Weekly*, annual number, February 1979.

Rankin, Mary Backus 'The Emergence of Women at the End of the Ch'ing, the Case of Ch'iu Chin', in M. Wolf and R. Witke (eds) *Women in Chinese Society* (Stanford, 1978. First edition 1975).

Reform Movement of 1898 (Foreign Languages Press, Peking, 1976). (Pamphlet)

Rhys Davids, Caroline A.F. *Psalms of the Early Buddhists. Vol. 1. Psalms of the Sisters, Pali Text Society* (London, 1909).

Rodinson, Maxime *Islam and Capitalism* (Suffolk, 1974).

———— *Marxism and the Muslim World* (Zed Press, London, 1979).

Roshanak and Faramarz 'The Veil and the Question of Women in Iran', in A. Tabari and N. Yeganeh (eds) *In the Shadow of Islam* (Zed Press, London, 1982).

Russell, Jane *Our George. A Biography of George Edmund de Silva* (Times of Ceylon, Colombo, 1981).

Said, Edward W. *Orientalism* (Vintage Books, New York, 1979).

Samin, Ahmet 'The Tragedy of the Turkish Left', *New Left Review*, no. 126, March–April 1981.

Sanghvi, Ramesh *Aryamehr: The Shah of Iran* (London, 1968).

Sanghvi, Ramesh, Green, Clifford and Missen, David (eds) *The Revolution of the Shah and the People* (London, 1967).

Sano, Noriko 'Japanese Women's Movements during World War II', in *Feminist International*, no. 2, Tokyo, 1980.

Savory, Roger M. 'Social Development in Iran during the Pahlavi Era' in G. Lenczowski *Iran Under the Pahlavis* (California, 1978).

Schram, Stuart R. *The Political Thought of Mao Tse Tung* (Pelican Books, 1969).

Schwarcz, Vera 'Ibsen's Nora: The Promise and the Trap', *Bulletin of Concerned Asian Scholars*, January–March 1975.

Sievers, Sharon L. *Flowers in Salt. The Beginnings of Feminist Consciousness in Modern Japan* (Stanford University Press, 1983).

Siu, Bobby *Women of China, Imperialism and Women's Resistance 1900–1949* (Zed Press, London, 1982).

Sivathamby, K. 'A Study of Arumuka Navalar', in *Social Science Review* (Colombo, 1979).

Soong, Ching Ling *The Struggle for New China* (Foreign Languages Press, Peking, 1953).

Spector, Ivar *The First Russian Revolution: Its Impact on Asia* (Prentice Hall, Englewood Cliffs, New Jersey, 1962).

Spence, Jonathan D. *The Gate of Heavenly Peace. The Chinese and their Revolution 1895–1980* (Faber & Faber, London, 1982).

Srivastava, Harindra *Five Stormy Years, Sarvarkar in London* (Allied Publishers, New Delhi, 1983).

Subido, Terroso *The Feminist Movement in the Philippines 1905–1955* (Manila, 1955).

Tabari, Azar and Yeganeh, Nahid *In the Shadow of Islam. The Women's Movement in Iran* (Zed Press, London, 1982).

Tambiah, S.J. 'Polyandry in Ceylon', in Christoph Von Fürer-Haimendorf (ed.) *Caste and Kin in Nepal, India and Ceylon* (Sterling Publishers, New Delhi, 1978).

Tekeli, Sirin 'Women in Turkish Politics', in N. Abadan-Unat (ed.) *Women in Turkish Society* (E.J. Brill, Leiden, 1981).

Thapar, Romila *A History of India*, Vol. 1 (Penguin Books, London, 1966).

Thomas, P. *Indian Women through the Ages* (Bombay, 1964).

Topley, Marjorie 'Marriage Resistance in Rural Kwangtung', in M. Wolf and R. Witke (eds) *Women in Chinese Society* (Stanford, 1978. First edition 1975).

Toprak, Binnaz Sayari 'Religion and Turkish Women', in N. Abadan-Unat (ed.) *Women in Turkish Society* (E.J. Brill, Leiden, 1981).

Truong, Thanh-Dam 'Women's Position in Vietnamese Society in Historical Perspective' (unpublished monograph, Institute of Social Studies, The Hague).

UNESCO, *Mustapha Kamal Ataturk* (Paris, 1963).

Vatikiotis, T.J. *The History of Egypt* (London, 1980).

Vavich, Dee Ann 'The Japanese Women's Movement — Ichikawa Fusae', *Monumenta Nipponica*, 22, no. 3–4, Tokyo, 1967.

Vien, Nguyen Khac *The Long Resistance* (Foreign Languages Publishing House, Hanoi, 1977).

Voice of Women, journal of the 'Voice of Women' group. Colombo, 1980.

Vreede-de Steurs, Cora *The Indonesian Woman: Struggles and Achievements* (The Hague, 1960).

Wada, Yoshiko 'Japanese Emperor System', in *Feminist International — Issues for Women East and West*, vol. 1, no. 4, 1978.

Wieringa, Saskia 'The Perfumed Nightmare — Some Notes on the Indonesian Women's Movement' (Working Paper — Sub-Series on Women's History and Development — no. 5, Institute of Social Studies, The Hague, 1985).

Wilber, Donald N. *Contemporary Iran* (London, 1963).

Witke, Roxane 'Mao Tse-Tung, Women and Suicide in the May Fourth Era', in *Chinese Quarterly*, no. 31, July–September 1967.

Wolf, Arthur P. 'The Women of Hai-Shai. A Demographic Portrait', in M. Wolf and R. Witke (eds) *Women in Chinese Society* (Stanford 1978. First edition 1975).

Wolf, Margery and Witke, Roxane (eds) *Women in Chinese Society* (Stanford University Press, California, 1978. First edition 1975).

Wolf, Margery 'Woman and Suicide in China', in M. Wolf and R. Witke (eds) *Women in Chinese Society* (Stanford, 1978. First edition 1975).

Woodsmall, Ruth Frances *Muslim Women Enter a New World* (New York, 1936).

————— *Women and The New East* (Washington, DC, 1960).

Wortham, M.E. *Mustapha Kemal of Turkey* (Boston, 1931).

Wright, Arnold *Twentieth Century Impressions of Ceylon* (Lloyd's Greater Britain Publishing Company Ltd, London, 1907).

Yeganeh, Nahid 'Women's Struggles in the Islamic Republic of Iran', in A. Tabari and N. Yeganeh (eds) *In the Shadow of Islam* (London, 1982).

Index

Zed Books Ltd

is a publisher whose international and Third World lists span:

- **Women's Studies**
- **Development**
- **Environment**
- **Current Affairs**
- **International Relations**
- **Children's Studies**
- **Labour Studies**
- **Cultural Studies**
- **Human Rights**
- **Indigenous Peoples**
- **Health**

We also specialize in Area Studies where we have extensive lists in African Studies, Asian Studies, Caribbean and Latin American Studies, Middle East Studies, and Pacific Studies.

For further information about books available from Zed Books, please write to: Catalogue Enquiries, Zed Books Ltd, 57 Caledonian Road, London N1 9BU. Our books are available from distributors in many countries (for full details, see our catalogues), including:

In the USA
Humanities Press International, Inc., 165 First Avenue,
Atlantic Highlands, New Jersey 07716.
Tel: (908) 872 1441;
Fax: (908) 872 0717.

In Canada
DEC, 229 College Street, Toronto, Ontario M5T 1R4.
Tel: (416) 971 7051.

In Australia
Wild and Woolley Ltd, 16 Darghan Street, Glebe, NSW 2037.

In India
Bibliomania, C-236 Defence Colony, New Delhi 110 024.

In Southern Africa
David Philip Publisher (Pty) Ltd, PO Box 408, Claremont 7735,
South Africa.